The Pocket Paderewski

A marvellous musician who was able to play magisterially but limpidly, full of charm and yet with forensic intelligence and insight. One can only regret not knowing sooner about this great artist.

— Dr. Leslie Howard

Distinguished pianist, composer and musicologist. Acclaimed performer of Liszt

Cahill plays throughout with irrepressible spirit and energy. The character of each piece is clearly projected and his appreciation of what the music is 'about' is faultless. It is easy to visualise his virtuoso panache.

— James Methuen-Campbell

International authority on Chopin interpretation

Cahill's playing is passionately driven, full of excitingly forthright strength, but with a formal grip and sense of cadence that give it true command, shot through with unmistakeable touches of originality and tonal nuance.

— Piers Lane

Australian pianist of worldwide distinction

Also by Michael Moran

A Country in the Moon: Travels in Search of the Heart of Poland
(Granta Books, London 2008)

Beyond the Coral Sea: Travels in the Old Empires of the South-West Pacific
(HarperCollins, London 2003)

Point Venus
(Brandl & Schlesinger, Sydney 1998)

Moran's writing is richly atmospheric with real depth and sparkle.
— C.J. Schüler, *The Independent*

There is no faulting his research, his integrity, or his ability to transport us.
— Anthony Sattin, *Sunday Times*

Triumphantly balances humour with scholarship.
— Robert Carver, *The Observer*

The Pocket Paderewski

THE BEGUILING LIFE OF THE AUSTRALIAN CONCERT PIANIST EDWARD CAHILL

MICHAEL MORAN

Australian Scholarly

First published 2016 by Australian Scholarly Publishing Pty Ltd
7 Lt Lothian St Nth, North Melbourne, Victoria 3051
tel 03 9329 6963 / *fax* 03 9329 5452
aspic@ozemail.com.au / www.scholarly.info

ISBN: 978-1-925333-88-6 HB / 978-1-925588-03-3 PB

Cover design Amelia Walker

To the memory of mine own
'Uncle Eddie'

'Youth dreams mad dreams, and rare is the man whose desires find perfect fulfillment. I have walked in the path of the makers of music and dreamed their dreams. It all seems so clear now. And I am content.'

The distinguished Russian-born pianist Arthur Friedheim (1859–1932), *Life and Liszt: The Recollections of a Concert Pianist* (New York 1961)

'You should never despise social life – *de la haute société* – I mean, it can be a very satisfying one, entirely artificial of course, but absorbing. Apart from the life of the intellect and the contemplative religious life, which few people are qualified to enjoy, what else is there to distinguish man from the animals but his social life? And who understand it so well and who can make it so smooth and so amusing as *les gens du monde*?'

'It's rather sad,' she said one day, 'to belong, as we do, to a lost generation. I'm sure in history the two wars will count as one war and that we shall be squashed out of it altogether, and people will forget we ever existed. We might just as well never have lived at all. I do think it's a shame.'

Nancy Mitford, *The Pursuit of Love* (London 1945)

CONTENTS

Edward Cahill

Private Cape Town Studio Recordings of Liszt and Chopin (1955)

Re-Mastered by Selene Records Poland

Pitch-corrected by Jonathan Summers, Curator of Classical Music at the British Library

(Author's Private Collection)

Internet Link: www.michael-moran.net/paderewski

Author Website: www.michael-moran.net

PREFACE

I shall never forget hearing the recordings of the pianist Edward Cahill for the first time during the millennium year. One Saturday evening spent at home alone in rainswept London I decided on an impulse to climb up into the attic and open the trunk of his effects I had inherited long ago. My mood that night was fearfully low as I was attempting to emerge from a blighted love affair. Depression about my future had also set in as I felt I had been studying the piano seriously for far too long without significant success. Seeking the warmth and reassurance of some connection with my family I brushed away the cobwebs suffocating the trunk and began to rummage through the detritus of his life. At the bottom I found some old tape recordings and took them downstairs in anticipation. My old Revox open-reel machine spun into life.

I shall always treasure the feeling of exhilaration on first hearing the individuality of the piano sound he created in his interpretation of *La Campanella* by Liszt. He performed the work as a spectacular tour de force of virtuosity with the greatest refinement of touch, vitality of tone, bell-like timbre and that feathery velocity reminiscent of the late nineteenth century giants of the keyboard. As a musician myself I was astounded at the quality of the playing and determined there and then I must research and write about his life. I was to uncover a universe of fascinating historical recordings, period detail and a career of relentless glamour and success. After a long delayed beginning, the quest for this family portrait was to take me six years.

The fragmentary material piled into that old cabin trunk was a chaotic jigsaw puzzle. It contained unsorted personal letters, journals, manuscripts, music reviews, scrap books, music, concert posters, concert programmes, newspaper articles, official documents, period photographs, a small piece of 16 mm film as well as 78 rpm shellac and tape recordings. Some newspaper reviews glued into the scrapbook were carelessly trimmed so as to be undated, unidentifiable or sectionally damaged, letters contained only the month and not the year they were written with illegible signatures. Photographs often did not identify the exotic subjects. The treasure chest had been collecting dust in the attic of my London flat for over thirty years.

Fortunately in 1968 I had spent some six months with him as a young man and discussed in depth his career, music and the piano. Now I asked myself whether there was sufficient material to construct an engaging biography of a long forgotten Australian concert pianist born in 1885 who was also a member of an unknown family? I feared no-one attempted biographies of such forgotten figures owing to the piecemeal nature of the sources. However I was determined to assemble this remarkable life.

Tantalising references had always hovered in the family of a 'legend', of 'a brilliant classical pianist who played for Queen Mary in London and the aristocracy of Europe during the glamorous 1920s.' As 'Uncle Eddie' had left Australia permanently in 1934 the family could never fully comprehend the depth of his achievement. Few details were known, family records scarce, his name rarely mentioned. No chronology of Edward Cahill existed until I tentatively began work. Establishing this with accuracy soon became the major challenge of the enterprise. Informed supposition was an occasional unavoidable necessity as it proceeded. Any inadvertent blunders are entirely due to my own lack of vigilance.

As time passed I gradually began to see 'Uncle Eddie' not only as a rounded personality but also very much 'a figure in the landscape' of his day, similar to those diminutive personages that populate 17th century classical landscape paintings by Claude Lorrain, Nicolas Poussin or Gaspard Dughet. I became increasingly consumed by the mysterious process of unravelling the poetry of his life as an artist and the society that nurtured him. I brought to light extraordinary coincidences and unsettling congruencies with my own life.

During this 'resurrection' I did not travel to all the destinations that comprised his itinerant lifestyle as his recitals spanned almost every continent and were often in prohibitively expensive exotic locations. Many countries have changed out of all recognition since his time as a result of war, partition or simple developmental change. Inevitably there are tantalising gaps as in all biographies. However I travelled extensively even obsessively in his footsteps encountering a multitude of astonishing places in what became in the end an amazing journey of musical and spiritual discovery.

Prologue

In the year 1891 a curly-haired boy runs along the sunny banks of a river in the early morning chasing a butterfly with his net. Dragonflies with electric blue abdomens and clear wings hover above the muddy water. If he stays very still they will even settle on his trousers for a few seconds warming themselves in the sun. He is a very happy little boy. He has carefully prepared his beer and treacle mixture the night before and smears it on the slim trunks of his favourite eucalypts and nearby bushes. This nectar attracts the butterflies and he can easily capture them in one swift arc. He loves the kaleidoscopic colours of nature. Singing to himself, he puts them in his killing jar. He then carefully folds them into small paper envelopes.

Later, before they dry and stiffen, he carefully pushes fine pins through the thorax and spreads the wings and straps them flat with strips of special paper onto the setting board. Later, when they dry, he displays them in the cabinet his grandmother had bought for him. In spring he loves to watch the huge migrations of the black and white Caper Whites drinking at the river banks. The fast Tailed Emperor, wings folded like a painted Chinese fan, feeds on the over-ripe figs and flowering citrus trees in their garden. In his bedroom he has a glass case of smelly, hairy, wildly striped caterpillars. He loves to watch them until the silver or green chrysalis forms and hangs from its silken pad on the twigs. He sighs with impatience, waiting for its radiant future. The beautiful adult creature finally emerges, shimmering in its fresh markings to begin its life of spectacular display. These he lets fly free.

He is not your normal little boy by any means. He is actually a bit of a show-off, like his butterflies. He loves sounds too; all sorts of sounds fascinate him. They thrill him. He collects old bottles and tins, in fact anything that makes a sound when you hit it with a stick. On this shabby orchestra, sitting in the dust, he performs for other children in the neighbourhood and his brothers and sisters who gather around. The grown-ups roar with laughter to see a very small boy rushing madly about hitting bottles and tins. Lizards scatter under the rocks; rosellas and black cockatoos flee to the trees. Then someone teaches him how to improve his sounds. They show him how by filling the containers with different quantities of water he can produce different notes. His tin can and bottle symphonies improve. He cannot be stopped.

After these first 'performances' in the dirt and dust of colonial Australia he learns the piano against his father's wishes from the wife of the milkman, goes from strength to strength musically and travels from continent to continent, culture to culture until he accomplishes his childish dream. He finally plays in recitals in London commanded by the Queen of England and later in the houses of all her aristocratic friends. The little boy's name is Edward Cahill and this is his story.

CHAPTER 1

LITTLE LORD FAUNTLEROY IN THE GERMAN POCKET

On the east coast of Australia in the State of Queensland, or 'Deep North' as some Australians call it, lies picturesque Moreton Bay, some twenty kilometres north of Brisbane. Captain Cook named but did not explore it on 15 May 1770 during his first voyage. 'This veritable Garden of Eden', teeming with fish, crustacea of all kinds, exotic flowers and colourful birds, subsequently became a ghastly penal outstation. Europeans began to settle the area, but the geography of impenetrable forest and river made farming difficult. This provided a challenge for the predominantly German, Prussian, English and Irish immigrants. The promise of a salubrious climate, orderly government, regular laws, excellent education and religious freedom were irresistible to many fleeing over-population, famine and poverty in Europe.

In 1862 John Davy, his wife Mary and his brother-in-law Francis Gooding emigrated to Queensland and established a sugar plantation between the Albert and Logan Rivers which they named Beenleigh after their old farm in Devon, England. The farm had been suffering severe financial difficulties despite the generally increased prosperity of agriculture in Britain in the mid-nineteenth century. In their new home they were soon growing sugar cane and manufacturing rum, a business which developed into the famous Beenleigh Rum Distillery. A small township subsequently evolved at the junction of five roads and flourished under the same name, Beenleigh.

In 1863 the thirty-year-old farmer and blacksmith Johannes Dauth, his twenty-five-year-old wife Caroline and their three children emigrated to Australia from Stöckheim, Brunswick, some three hundred kilometers north-east of Frankfurt-am-Main.

Germans living west and east of the River Elbe had suffered from an increase in population too large for the resources of the land and were facing economic disintegration. These were the boom years for emigration to Australia.

Only a few years before Queensland had been created a separate colony from New South Wales. The new colony required a labour force to populate its vast spaces. After lengthy consideration the family sailed on 22 September 1863 on the maiden voyage of the clipper *Susanne Godeffroy*. She put to sea from Hamburg and encountered a rough and stormy passage through the English Channel and particularly high seas around the Cape of Good Hope into the Roaring Forties. 'Long ridges of water ran high and fast' which damaged the masts.* Passengers often landed looking 'like they had been in the grave for a week and dug up' reported one migration official. The ship anchored in Moreton Bay over four months later. All the Dauth children survived and a baby was born to Johannes and Caroline whom they named Mary. This infant, so romantically 'born at sea', somehow managed to survive the long voyage and would ultimately become the mother of the brilliant Australian pianist Edward Cahill.

Upon arrival Johannes settled in the New Year first at Eagleby (also known as 'German Pocket') but soon moved to nearby Beenleigh where he became one of the earliest settlers. He opened a blacksmith's shop and built a residence in George Street. Germans were highly respected as hard workers and he became successful supporting his family in relative comfort.

By the mid 1870s Beenleigh was a thriving rural business centre, the main town of the Logan and Albert districts. Queensland had the largest number of German-born residents in the Australian colonies. A school opened in 1871 and one of the Dauth family was among its first pupils. The Beenleigh Hotel was soon established on the corner of George and Main Streets 'a handsome new two storey building ... which will favourably compete for accommodation

---

* I am indebted for most of the early history of Beenleigh to Anne McIntyre of the Logan River & District Family History Society Inc. who assisted me greatly in my research and also published *They Chose Beenleigh: A Tribute to the Immigrant Landholders and Pioneers of the Beenleigh and Eagleby, Queensland, Australia prior to 1885* (Beenleigh 2009), Sailings, p. 47.

and situation with any hotel in the colony out of Brisbane'. By 1885 the population of the town had risen to over four hundred. Although Queensland was not noted at this time for its cultural activities, the presence of the German community and their love and talent for music meant there was substantial support for the building of the School of Arts.*

Edward Cahill's father was born in 1857 on the border of County Tipperary and Laois County (formerly Queen's County) Ireland. The Great Famine of 1845–9 had devastated landlocked Queen's County. Thousands died and many were forced to eat anything they could find. The magistrate Nicholas Cummins described his visit to the hovels of Skibbereen in West Cork

> In the first, six famished and ghastly skeletons, to all appearances dead, were huddled in a corner on some filthy straw, their sole covering what seemed a ragged horsecloth, their wretched legs hanging about, naked above the knees.†

Thousands of inhabitants looking for a better life fled the Great Famine and emigrated to America, Canada or Australia, the Cahill family among them.‡ Edward Cahill Senior was resident in colonial Queensland by 1869. In March of 1881 he was reported to have captained the Tambourine Cricket Club against Upper Logan and knocked up a creditable score as an excellent 'all rounder'. On the Prince of Wales's Birthday the following year he played for Beenleigh as a wicket keeper and fielded and batted outstandingly. He was remembered in the town with much affection as a jovial Irishman with a rough sense of humour.

By the 1880s the economy of this vast colony had moved into positive cycle. However the colony of Queensland remained 'a rather puzzling mixture of success and failure.'§ Many immigrants felt misled by the rosy expectations their agents had given them. Unskilled labour faced a bleak future, but those who commenced

---

* The School of Arts Movement originated in Scotland and spread throughout the English-speaking world in the mid-nineteenth century.

† *The Times* of Christmas Eve 1846 quoted in Thomas Keneally *The Great Shame: A Story of the Irish in the Old World and the New* (London 1998), pp. 129–31.

‡ Between 1841 and 1861 Queen's County lost almost half its population from 154,000 to 90,600.

§ Raymond Evans, *A History of Queensland* (Cambridge 2007), p. 111.

'the fierce battle with nature to form things'* could save and prosper if their health stood up to the rigours of the climate.

In November 1884 Edward Cahill Senior and Mary Dauth married in Brisbane and took up residence permanently in Beenleigh. Despite the economic gloom, he took over as the 'Licensed Victualler' of the Beenleigh Hotel in April 1894, renting it for 30/- per week.† For the previous five years he had been the licensee of the nearby Yatala Hotel about three kilometres from Beenleigh. His new hotel became the centre of the town's social life and the haunt for regular meetings of the local cricket club, jockey club and rifle association. The booking office and staging post for the legendary Cobb & Co transport and Royal Mail coaches was situated in the hotel. 'Incidents' in the life of the town tended to happen there. One anecdote tells of a day when a young man working in the cane fields near Eagleby felt a prick on his ankle and realised he had been bitten by a snake, probably the dreaded Coastal Taipan. Despite the swift efforts of the local Dr Sutton he died under 'the best medical supervision' in a room at the Beenleigh Hotel.

Edward Cahill Junior was born almost exactly a year after their marriage on 10 November in the boom year of 1885. Mary Cahill bore a child every year for the next eight years. She was to survive this gruelling experience without serious illness and only one was to die as an infant. In time the Cahills built a house they called 'Roscrea', which became a landmark in Beenleigh. The residence was named after the town near the border of Laois County and County Tipperary where Edward Cahill Senior was born.

The area around Beenleigh is quite flat, dotted with shrubs and eucalypts such as Ironbark and Forest Red Gum. Despite being only twenty kilometres from the Pacific Ocean, the town is stiflingly hot in summer. The Albert River where Eddie hunted butterflies still takes its slow and picturesque course through the rather arid landscape. When I visited Beenleigh there was no evidence of the site of the distinctive Cahill family home. Undoubtedly Roscrea would have been characterized by broad verandas shaded by a large, graceful Dutch gable roof of shingles or corrugated iron. Sadly I could find

---

* Evans, *A History of Queensland*, p. 110.

† Around £150 in 2015.

no photograph of it during my extensive research. However a few of the buildings Eddie would have known as a child are preserved in what is known as Old Beenleigh Town, an historical village situated on the outskirts of the town's modern suburban sprawl. I attempted to reconstruct this early Australian community in my mind's eye but it was an almost impossible task. Born in 1885 Eddie would find modern Beenleigh unrecognizable.

* * *

Eddie's grandmother and mother were both particularly fond of music. As he grew older he spent hours experimenting with the sounds on his grandmother's old piano, one of the few refined features of their colonial life. She wanted him to learn to play and spoke secretly to his mother about it. His father had no interest in butterflies or piano playing. 'You women will spoil the boyo. The piano is for colleens! Your sisters can learn the piano if they want. He should learn to ride and shoot like a man!'

At the age of five, his mother decided he should begin lessons at his grandmother's house with the milkman's wife. She could play fluently and taught the boy to read music. A few times a week during her round she would tie up the horse, leave the milk cart outside and slip into his grandmother's house to give Eddie a half hour 'secret' lesson. Our 'jovial Irishman' did comment rather unfavourably however when he saw his young son early one morning enthusiastically trotting down the dusty country road between the weatherboard houses dressed in a red velvet Little Lord Fauntleroy suit, his hair carefully pomaded and curled. He threatened to beat him black and blue. 'My mother loves him so much!' his wife assured her husband when he expressed exasperation and returned to the bar to serve some thirsty sun-burned pastoralists. Eddie seemed to know, seemed to have always known, what he wanted to do with his life. That was, of all unlikely things in this region of pitiless heat, pioneers and heartless bush, to be a musician and above all to play the piano. Eddie adored these lessons with the intensity of a vocation.

He was enrolled at the state primary school and was popular with his classmates. The teachers in the small school felt he was above average intelligence for his age. He seemed to be able to instantly communicate his friendliness, good temper and general happiness with life to everyone. Even at this early stage he was a particularly charming child. By the age of eight, the piano playing was coming along well and the lessons became far less of a secret, in fact the whole thing was rather out in the open. He was making extraordinary progress, far beyond what might be considered normal for a child of his age and far beyond the skill of Mrs Bale the milkman's wife. 'Lost in the music!' she said one day. 'Naturally gifted!' she exclaimed on another.

Occasionally, now that he was old enough to keep quiet and cease fidgeting, his mother would take him to a concert at the School of Arts. There was an unusual degree of sophisticated cultural life in this small, isolated town, a place which surprisingly nurtured his dreams. His father was becoming increasingly irritable as the boy reached puberty. He had hoped 'the boyo' would eventually 'grow out of it' and come into the hotel business. 'Music is no career for a man son! Musicians are unhappy, hopeless fellows. If you keep this up you'll end up in the gutter. Wake up to yourself!'

The boy did not seem to care. Every time he sat on the piano stool he could imagine huge crowds of people listening to him in great halls, idolising his performance. He had particularly small hands but wonderful dexterity and an engaging natural way of playing. He also seemed to have what was known as 'perfect pitch', a mixed blessing in some respects, and could improvise his own tunes on any melody that was given to him by members of an audience. In a diary reminiscence written for a radio broadcast made in Sydney as he approached middle age he underlined '*I was a very happy little boy*'. But in reality he contemplated with horror the idea of working in his father's hotel among the rough drovers, cane cutters, cattlemen and rum drinkers.

One of the worst decades in Australian history opened as he began at the rural primary school in Beenleigh. From 1891–96 a severe economic depression crippled the country and was immediately followed by one of the longest-lasting droughts in the colony's history lasting from 1898–1905.* Unemployment reached catastrophic levels. White settlers clashed with Aboriginals and

* Evans, *A History of Queensland*, p. 124.

Melanesian 'Kanakas' who were deemed to be a 'doomed race of Heathens'. Local papers brayed 'no white woman is safe'. By the close of the century the lives of many immigrants and hundreds of thousands of native people had been sacrificed in a genocidal mayhem that had lasted for years.*

* * *

As the eldest son, Eddie was expected to take up a trade after leaving school at fifteen. It is hard to imagine an environment less conducive to becoming a pianist than the Queensland of the early 1900s for such a cultured, aesthetic young man. The family decided that an excellent beginning for someone of Eddie's sensitive temperament would be as a draper's assistant in his father's drapery business a few doors down from the Beenleigh Hotel. Wanting to please rather than follow the summons of his heart, he agreed to take up this dull trade. Each morning he swept the floor of the shop and sprinkled it with fresh damp sawdust, raised the blinds on the front window and adjusted the headless manikins freshly dressed by an eccentric window-dresser. In the evening he lit the oil lamps, which turned the shop into a glowing cavern with pockets of mysterious darkness. He learned to cultivate the charm of the professional salesman. He exuded a natural appeal which impressed the appreciative English colonial ladies who were keen to keep up appearances and deck themselves out in copies of the latest London or Paris fashions. For physical relaxation he played lawn tennis at the weekend, a choice over Rugby Union football which was considered askance by the men of Beenleigh. Yet he managed early each day to fit in an hour or more piano practice at his grandmother's house and even more on Sundays.

He was already twenty-five when, by now a fully fledged draper, he decided he could not stand working in the shop a minute longer, even as the manager. He was chronically tired of measuring out lengths of cloth for elderly women with endless discussions of price. He could hardly wait until the doors closed for the day and he could rush to the joys of the piano and practise like a demon. He had given what might be considered his first piano

* Grimly detailed throughout Evans, *A History of Queensland.*

recital in the School of Arts in 1907. But as he lay in bed at night listening to the raucous shouts from the verandah of the hotel, the drunken carousing in the streets, he planned to run away to Brisbane, embark on a ship bound for Europe, burn the shop down, anything to escape the drudgery that stretched endlessly before him. He wanted adventure, glamour and fame, the adulation of the glittering crowd as a performing musician. He was unashamedly convinced of his talent.

* * *

In 1909 Queensland celebrated its 50th year as a separate entity with a Jubilee Exhibition at the annual Brisbane Agricultural Show in the Botanic Gardens and the official opening of the University of Queensland. Eddie decided to enter the piano competition which was part of the celebrations. The event was judged by a Professor Ives. Eddie was proclaimed the 'Piano Champion Solo' for his performance of a Schumann *Novelette* and he was awarded a gold medal in addition to some prize money. This victory was followed by some serious tuition with a mysterious Miss Hilda Roberts, a Brisbane pianist who introduced him to the acclaimed method pioneered by Tobias Matthay in London.[*] These lessons gave him the self-confidence to seek new endeavours and challenges in music.

The early silent cinema had always fascinated Eddie as a teenager. He used to avidly attend the screenings of short documentaries and comedies at the School of Arts in Beenleigh and also played for Beenleigh Pictures, the firm who screened silent pictures there. Often too he played for the dance that followed. In the early newsreel of the spring meeting of the Melbourne Cup filmed by the Frenchman Marius Sestier, he was captivated by the glamorous crowds of women in ornate Edwardian lace dresses.[†] Eddie had

---

* Tobias Matthay (1858–1945) was an outstanding English pianist, teacher, and composer. He studied at the Royal Academy of Music under the composer and pianist Sir William Sterndale Bennett and taught there from 1876 to 1925 as Professor of Advanced Piano. The English virtuosi Myra Hess, Clifford Curzon, Moura Lympany, Harriet Cohen and Irene Scharrer were but a few of his outstanding pupils. He founded a piano school in 1905 and published several books on technique.

† The Frenchman Marius Sestier (1861–1928), came to Australia from India in 1896 and made some of the first Australian films and screened them at the Salon Lumière in Sydney.

his first taste of the bewitching theatre of royalty and upper-class life, the endless procession of elegant carriages, superb horses and court uniforms and cocked hats fluttering with ostrich feathers in the 1901 documentary *The Inauguration of Australia.* At thirty-five minutes it was one of the longest films of the time made anywhere in the world. On one cloth-buying trip to Brisbane in 1907 he saw 'Australia's Greatest Drama', *The Story of the Kelly Gang,* at the Centennial Hall, the world's first full-length feature film advertised as being 'over a mile in length' and 'over an hour in duration'.* The piano accompaniment included a 'Lecturer' who explained the story and characters using a pointer. Voices behind the screen added dialogue. A kookaburra had been trained to laugh when a limelight lamp shone on it.

He slowly became aware of a possible avenue of escape from the drapery. One day a horse-drawn travelling picture show arrived in Beenleigh. A number of these forgotten touring companies wandered the vast outback of Australia offering silent cinema entertainment. Isolated towns lacking in electricity and the phonograph meant these shows were tremendously popular. They often mixed vaudeville acts with short films projected by limelight. Music was a vital ingredient although during the projection there was a good deal of mechanical noise. Devastating explosions were always likely. 'Going to the pictures' was an adventure in the early years of the Australian silent cinema, for both the audience and the projectionist.

He considered the job of 'picture pianist' something he could easily accomplish and auditioned for the Irish manager of a travelling show called *Flaniken's Films* that had just lost its accompanist. At the audition he improvised with great élan and spirit for *The Eureka Stockade.* The company presented silent stars such as Charlie Chaplin, 'Fatty' Arbuckle and Mabel Normand as well as the rough and tumble of the Keystone Cops to entertainment-starved outback audiences. Eddie would also provide the music for the dance that followed the show.

To the shock and dismay of the entire Cahill family, Eddie excitedly accepted the offer of this poorly paid, uncomfortable job

* *The Story of the Kelly Gang* was photographed for J. & N. Tait by the talented Millard Johnson and William Gibson and first shown in Melbourne on Boxing Day 1906.

with *Flaniken's Films* travelling the outback as an accompanist. He was beside himself with delight. The itinerary would take in much of central Queensland and northern New South Wales. This was to be his first professional musical engagement and the beginning of an enduring love affair with the stage and travel. His father was bitterly disappointed having purchased the Beenleigh Hotel in 1909 and radically remodelled the exterior. He had hoped Eddie would take over when he retired.

The evening programme could be a five-reel feature with two or three shorter comedies or 'scenics' as they were known. A singer travelling with them performed songs by the renowned Scottish entertainer Harry Lauder or popular numbers such as *Meet Me To-night in Dreamland* or *I Wonder Who's Kissing Her Now* accompanied by lantern slides. As he toured with silent pictures Eddie learned how to 'work' an audience, to strongly communicate intense emotion with music. The type of vaudeville act that might accompany the films is breathlessly described in an advertisement in the *Barrier Miner* of 8 January 1912, published in the rough and isolated outback mining town of Broken Hill in far west of New South Wales where 'Mr Eddie Cahill (A.R.A.M. Gold Medallist) and pianologist will preside at the instrument'.

> 'Ching Sung Loo, the Chinese magician, is one of the star performers with his pretty lady assistant. His stage setting is said to be a blaze of Oriental grandeur. He does not speak during the performance, but glides about the stage stealthily and mysteriously. It is claimed that he makes steaming coffee from apparently nowhere, which is freely distributed to the audience; that he raises a lady into mid air utterly defying the laws of gravitation and places her on the points of three swords; that he raises a large bowl of water with living fishes in it from nowhere; that he shoots an arrow through a lady's body, changes wine into water; and that the climax is reached when he eats paper and cotton wool, and the next moment clouds of smoke and streams of sparks issue from his mouth. Then he allows a rifle to be fired point blank at him, and he catches the bullet, which has been previously marked for identification purposes by one of the audience.'

In time, books of musical suggestions were published such as the *Edison Kinetogram* to assist pianists and orchestras in their accompaniments.* Eddie learned to project his feelings directly through the piano in a variety of musical styles. Sinister and uncanny mood music for the night, *agitato* running passages for high tension dramas, seductive touches for the warmth of love, the disturbing chords of jealousy, heavy masses heralding impending doom, the grandeur of heroic combat or the tumult of battle. Eddie was talented at this task, had excellent technique, was a good sight-reader and knew a great deal of music by heart. It was a hard school but an invaluable apprenticeship. He felt that exploring the beauty of the Queensland countryside was ample compensation for the meagre pay.†

It was not long before Eddie found himself in a more permanent position conducting an orchestra of eight at the King's Pictures and the historic Princess Theatre in Brisbane. A lone pianist can watch the screen and improvise whereas an orchestra cannot accomplish this as an ensemble. One of the earliest scores composed especially for a silent film was by the French composer Camille Saint-Saëns for *L'Assassinat du Duc de Guise* in 1908. Eddie was required to compile music from the classical scores of one composer or order selections from a number of composers to suit the emotional hue of the film. This technique reached its apotheosis in 1925 with the legendary score written by Edmund Meisel for *The Battleship Potemkin* directed by Sergei Eisenstein.‡ The director wrote 'The audience must be lashed into a fury and shaken violently by the volume of the sound … this sound can't be strong enough and should be turned to the limit of the audience's physical and mental capacity.'

On a less dramatic scale, Eddie believed that the music should not simply be background but become part of the fabric of the film itself. Such an idea was most unusual at the time and sadly his work in this area has not survived. One of his favourite silent features was *The Cheat* (1915) an early silent directed by Cecil B. DeMille starring

---

* A beacon in the dearth of well-researched academic studies of the history of music in the silent film era is the excellent and informative *Music and the Silent Film: Contexts and Case Studies 1895–1924* by Martin Miller Marks (New York 1997). Quoted p. 72.

† A charming film of life on the road in an Australian travelling picture show in the early 1900s is *The Picture Show Man* (1977) directed by John Power and starring Rod Taylor, John Meillon, Judy Morris, John Ewart, Patrick Cargill and Harold Hopkins.

‡ Edmund Meisel (1894–1930) is a neglected Austrian composer who was a pioneer and a truly *avant-garde* artist in his approach to silent film music.

Fannie Ward and the Japanese actor Sessue Hayakawa. Famous for its dramatic low-key lighting, it explored the taboo of an extra-marital intrigue through erotic Orientalism, female masochism and forcible seduction. In one harrowing scene the flesh of the female character is branded like a prize heifer by the seducer in a gesture of possession. This would no doubt have required a significant leap of musical invention for the young pianist, inexperienced in such passions as were most of the audience.

* * *

Eddie's work in the silent cinema was the beginning of his artistic career. However whilst inhabiting the world of celluloid dreams, roaming the outback and playing in darkened cinemas Eddie did not really take much note of the worsening world situation. It was reported on 28 June 1914 that a European town called Sarajevo was in mourning for an Austrian royal personage who had been shot by a lunatic. Tributes to the nobleman, the Archduke Franz Ferdinand, were paid by the British House of Commons. Sir Oliver Lodge, on his way to Melbourne in July for the meeting of the British Association, said it was most regrettable that Britain should fight over 'a little bother in Serbia.'

The gravity of the European crisis was overlooked in general in Australia as other matters were distracting the public. Dame Nellie Melba was on her way home. Through her influence the Commonwealth Government had acquired the Marconi patents for wireless broadcasting. Australia was beating Canada in the Davis Cup and Maurice Guillaux was setting out to carry air mail from Melbourne to Sydney, then the longest air mail flight in the world. When war was actually declared the *Sydney Morning Herald* drew itself up

> 'Above and beyond everything our armies will fight for British honour. It is our baptism of fire.'*

Eddie had chosen not to enlist for the Great War despite the pressure exerted by his younger and more jingoistic brother James. He did not particularly dislike Germans – his mother was one. The

* *Sydney Morning Herald*, Thursday 6 August 1914, p. 6.

whole idea of hatred, death and killing were abhorrent to him. The war had silently crept up on most people. His mother was secretly relieved. She had suffered and wept enough when his brother James had enlisted in 1916. Another son heading towards the trenches would have been too much to bear. His Irish father was strangely non-committal, yet he seemed to exert an invisible pressure on his artistic son not to be a shirker and do his duty.

Eddie never forgot the shame of being handed a white feather in full view of the drinkers outside his father's hotel by one of the pretty Beenleigh girls*. For the entire period of the war he felt neurotically divided between the responsibility he felt towards his artistic calling and a nagging guilt for failing to enlist. An idea of the prevailing attitude to culture is contained in the earliest newspaper mention of Eddie in the *Darling Downs Gazette* of Saturday 19 June 1913. He is referred to as 'the brilliant young *pianiste*' in a society gossip column entitled *Le Beau Monde,* the writer having adopted the moniker 'Pansy'. Of his concert in Toowoomba on 21 July a perceptive columnist was one of the first to describe qualities that remained throughout his career

> Mr Cahill's technique lacks nothing in accuracy, his taste is excellent and he has the enviable facility of making the audience firm friends by his unassuming manner and undoubted facility.†

The German Dauth immigrant side of his mother's musical family were silently marginalized as 'enemy aliens' although not interned during the Great War. The discrimination did not reach the heights it did in England where even dachshund dogs were attacked in the street. Some five percent of the population of Queensland was of German heritage, yet the state had a more moderate policy towards internees than most other Australian states. Overall, the pressure of immigration remained an inflammatory issue. The town of Innisfail was described by the notorious *Smith's Weekly* as 'a town of dreadful dagoes … a filthy foreign scum oozes from its highways.'‡

---

* Being handed a white feather was a sign that the giver regarded you as a coward for not enlisting in the Great War.

† *Darling Downs Gazette,* 22 July 1913, p. 6. At this concert Eddie performed Liszt's Hungarian Rhapsody No. 12, the Chopin Nocturne Op. 27 No. 2 and Prelude in C minor Op. 28 No. 20 as well as the Scherzo-Caprice Op. 22 by the now forgotten French composer Benjamin Godard (1849–95). At this time he played Gors and Kallman German pianos.

‡ Quoted Evans, *A History of Queensland,* p. 176.

* * *

Another of Eddie's few brief periods of formal study of the instrument entailed six months in 1912 with a Mr J. A. Johnstone of Melbourne, described by the *Queenslander* newspaper as being 'a musician of broad views and great knowledge, a clear and commonsensible thinker and writer on musical subjects, and altogether one of the best equipped teachers in Australia.' Overflowing with natural talent Eddie was largely a self-taught musician with the sustaining vanity that accompanies such gifts. He had left the family nest and was now committed to making his living from music, specifically piano playing.

Early in 1914 he was to be introduced to a man who would change his professional life considerably. The English-born singer, variety artist, entrepreneur and businessman Edward Branscombe had arrived in Australia in 1896 with the English Concert Company. He had been a solo tenor at Westminster Abbey during much of the 1890s, but his career is primarily associated with Australia. In 1901, following a tour of South Africa, Branscombe assembled the Westminster Glee Party and toured the Commonwealth performing a repertoire of English part songs, glees, and madrigals. In addition to his role as soloist, he acted as music director, conductor, and arranger.

Unlike Britain where the musical hall and vaudeville attracted fairly exclusively working-class audiences, the average Australian audience comprised a considerable mix of classes and tastes. Australian theatre was not exclusively preoccupied with bushrangers, convicts and the harsh life of settlers in the outback although they took their rightful place as a reflection of the country's history. Variety acts and plays from abroad were equally if not more popular than the home-grown product.

Branscombe pioneered the use of open-air venues in Australia with his 1909 season at the Melbourne seaside suburb of St Kilda. Open-air garden theatres were subsequently opened in Brisbane and other state capitals. By 1911, Branscombe had put together a number of troupes under the generic title 'The Dandies', the name reflecting the elegant style of costuming and stage decoration. Each troupe, comprising around a dozen performers and a music director/pianist, was distinguished by a colour. Beginning with the Orange Dandies, subsequent companies evolved in the manner of the rainbow to be the Green, Pink, Red, Violet, and Scarlet Dandies.

These companies maintained a significant presence around Australia throughout the First World War, and in this respect played a particularly important role in the country's cultural development, particularly in the smaller, more far-flung capital cities. They employed more than sixty performers at a time and each troupe had an almost exclusive repertoire of many original songs. They presented new material each season. The performers were experienced, multi-talented professionals from the worlds of music hall, vaudeville, or musical comedy. Eddie was taken on as the music director and pianist of the Violet Dandies for the 1914–1915 season and the Orange company from 1916–17. The Orange Dandies had orange and black stage decorations and the men in the troupe wore evening suits faced with orange silk. He greatly respected Branscombe's attention to detail and musical knowledge.

The home of the Brisbane cast was the Cremorne Theatre on the banks of the Brisbane River. The great Polish pianist Ignacy Jan Paderewski performed there on his tour of Australia and commented favourably on the musical discrimination of Brisbane audiences.* Eddie performed more serious classical works as well as vaudeville accompaniments, some composed by himself. In popular venues such as the Exhibition Gardens in Adelaide he was sometimes restricted to an upright piano by limited stage space. He loved Weber and performed the *Invitation to the Dance* with vocal accompaniment as well as the Konzertstück in F minor and the Grieg Piano Concerto A minor with his sister Lily (also an excellent pianist) who performed the keyboard reduction of the orchestral parts on a second instrument.

Glittering confections played with his characteristic élan and panache such as the Grand Polka de Concert Op. 1 by the forgotten American composer Homer Newton Bartlett were tremendously

---

* Ignacy Jan Paderewski (1860–1941) was a Polish pianist, composer, politician and statesman who battled for Polish independence. He was well known and deeply respected on a global scale for both his musicianship and as a statesman. He was the prime minister and foreign minister of Poland in 1919, and represented Poland at the Paris Peace Conference in the same year.

popular.* The fine pianist Harold Bauer, a pupil of Paderewski who performed with Pablo Casals and Fritz Kreisler, was touring Australia early in 1913.† He was greatly impressed with Eddie's playing and encouraged him to study in Paris. The outbreak of war and financial constraints prevented any serious consideration of this idea.

The *Brisbane Courier* described what an audience might experience in this type of early Australian theatre during the capricious summer weather:

> Open-air entertainments are delightful on summer evenings in Brisbane, and the popular 'Cremorne' theatre, situated on the river bank, South Brisbane, facing the south-east, and open to the cool breezes, is always a favourite resort. During the cool evenings, and when the weather is threatening or unpropitious, the popular theatre is converted into a huge canvas hall, and completely enclosed in waterproof awnings and side screens which afford protection against inclement weather.‡

A decisive meeting came about during this happy period when Eddie met the lyric tenor George Brooke (b. 1886), also a performer with the Violet and Orange Dandies. Eddie was very taken with his superb voice and together they performed English art songs, German *Lieder* and in particular Negro spirituals of which George was particularly fond. He had studied singing in Melbourne under a Professor Frederick Beard. The British minstrel show was enormously popular in Australia at this time and the more artistic and spiritual forms of its expression were greatly appreciated by 'cultured' audiences. In a broadcast for the BBC in the 1930s Eddie reminisced about his first meeting with George Brooke

> I met my fate in the person of George Brooke. He became my partner in every musical venture, and my life-long friend. He had previously been a clerk in a bank but found it so desperately boring he decided to pursue his dream of being a singer. I had gone over to Manly one warm summer evening to see the Dandy Show. There were about a dozen performers in the company which appeared to be a very popular one. But George

* Homer Newton Bartlett (1845–1920) born Olive, New York. A pianist and composer considered one of the finest of American musicians.

† Harold Bauer (1873–1951), a notable pianist born in Kingston upon Thames to a German father (a violinist) and an English mother.

‡ *Brisbane Courier*, 22 September 1917, p. 12.

Brooke the singer was even then the star attraction of the show. A man with expressive dark eyes and a smile that disclosed teeth of dazzling whiteness, he was noticeable on the platform by a certain aloofness, an expression almost of boredom, when he was not actually singing. The moment he opened his mouth he appeared to become another person, and seemed to exert on his audience, quite without effort, an extraordinary personal magnetism.

The atmosphere of the crowded audience changed imperceptibly as he sang his first number. People sat silent, attentive, not a dress rustling, not a cough or movement. He sang a simple ballad *The Empty Nest.* Another artist might have rendered it sugary sweet, an ordinary song. This young man lifted it into the realm of true art. I knew then he was destined for greater things than a Dandy show. It was not long now before I was in the same show playing for Brooke, and this was the beginning of a great partnership that lasted until his untimely death.

George, although he knew as well as I did, that he 'had the goods' was always more apathetic in business than I was and it was becoming more and more the rule between us for me to be the battling member of the firm. That was the difference in our respective temperaments. It has always been my way to rush in where angels fear to tread, but George was more of the 'live and let live' type. 'Leave it to Ed' in business matters was his slogan. He had less sense of money than anyone I ever knew. I have even known him to start out to do our household marketing with a five pound note returning with five pounds in change and an armful of purchases! 'Why worry?' was his motto and yet strange to say, he was wonderfully accurate and painstaking in things of real importance he wanted to carry through. It was always left to Brooke to look after the cash. In the job he was quite in his element, never made a mistake in the reckoning and never lost sight of it until it was safely in the bank.'

Another consequential moment occurred early in 1915 in Adelaide on one of their earliest Australian tours with the Dandies when Eddie and George met Dame Nellie Melba.* Eddie continues in a broadcast reminiscence

* Dame Nellie Melba (1861–1931) was an Australian operatic lyric soprano of incalculable fame and renown in her day. She became one of the most famous singers of the late Victorian period performing for Royalty across Europe, the Tsar of All the Russias and Leo Tolstoy. She was the first Australian to achieve international recognition as a classical musician and became a household name. She actively supported her compatriots, like Eddie and George, if she felt that they, as she put it rather bluntly, 'had the goods'.

'The diva at that time was giving a series of concerts in the Exhibition Building – a great barn of a place – in whose pleasant gardens our own show was also holding a season in the open air. We frequently said to one another 'What a bit of luck it would be for us if we could induce Melba to hear our work.' The idea grew to be a sort of superstition in our minds. If Melba would hear us and approve, all would be well. I remember the clock striking 12 on the night when we finally sealed a letter containing our request to Melba to give us a private audition and I said to Brooke 'Surely that is a good omen for us.' George was just as keen on the idea as me, but, as usual I did all the talking!'

Next morning we were summoned to Government House, where Melba was staying as the guest of Lady Galway.* I had heard Melba sing. How can I describe her voice? To me it was as sparkling as silver. There was a coolness about it. It is almost impossible to describe the beauty of it. I can never forget that haunting white quality, or should I say that perfection of tone in *Salce, Salce* the Willow Song sung by Desdemona in Verdi's *Otello.* Meeting her face to face on such an important mission was a very different matter. We knew of her erratic temperament, her moods, her sudden likes and dislikes, How would she act towards us?

Punctually at the appointed time Melba came into the drawing room with that quick, forceful step of hers that was so characteristic. We had heard from Lady Galway that Melba was exhausted under the strain of the previous night's concert, but there was no evidence of it in her appearance. She immediately asked us to begin. I played one of my favourite works, the dramatic Bach-Tausig Toccata and Fugue in D minor and Brooke sang the German *Lieder* that he loved so well. Before Melba had spoken we both felt she was interested in our work. In her abrupt, spontaneous way she asked me to also play some work at two of her concerts.

As we were about to leave she said 'Always keep something in reserve. Never give the public all you have.' This of course was of great value to me as a professional pianist. Subsequently

---

* Lady Galway (1876–1963), Marie Carola Franciska d'Erlanger, was a Baroness and the only daughter of the Irish Baronet Sir Rowland Blennerhassett and Countess Charlotte Julia de Leyden, a biographer and historian from Bavaria. She married Lieutenant-Colonel Sir Henry Lionel Galway, KCMG, DSO (1859–1949) who was the spectacularly controversial Governor of South Australia from April 1914 until April 1920. During the Great War the Governor stirred up resentment against Australians of German descent despite the fact his wife was half German.

> Melba said to Brooke 'You must both go to London after this terrible war is settled. Better to be a lamp post in London than a star in Australia.' Naturally this gave us great heart. Melba had enormous strength of character. The *Queenslander* newspaper commented on the success abroad of Percy Grainger. Of the remark made by Madame Melba the paper observed 'Paderewski is still on the throne, but the world is wide, and there is plenty of room and reward for pianists of exceptional quality.'
>
> When the time came she promised to give us letters of introduction to her manager in London and something special to my heart, a letter of introduction to the great Russian pianist Vladimir de Pachmann.* At the time he was considered one of the greatest Chopin interpreters in the world. I always likened Melba to a Roman Emperor.'

Performing with George he found it easier to calm his nervous tension. Described as 'bright, alert, happy and breezy in speech, quite modest in regard to his attainments but an enthusiastic music lover'† he occasionally and surprisingly suffered stage fright. They gave many concerts as a duo all over Australia to great acclaim in addition to their Dandies contract. The 'sharing' of musical discoveries rather than 'presenting' music would be the source of their continuing popularity. Their work with the Dandies helped them achieve a remarkable balance in skilful programme design within a variety of musical genres. A Schumann *Novelette* or the Chopin *Grande Valse Brillante* might jostle surprisingly well with the popular and stirring Maori song *Waiata Poi*; a Liszt Hungarian Rhapsody may follow a Negro spiritual; serious Schubert *Lieder* or Puccini operatic arias hold hands with charming salon piano pieces by the largely forgotten composers such as Cécile Chaminade‡, Amilcare Zanella§ or Benjamin Godard.

* The Russian pianist Vladimir de Pachmann (1848–1933) was regarded as one of the greatest pianists of his day and considered by his public as the greatest interpreter of Chopin. He was possessed of extraordinary eccentricities during performances, often engaging the audience verbally, describing how he was playing, even praising himself lavishly and audibly in mid-piece. 'Excellent Pachmann!'

† *Prahran Telegraph*, 5 February 1916, p. 4.

‡ Cécile Chaminade (1857–1944) was a now largely forgotten French composer who had an extremely successful career performing her own works with inimitable Parisian *chic* and *panache*.

§ Amilcare Zanella (1873–1949) was an Italian composer and pianist who became famous in Argentina and later Director of the Conservatoire at Parma and then later a renowned musical figure at Pesaro on the Adriatic coast of Italy.

Not all the reviews were glowing ('Mr Cahill's fingers work faster than his feelings. He necessarily was not so successful where a deep note of feeling has to be sounded, but in others he was delightful ... Mr Brooke also is too obvious in his intentions', wrote the rather mean-spirited music critic of *The Argus* in Melbourne in November 1917). It was slowly becoming clear that if their star was to rise, a period of 'study overseas', preferably in London, would be the next sensible step.

Eddie was a neurasthenic individual, super-sensitive to criticism, and towards the end of 1917 had a complete nervous breakdown. This was the first of a number he suffered throughout his life that hints at a manic-depressive personality or bi-polar disorder. The source of his anxiety was perhaps only partly the result of his fear of audience and critical reaction to his playing. There was the prolonged guilt associated with not enlisting and grim apprehensions for his brother fighting at the front. As my researches deepened I began to wonder about his sexual orientation. In this censorious time it may have given him worsening inner conflicts. Certainly he was afflicted with what is now known as 'free-floating anxiety', generalised worry out of all proportion with the risk. Anxiety was the first inherited familial aspect of his personality I noticed in myself.

It was thought by the Dandy company that Eddie would need to give up the concert stage for at least a year. However, being a resilient personality and at base a bubbling optimist, he turned matters to his advantage, even attracting a fee for a newspaper testimonial praising the manufacturers of Elliott's Beef, Iron and Malted Wine which apparently restored him to mental health 'I am back at my piano again and now feel as ever I was. Your wonderful tonic is a real 'pick me up' saving me weeks of illness.' So well in fact that he gave a 'heartily applauded' charity concert for the State War Council's Appeal Fund at the Town Hall in Melbourne in March 1918.

The Armistice with Germany was signed on 11 November 1918. Eddie and George were suffering chronic financial need and cast about them for further opportunities. Eddie had become deeply depressed over the deaths in a single year of his brother James from influenza and his beautiful sister Mary, beloved for her selflessness, from acute rheumatism. A sense of mortality now lay heavy upon him. Unemployment was a chronic immediate post-war problem in a land hoping to become in the words of the British Prime Minister Lloyd George, 'fit for heroes'.

Now that the war seemed to be haltingly drawing to a close they decided to leave the Dandies and take the risk of setting up alone as the Cahill-Brooke Concert Party. An account of a concert in the Brisbane *Daily Standard* of April 1917 indicates initial difficulties

> The Centennial Hall on Saturday night was too small to accommodate the enthusiastic audience that greeted them. The need for a decent hall for this class of entertainment was never so apparent as on this occasion. The promoters did their best to hide the 'dinginess', but were powerless to eliminate the noise of clicking billiard balls and roisterers in the backyard adjoining the hall. A tin of rubbish and offal made its presence felt in the outside passage until a soldier volunteered to remove it. Apart from these disadvantages the acoustic properties for vocalists are bad.

After a generally successful Australian tour (where the *Moonlight* Sonata was usually considered the high point) the primary critical observation, apart from their exhibition of great talent and attracting insistent encores, was that their immense popularity stemmed from 'playing to suit the tastes of lovers of all classes of music'. Not all was cherry blossom. Classical music critics called for more seriousness from Eddie and more spontaneity from George. Yet most agreed on their tremendous musical promise. It was widely considered that Eddie would become one of the greatest pianists Australia had produced since Percy Grainger.

They were soon engaged by the famous Canadian impresario Frederick Shipman, who managed the tours of such stars as the Australian soprano Dame Nellie Melba and the Austrian violinist Fritz Kreisler. He planned an unprecedented tour of India and the Southeast Asia. After it was concluded and they were financially secure, they could follow Dame Nellie Melba's advice and set sail for that ultimate goal of colonial classical musicians seeking to prove and improve themselves, the great metropolis of London.

CHAPTER 2

OF MAHARAJAS AND PALACES

It was my songs that taught me all the lessons I ever learnt.
Rabindranath Tagore, *Gitanjali*

Frederick Shipman harboured immense ambition for the Cahill-Brooke Concert Party. He conceived the longest musical concert tour of the Southeast Asia and India ever attempted by Europeans. Over a period of more than a year, at times together with the operatic soprano Rita Erle (formerly Rita Kirkpatrick) and lyric soprano Miss Josie Westaway (the beautiful young soloist of St Mary's Cathedral choir Sydney), they would tour India, the Philippine Islands, Siam (Thailand), Borneo, Sumatra, Java, Kashmir and Burma (Myanmar). In late September 1919 after a lavish farewell party thrown by Miss Westaway at her parents' home, they embarked on the SS *Montoro*, a comfortable passenger vessel that plied between Australia, India, Java and Singapore. The paper streamers connecting them to friends and relations stretched taut and snapped. A great adventure lay ahead.

Their first taste of the exotic East came unexpectedly in Darwin itself as they were marooned there for three dull weeks waiting for a passage. In 1919 Darwin was an unprepossessing town prone to periodic destruction by cyclones. Unemployed Chinese, Europeans and Japanese lolled in the stifling heat. Bullock carts and camel trains passed lethargically along the wide streets while the occasional bean seed planter in a white sola *topi* and tropical suit emerged onto a wooden balcony. The evening before they sailed, an excited Eddie and George gave a concert using an ancient piano in a dilapidated 'concert hall'.

The voyage was smooth and uneventful, the gentle thrum of the engines reassuring, the movement of air on deck refreshing during velvet tropical nights. Their first appearance in 'the East' *en route* to India was at the imposing Victoria Theatre in Singapore for two nights on 22 October and 24 October. A few months before their arrival a statue of Sir Stamford Raffles had been erected before the tall signature clock tower to celebrate the centenary of the founding of Singapore.[*] They then sailed on to Bangkok for a brief appearance while the ship took on stores and cargo. Reviews of these concerts appear not to have survived. They would give further performances on the return voyage to Australia after their extended tour of India.

After reaching the Bay of Bengal some hundred miles from Calcutta (Kolkata) Port, a highly skilled and immaculately dressed pilot boarded the ship with his assistant. He guided the ship through the swift and treacherous currents of the Hooghly (Hugli) River past the ruins of a Portuguese Fort to the berth at Diamond Harbour. Kipling described it as 'the most dangerous river on earth' with channels swollen with 'the fat silt of the fields'.[†] Eddie and George were taken by car from here to the Grand Hotel. They would perform their first recital of the tour at the dazzlingly white imperial Calcutta Club.

Calcutta (Kolkata), known as the 'City of Palaces' had been the colourful and exotic capital of the East India Company and British Raj for over a hundred years. The imposing Calcutta Club had been founded in 1907 by Lord Minto[‡] successor to Lord Curzon as Viceroy of India[§]. Minto, a keen hunter (his shooting party bagged 4,919 inedible sand grouse in two days in 1906), once commented in a burst of imperial pride 'The *Raj* will not disappear in India as long as the British race remains what it is …'. Wandering about in the enervating heat they admired Dalhousie Square (the present Benoy-Badal-Dinesh Bagh), the classically columned administrative centre of the city and the former headquarters of the East India Company.

* Sir Thomas Stamford Raffles (1781–1826) was a British statesman most famous for his founding of Singapore on 6 February 1819. His legacy lives on along with his name.

† '*An Unqualified Pilot*' from Rudyard Kipling *Land and Sea Tales* (London 1923), p. 35.

‡ Gilbert John Elliot-Murray-Kynynmound, 4th Earl of Minto (1845–1914) Viceroy of India 1905–10.

§ George Nathaniel Curzon, 1st Marquess Curzon of Kedleston (1859–1925) was the pre-eminent Viceroy of India 1899–1905.

Like many young men of the day, the most Eddie and George knew of the city (and perhaps of the entire country) was that notorious myth of Empire, the 'Black Hole of Calcutta'.

Eddie was enraptured by the former capital and its extensive parks. They strolled through the hazy European Quarter along wide avenues of classical Palladian architecture. The Royal Botanic Gardens, perhaps the finest in the Empire, were situated on the opposite bank of the Hooghly River. They admired the Great Banyan, traveller palms, mangoes, feathery casuarinas and mahogany. At the entrance to Government House a monumental classical arch was crowned with a British lion, its paw possessively resting on a globe in a statement of invincibility. They explored the poor areas and dusty markets, the air beguiling them with spices and the aroma of rich roasting coffee.

It was a particularly sensitive time for a concert party to be touring India. By the time of their visit cracks in the edifice of imperial domination had inexorably begun to widen. The storm clouds of Indian nationalism were gathering. The Cahill-Brooke Concert Party had arrived to entertain but the Anglo-Indian administrators were teetering on the brink of profound change.[*] Ghandi had transformed the Indian National Congress into a powerful force demanding home rule. Our entertainers had sailed into a fraught political atmosphere.

Both Eddie and George believed that audiences wished primarily to be amused, women being far more sympathetic to music than men. This would certainly have been the case in colonial India. British men were judged on their preference for 'hard bodily exercise', their ability to ride, hunt game, show skill at pig-sticking, shoot and talk about tigers. These jungle wallahs preferred 'knocking about in stained brown raiment' and waking up for breakfast in virgin undergrowth to listening to classical music. When the blunt Irish-born Viceroy Sir John Lawrence[†] learned that one benighted Civilian had brought a piano out to India he swore to 'smash it' for him.[‡]

---

* In the nineteenth and early twentieth century the term 'Anglo-Indian' was defined by the *OED* as 'Of mixed British and Indian parentage, of Indian descent but born or living in Britain, or (chiefly historical) of British descent or birth but living or having lived long in India'.

† Sir John Lawrence (1811–79) was a British statesman who served as Viceroy of India 1864–69.

‡ Members of the Indian Civil Service were known as 'Civilians'.

However, scattered among the prospective audience were the Collectors and Civilians of the Imperial bureaucracy.* They were the minority of cultured Oxford men, some even intellectuals, who read Plato, Horace and Homer whilst in India. Some studied and made significant contributions to knowledge of the languages and ethnography of the subcontinent. Most contributed significantly to advancing the infrastructure in India, ruling by a curious mixture of discipline, military might and moral force.

The Calcutta Club concerts were highly successful (discounting the wayward tuning of the piano) with many encores being enthusiastically demanded. As well as performing his usual Liszt rhapsodies, Chopin polonaises and nocturnes, Eddie realized it was close to Christmas. Many in the audience were separated by their colonial duties from the comforting drawing room fires and festive cheer of 'Home'. To conclude the classical section of his concerts Eddie performed the novelty piece 'Trinity Chimes' by the American composer Walter Decker. In this astonishing piece 'Silent Night' alternates with 'Come All Ye Faithful' in the bell-like upper registers of the piano, the charm and amusement of which was augmented by George ringing hand bells. This reminder of an English Christmas was rapturously received.

* * *

A long train journey hugging the coast of the Bay of Bengal took them through heat and dust to Madras (Chennai) on the Coramandel Coast, the landscape a mixture of palms, lagoons and white beaches. The climate of Madras was debilitating so the city was not a popular posting. The new, large capacity Wellington Cinema in the suburb of Tana welcomed them for a week-long season. Eddie received glowing reviews praising his musical temperament 'which enables him to give interpretations of compositions which are full of expression, which seek to convey the meaning the composer intended to convey.' He was forced to perform on an indifferent baby grand piano with sweating, slippery fingers. The *Madras Times* wrote: 'The chief praise must

* A 'Collector' was a principal position in the executive branch of the Indian Government (Indian Administrative Service).

undoubtedly be given to Mr Cahill. He played magnificently, and the memory of at least one item, Zanella's *Minuetto* will remain with us for a very long time.'* Eddie also played the *Moonlight* Sonata, the famous Rachmaninoff Prelude in G minor and some minor salon works of his own composition.

* * *

A week-long season in Bangalore (Bengaluru) left them exhausted. The company were lodged in the fine West End Hotel. In the city Cubbon Park was named Rotten Row in a nostalgic reference to London's fashionable ride in Hyde Park. Eddie was far more of a mannered aesthete than George and enjoyed what he called 'the charm and extravagance of imperial life'. The heat and exotic atmosphere excited his libido as he picnicked with ladies in Meade's Park and listened to imperial military bands. George found the English rulers pretentious and often refused to accept formal invitations to white tie dinner parties. The need to adapt to English colonial manners soon led to frayed tempers. In addition a platonic romance seemed to be blossoming between Eddie and 'the particularly charming' soprano Josie Westaway. George sang duets with her and discovered his own heart similarly engaged. This lead to the boys leading rather separate social lives.

The testimonials from Dame Nellie Melba gave them *carte blanche* to the highest cultural circles. Eddie was praised for possessing 'the characteristic modesty of a true artist'. George was praised for the adventurous variety of his songs ranging from Schubert *Lieder* to Negro spirituals. In an interview he commented that as artists they wished to attract the casual lover of music, 'the one who says he knows nothing about it but just likes it.'

* * *

The pleasantly mild winter weather continued until the end of January 1920. The steam locomotive of the Guaranteed State Railway Company pulled into the largely deserted fortress-like railway station at Secunderabad carrying the concert party to their

* The Tempo di Minuetto No. 1 Op. 29.

next engagement. This small town, founded as a British cantonment at the turn of the eighteenth century, is separated from its better known twin sister Hyderabad by beautiful Lake Hussain Sagar.*

Eddie and George performed at the Secunderabad Club, one of the five oldest clubs in India and at that time reserved exclusively for British officers and their wives and families. Enthusiasm greeted what was clearly an 'event to pass the weary hours'. After the concert the audience clamoured for a return of the touring company. The local paper wrote pointedly

> 'As a rule touring parties that come to small stations like ours are attended only by people who can think of nothing else to do or dinner parties the hostesses of which do not feel able to entertain their guest after the meal. This was not the case on Monday.'

The travelling concert party were almost living on trains breathing in gritty smoke for hours. From Secunderabad they travelled on a narrow gauge railway into the thankfully cool nights of Poona (Pune). Pune is situated in Maharashtra at the confluence of the Mutha and Mula rivers, occupying a strategic position on the trade routes between the Deccan and the Arabian Sea. Poona was one of the best rest stations in India because of the climate, the gymkhana, the charming balls and 'jolly regattas' celebrated on the river.

The concert party performed at the weatherboard Gymkhana before a mixed audience of graceful ladies and stiff military officers. The 'Poona Season' began in June so they had arrived at an unfashionable time. Eddie worried about an initially 'deep silence' that reigned after each item. Society in Poona was rather straight-laced at any time but at the conclusion the audience erupted into 'tumultuous applause'. The concerts were reviewed as 'a musical treat of a very high order.'

Eddie was curious to explore the other side of town, the alternative world of their 'official' engagements. The Imperial Poona lifestyle was in shocking contrast to the indigenous area, still locked into the Peshwa era. He noticed no broad roads here, simply unsealed tracks, numerous Hindu temples, a labyrinth of suffocating alleys and lanes swirling with dust and dirt. Stinking

* A cantonment was a permanent military station.

latrines were placed at the entrance to houses for the convenience of the sewage collectors creating terrible discomfort to those entering or leaving the dwellings. At night a shattered collection of kerosene lamps gave fitful illumination to the human shadows that flitted past seeking the safety of home.

* * *

From Poona to Bombay (Mumbai) was but a short distance. They experienced a certain 'Grandeur of Arrival' at The Victoria Terminus, an imposing Venetian Gothic Revival building enlivened by exuberant Indian decoration. They were taken by horse-drawn carriage to the extraordinary Watson's Esplanade Hotel, the grandest in the city. Poverty and wealth lay in close proximity; beautiful women and tall athletic men gave a theatrical atmosphere to street life.

Watson's Hotel had been fabricated in wrought and cast iron by the Phoenix Foundry Company in Derby, shipped out and assembled on a wide Esplanade. One writer referred to the skeleton of the exceptional structure 'like a huge birdcage had risen like an exhalation from the earth.'[*] The floors were of precious teak, mahogany and Minton tiles. There was a central atrium with a restaurant, drapers, tailoring shops, drawing rooms and billiard rooms located below the hotel accommodation.

Eddie and George took small rooms in the upper story reserved for 'bachelors and quasi-single gentlemen'.[†] The reception cannot have been so different for them than when Mark Twain stayed at the hotel at the turn of the twentieth century. He described his own arrival at Watson's in his wonderfully prolix travelogue *Following the Equator*

> The lobbies and halls were full of turbaned, and fez'd and embroidered, cap'd, and barefooted, and cotton-clad dark natives, some of them rushing about, others at rest squatting, or sitting on the ground; some of them chattering with energy, others still and dreamy; in the dining-room every man's own private native

* James Douglas, *Bombay and Western India: A Series of Stray Papers,* 2 vols, 1893, vol. 1, p. 218. The hotel was the first pre-skyscraper, multi-storey habitable building in the world in which all loads, including those of the brick curtain walls, were carried on an iron frame.

† *The Times of India,* 14 February 1870, p. 2.

servant standing behind his chair, and dressed for a part in the Arabian Nights ...*

Kipling fictionalized the hotel in two of his stories.

The first concerts Eddie and George gave were at the Bombay Gymkhana, originally a cricket pavilion that had grown into an exclusive club for British officers. After their evening and lunchtime concerts, which were extremely popular, they would relax, sip their Pimm's or take a 'peg' of whiskey and watch a cricket match from the spacious veranda.† Fans revolved lethargically in the high wooden ceilings. Their customary mixed musical program was 'ferociously applauded'.

The *Bombay Advocate* wrote that the customarily decorous audience were given to 'enthusiastic cheers mingled with outbursts of applause when Mr Edward Cahill, the talented Australian pianist, finished his second number'. The response bordered on an actual ovation by the colonial 'men of action' normally bored to tears by piano playing. George was considered to have a 'fine platform appearance' and 'a limpid quality of tone and fine phrasing'. Xaver Scharwenka's spirited Polish Dances were tremendously popular, as was the *Miserere* scene from *Il Travatore*. As well as Chopin polonaises Eddie repeated the novelty piece 'Trinity Chimes' with George once again enthusiastically setting to on hand bells. The nostalgia thus evoked almost brought down the house. They had also been secured for a long run of performances at the magnificent and relatively new Royal Opera House, the interior adorned with crystal chandeliers, precious marbles, cane seating and behind the stalls, rows of boxes with notorious couches.

The *Bombay Chronicle* perceptively noted that 'Mr Cahill tries to arrange his programs that it may have a crescendo of interest, and by arousing the imagination to appeal to the casual theatre-goer as well as the trained musician.' The hall was crowded to hear his 'renowned singing tone' in a selection of Mendelssohn's *Songs Without Words* and to appreciate his lightness and elegance in the *Andante and Rondo capriccioso*. They leapt to their feet after

---

* Mark Twain, *Following the Equator: A Journey Round the World* (Hartford, Connecticut 1897), p. 348.

† A 'peg' was a miniature jug for a measure of alcoholic drink in colonial India. Also known as a *chota-peg*.

the dramatic and popular Liszt Hungarian Rhapsody No. 12. 'His mastery of the piano suggests genius rather than talent. He is destined to become famous.' Eddie commented on the intense musicality of the large number of Bombay Parsis who patronized their concerts, one family attending eighteen performances and following them to other points of call around the country.[*]

* * *

The Viceroy at the time of their visit to Jaipur was the much decorated Frederic Thesiger, 1st Viscount Chelmsford[†], 'a lofty patrician with a Merovingian disdain for interference in any business at all and a man in the hands of his own officials.'[‡] He had been a controversial Governor of Queensland from 1905–9 before being appointed Viceroy by George V in 1916. The soundness of his judgment was often called into question. Despite the grandeur and power of their position, the Viceroys were not always from the absolute top flight of administrative British talent. The enormous Rajputana Agency area was referred to disparagingly in personal letters as the 'Great Sloth Belt'. The concert party had been invited to give a single concert of classical music before the Maharajah of Jaipur, HH Maharajadhiraja Sir Madho Singh II[§]. The Viceroy also communicated a wish to hear the Queensland pianist.

An adopted son of the Maharajah HH Ram Singh II[¶], HH Madho Singh II was a just and progressive ruler. He extended the superb Rambagh Palace to lavishly accommodate guests. It had its own polo field attached to the pleasure gardens. Lord Curzon had a particular respect for this ruler who had made an historic visit to England in 1902 to attend the coronation of King Edward VII, now Emperor of India. Mounted Indian colonial troops had made the

---

* The Parsis are an ancient minority Persian Zoroastrian racial group who fled religious persecution in Iran in the 10th century to settle in India, mainly in Bombay. They were particularly loyal to Britain during the period of Empire and their outstanding character qualities, moral stature and advanced culture were greatly respected by the imperial powers. The conductor Zubin Mehta is and the popular singer Freddie Mercury was a Parsi.

† Frederic John Napier Thesiger, 1st Viscount Chelmsford (1868–1933), Viceroy of India 1916–1921.

‡ Nigel Collett, *The Butcher of Amritsar: General Reginald Dyer* (London 2005), p. 324.

§ HH Maharajadhiraja Sir Madho Singh II (1880–1922).

¶ HH Maharajah Sir Ram Singh II (1835–80).

event into a superb pageant. To accommodate his orthodox Hindu lifestyle he chartered an entire P & O liner modified to include a temple to Krishna. Master silversmiths had cast two vast polished *gangajalis* (water containers) from some 14,000 silver coins filled with hundreds of gallons of sacred Ganges water for drinking and bathing while abroad.

For their first concert in overwhelmingly sumptuous surroundings, the Maharajah sent two Sunbeam motorcars to collect the concert party. For the second concert he despatched a richly caparisoned elephant. When entering the palace by motorcar they had wondered at the imposing gate what appeared to be a doorbell mounted high above the ground. Seated in the opulent *howdah* perched on the back of the elephant its high placement became clear. The Maharajah, as Eddie noted, festooned in 'more precious jewels, pearls and priceless fabrics than I have ever seen in my entire life' appreciated the performance. George almost caused a serious incident of etiquette before they began to perform by investigating in a mood of vague curiosity what was behind the Purdah Curtain in the Durbar Hall. The private secretary to the Maharajah rushed across preventing the cultural calamity of George gazing upon the ruler's wives concealed there to hear the concert. Eddie and George in wonderment finally rested in the palace as honoured guests, touring and admiring the beauty of this princely city with its pink sandstone palaces and beautiful gardens.

* * *

By the end of March 1920 the weather was heating up to an uncomfortable degree and the company were pleased to learn that after an unnoticed concert they gave in New Delhi, their next point of call would be the cool, pleasure-loving hill station of Mussoorie.

Rudyard Kipling wrote of Mussoorie in *Kim*:

> 'Who goes to the hills goes to his mother.'
>
> Under the great ramp to Mussoorie he drew together as an old hunter faces a well-remembered bank, and where he should have sunk exhausted swung his long draperies about him, drew a deep double-lungful of diamond air, and walked as only a Hillman can. Kim, plains-bred and plains-fed, sweated and panted astonished.

As summer strengthened rendering the plains a sweltering crucible, the British, especially the women, fled the relentless heat like migrant birds. They settled in the clubs, hotels and rented houses of the hill stations of the Punjab from April to the end of June. Many single girls in optimistic and party mood were 'fishing' for a suitable aristocratic sun-burnished officer on leave when they made the two thousand metre ascent to beautiful Mussoorie, the 'Queen of the Hills'. The husbands were abandoned to 'do their lofty duty' and baked on the plains while their wives adopted a young 'bow-wow' for the duration.* Mussoorie had a 'rather naughty' reputation for theatricals and loose moral behaviour. Here individualism was allowed a freer rein than the more famous and 'proper' Simla, the official summer capital ironically known as 'The Abode of the Little Tin Gods'.

The variety of its scenery and spectacular views marked it out from other hill stations. Mussoorie had two breweries, a polo field, a small golf course and at the glamorous centre of social gatherings, the Himalaya Club and the Happy Valley Club. Anglo-Indian bungalows, decorated with hanging baskets of sweet peas and geraniums, were named with nostalgic Englishness Holly Mount or Rosemary Cottage. At Stiffles Restaurant the tables overflowed onto the summer pavements. The restaurant had once catered for the visit of the Princess of Wales, later to become Queen Mary. Balls, dinners, theatricals and tea parties attracted all manner of respectable and louche aristocracy. Lovers languished in the exoticism of the East longing for leave. Maharajahs built summer residences in the guise of French chateaux.

The Cahill-Brooke Concert Party were in great demand as by the early 1920s the hill station had become the epitome of the 'roaring twenties' in India. Dance teachers of German origin conducted classes on the finer points of ballroom dancing. After travelling by train from Delhi to Dehra Dún, the concert party were taken up the serpentine road to the main town by *tonga*.† Fragile railings were

* A 'bow-wow' was an admirer who with the greatest rectitude would do all those little tasks a colonial lady so often required – fetching, carrying, standing on attendance for wants and needs, dealing with Indian tradesmen, providing company and status at afternoon tea, balls, soirees and so on.

† A romantic horse-drawn carriage.

the only barrier against terrifyingly precipitous drops. The first motorcar only managed to reach Mussoorie in 1920. They stayed at the fashionable Savoy Hotel, a place with a certain 'reputation'. The American writer Lowell Thomas, who spent several weeks with Lawrence of Arabia in the deserts of Palestine, visited Mussoorie in 1926 during his extensive travels in India. In his book *The Land of the Black Pagoda* he wrote of what became known as the 'separation bell' at the Savoy. He laconically observed:

> 'There is a hotel in Mussoorie where they ring a bell just before dawn so that the pious may say their prayers and the impious get back to their own beds.'

* * *

The parents of many British children were not sufficiently well off to send them to public school in England. Mussoorie had an equable climate, crystalline air and was more easily accessible than many hill stations. As a result many fine boarding schools opened to satisfy this demand for education. The teachers were recruited in England and the first students were mainly the daughters of British officers.

The concert party had been invited to perform at Woodstock School, which at that time functioned as a finishing school for well-bred young ladies. Since its foundation in 1854, excellence in music had been a priority and the students and their guests were highly appreciative of Eddie's mastery of the piano.* The programme was similar to others on the tour but Chopin's so-called 'Military' Polonaise was a particular hit together with Liszt's stirring Hungarian Rhapsody No. 2. Eddie was surprised at their depth of knowledge as they requested specific works by Schumann, Bach, Beethoven, Debussy and even Borodin. George sang Grieg and Schubert songs as well as those of a more religious nature such as 'Angels Guard Thee' and 'Song of Thanksgiving'.

Throughout his life Eddie preserved great enthusiasm for the talent of the rising generation. The musical education of the

* Woodstock School continues to thrive. In 2015 it had five hundred pupils from almost thirty different nationalities. It is considered one of the finest schools in India and its music department now has an almost legendary reputation for excellence.

young was often at the forefront of his thoughts. He accompanied this recital with a short detailed talk on each composer and his inspiration in composing the piece. Vain certainly but never an egocentric performer, he cultivated a strong personal interaction with the audience.*

* * *

While wandering Bombay between their concert engagements, the concert party had witnessed various street disturbances. They had been subject to mysterious personal taunts. They discovered these insults were the direct result of the turbulent atmosphere in the town of Amritsar, some three hundred kilometres distant. The reverberations of an atrocity that had recently occurred there destabilised the entire country and was the catalyst that began the disintegration of the British Empire in India.

The reflection of a golden temple trembled in the breeze on the surface of the lake known as Sarovar (Holy Pool of Immortal Nectar). Turbaned Sikhs in scarlet robes sat cross-legged on carpets in the shade of spreading trees in contemplation and prayer. Eddie was rendered speechless by the sight. More thoughtfully he found it difficult to believe that only a year before, this holy city, the spiritual and cultural heart of the Sikh religion, had witnessed an unparalleled act of savagery. As Herbert Asquith, former Prime Minister, put it to the Hunter Committee in 1920 'There has never been such an incident in the whole annals of Anglo-Indian history, nor, I believe, in the history of our Empire, from its very inception down to the present day.'†

Mounting disorder in the Punjab had been fertilised by the passing of the notorious Rowlatt Act of March 1919 in response to perceived threats of revolutionary terrorism. Suspects could be imprisoned without trial or legal representation for up to two years. The spectre arose of a repeat of the vicious Indian Mutiny and Cawnpore Massacre of 1857, outrages that were deeply etched into the British imperial psyche. In the face of political activism

* I am indebted to Ganesh Saili and his book *Mussoorie Medley: Tales from Yesteryear* (New Delhi 2010) for my descriptions of old Mussoorie. All the perfumes and spices of India erupted from the wrappers when I unpacked this book from the post in Warsaw.

† Hansard: Punjab Disturbances. Lord Hunter's Committee, HC Deb 8 July 1920, vol. 131.

in Amritsar, the officer in command of the area, the coercive and psychologically unbalanced Brigadier-General Reginald Dyer, issued stringent proclamations against public meetings. Any assembly would be fired upon without warning, a proclamation ineffectively communicated to the populace at the time.

By April 1919 British civilians in Amritsar were being subjected to terrorist acts, looting and murders. On the evening of 13 April several thousand Indian men, women and children had assembled for a meeting in a walled open space of the town known as Jallianwala Bagh. Dyer felt this group posed an unacceptable threat to law and order. He arrived in his Rolls-Royce armoured car with a small body of carefully selected Gurkha and Pathan troops whom he knew felt little affection for Punjabi civilians. He lined his men up and without prior warning ordered them to open fire on the unarmed crowd. The firing continued uninterrupted for ten to fifteen minutes with panic-stricken knots of people wildly fleeing bullets, unable to escape in any numbers from the enclosed walled field. He ceased firing only when the ammunition ran out, leaving hundreds dead and perhaps a thousand or more wounded.

He subsequently imposed a curfew which effectively prevented recovery of the dead, dying and wounded. 'I thought I would be doing a jolly lot of good and they would realize that they were not to be wicked,' he commented during the official investigation of the incident. The effects of doing 'my horrible, dirty duty' (as Dyer put it when he was relieved of his post) can hardly be overestimated. Huge support was given to Dyer by the British in India, at home and by the Army. This compliance with such savagery alienated Indians previously respectful of British moral prestige. The atrocity galvanized Gandhi and the Indian National Congress. He remarked after the long drawn out official enquiry 'We do not want to punish General Dyer; we have no desire for revenge; we want to change the system that produces General Dyers.'

When Eddie and George arrived in Amritsar to give a concert barely a year later in April 1920, Dyer had just embarked for England in disgrace. A profound legacy of hatred remained and they were justifiably worried about appearing in such a light matter as a classical concert in these volatile surroundings. However exercising a degree of personal courage they 'soldiered on' and the evening performance passed off peacefully enough. Those British civilians and officers who attended said it was a welcome emotional release from the 'trying times' they were then experiencing.

* * *

Another long train journey followed through Rawalpindi to ancient Peshawar and the Jamrud Fort on the North-West Frontier at the entrance to the Khyber Pass that connects Afghanistan and Pakistan. While changing trains they noted with alarm a rough placard nailed up at Peshawar station. Eddie copied it into his notebook:

> 'Active resistance will crush the viper's head. Burn their offices, mutilate their railways and telegraphs, induce the police and Army to work with you and slay these dogs of Britain everywhere you find them.'

They continued the short journey to the fort in a 'blue funk' as Eddie put it. He had read of the perennially imminent Russian threats to British India at this place, the Great Game as it was known, but tried rather to concentrate on the music he would play, drumming his fingers on the dusty seat back of the railway carriage. The line passed through awe-inspiring mountains, tunnels and over bridges and deep culverts. Fierce local Afghan tribesmen perched on the cowcatcher. Eagles swooped and at night the jackals howled.

It is scarcely credible that a concert of European classical music was being given in this fortress during the Waziristan campaign surrounded by colourful *caravanserai* plying the Silk Road. The battered piano in the fort had not been tuned for years and Eddie finally abandoned his solo numbers leaving the floor mainly to George who sang stirring tunes to a gentle accompaniment. The officers and troops were delighted. The soprano Rita Erle had by this time returned to Australia, exhausted by the debilitating heat, Eddie and George continuing the tour as a double act.

* * *

The red tongue of the Hindu Goddess Kali sprang from her mouth in shame, the black female figure with flailing arms was surrounded by fire. Her powerful eyes skewered one's heart as she stood on the indigo body of her husband, the Hindu deity Shiva. The image wore a necklace of skulls. The street down which Eddie was walking contained this forbidding mural, a dark and narrow alley littered with refuse and reeking of ordure, dissolution, death and decay yet the nearby bazaars teemed with life and colour. Bright stalls sold a riot of mortuary paraphernalia. Pilgrims wearing perfumed garlands of flowers prayed at tiny wayside shrines or passed in crowded knots seeming to flow like the tide towards the banks of the Ganges, like tributaries of the great river itself. Ascetic holy men (*sadhus*) were covered in ash with matted, dusty, hennaed locks, long beards and fierce expressions.

By early May 1920 the Cahill-Brooke Concert Party had reached Kashi (Benares or modern Varanasi) the spiritual capital of India, a city associated with death and its transcendence. They had travelled by train for days on the East Indian Railway from Bombay, some 1600 kilometres. This ancient site has produced great writers, thinkers, philosophers and a remarkable school of music, a city famous for its woven cloths and ornate silks. The British writer, photographer and painter Richard Lannoy describes it 'a state of mind' rather than a place. The Maharajah of Benares would be their host and they would play for him.

Eddie Cahill was a concert pianist but also a man possessed of a passion for exploration and insatiably curious about unfamiliar cultures. He drifted through the pungent haze that lay over the city, clambering down myriad steps through dizzying levels of complexity, passing ornately carved pinnacles of blackened temples, terraces, the bastions of palaces, arcaded blocks, cracked platforms, crumbling walls of brick, pyramids, domes, patios and hanging gardens with withering plants, desiccated leaves fluttering onto filigreed cast-iron balconies. Large grey monkeys skipped about.

Suddenly the Ganges, the colour of old gold, lay before him. Beneath the terraces at the water's edge a panoply of tattered woven leaf parasols sheltered bathers and Brahmins from the sun. On platforms over the water, men exercised in incredible postures or swung heavy batons. Temple bells mixed with chattering voices. The colours of draped cloth – yellow, mauve, saffron and green – radiated a festive atmosphere of a floral display while clouds of pigeons whirled in spirals. There was a solemnity, even nobility, in the draped figures of women carrying polished brass pots glittering in the sunlight.

Early one morning Eddie and George took a boat and glided down the Ganges at sunrise. The entire river bank was thronged with bathers and the river itself dotted with boatmen disposing of remains or ashes. An occasional corpse or dead dog floated past. The water was clearly polluted yet the pilgrims drank of it to purify themselves, believing it miraculous. The panorama reminded Eddie of Arcadian classical paintings by Poussin or Claude, Carthage in ruins. In the evening the shore was lit fitfully with oases of light. These were the Burning Ghats* of Kashi, the most exalted of them being the Ghat of Manikarnika.

In a mental state bordering on horror they saw wooden biers, shrouded bodies roped to them then immersed in the Ganges and allowed to dry. A pyre of selected woods was constructed, the body reverently placed upon it and lit with a flaming torch after incantations had been intoned. Waves of heat and smoke carrying the sound and smell of flames devouring flesh rose to the visitors' viewing towers where they stood. Funeral priests moved through the haze like phantoms, striking the corpses with batons. Eddie was aghast to hear the cracking of the skull with a bamboo pole, to release the soul. They watched the compelling scene with fascination, their inexperienced natures stunned by the sight.

Eddie and George were to perform at the magnificent eighteenth-century Ramnagar Fort before HH Maharajadhiraja Sri Sir Prabhu Narayan Singh Sahib Bahadur and his guests[†]. He had been created Maharajah of Benares of the new Princely State by the British in 1911 and had been granted a personal salute of 15 guns. This imposing and exotic red sandstone confection of Hindu and Islamic architecture is situated some fourteen kilometers from Varanasi on the opposite bank of the river. Monumental walls and bastions reminiscent of crusader castles line the river front. Airy open formal courtyards, fountains and carved arcades adorn the interior spaces.

* A ghat is a defined length of river frontage between some 30–200 yards long. Most are in the form of terraces of steps leading down to the River Ganges. The 'Burning Ghats' are those where corpses are cremated.

† Lt. Colonel HH Maharajadhiraja Kashi Naresh Sir Prabhu Narayan Singh Sahib Bahadur (1855–1931).

The Maharajah lavished gifts of diamond-encrusted cigarette cases and diamond cuff links upon them and placed his magnificent Rolls-Royce Silver Ghost at their disposal. Early motoring in India was a dramatic activity as they discovered *en route* to their concert. As the car made its stately progress past bullock carts, their occupants tumbled out in fear onto the road, the animals plunging into nearby ditches at the manic blowing of its klaxon. The 'Spirit of Ecstasy' wafted past sacred cows and elephants, supplicants before wayside altars, screaming children and colourfully turbaned pilgrims. Dogs fearlessly charged the car head on emerging unscathed from beneath barking wildly in the choking dust. One of the British guests, a Deputy Collector, told them of an elderly Indian woman walking in the middle of the road who was run over and killed by a speeding car carrying the Nizam Mahbub Ali Pasha of Hyderabad. His Highness being troubled by the event sent a generous gift to the family. Observers noticed that from then on whenever the Nizam went driving the road suddenly filled with the elderly poor placed there by impecunious and optimistic relatives.

The concert was a great success and an historic occasion. They performed in the opulent Durbar Hall within the Maharajah's palace, a room lined with precious marbles, brocades of silver and gold, inlaid ivory furniture, a sandalwood throne, crystal chandeliers and tiger skins. For the first time in the history of the palace Eddie performed Chopin, Liszt, Beethoven and Chaminade whilst George sang Schubert and Brahms *Lieder,* English art songs as well as Negro spirituals. A Hindustani late-night *raga* native to Benares was movingly performed on the *sarod, mridangam* and *tabla* at the conclusion of their concert.

CHAPTER 3

'THE EAST OF THE ANCIENT NAVIGATORS'

The Cahill-Brooke Concert Party were exhausted from their Indian tour as they again boarded the SS *Montoro* in Calcutta bound for a reappearance in Rangoon (Yangon), Bangkok and Singapore on the return voyage to Australia. The tour of India was reported to be one of the most successful ever attempted by Western classical musicians. They looked forward to resting on the ship in the cool sea breezes. However the water was as still as glass, the sky leaden and the air oppressive. The listlessness, irritable moods and lack of sleep engendered in the deep tropics enervated them, yet Eddie enjoyed the sense of impermanence created by travel. It gave him a heightened sense of reality. George, a more grounded personality, often found himself irritated by the closeness and Eddie's fluctuating moods.

Rangoon. The heat, humidity and thunderstorms of May 1920. The opulent Golden or Shwedagon Pagoda nestled among the palms, its pinnacle dominating the skyline of the city from every angle. Somerset Maugham referred to it as the 'sudden hope in the dark night of the soul'. Eddie wrote in his travel journal of the vibrant colours of the city, crammed to bursting with golden pagodas and Chinese temples.

> I feel I have entered a sort of paradise. The Queensland coast is beautiful but the sense of the exotic East is very strong here. The air itself seems perfumed. How Debussy would have loved this place and painted it in impressionistic sound pictures! The refined Burmese dancing girls wear lilac, pink, green and lapis lazuli silks and ornaments. They have a natural elegance of carriage, graceful hand movements and seductiveness imitating mystical birds or guardian spirits, all moving in a manner as beautiful as a musical phrase.

During the Calcutta season Josie Westaway had met an admirer, the dashing Captain H.A. Keywood. Unknown to the boys they had become secretly engaged during their appearances in Quetta in Balochistan (now Pakistan). Keywood ardently followed the party to Burma (Myanmar) where the couple were married in Rangoon in a small but picturesque ceremony.

Reluctantly the happy party broke off touring the resplendent sights to prepare for the concerts at the Gymkhana Club. The *Rangoon News* wrote of their second concert: 'Saturday night's audience was larger and even more enthusiastic than that on Friday ... Cahill showed his mastery of the instrument.' Eddie and George slept on board ship for the few nights of their stay. They impatiently waited for the stevedores to load fuel, mail and supplies before sailing on to Singapore and a short season at the legendary Raffles Hotel. With the marriage and departure of the *femme fatale* their own relationship resumed its usual friendly course.

* * *

Although certainly no intellectual, Eddie had always been a great reader and was particularly fond of the novels of Joseph Conrad. Lazing in a deckchair on a rare sparklingly clear day at the beginning of the southwest monsoon of late May 1920, he marked a passage in a dog-eared copy of the narrative story *Youth* as they sailed close to the coastline of the Malay peninsula to take up their engagement at Raffles.

> The fronds of palms stood still against the sky. Not a branch stirred along the shore, and the brown roofs of hidden houses peeped through the green foliage, through the big leaves that hung shining and still like leaves forged of heavy metal. This was the East of the ancient navigators, so old, so mysterious, resplendent and sombre, living and unchanged, full of danger and promise.*

When in 1819 Sir Stamford Raffles signed a trade treaty with Sultan Hussein Shah on behalf of the British East India Company, the current idea of Empire was rather more idealistic than our later corrupted perception of it. He wrote

* Joseph Conrad, *Youth* (London 1902) pp. 45–6.

> If the time shall come when her empire shall have passed away, these monuments will endure when her triumphs shall have become an empty name.'*

Raffles remains one of the great symbols of British imperial colonial life and yet it was founded neither by Sir Stamford Raffles or any other British national. Four sharp entrepreneurial Armenian brothers, the Sarkies, recognised the trade potential of the port. They purchased the Raffles Girls' Boarding School in Singapore to convert to a hotel. Raffles opened in 1887. Rudyard Kipling, an early distinguished guest, commented 'the food is as excellent as the rooms are bad.'

In time the port of Singapore grew to become the seventh biggest in the world. Opium dens rubbed shoulders with luxury hotels. Between 1897 and 1899 Raffles was extensively renovated transforming the modest hotel into 'The Savoy of Singapore'. Renaissance-style architecture with cool verandahs, a vast columnar dining room paved with Carrara marble, bronze statues and sweeping staircases illuminated by 'decadent' electric light. Fans circulated lazily although *punkahwallahs*† were retained to foster an exotic Eastern atmosphere. Fortunately the last Singapore tiger had been shot under the billiard room in 1902.

Eddie and George were collected from the ship by hotel *jinricksha* for their concert season. Their suite had its own sitting room, bedroom and dressing room with an attached bathroom and direct telephone, luxuries unheard of outside the great European capitals. They looked forward to 'all the comforts of home' with an English breakfast of porridge, bacon and eggs or kippers followed by tea, toast and rough-cut Seville orange marmalade. Later in the day a *tiffin*‡ would be served.

The 'Bright Young Things' of Singapore had begun to patronise Raffles in the 1920s and tea dances had become de rigueur. An orchestra played every night. The atmosphere of the city tended to the morally casual. In the exaggerated class-conscious atmosphere

---

* Quoted in James Morris, *Pax Britannica* (London 1968) p. 154.

† A 'coolie' who moved a large hinged fan attached to the ceiling above the hotel guests via a pulley system. At Raffles they were operated with sublime lethargy by way of a string attached to the big toe.

‡ A light afternoon meal often of delicately curried dishes originating in British India.

of the Straits Settlement, white tie and tails together with long ball gowns were insisted upon even in the stifling humidity. Eddie and George with their vaudeville experience kept everyone entertained. They sweated through the night and failed to sleep in the afternoons. In competition with their classical repertoire, jazz was the predominant musical passion at Raffles.

The entertainment provided by the Cahill-Brooke Concert Party was particularly welcome in an atmosphere of colonial *ennui*. The sheer enthusiasm that greeted these two talented musicians, the relief from boredom they offered, comes as no great surprise. The *Singapore Times* wrote

> Because his name does not end with a 'ski' or a 'vitch' some people would think that Mr Cahill's playing would not compare with that of the great foreign pianists but the pitch of enthusiasm aroused last night soon dispelled this idea. He is undoubtedly the best pianist heard in Singapore for many a rainy year.

Eddie and George were a close team both emotionally and musically, discussing and noting accounts of the formidably eccentric colonial characters they encountered. Many distinguished writers were to paint literary portraits of such bizarre personalities. Somerset Maugham described the White man in Malaya as 'a pale stranger who moves through all this reality like a being from another planet … they are bored with themselves, bored with one another.'*

One such eccentric they encountered was a commanding figure who haunted the Raffles Bar of an evening. The archaeologist and anthropologist Professor Pieter van Stein Callenfels was a distinguished graduate of Leiden University.† He was rumoured to have eaten human flesh when living among the cannibals of Sumatra. This giant of a man entered Raffles mythology by insisting on quarts of beer and consuming ten bottles of gin at breakfast. According to one report 'his monstrous body heaved and shuddered like a shaken blancmange'. Arthur Conan Doyle modelled Professor Challenger on him in his novel *The Lost World.*

Raffles was probably where Eddie also first made the

---

* Somerset Maugham, *A Writer's Notebook* (London 1949), Readers Union Edition, 1951, p. 169.

† Pieter van Stein Callenfels (1883–1938).

acquaintance of the notorious and glamorous Russian physician Dr Serge Voronoff who grafted monkey glands (thyroid and testicles) into humans in pursuit of the secret of eternal youth. Little did he realise at the time what an important role this mournful-looking individual, accompanied in the tropics by a statuesque young blonde, would play during his own declining years on the Côte d'Azur.*

* * *

After this entertaining season of concerts the Cahill–Brooke Concert Party took passage in late May 1920 on a Danish freighter from Singapore to Bangkok. Officials in white ducks and solar *topi* leaned against the rails of the promenade deck, gazing vacantly out to sea. Siam (Thailand) had held its mysteries in the European imagination for centuries. Eddie was increasingly attracted to the high social status and luxurious lifestyle of the aristocratic audiences that patronized them in Southeast Asia. They had been summoned by His Majesty Vajiravudh Rama VI, King of Siam to play Chopin and sing at the Grand Palace in Bangkok.†

As Crown Prince, Rama had led a remarkably cosmopolitan life, opening up his previously isolated country to foreign influence. He represented his father in Europe for the first time at the Diamond Jubilee of Queen Victoria and subsequently at her funeral. He also attended the coronations of King Alfonso XIII of Spain as well as King Edward VII and his consort Queen Alexandra in England. He invited many crowned heads of Europe to his own coronation ceremony in 1911, the first time foreigners had been invited to any royal event in Siam. Educated at Sandhurst and Christ Church Oxford he was a member of the notorious Bullingdon Club and read law and history. Unusually fascinated with the eighteenth-century history of Poland and the piano music of Fryderyk Chopin, in 1901 at the age of twenty he published the recondite volume *The War of the Polish Succession.* In 1904 he temporarily became a monk according to Siamese tradition. After accession to the throne in 1910 he carried through many wide-ranging reforms, in the face of fierce

* Ilsa Sharp, *There is Only One Raffles: The Story of a Grand Hotel* (London 1981), pp. 101–3
† Vajiravudh Rama VI, King of Siam (1880–1925).

opposition from the aristocracy.

During the Great War this Anglophile brought Siam in on the side of the Allied Powers. He became effectively the father of modern Thai nationalism. A gifted writer and poet he produced modern novels, short stories and plays. He translated three Shakespeare plays into Thai – *The Merchant of Venice, As You Like It* and *Romeo and Juliet*. After a remarkably colorful sex life and many tragic love affairs involving various marriages, broken engagements, concubines and homosexual lovers, he passed away in November 1925, a mere two hours after his only daughter was born. Such was the remarkable man for whom Eddie and George were to play and sing in private audience.

The exoticism of the palace and its opulent interiors were breathtaking. Tears formed in the eyes of the King as Eddie played Chopin nocturnes on a fine English Broadwood grand. The nationalist spirit of the polonaises seemed to inspire the king with a curious fervour. He leant forward attentively on his throne at climactic moments. His love and knowledge of European music also became apparent as the unaccustomed harmonies of Schubert and Schumann songs filled the oriental space.

Their concert of undemanding classics was also very successful in the rather less august surroundings of the Bangkok Sports Club. George was singled out for particular praise by the Siam *Observer*: 'We have never heard a tenor whose enunciation was so perfect or who so manifestly sets himself to interpret the meaning, the spirit, the message of a song.' Eddie's charismatic personality was favourably commented on, but so too was the frightful state of the piano.

The *Observer* continued:

> That he should attempt one of Liszt's Hungarian Rhapsodies for example, on a piano which seemed likely every minute to fall to pieces left one aghast; yet he scored perhaps his greatest triumph here. If Bangkok does not pack the halls at the remaining place, then it may be set down as a soulless place and a disgrace.

Without complaint Eddie always dealt with the unpredictable instruments he often encountered.

* * *

Eddie and George paced the deck of the steamer *Kuching* taking their morning constitutional. An early morning thunderstorm had cleared the air. The soft tropical sunrise over Sarawak revealed distant mountains framing a wide bay dotted with islands. Mount Santubong rose almost a thousand meters directly from the northern end of the bay. The two friends had almost recovered from their concert a few days earlier at the Jesselton Hotel in Jesselton (Kota Kinabalu), the capital of the West Coast Residency of the British Protectorate of North Borneo. They found the exoticism of the location tremendously exciting. The concert took place on the broad verandah among the British officials of the British North Borneo Company reclining on rattan chairs in white ducks sipping gin *pahits*.

Western classical music was unexpectedly accompanied on instruments by hundreds of local Bajau people known generically as the 'Sea Gypsies'. These native peoples, dressed in bright cloth and ornamented with seashells and turtle shell, had come ashore from their boats and were sitting on the grass outside the hotel. The men played drums while the women enthusiastically performed on suspended brass gongs and large wooden xylophones. They completely drowned out the romantic melodies of Chopin and gave Eddie moments of great hilarity. His inborn sense of Irish theatre played up to this 'spontaneous madness'. The Liszt piano pieces and Maori songs attracted even more frantic beating on the drums and gongs. An unprecedented scene unfolded with dances, singing and general gaiety. The eruption of such wild spontaneity exhausted Eddie and George. 'What a devilish racket but such fun! This is living! More please!' Eddie noted in his journal.

* * *

Some weeks before, during one of the regular tea dances at Raffles in Singapore, Eddie and George had encountered HH the Ranee Sylvia Brooke*, daughter of Reginald Brett, 2nd Viscount Esher†

* Sylvia Brooke née Brett (1885–1971).

† Reginald Baliol Brett, 2nd Viscount Esher (1852–1930) 'Reggie' was an historian and

and wife of the third and last White Rajah of Sarawak, Vyner Brooke*. This wild eccentric lady was slowly but surely building a reputation for cultivated outrageousness. In later life she adopted a flamboyant Hollywood-inspired social style, wrote books, painted, piloted wood and wire biplanes and led a Technicolor love life of outstanding mendacity. The popular press adored her.

Opinions could be mixed however as evidenced by two MPs sent from Westminster to sound out local opinion as to the possible cession of the Kingdom of Sarawak to Britain. The Labour MP D.R. Rees-Williams thought she had 'brought the charm of Mayfair to the Tropics and some of the exotic perfume of the Tropics to Mayfair.' The Conservative MP David Gammans however objected to her dancing with prostitutes at the Cathay Cabaret in Kuching, remarking in a private memo to the Secretary of State: 'She has these girls to the Palace and paints their pictures. A more undignified woman it would be hard to find.' Sex in marriage she once described to her sister Doll 'As an act it is both ridiculous and awkward, and I take a very poor view of it indeed.' Despite her physical aversion to 'the act' three 'dangerously beautiful' Brooke daughters were produced during the marriage. They would add to their mother's fitful lustre by marrying eight times between them including an earl, a band-leader and an all-in wrestler.†

During the cocktail hour one evening Eddie and George had found themselves chatting animatedly to the Ranee, lubricated by quite a few of the hotel's notorious Singapore Slings, a drink invented by a Raffles' barman, a Hainanese immigrant named Ngiam Tong Boon. They were tipsily attempting to trace a highly unlikely family connection via surnames between George Brooke and Vyner Brooke. When she learned of their coming concert in North Borneo and later heard them perform at the hotel, she

---

Liberal politician. This rather modest description entirely belies the extraordinary 'behind the scenes' influence of this *éminence grise* on virtually every important aspect of British government and royal policy of the day. The marriage had its moments.

* Charles Vyner Brooke GCMG (1874–1963) the third and final White Rajah of Sarawak was born in London. His life is more than worthy of the wildest fiction.

† I am indebted for details of Sarawak and Sylvia to Philip Eade, *Sylvia, Queen of the Headhunters* (London 2007). The detailed history of the Kingdom, the relationship of Sylvia and Rajah Vyner Brooke and the antics of the rest of the remarkable Brooke family is chronicled in this hugely entertaining volume.

insisted that they give a concert at the Astana Palace in Kuching, the capital of the Brooke's jungle kingdom.

The Cahill–Brooke Concert Party thus found themselves on a tramp steamer sailing down the Malaysian coast of the South China Sea. Steaming up the Sarawak River towards the capital Kuching they passed small Dayak villages clinging to the muddy banks. Scattered groups of amber-skinned women and children stood motionless in the sea as the steamer passed, figures in a landscape of mangrove swamps, screeching monkeys and head-hunter's jungle. Eddie and George were taken ashore to the landing stage by canoe.

Sarawak in 1920 was a brilliant and entertaining British colonial anomaly. Originally part of the Sultanate of Brunei, it was ceded to the British adventurer James Brooke in 1842 as a reward for assisting the Sultan put down a local rebellion.* As the first White Rajah, James ruled Sarawak as his personal kingdom and greatly increased the area under his control. However by May 1946, submerged in an intrigue of bureaucratic smoke and mirrors, Sarawak had become the last colonial possession to be acquired by Britain. The Astana, where Eddie and George were to perform, had been built by the acerbic second White Rajah, Charles Brooke.† The Ranee Sylvia Brooke was musical and played the piano. Before her marriage she was the percussionist of the Grey Friars Orchestra, a band made up entirely of eligible young girls. This band had been cunningly formed by Margaret de Windt, the mother of the future Rajah, Vyner Brooke, in order to provide potential spouses for her three shy sons. The idea was successful.

The Brookes had a unique relationship with the Dayak head-hunting chieftains and their people. Many hundreds assembled in the beautiful gardens of the Palace in the late afternoon before the

* James Brooke (1803–1868) the first White Rajah of Sarawak was born in Benares, India. He never married. Like many adventurers associated with the British East India Company his actions in Sarawak were directed to expanding the British Empire, assisting the local people (by whom he was treated as a type of deity) in fighting piracy and slavery and expanding his own personal fortune in the process. Brooke features in much English literature including *The White Rajah* by Nicholas Monsarrat and Joseph Conrad's *Lord Jim* as well as the Kipling short story 'The Man Who Would be King'.

† Charles Brooke (1829–1917) the second White Rajah of Sarawak was born in Burnham, Somerset in England. He ruled Sarawak from 1868 until his death. He adopted similarly stern patrician values to his uncle James and improved the lot of the native peoples of the region and suppressed the passionate head-hunting activities of the Dayaks.

concert. Vyner was a passionate gardener and the native people sat almost suffocated by the heady perfume of gardenias, tuberoses and frangipani. Again Chopin and Schubert were accompanied by brass knob gongs, xylophones and drums. Sadly, the *Sarawak Gazette* has left us no account or critical musical assessment of the concert. Eddie and George were not particularly dejected to leave the poor instruments and the disappointing rooms of the dilapidated Astana.

* * *

As the ship left Sarawak and crossed the Java Sea to their next engagement, plumes of ash billowed into the sky from volcanic craters along the 'Ring of Fire'. The Cahill-Brooke Concert Party would soon berth at the port of Batavia (present day Jakarta), the capital of the Dutch East Indies (Indonesia) known ominously as the 'Graveyard of Europeans'. Javanese natives dressed in colourful *batik* caps and Dutch traders in white duck crowded the wharf. They were driven with their luggage by 'fast' motor coach a few miles to Weltevreden and the Hotel Des Indes. The entrance to this luxury establishment was alive with a flurry of red parasols and batik sarongs, motor vehicles, two-wheeled pony traps and *bakeks*, a type of rickshaw. They were checked into a private bungalow in the extensive grounds. Huge banyan trees (considered holy by the Javanese) grew in the front garden. Festooned with the tendrils of creepers, the branches were full of tiny chirruping birds. Both musicians had begun to feel the uncomfortable heat. 'It is as if we are being slowly cooked!' exclaimed Eddie.

Reviews of these concerts have not survived, but we know they performed in the hotel alongside the tremendously popular Mr Podinovsky's Russian Quintet, which provided nightly dance music. They also performed at the Concordia Club and the Box Club. Eddie gave a successful recital including Mendelssohn's *Andante and Rondo Capriccioso,* Schumann's *Aufschwung* from the Fantasiestücke Op. 12, the second Novelette in D major, and the *Staccato Caprice* by the forgotten Austrian composer Max Vogrich.*

* Max Vogrich (1852–1916) was born in Hermannstadt, Transylvania (now Sibiu, Romania). A childhood prodigy, he was an acclaimed pianist by the age of 14. He studied

Probably as a result of years spent in the drapery at Beenleigh, he always dressed in a dapper almost exhibitionist style. After the well-attended afternoon concert at the historic Harmonie Club he spent some time shopping at Oger Frères, a fashionable gentlemen's outfitters. Throughout his life Eddie would remain proud of his appearance, taking a perfectionist, almost a prissy care of details and vainly attempting to cultivate the wild mane of hair so characteristic of the 'inspired virtuoso'. One evening they watched with fascination the traditional *Wayang kulit* or puppet theatre which had been erected in the hotel garden. For many hours human desires and destinies are acted out by the puppet master, the shadows being cast on a screen illuminated from behind. The drama is accompanied by a small *gamelan* orchestra*.

The train travel they had experienced during their concert tour of India had by now become a source of allure to both our artists. Java did not disappoint as they boarded the train to make the long, hot journey to Solo (Surakarta) in Central Java. The carriages were quite open for coolness, and native Javanese seemed to be hanging from every window and door. But these steam trains were fired by wood not coal. This meant that glowing cinders as well as smoke were constantly blown into the carriages burning holes in one's clothing. It was now the end of May and the wet season had drawn to a close.

Java was divided into two royal capitals, both descended from the Mataram kingdom: the Sultanate of Yogyakarta and the Sultanate of Surakarta (Solo). Eddie and George had been invited to perform and also attend a *gamelan* concert and *Wayang orang* classical dance at the Palace of the Royal Court or Keraton

---

in Leipzig under Carl Reinecke, Hans Richter, Moritz Hauptmann and Ignaz Moscheles, completing his studies in 1869. From 1870 to 1878 toured continental Europe, South America, and the United States. From 1882 to 1886 he toured and taught in Australia. He died in New York. His forgotten works include operas, an oratorio, cantatas, several masses, symphonies, violin and pianoforte concertos and sonatas besides duets, songs, and chamber music.

* A very particular musical ensemble of percussion instruments particular to Indonesia. Generally from the islands of Bali or Java it comprises a variety of instruments such as metallophones, xylophones, drums and gongs, bamboo flutes and bowed and plucked strings. Vocalists may also be included. The tuning, rhythm, intervallic structure and notation of a gamelan orchestra is extraordinarily complex. Many of the greatest 20th century Western composers such as Olivier Messiaen were influenced by *gamelan* music.

Surakarta Hadiningrat at Solo in Central Java.

Their host, Susuhunan (His Exalted Majesty) Pakubuwono X, wore a black cap with gold bands with what appeared to be a curious mixture of Western dinner jacket and an elegantly patterned *batik* sarong, slippers and a short sword decorated with flowers. Eddie wrote to his sister.

> It is so strange to see this mixture of Eastern and European styles jumbled together! Decorations, waistcoat and sash, enormous rings, even a watch chain as we are used to in the West yet also wearing a gem-encrusted turban and jewelled slippers. His consort looked far less splendid. The peacock and the hen in short!

The audience comprised Dutch administrators and 'various aristocratic Javanese personages'. The concert was followed by traditional refreshments of spiced tea, coffee or chocolate with tiny sweet rice cakes sprinkled with coconut.

A *gamelan* orchestra of native musicians then assembled. They accompanied a *Legong* dance by two prepubescent female dancers in fabulously ornate gold costumes moving in a sort of trance as Eddie described it 'like butterflies visiting flowers', fluttering wide-open eyes, elegant fingers curving in arabesques and tiny intricate foot movements. There was also a chorus of male and female singers.

He admired the extreme beauty of the male dancers who followed, their ravishing costumes, the gem emblazoned *kris* tied with a silk band to their waist, their smooth amber skin, the kohl-shadowed eyes that accentuated their noble profiles and the sensuality of their movement. After the concert Eddie and George left the palace in the cool of the late evening and wandered under the oil lamps that hung from the banyan trees. They were in a dream, feeling as if they had visited the enchanted realms of a fairy tale.

Their long tour was concluded. As they sailed back to Australia on SS *Montoro* in late November 1920, they watched fascinated as the distant volcano Mount Bromo spewed a huge plume of ash and pumice. Eddie's taste for the glamorous luxuries of royal patronage was firmly established on this early, sublimely exotic voyage into the heart of India and Southeast Asia.

* * *

Their return to Beenleigh after so many months of epicurean delights and adulation could only have come as an anticlimax. The sumptuous gifts from their Asian journey that he proudly displayed made a great impression in provincial Beenleigh. Diamond-encrusted cigarette cases and ruby cuff-links were not a common sight in small Australian towns. The voyage had also deeply impressed him musically and would contribute to the development of his repertoire. He began to study Debussy's *Estampes* (*Prints*) in particular the first, entitled *Pagodes,* with its evocation of the *gamelan* orchestras he had so recently heard.

After being treated with oriental obsequiousness and acknowledged as a musical celebrity it was difficult for Eddie to accommodate to the harsh realities facing the state of Queensland in the early 1920s. The idea of an Australian Federation of States, which had come into force on 1 January 1901, had not been received enthusiastically by what was now defined as the 'State' of Queensland rather than the 'Colony'. Many Australians had been traumatized by the sacrifices of the Great War, in particular the disastrous Dardanelles Campaign. The Australian casualty rate after the Great War stood at almost sixty-five per cent, among the highest of any Empire country. At one and a quarter per cent of the population, almost every family had been affected including Eddie's own. This volatile political mood was hardly conducive to the creative arts.

The pianist showed no interest in politics, the burgeoning Labor movement or the rise of Australian nationalism. Eddie was a confirmed aesthete. He was no tough farmer's son facing flood and drought, the infestation of prickly pear, venomous snakes or the cane toad. He was never a real 'cobber'. His diminutive stature and artistic temperament only sharpened his sense of being an outsider. 'Only girls play the piano, mate!' was contemptuously thrown at him on more than one occasion.

> The state registers a highly masculinist culture, stemming from its penal origins and the pioneering of harsh terrain: rambunctious, brash, violent and larrikin. Women were shown their place … A land always hard like an anvil of survival; a climate in most

weathers equatorial, capricious and punishing; and everything befitting living *in extremis* – the sharper chromacity, the inordinate lushness or barrenness of nature, the roar of insect noise, of cyclone and bushfire, the overbearing humidity and distance - monotonous limitless horizons of red, powdered earth, all drenched in blazing light.*

The first concert appearance of Eddie and George in Australia after the India and Southeast Asian tour was in February 1921. As part of a wide-ranging concert tour of the country they were billed with the variety vaudeville act known as *The Sparklers* (songs, popular operatic arias, comedians and ballet) in Brisbane's Palace Gardens Theatre. The audience was large and rather distinguished. The English Governor of Queensland, Sir Matthew Nathan, a soldier and civil servant attended, together with his 'suite' and the Labor Premier 'Red Ted' Theodore (a fierce Labor man) as well as the Mayor of Brisbane. The *Brisbane Courier* made a comment on Eddie's performance of the Liszt Hungarian Rhapsody No. 2 which illustrates how popular entertainment of the time teetered on the cusp of change from being simple entertainment to being appreciated as more musically serious.

> Mr Cahill credited his listeners with an elevated musical taste ... he exhibited originality of style without extravagance, and was polished without affectation ... While he interprets the most classical works, he also contributes the more popular numbers, and thereby meets with the approval of audiences.

Eddie's popular father died in May at a youthful 64 and was much lamented by the local community and his family. In November 1921 Eddie and George had luncheon at Government House in Melbourne with the 'cheery-faced' Governor of Victoria, George Rous, 3rd Earl of Stradbroke and his volatile and rather informal wife Countess Helena, Lady Stradbroke.† They were able to renew their acquaintance with another guest at this luncheon, Dame Nellie Melba. The introductions they made at this social event were to be of the utmost importance to their future careers.

---

* Evans, *A History of Queensland*, p. 270.

† George Edward Rous, 3rd. Earl of Stradbroke (1862–1947) was the 15th Governor of Victoria, Australia. Helena Violet Fraser (?–1949) was the daughter of Lt.-Gen. James Keith Fraser. She was one of Eddie's most important patrons from the very beginning of his concert career. She married George Rous in 1898 and was created a DBE in 1927.

Lady Stradbroke was to give them substantial patronage and letters of introduction before they travelled abroad.

After much deliberation on the grim employment prospects for them in Australia and encouraged by patrons and friends, Eddie and George finally decided to take that great leap into the unknown for colonial Australians – a passage to London. At the time most Australian musical artists of any talent were forced to travel abroad to study and gain experience. They announced that they had decided to leave Australia for London at the beginning of 1923.

Eddie always planned concerts with a high degree of marketing panache. For the beginning of the 1922 season he proposed an extended series of 'Farewell Recitals' around Australia and New Zealand. Using his personal charm and pianistic talents, Eddie throughout his career ruthlessly cultivated his social contacts particularly with the enthusiastic wives of distinguished citizens.

Their first 'Farewell Concert' was arranged in the Assembly Hall, Melbourne for 2 December 1921 under the patronage of the Lady Stradbroke and in the presence of Dame Nellie Melba. At the Grand Opera House Wellington on the New Zealand leg of their farewell tour they appeared on the same programme as the great Ella Shields.* Shields was an American-born vaudeville star, a diminutive male impersonator whose first husband wrote her famous comic signature tune *Burlington Bertie from Bow*, 'a study of genteel vagabondage from its best angle'. She was billed as 'young and pretty with a lad-like figure, modestly controlled, and yet boyishly virile ... [she] puts pep into the most jaded audience'.† She also enthusiastically encouraged them to go to London.

Eddie was becoming increasingly serious about music and tiring of the kaleidoscope of acts that appeared on their programmes. The variety might include 'Harko' the Comedy Cartoonist, 'Togo' the Miraculous Japanese with Sensations of the Orient, 'Nancy Cook' the Winsome English Soubrette with Handsome Frocks, a Dialect Comedian of Pantomime Fame. And yet the silent cinema and music hall had given Eddie a unique and extraordinary apprenticeship for

---

* Ella Shields (1879–1952).

† Julie Andrews performed this song with great panache in the 1968 movie *Star* directed by Robert Wise.

becoming a serious classical pianist. Colourful and rowdy audiences trained him to significantly project his personality, subdue his stage fright and carefully plan the entertainment content of his programs.

The *Sunday Sun* reviewed a concert in Sydney at the Tivoli Theatre with the manly vigour of a Regency pugilist:

> Edward Cahill, a pianist of quality, proved that he could get a half-Nelson on vaudeville patrons, and hold them enthralled. With Cahill was George Brooke, who sings with fervor, and will be the idol of many a matinee girl.

Their appearance at the Hibernian Hall in Cairns in August 1922 that was excitedly anticipated. The advertisement enthused

> 'Hear the Famous Australian Artists prior to Departure for London and Paris. Dame Nellie Melba wires: *'Best Wishes for Success of the Tour'.*

The two farewell concerts in September at the Theatre Royal in Rockhampton were extensively reviewed by the *Morning Bulletin*. The paper enthusiastically predicted that in his wonderfully varied program Eddie was 'on the high road to considerable eminence as a pianist ... [with] the true touch of a master.' Further concerts at the Tivoli Theaters in Melbourne and Sydney followed before their final embarkation for England and London. George was presented with a handsome tribute from the famous English contralto Dame Clara Butt. She considered him 'the most artistic singer I have heard since coming to Australia'. Their voyage to 'the Mecca of Music' would take them some six weeks.

CHAPTER 4

BACH AND OTHER FEARFUL WILDFOWL

They leave us – artists, singers, all –
When London calls aloud,
Commanding to her Festival
The gifted crowd.
From overseas, and far away,
Come crowded ships and ships – ea,
With scornful lips.
For Her, whose pleasure is her law,
In vain the shy heart bleeds –
The Genius with the Iron jaw
Alone succeeds.

When London Calls, Victor Daley*

Cabin trunks marked 'Wanted on Voyage' were manhandled into their First Class cabin, the rest safely stowed in the bowels of the SS *Naldera*. In January 1923 nearly all the Cahill family and many distinguished folk from Beenleigh made the long, dusty journey to Sydney to see them off to London. Their emotions were in turmoil as evidenced by many sleepless nights. This would be a true leap into the dark. England to most Australians of the time remained profoundly the far away 'mother country'.

They were carrying letters of recommendation to many influential members of London Society. The bastions of correct form could not have been breached in any other way. One from Lady Stradbroke, wife of the Governor of Victoria, another from the Labor Premier of Queensland and one-time gold prospector, 'Red Ted' Theodore. Recommendations came from the vaudeville performer Miss Ella

* Victor Daley (1858–1905) was an Australian poet who represented the 'Celtic twilight' school of poetry.

Shields and Robert Courtneidge.* Finally the ultimate open sesame for any musical artist visiting London, a letter of recommendation from Dame Nellie Melba herself. 'Better to be a lamppost in London than a star in Australia,' she had waspishly commented when she heard them at Government House Adelaide in 1917. 'You boys have the goods,' she said in her most robust style. 'Go to London where there is a market and sell them.' Melba did not bequeath her patronage lightly.

Eddie and George arrived in London in February in the dark and damp cold of mid-winter. At last they could boast that they had sauntered down the Strand, the urgent goal of so many colonials visiting the capital for the first time. Clammy, atmospheric fog replaced the pure light of Australia. Passers-by materialised threateningly and were mysteriously absorbed into the gloom. Before they encountered the consolations of smart society, the climate convinced Eddie for some time that he had made a terrible mistake. Yet London in 1923 was a brilliant city. For two young Australians from a small country town it was a heart-stirring experience.

> I looked at London, astonished by its size and by the millions of people in it. Could it be possible, I asked myself, that anyone would want to hear me play the piano. An unknown young man from a tiny place in Queensland. The idea was fantastic! Well, perhaps not quite so fantastic.

* * *

Before the outbreak of the Great War, tensions in Europe had risen to an explosive level. Her Highness Princess Marie Louise (a granddaughter of Queen Victoria and a later patron of Eddie and George) relates an extraordinary incident that took place when her second brother, Prince Albert of Schleswig-Holstein was sailing on the Emperor's yacht to Norway. She told Eddie of the bizarre incident and later related it in her memoirs

> I can say in perfect truth: the Emperor did not want the war … when the Emperor was shown the telegram sent to Serbia

* Robert Courtneidge (1859–1939) was British theatrical manager-producer and playwright and father of the famous actress and comedienne Cicely Courtneidge (1893–1980).

by Berchtold, he was terribly upset ... when his agitation had calmed down he turned to my brother and said, 'Abbie, let us go and wash the dogs'. So they retired to the Emperor's cabin, took off their coats and scrubbed the dachshunds.*

Five years after the armistice, the English society into which Eddie and George had now moved was in a state of profound transition. Many members of the aristocracy and middle classes would never regain the luxurious standard of living they enjoyed before the war. However opera had returned to Covent Garden six months after the conclusion of the hostilities with a gala performance of Puccini's *La Bohème* with Nellie Melba singing the part of the seamstress Mimi.

The thousands of hated war profiteers who had avoided mud, rats, flies, corpses, mustard gas and shrapnel were now thriving in positions of power and influence. Sorrow had touched almost every family in the land. The distractions and escapist pleasures of cricket, football matches, the public house, the *palais de danse* as well as the variety theatre gradually became irresistible attractions. No one ever wanted to fight again. 'The vulgar, disgraceful, over-fed, godless social order that we call Edwardian was finished.'†

Eddie and George, using their influential letters of introduction, hoped to soon be frequenting High Society. The younger generation of aristocrats had been enthusiastic for war. The rhetoric of German 'frightfulness' (the killing of civilians) was an irresistible a goad to action. They had sped eagerly into battle and been slaughtered, blinded or otherwise maimed, their families later financially ruined by 'super-tax' and crippling death duties. One soldier of the British Expeditionary Force had written: 'A lot of ships were needed to bring the British Army to France. Only two will be needed to take it back, one for the men and the other for the identity discs.' Lady Diana Manners, considered the most beautiful woman of the age and a member of the 'wildly avant-garde' and 'outrageous' group known as 'The Corrupt Coterie' lost almost all the young men she had ever loved.‡ As many young aristocratic women, Diana was working as a nurse among the wounded in the frightful conditions

* Her Highness Princess Marie Louise, *My Memories of Six Reigns* (London 1956), p. 178.

† Kenneth Clark (Lord Clark of *Civilisation*) in *Another Part of the Wood* (London 1974), p. 41.

‡ Angela Lambert, *Unquiet Souls: The Indian Summer of the British Aristocracy* (London 1984), p. 149.

of Guy's Hospital in London. 'Our pride was to be unafraid of words, unshocked by drink and unashamed of 'decadence' and gambling – Unlike-Other-People, I'm afraid.'* She was later to become one of the most loyal patrons of Eddie's recitals in both London and Paris. The war for Diana was 'a gruesome soul-shattering end to the carefree life I knew.'†

However, on the surface life little appeared to have changed among the privileged classes. The London Season continued undiminished although the aristocracy were slowly abandoning their London mansions and retreating to the country. Lady Circumference comments in Evelyn Waugh's *Decline and Fall* 'Well, we all feel the wind a bit since the war.' The aristocratic behaviour of society in London was being replaced by a type of louche New York café society. Patrick Balfour, Lord Kinross, describes the changes:

> In so far as the 'twenties can be defined they were a period of change: from quails in aspic to eggs and bacon, from champagne to lager, from coal fires to electricity, from mansions to mansion flats, and from balls to cocktail parties; an age in the course of which peers became Socialists and Socialists became peers, actors and actresses tried to be ladies and gentlemen and ladies and gentlemen behaved like actors and actresses, novelists were men-about-town and men-about-town wrote novels, persons of rank became shopkeepers and shopkeepers drew persons of rank to their houses, the Speed King supplanted the Guards Officer as the *beau idéal* of modern woman and modern woman herself grew each day slimmer and slimmer – and slimmer … It was an age in which traditions of the old dovetailed into the ideas of the new.‡

* * *

At first Eddie and George stayed in a small hotel near Victoria Station before taking up residence in early spring at 26 Randolph Crescent, Maida Vale in West London. Known as 'Little Venice' it is a unique combination of affluent white-stuccoed mansions,

---

* Diana Cooper, *The Rainbow Comes and Goes* (London 1959), p. 82. This volume of memoirs is one of the most moving personal accounts of the destruction by the Great War and the halcyon sunset days of aristocratic Edwardian England.

† Ibid., p. 112.

‡ Patrick Balfour, Lord Kinross, *Society Racket* (Tauchnitz Edition, Leipzig 1934), pp. 59–60.

patio gardens and lush greenery reflected in the water of picturesque canals.

The betrothal of the twenty-eight-year-old Prince Albert, Duke of York to Lady Elizabeth Bowes-Lyon was announced shortly after they arrived. The Royal Wedding would be on 26 April 1923. One of the letters the boys were carrying was from Lady Stradbroke. It opened the doors to No. 7 Carlton House Terrace, the home of the Hon. Lady Herbert.* Although no longer young, this American hostess had married into a distinguished English family. From her drawing room overlooking The Mall, Eddie and George watched the plumed cavalry and splendid carriages of the wedding procession to Westminster Abbey. Here they were introduced to an assortment of fashionable hostesses and members of the aristocracy. Later they lost themselves in the vast throng that greeted the royal couple who appeared on the balcony of Buckingham Palace beside the regal, almost austere figure of Queen Mary.

> The bride wore a medieval-style chiffon moiré wedding dress embroidered with silver thread and pearls and incorporating sleeves and train of Nottingham lace. Afterwards the happy couple left to spend their honeymoon at Polesden Lacey, country home of the Royal family's intimate friend, Mrs Ronnie Greville.†

'Lilibet' surprisingly did not wear a tiara. The groom known to the family as 'Bertie' wore dress uniform in blue-grey, that of a Group Captain in the Royal Air Force.

Another letter from Lady Stradbroke introduced them to the conspicuous Dowager Marchioness of Linlithgow.‡ She invited

---

* The Hon. Lady Herbert (d. 1923) was born Leila 'Belle' Wilson, a New York heiress. In 1888 she had married Sir Michael Henry Herbert (1857–1903) who had been British Ambassador to the US in the final year of his life. She had the reputation of attempting to be more English than the English and represented the increasing society influence of a growing number of American London hostesses. Sir Michael came from a distinguished family whose seat was magnificent Wilton House near Salisbury in Wiltshire, arguably the most beautiful country house, gardens and grounds in England. Many English historical films have used scenes set in the famous Inigo Jones Double Cube Room at Wilton (*Barry Lyndon, The Madness of King George, Pride and Prejudice, Mrs Brown*).

† Andrew Barrow, *Gossip: A History of High Society from 1920 to 1970* (London 1978), p. 16.

‡ Hersey Alice Mullins, Marchioness of Linlithgow (1867–1937) was the wife of John Hope, 1st Marquess of Linlithgow (1860–1908) who, as the 7th Earl of Hopetoun, was the 8th Governor of Victoria (1889–95) and a highly controversial 1st Governor-General of Australia (1901–3). Lady Hopetoun's private character was less formal than her public one. She was a keen angler, an expert horsewoman and an enthusiastic hunter. She was a crack

them to a luncheon for 'at least fifteen' smart London hostesses and they left with seven engagements at one hundred guineas each.* They could hardly believe their good fortune.

The year they arrived in England was eventful. February 1923 saw the glories of Tutankhamun's tomb in the Valley of the Kings revealed and in April some 200,000 fans packed the new Wembley Stadium for the first Wembley FA Cup Final. In politics May saw Bonar Law resign his brief premiership of less than a year and Stanley Baldwin appointed Prime Minister. In June the great racehorse Papyrus won the Derby and in July wives were allowed to petition for divorce. October witnessed Southern Rhodesia become a self-governing colony. 'Popular' music, the craze for jazz and the associated abandoned life style of drink, drugs and sex was emerging. John Cobb was racing a ten-litre *Delage* and Count Louis Zborowski his *Chitty-Bang-Bang* aero-engined monsters at Brooklands motor racing circuit. Many BBC regional stations began broadcasting and the first transatlantic radio broadcast between London and New York took place. The wireless celebrated its first birthday.

The contacts made at the royal wedding led to their first informal engagement. Before their official concert tour they provided a modest entertainment in aid of the District Nursing Association in the village of Great Horwood. This small concert in the village hall was arranged by a Mrs Frederick Denny of Horwood House, who had founded the association as part of her charitable works. 'Such piano playing had never before been heard in the village ... every piece was of course encored.' observed the local reporter.

The impresario Frederick Shipman, who had arranged their Southeast Asian and Indian Tour, had organised various public engagements at variety theatres throughout England and Scotland. In the few months before their first appearance at the Alhambra in Glasgow they set about shopping for elegant clothes in Jermyn Street and spent a small fortune on costly silk top hats, detachable collars and cuffs, white tie, tails and morning suits, all de rigueur

---

shot, even though shooting was then considered an unusual activity for a woman and disapproved of by Queen Victoria. She was also a photographer and an artist in cartoons, caricatures and watercolours.

* 100 guineas in 1923 was worth over £5000 at 2015 values.

for formal London occasions. Eddie's experience as a draper had given him impeccable taste in clothes. The gift of diamond cuff-links and shirt studs from the Maharajah of Jaipur could at last be put to good use. They wandered the teeming Caledonian Market in North London and were offered bowler hats, brass doctor's plates and a skeleton in a box.

Attendance at the royal wedding also led to their first society appearance in April arranged by a mysterious Mrs Webster at 25 Tedworth Square, Chelsea. Being merely 'young colonials' they felt particularly nervous performing before a distinguished collection of countesses, dowagers, duchesses, lords and their ladies. Eddie suffered from nerves and had a special mixture concocted in Soho supposedly to suppress stage fright. George was of a more sanguine temperament. They both harboured the undeserved Australian cultural inferiority complex faced with the English aristocracy, a common affliction in the early days of Federation, something not shed nationally until much later.

> He knows that although his erudition may be sound, his clothes faultless, and his hands as clean as his linen – though he may have much knowledge, much tact, much eloquence, much refinement – his acceptance among the people who can trace their descent for a couple of centuries will be achieved in spite of, and in no way because of, the land of his birth.*

The Times review of the concert was not particularly encouraging, praising Eddie's performance of Schumann's *Aufschwung* but deciding the Chopin Nocturnes and Waltzes were not sufficiently *cantabile*. George's lyric tenor voice was praised but not his selection of English art songs. The *Morning Post* felt they made 'a favourable impression' and 'applauded some excellent singing and piano playing.' This appearance led to other social engagements such as at the home of the fashionable Mrs Ernest Guinness wife of the Hon. Arthur Ernest Guinness who lived at Grosvenor Place. She is now best remembered as the mother of the 'Golden Guinness Girls', the brightest and most notorious of the 'Bright Young People' of the 1920s.†

---

* Alfred Johnson Buchanan, *The Real Australia* (London 1907), p. 303.

† Her magnificent 1912 portrait by the eminent artist Frank Dicksee expresses the confidence and opulence of the Edwardian era perhaps more than any other.

They opened their United Kingdom public season in one of the best-equipped theatres in Britain, the Alhambra Variety Theatre in Glasgow on 9 July 1923.* It was able to accommodate almost three thousand people and considered to be the most modern theatre in Britain. Specialising in variety shows, stars such as Harry Lauder, Cicely Courtneidge, Jessie Matthews and Ivor Novello had appeared there. The Australians received star billing. Two days before, the *Weekly Record* had revealed under the headline '*Wizard Pianist*' that Eddie had 'the smallest pair of hands among the world's pianists' and could barely stretch an octave. However they assured prospective audiences that once 'the pocket Paderewski' had arranged the piano stool to accommodate his diminutive stature 'there is not one masterpiece in the world of music that will deter him'.

The heyday of the music hall and variety theatre was slowly fading after the Great War as the age of the cinema began to flourish. In November, a theatrical agent shot himself in the Golden Gallery at the top of the dome of St Paul's, after his business had been ruined by the cinema. The greatest architect of those sumptuous Edwardian jewel-box interiors, Frank Matcham, had died in 1920. Many superb theatres were demolished. 'The boys' appeared twice nightly to disappointingly mixed reviews. Shortly after however as some compensation, they were warmly received in Birmingham at the Grand Music Hall.

* * *

Their London concert season that year began in grand style with their attendance in morning dress at an Afternoon Party in the grounds of Buckingham Palace on 26 July 1923. This was a charming affair with green and white striped refreshment tents and white marquees set out in the gardens of the palace with excellent tea and 'cucumber sandwiches the size of a stamp and cake' as Eddie noted. Various military bands provided festive entertainment as distinguished guests were formally presented to the King George and Queen Mary under an awning. Later the King and Queen wandered among the

* The Theatre opened in 1910 and was designed by architect, Sir John James Burnet. It was built on the site of the popular Waterloo Rooms, which had previously been Wellington Street Church. The name derives from association with the Moorish palace in Granada.

guests, stopping to chat briefly now and again.* After receiving such invitations so soon after his arrival in England, before long Eddie began to be driven by ambition and a degree of social snobbery. Although outwardly advocating the maintenance of a natural style without affectation and determined not to conceal his Australian accent, he began to fill an address book that by the end of his career in London would appear like a concise edition of Debrett's.

Their modest London concert debut was held over the August bank holiday at the Victoria Palace Theatre. The audience were enthusiastic, and 'cooees' mingled with the applause.† Again the official reviews were mixed. Eddie was thought rather begrudgingly to 'play the piano with plenty of skill if a little mechanically'. But the *Daily Telegraph* wrote 'Edward Cahill is a pianist of unusual skill and talent, whose spirited playing delighted last night's audience. He has a most delightful staccato touch.' Concerning George, *The Times* had 'Nothing but praise for his attractive voice' although he was thought to be wasting his talent on 'hackneyed songs'. The *Pall Mall Gazette* was more forthcoming: 'Their reception after the performance was extraordinary; although they were called before the curtain several times the audience could not have enough of them, and actually stopped the following item in order to have a speech.' Their fiercely loyal housekeeper, a typical East End Londoner, attended this concert. She was sitting in the gallery. Eddie's diary relates her conversation

'They all loved yer!'

'How do you know?' asked Eddie

'Well, I stood at the door comin' out an' I said 'How'ed you like 'em?'

'We loved 'em!' they said.

'They was lucky. If they 'adnter, I'd a walloped 'em!

This season was followed by appearances at the London Alhambra in Leicester Square. Here they appeared alongside Lee

---

* In the 1920s the Buckingham Palace garden parties were more pleasant, exclusive and less crowded than today.

† 'Cooee!' is a shout used in the Australian bush to attract attention. Loud and piercing, it can carry over long distances. The word means 'come here' from the Dharug language spoken by the now extinct Aboriginal people from the Sydney area. One of the Sherlock Holmes mysteries entitled *The Boscombe Valley Mystery* is solved when Holmes recognizes 'cooee' is an Australian word.

White and Clay Smith.[*] Decorated in the Moorish style, the venue was 'the most comfortable theatre in London' according to Kenneth Clark of *Civilisation*.[†] The London *Morning Post* referred to George's voice 'of almost honey sweetness and possesses the art of absolutely clear enunciation ... They do not want to draw only the trained musician but to interest the casual lover of music. Consequently their repertoire consisted of both popular and classical numbers, drawn from the best sources. Their success was immediate.'

A season at the London Coliseum followed. The *Star* commented patriotically with fresh wounds clearly uppermost in their mind, appreciative of the war support shown by Australia

> 'Australia will be There' was the song of the War, and last night, two Australian artists were there too – with a splendid reception. Both are admirable artists and were a big success.

They appeared alongside the great Japanese actor Sessue Hayakawa.[‡]

They also appeared at the celebrated London Palladium National Sunday League concerts and also at the Boosey Ballad Concerts at the Albert Hall and the Queen's Hall. Eddie reflected later in life that when he looked down at the audience of thousands from the stage of the vast Albert Hall he felt his heart almost bursting as his childhood dreams of becoming a concert pianist had all come true. The National Sunday League concerts had been established, as the secretary Henry Mills stated, 'generally to promote intellectual and Elevating Recreation on that Day'. The *Daily Mail* reported they were so enthusiastically received 'they could scarcely leave the stage'. The critic further noted the growth of their astonishing popularity after having only spent a short time in England.

---

* Lee White (1886–1927) and Clay Smith (1885– ?) were an American husband-and-wife Vaudeville team. White and Smith, who are credited with giving Gertrude Lawrence her start in show business, at one time owned and operated London's famous Strand Theatre.

† Clark, *Another Part of the Wood*, p. 72. He visited the Alhambra as a schoolboy to see a Diaghilev ballet after a painful session at the dentist.

‡ Sessue Hayakawa (1889–1973) was a Samurai and a brilliant Japanese actor of both the silent film era and the talkies. In the late 1920s he was as well known as Charlie Chaplin and Douglas Fairbanks. He was one of the highest paid stars of his time. Hayakawa is best known as Colonel Saito in the film *The Bridge on the River Kwai*, for which he received an Academy Award nomination for best Supporting Actor in 1957. This remarkable man was also a theatre actor, film producer and director, screenwriter, novelist, martial arts expert and ordained Zen Master.

Being unused to criticism of any significant kind on their concert tours of Australia, India or Southeast Asia, some of the less positive official reviews came as an unwelcome shock. In London Eddie had already attended a number of piano recitals by internationally famous pianists, something normally denied him in Australia. He heard the superb violinist Fritz Kreisler and the pianist Ignacy Jan Paderewski at the Albert Hall, both of whom he admired greatly. He managed with his persuasive charm to engage Paderewski's agent, a Mr L.G. Sharp, to arrange a few suitable alternative venues for them. Because of his small stature Mr Sharp began to refer to him as 'the pocket Paderewski ', a nickname that stuck.

At the Queen's Hall Eddie heard the almost forgotten but brilliant Ukrainian-born Russian pianist Leff Pouishnoff*, who specialized in Chopin. Pouishnoff had escaped the Bolsheviks during a concert tour of Persia and had arrived in England only a year before Eddie. His career had been suffocated by the Great War and the Russian Revolution, but after settling and performing in London he was greatly acclaimed. Eddie was influenced by Pouishnoff's refined touch and sophisticated nuance, a technique in performing Chopin that never lapsed into effeminacy or sentimentality. He also greatly admired the famous Ukrainian-born pianist Benno Moiseiwitsch and naturally the Pole of genius Arthur Rubinstein, a pioneer of the modern performance aesthetic and only two years younger than Eddie. The remarkable but forgotten Belgian pianist and composer Arthur de Greef was also performing in London at that time. De Greef had studied in Weimar for two years with Franz Liszt. Eddie loved the sparkling, light elegance and charm of the Chopin *Grande Valse Brillante* in E-flat major he heard.

Eddie, despite his great natural gifts, now realized that he must work and study harder than ever to make his mark as a serious concert artist. He must improve his technique and significantly enlarge his repertoire if he was to be noticed at all as a virtuoso pianist in the great capital. He now began to practise in earnest. He was worried that success seemed to have come rather late in life and that his Australian beginnings were a mixed blessing.

---

* Leff Pouishnoff (1891–1959), a pupil of the renowned pianist and teacher Annette Essipova, a pupil and subsequently wife of the great Polish pedagogue Theodor Leschetizky. In 1938 the first pianist to be televised.

* * *

Eddie and George did not fall into a fit of the dismals at the lukewarm reviews, but courageously decided to take positive action and organise some serious music lessons. This was particularly challenging for Eddie as a mature pianist but rather less challenging for George. Although Eddie had been a child prodigy, astonishingly neither artist had had any significant degree of formal musical training and yet both had been hailed on their tours as among the finest of musicians. Eddie was now thirty-eight and George thirty-seven, although Eddie was extraordinarily youthful in appearance with an exuberant a personality that belied his age. He often fibbed about it, neatly subtracting a remarkable thirteen years in official but clearly unverified documents.* Like many Australian artists they were unprepared for the high standards and criticism of the London music critics.

Fortunately the letters of recommendation from Dame Nellie Melba opened distinguished musical doors. In May she had written to them personally from her sumptuously furnished house at 15 Mansfield Street W.1 The letter on elegant pale blue paper reads

> May 30th 1923
>
> Dear Mr Cahill,
>
> I am writing this letter to wish you every success in England. It is always difficult for new-comers to begin, but I feel sure that once you get a chance you will make good, as you did in Australia.
>
> Yours very truly
>
> Nellie Melba

She was seriously ill at the time and this letter indicates great generosity of spirit.

Eddie managed to be accepted for a series of lessons with the great English pedagogue Tobias Matthay. He had already profitably encountered this method with Miss Roberts in Brisbane and was now an acolyte at the source. This teacher concentrated on tone production and touch, analysing the muscular minutiae of

* A true copy (No: 61189) of his Colony of Queensland Birth Certificate (Extracted 27 February 1962) certified by Registrar-General Timothy Francis de Sales Scott, confirms his Date of Birth as 10 November 1885 at Beenleigh.

finger and arm movement involved with the pianist's interaction with the keyboard. This was of great importance to Eddie as he had very small hands that could barely stretch an octave yet play much Liszt and Chopin with ease. In the past many had marvelled at his authoritative performance of the Bach/Tausig Toccata and Fugue in D minor, BWV 565. They were even illustrated in the Melbourne *Table Talk* journal in an article entitled 'Hands and the Man – Can they Stretch an Octave?' Like the hands of Chopin, when the physical need arose a remarkable flexibility of ligaments and muscles allowed his hands to stretch and open, uncannily resembling a snake swallowing a bird. He began to perfect a touch and tone of delicacy, evenness and velocity typical of the late nineteenth century school of pianism. Performance suggestions were offered by Matthay in a generous, kind and illuminating manner. His predominant maxim was 'Never touch the piano without trying to make music.'

George took advice in programming and also lessons in voice production from the great English romantic art-song composer Roger Quilter.* Their meeting with his elder sister Mrs Frederick Denny was to be of incalculable consequence for their future London careers. He also managed to arrange lessons in London with the outstanding composer of romantic songs Guy D'Hardelot.† This was the *nom de plume* of the exotic Helen Rhodes (née Helen Guy) born of a French mother and English father in an ancient castle near Boulogne-Sur-Mer once lived in by Henry VIII and Anne Boleyn. She was also to play an important part in their forthcoming musical careers.

However perhaps the most important teacher for George at this

---

* Roger Quilter (1877–1953) was born in Hove in Sussex. This neurasthenic, fastidious but tremendously gifted English composer was born into an aristocratic family and, unusually for a composer, was educated at Eton. He attended the Hoch Conservatory in Frankfurt together with Percy Grainger and Cyril Scott. He was a prolific composer of the English romantic art song as well as orchestral music. He accompanied George Brooke at the piano on a number of occasions.

† Guy D'Hardelot (1858–1936) studied at the Paris Conservatoire and was much praised by Gounod and Massenet. The great French operatic soprano Emma Calvé did a great deal to popularise her songs. That rare creature, a woman composer of masterly refinement and form, she was cultivated and befriended by members of the English aristocracy such as Lady Diana Cooper. Her most famous love song *Because* has been recorded by all the great tenors from the dawn of recording.

time was Baron Raimund von Zur-Mühlen who lived on the South Downs at Steyning in Sussex.* He was one of the last personal links with the romantic school of German *Lieder* composers – Schubert, Schumann, Brahms, and Wolf – and the greatest concert tenor of his day. This magnificent singer was possessed of a noble style and wonderful *Vortrag* which powerfully moved the hearts of his listeners.† He was also a great teacher with whom many well-known artists had studied.

> Clara Schumann regarded him as a special exponent of her husband's songs, and he was her guest for nearly a year at Frankfurt, studying and singing Robert Schumann's songs, inspired by her wonderful playing and guided by her intimate knowledge of the music. This phase of study undoubtedly explains the insight Mühlen displayed in the interpretation of Schumann's *Lieder*, not only from the vocal point of view, but in his feeling for the dynamic shading and inner meaning of the accompaniments. (How one remembers him saying, 'No! No ! Kinder, that is not the way! Clara's darling fingers would play it so,' indicating the exact shading he required.')‡

Aristocratic circles in Berlin adored his *Liederabend* recitals. Bismarck, amid scenes of great enthusiasm, placed upon his brow a beautiful silver laurel wreath, inscribed with the words, 'To the Prince of Singers, Raimund von Zur-Mühlen'.§ At one concert Brahms shouted: *'Endlich, endlich habe ich meinen Sänger gefunden!'* ('At last, at last, I have found my singer!'). Mühlen mainly concentrated on strengthening George's upper voice without forcing the sound. The distinguished teacher had found Australian voices to be generally excellent. George was able to concentrate on interpretation from the outset.

The boys now worked hard at assembling programmes that achieved a rare balance between the seriously classical and the merely charming. Never trite, the collections of songs and piano pieces always reflected the innocent sensibility and sentiment that

---

* Baron Raimund von Zur-Mühlen (1854–1931) was born in what is now Viljandi in southern Estonia, formerly Fellin a town belonging to the Hanseatic League.

† *Vortrag* was the period style of the interpretation in question.

‡ From the extensive tribute upon his death by H. Arnold Smith 'Baron Raimund von Zur-Mühlen: The Passing of a Great Artist', *The Musical Times*, Vol. 73, No. 1070 (1 April 1932), pp. 316–20. A fine essay indeed.

§ *The Musical Times*.

suffused music that preceded the Great War. They avoided the easy seductions, irresistible decadence and effortless wooing of the audience by jazz that was the contemporary rage. Instead George chose to sing Negro spirituals, many of them refined works of art, which were received with admiration by all social classes. Many of the songs and piano pieces they chose were by now forgotten composers. Eddie and George regarded the musical discernment of variety theatre audiences with a respect they clearly appreciated.

A newspaper debate erupted on their first appearance at the Victoria Palace in London. It was begun in the *Sunday Times* under the title *Art and the Public* by the acerbic and distinguished theatre critic and diarist James Agate. He posed a question and raised an issue

> How far must he [a musician] temper the wind of his artistry to a public, the marrow in whose bones may be supposed to freeze at the bare mention of the classics? Compromise is normally the solution. The artist prints on his programme Bach, Rimsky-Korsakov, Scriabine [*sic*] and other fearful wildfowl. But there is no need for alarm ... public taste is not so low as those who cater for it insist.*

He then turned to the performance of the two young Australians: 'I have no doubt these two young artists were anxious to preserve their musical souls provided this was not at the expense of the audience … let me say here that they broke fewer promises than is customary.' They had been recalled many times. He observed in his characteristic ironic style that the audience were as highly delighted by Eddie's performance of the 'enchanting' Józef Wieniawski† *Valse*

---

* James Agate, *Sunday Times*, August 1923. James Agate (1877–1947) was the supreme British diarist between the wars cast in the mould of Samuel Pepys. He was also a pungent theatre critic for the *Manchester Guardian*, the *Sunday Times* and the BBC. His diaries were published in nine volumes under the title *Ego*. He believed in chronicling the minutiae of life which he felt would outlive politics in future human interest. How right he was.

† Józef Wieniawski (1837–1912) was a child prodigy, pianist, composer for the piano and brother of the great violinist Henryk Wieniawski. They often performed together in concert. He studied at the Paris Conservatoire, for three months with Franz Liszt in Weimar in 1855 and finally in Berlin from 1856–8. He taught and performed in Warsaw and Lublin until life became unbearable under Russian occupation whence he fled to Brussels with his wife and family where he died in 1912. This *Valse de Concert* was not popular with musical critics of the time but its infectious sparkle and melodic charm was tremendously popular with audiences. A good example of Eddie's understanding of what contemporary audiences desired.

de Concert in D-flat major 'as if the pianist had blacked his face and banged out *Back-back-back to Mazawattee* to the accompaniment of hysterical saxophones.'* Clearly Agate remained singularly unimpressed by the current jazz madness sweeping London.

Eddie had failed to perform the promised Konzertstück by Weber. Agate, in a peculiar lapse of musical taste, did not regret this, but felt that their choice of songs was prosaic. He regretted the replacement of Maori songs and some promised songs by Roger Quilter with 'more popular fare'. He felt this caution came from a significant underestimate of the tolerance of the music hall audience for the classics. One correspondent in this debate pointed out how a music hall performer needs to be 'a psychologist of no mean order' and carefully plan the sequence of the programme 'so that the changes are rung from one number to another with the maximum of effect'.

James Agate was not a music but a theatre critic, an occupation which had brought him that particular evening to the Victoria Palace. A perceptive man, he had unwittingly touched upon the crux of their London dilemma. How could they earn a living against the stiff competition of the music hall and still develop as serious classical musicians when confined to performing in popular venues? Most of their previous experience had been on the Australian popular vaudeville circuit. Their personalities and stage presence had flourished there. Agate concluded his article with a further question that shifted the blame from the performers to the organisers: 'Is the taste of the public low? Perhaps. Is it as low as the managers of our theatres, music halls and picture palaces pretend? No! A thousand times no!'

Increasingly Eddie and George included classical music in their programmes even on the variety theatre circuit. This dilemma goes a long way explaining why, when given the opportunity, they assiduously cultivated the more lucrative and less musically compromising engagements offered by High Society. Chopin himself had cultivated the same social class upon his arrival in Paris in 1831. Eddie almost immediately attracted the same type of aristocratic female support in the London of a different age. They would not have long to wait for social and musical success of no small order.

* Agate, *Sunday Times.*

* * *

The New Year celebrations of the momentous year of 1924 began with fireworks, champagne, the first Labour Government in history under Ramsay MacDonald and the suicide of the distiller Sir John Stewart in the baronial hall of Fingask Castle, Perthshire – the first of many suicides that year as more businesses began to fail. The Maharajah of Patiala took the entire fifth floor of the Savoy, over thirty-five suites of rooms and was reputed to wear underpants costing £200 a pair.* The great British Empire Exhibition was opened at Wembley by King George V and some ten million visitors would see this remarkable event before it closed. Fear of Bolshevism culminated in the forged Zinoviev letter scandal, which destroyed the government of Ramsay McDonald in October and brought the Conservative party to power with Stanley Baldwin as Prime Minister.†

One of Eddie's favourite novels was published that year. Michael 'every other inch a gentleman' Arlen published the 'hard-boiled' first modern bestseller *The Green Hat.* The heroine Iris Storm drives a matchless yellow Hispano-Suiza and shockingly for the time *enjoys* casual sex. With killing effrontery she comments 'It is not good to have a pagan body and a Chiselhurst mind … hell for the body and terror for the mind.'

Change was certainly in the air. Next to America, Russia was the country that preoccupied the imagination of Londoners at this time. It is hard to overestimate the excitement caused by any arrival in London of the immortal Russian ballerina Anna Pavlova. To attract a wider audience for the 1924 London season directed by Serge Diaghilev, the electrifying Ballets Russes starred in a variety bill at the London Coliseum in a production of the ballet *Le Train Bleu.* A reporter wrote 'It is as difficult to get a seat for 'The Blue Train' as it is to get a seat for the thing itself during the height of the Riviera rush.'

Eddie and George adored this light and fluffy confection, a French modernist ballet which celebrates fashion yet criticizes

* £200 in 1924 is the equivalent of £10,000 in 2015. Was the underwear woven with gold thread perhaps?

† The details of the fascinating story of the Zinoviev Letter is contained in Chester, Fay & Young, *The Zinoviev Letter* (London 1967).

superficiality, set in a chic French beach resort on the Côte d'Azur. Bathing costumes, tennis and golfing outfits were designed by 'Coco' Chanel, music by Darius Milhaud, a libretto by Jean Cocteau, the curtain painted by Picasso with the added attraction of charming acrobatic dancers. This 'sporting ballet' for *Les Poules* and *Les Gigolos* was created for the 1924 Paris Olympics by Bronislava Nijinska (Vaslav Nijinsky's sister) and was choreographed to show off the acrobatic prowess of the dancer Anton Dolin. Diaghilev's programme note is amusing: 'The first point about *Le Train Bleu* is that there is no blue train in it. This being the age of speed, it already has reached its destination and disembarked its passengers.'* Everyone thought the ballet 'perfection'. Harold Acton wrote: 'one had to sit through the antics of jugglers, trick-cyclists and acrobats, before the curtain rose on a single ballet.'†

'The boys' never lost sight of the fact they were essentially entertainers. There was no shame attached to performing at such popular, commercial venues in London in the 1920s. The year 1924 was also a momentous one for Eddie Cahill and George Brooke. It began inauspiciously with variety theatre performances at the raucous Empire Theatre Newcastle and the Empire Theatre Liverpool. The *Liverpool Courier* commented on Eddie's playing: 'He confined himself rather too much to the virtuosic branch of his art. His accompaniments to Mr Brooke's singing showed the more artistic player.' Clearly achieving the right musical balance was proving a challenge in the rugged north. They then toured gentler Brighton, appearing at the Sunday Concerts at the Winter Garden, Bournemouth under Sir Dan Godfrey and at other south coast 'watering places' to far greater acclaim.

Eddie had one curious interest seemingly at odds with being a classical musician. He was interested in motor racing, had even done a little in Australia and arranged to visit the Brooklands circuit over Easter. He felt a connection between the two forms of risk-taking – one with Liszt at the limits of the keyboard concertizing and the other at the limits of a fast car on a race track. The adrenalin rush that resulted from the proximity of an accident, of danger,

---

* An excellent full account of the ballet and a modern production, *New York Times* Dance Feature, 4 March 1990.

† Harold Acton, *Memoirs of an Aesthete* (London 1948), p. 85.

stimulated his rather neurotic temperament. A moth attracted to the flame.

The great golden age of sports car racing was flourishing in these years, although the track itself had been open since 1907.* In Australia the Cahill family loved the new Dirt Track motorcycle racing, in particular Eddie's sister Elizabeth, an unlikely interest for an operatic soprano.† This popular sport was begun by Australian farmers racing motorbikes around rough oval circuits in the early 1920s. 'Bessie' had written to Eddie after reading about motorcycle racing at the new Brooklands track and suggested he should go while in London and report back to Beenleigh. After all, she had read that Brooklands attracted wealthy aristocrats and one never knew who Eddie might encounter.

In May 1922 HRH the Duke of York, mainly interested in motorbikes, had called a Brooklands Royal Meeting. 'The Duke was greeted by the Earl of Athlone and a Persian carpet was laid out on the track when he arrived. The Duke had entered his chauffeur, S.E. Wood, riding a 350cc Douglas and a 988cc Trump-Azani. Brooklands racing at that time was organised along horse-racing lines. He wore the Duke's colours (a scarlet jersey with blue stripes and sleeves like a jockey) but was unfortunately unplaced in his races.'‡ Eddie attended the 1924 Easter Meeting where the Polish aristocrat Count Zborowski drove incredible aero-engined giants in battle, becoming airborne on the famous but uneven concrete banking. Zborowski pitted his monstrous 27-litre Higham Special against the 21.7-litre Fiat 'Mephistopheles' of Ernest Eldridge and 'Le Champion' driving the 20-litre Isotta-Maybach.

Society concerts continued to increase apace. They were asked

---

* Brooklands had been built on land near Weybridge in Surrey by an early motoring enthusiast Hugh Locke King. It was the first purpose-built car racing circuit in the world. He finally decided on a 2¾ mile banked oval course 100 ft wide around his estate where British cars could be tested and raced. This vast and pioneering undertaking put his financial future into doubt but Brooklands became one of the most famous racing car circuits of all time.

† Elizabeth Moran (née Cahill, 1888–1963) was the author's paternal grandmother. He well remembers her taking him as a young boy every weekend to the Brisbane Speedway to watch cinder track motorbike and Midget car racing. She was addicted to this unlikely sport and the smell of hot Castrol R oil. He still finds it exciting.

‡ David Venables, *Brooklands: The Official Centenary History* (Yeovil 2007), pp. 83–4. A brilliant illustrated book on the history of Brooklands covering the cars, motor-cycles and aircraft.

to support many causes that might have led more thoughtful and politically committed artists to question the moral, even political implications of participation. In May, Lady Violet Astor 'lent' 18 Carlton House Terrace for Eddie and George to give the first of many concerts to raise funds for the Southern Irish Loyalists' Relief Association. Princess Louise, Duchess of Argyll*, had come especially to thank 'Mr Cahill and Mr Brooke' for 'arranging such a delightful concert'. British loyalists were suffering in southern Ireland after the Irish War of Independence and the establishment of the Irish Free State at the end of 1922. Clearly Eddie with his Irish background felt his future concert career in High Society, a trajectory that implied support of the British 'enemy', was of far greater importance than the independence movement of his ancestral countrymen.

*HRH The Princess Louise, Duchess of Argyll (1848–1939) was the sixth child and fourth daughter of Queen Victoria and Prince Albert.

CHAPTER 5

A COLLAR OF DIAMONDS

At the end of May 1924 Eddie and George were invited through the good offices of the Dowager Marchioness of Linlithgow to a dinner and to perform at a sumptuous banquet at Lansdowne House.* This glamorous dinner was attended by members of the Royal Family (the Duke and Duchess of York, Prince Henry and Prince George) and hundreds of titled and distinguished guests. They dined off gold plate and chose from an ornate French menu offering among other confections *Les Coûpes d'Artagnon, Les Suprêmes de Volaille Princesse* and *Les Délices des Dames.* G.H. Mumm 1913 champagne was served throughout, with Royal Tawny Port, liqueurs and cigars. The banquet was held to present scrolls marking the endowments of beds in the new University College Obstetric Hospital. The band of the Grenadier Guards, the pipers of the Scots Guards and a Welsh male choir performed. 'The boys' gave what was quickly becoming their standard programme at the conclusion of the banquet.

It was a long way socially, a near incomprehensible distance, to Lansdowne House from the sheep stations of rural Queensland

> There is not a woman, scarcely a man among us who does not bear witness, in the way he dresses, or dines, or parts his hair, or takes the hand of a lady in a ball-room, that he is a humble imitator of the example set him by people who live in large houses and flourish in the pages of Debrett. There is not a man outside this narrow pale, be he English or Australian, who could walk along Piccadilly in the company of two members of the aristocracy, effete though that aristocracy may be, without a sense of elation bordering on vertigo.†

It was after this banquet and before they were due to open on 16

* Lansdowne House was originally designed and built in 1763 by Robert Adam for the Marquess of Bute.

† Buchanan, *The Real Australia*, p. 26.

June 1924 at the Victoria Palace Theatre in London that Eddie made a decision that was to have crucial consequences.

> Among the introductions I carried with me from Lady Stradbroke was one to a member of the Royal Household. I posted it fearfully one night in a red pillar box, glancing timidly at the address 'Buckingham Palace', and I went back to my flat in Maida Vale wondering whether the letter would be safely delivered and if I should get a reply.
>
> In a few days it arrived. I could hardly believe my eyes! Sir Edward Wallington, Knight Treasurer to Queen Mary, had summoned me to Buckingham Palace.* What should I do? What should I wear? How should I behave? I didn't know. I had no-one to ask. Never has anyone felt so young and helpless, so raw, so much a denizen of the outer fringes of Empire. I could hardly eat for days. I took long London 'bus rides on the open top deck to soothe my nerves. When it was cold and rained I pulled over the oil sheets and felt cosy. Eddie Cahill, a young pianist who only a year ago had been happily lost in sunny Australia was now invited to go to Buckingham Palace and would probably be asked to play to the King and Queen. At least, so I hoped.
>
> The day arrived when I walked down The Mall to the palace. A sentry in a scarlet tunic, and with a huge bearskin on his head, paid no attention to me as I entered the gates but a policeman stopped me. Whom did I wish to see? I told him. He saluted and I walked across the enormous forecourt to a door on the right of the palace. Sir Edward Wallington quickly put me at my ease. Footsteps were heard outside the door. 'The Queen,' Sir Edward murmured reverentially. I was told that Her Majesty wished to hear me play and would I attend a concert to be arranged at 69 Brook Street, Mayfair the home of Lady Harcourt. Was I agreeable? Yes, I stammered. I was delighted! And I walked out of Buckingham Palace treading on air. I wondered how my nerves would last out until the day of the concert.
>
> I soon received a letter from the Secretary to Viscountess Harcourt that said: 'The Queen is dining with the Dowager Viscountess Harcourt on July 1 and has informed me through her private Secretary that she would like to hear you play …'
>
> I had been asked to play for half an hour. What should I play? I decided on Chopin.

* Sir Edward William Wallington (1854–1933) had a significant Australian career before his service to the Royal Household. This almost certainly influenced his decision to summon Eddie to the Palace.

In the meantime, the two artists prepared another season of entertainment at the Victoria Palace.

Eddie continues his account of the royal adventure

> When the day of the concert at last arrived, I again spent shilling after shilling taking 'bus rides all over London to try and forget the ordeal that awaited me that evening. But it was no good. Nerves are terrible, but I have never met an artist without them.
>
> That night I found myself at 69 Brook Street. Crystal chandeliers blazed down upon the kind of audience I had always seen in my boyhood dreams. Queen Mary, with a collar of diamonds at her throat and a tiara, sat in the front row with the Viscountess Harcourt*. Behind her, blazing with real jewels and tiaras, sat the cream of the English aristocracy, the wives of ambassadors and many men and women distinguished in public life. I walked out to the piano, made my bow to the Queen and played a Chopin Nocturne.
>
> At the end of the concert, pressed to play more, I decided to play a little thing I had arranged on the boat coming over to England from Australia. I called it 'The Musical Box'. As soon as I had played the final note, Lady Harcourt came up to me and said that the Queen wished to speak to me. She was gracious and recalled her impressions of Australia saying her favourite city was Brisbane.
>
> She made no mention of our statesmen, but what impressed Her Majesty most of all were some of the strange creatures that went on two legs – she could not recall the name – but with an undulatory wave of the Royal Forearm she indicated 'the things that go this way' – meaning kangaroos. She wondered if they still had them. She asked about 'The Musical Box' in such a simple friendly way that I found myself talking to her without the slightest embarrassment. I told her that while I was aboard ship, I heard a little girl playing with a musical box and the thin tinkle of the tune got into my head, so that I went to my cabin and wrote it down. The Queen smiled. We had been talking for about fifteen minutes.
>
> To me, Queen Mary symbolised all that a real Queen should be. She was regal but shy, possessed warmth of personality but great dignity. She loved precious jewels and wore them with supreme confidence.

* Mary Ethel Harcourt née Burns (? –1961), the daughter of an Anglo-American banker, married Louis Vernon Harcourt, 1st Viscount Harcourt (1863–1922) in 1899.

> From that moment the doors of all the great houses in Mayfair were open to me. I think I am right in saying I started a vogue for Salon concerts in private homes which lasted from 1923 to 1937, just before the outbreak of the war. This is an era which has vanished but what great memories that era has for those who played some slight role of importance in it.

This dinner and entertainment took place on 1 July 1924 and the guest list was indeed distinguished.* The Queen had not been 'out to dinner' for many years. It is curious, a sign of his artistic vanity perhaps, that in this gushing reminiscence Eddie makes no mention of his musical partner George Brooke, who also performed after dinner for the Queen. He also failed to note the presence of the celebrated and glamorous Parisian pianist Madame Caffaret, who performed 'Pianoforte Selections' that evening. In addition, the English art song composer Roger Quilter accompanied the celebrated lyric tenor Roland Hayes, one of the first African-American male concert artists to receive wide acclaim.

A wonderful evening by all accounts. The Dowager Viscountess Harcourt was wearing the famous Boucheron Harcourt tiara and necklace. In gold, silver, emeralds and diamonds it was one of the most glorious tiaras in the age of tiaras. It says a great deal for the talents of Eddie and George that they were invited to join such august musical company. There was a fanatical enthusiasm for jazz then sweeping London among the 'Bright Young Things'. Lady Cunard's daughter, the notorious shipping heiress Nancy Cunard, scandalised her mother by openly living with her Black lover the jazz musician Henry Crowder. Allegedly over lunch the acerbic Margot Asquith asked her mother Maud 'Emerald' Cunard, 'What is Nancy up to? Is it dope, drink or niggers?'† The old aristocracy invited the rather more artistically distinguished African-American singers to perform Negro spirituals.

Eddie and George left with a host of future invitations to play

* Apart from Queen Mary honouring Viscountess Harcourt with her company, among the many guests in attendance at this dinner were the Duchess of Norfolk, the Earl and Countess of Bessborough, the Earl and Countess of Buxton, the Earl and Countess of Chesterfield, Viscount and Viscountess Willingdon, Countess Fortesque, the American Ambassador and Mrs Kellogg, Sir Edwin Lutyens the great architect, Sir George Frampton the noted British sculptor and Sir Campbell Stuart, Deputy Chairman of The Times Publishing Company.

† Quoted in Angela Hughes, *Chelsea Footprints: A Thirties Chronicle* (London 2008), p. 132.

in the great Mayfair mansions of the day. More importantly their appearance had been mentioned in the Court Circular. As they made their way home in an elated state, they were almost certainly unaware of the most notorious politico-sexual scandal of the 1920s that had rocked the address 69 Brook Street and the Harcourt family only two years before. Louis Harcourt, known as 'Loulou', the 1st Viscount Harcourt, was discovered dead in his 'Loulou Quinze' dressing room. He had committed suicide by gulping down an entire bottle of a sleeping concoction known as Bromidia.

Although the marriage had appeared outwardly respectable, 'Loulou' was a sexual predator, an enthusiastic paedophile. In the autumn of 1921 he had '*pounced* on an Eton boy who, with his mother, was visiting Nuneham Court, the Harcourts' country house in Oxfordshire. Thirteen-year-old Edward James told his mother of the advances of 'a hideous and horrible old man'. She gossiped about the incident in society and it finally came to the notice of the police. The British genius for tasteful camouflage concealed the grim details of the affair and the coroner delivered a verdict of 'death by misadventure'. Loulou's extensive child pornography collection disappeared without trace.* Music would continue to console Lady Harcourt after the family moved to Oxfordshire and Eddie continued to give recitals at Nuneham Court throughout the 1930s.

* * *

I have been a member of the Eccentric Club in London for some years. Family traits are seemingly carried in the genes. By extraordinary serendipity in March 2012 I was to have dinner in the same house, 69–71 Brook Street Mayfair, in the very same room as 'Uncle Eddie' had given his recital for Queen Mary. The dinner was to be given in the presence of the club patron and royal of my own day, Prince Philip, Duke of Edinburgh together with Lord Bath and Lord Montagu of Beaulieu and about 60 distinguished fellow club members. We ate in the opulent former Ballroom, surely one of the

* This account of a famous scandal of the time, not covered in the contemporary press but familiar to 'those in the know', is taken from the detailed description in Matthew Parris, *Great Parliamentary Scandals* (London 1995), pp. 84–6.

most outstanding interior survivals in a private London house.* The menu was chosen by HRH The Prince Philip himself and Piper-Heidsieck champagne was served throughout. I felt the evening to be an extraordinary coincidence 88 years after my great-uncle had played here.

Before dinner over an aperitif I had briefly spoken to Prince Philip. I explained something of my great-uncle.

'Your Royal Highness, my great-uncle Edward Cahill played Chopin for various members of your extended family in the 1920s. Queen Mary in this very room in 1924, also Princess Beatrice, HH Princess Helena Victoria and others'.

He listened attentively and then remarked with characteristic irony before quickly turning away to the next interlocutor.

'Well ... lucky for *them*!'

* * *

Another Afternoon Party in the grounds of Buckingham Palace at the end of June was followed by a recital at 'Number One, London' in the Waterloo Gallery at Apsley House.† At the time this was the most famous privately owned gallery in the world. The Duchess of Wellington had invited a number of foreign ambassadors to view the gallery and asked Eddie and George to come earlier for tea and to discuss the music they would play. They were the first Australians ever to perform there. Eddie spoke of this recital with the greatest pride throughout his life.

Both artists were fond of horse racing and in late July donned their panamas and motored down to West Sussex for 'Glorious Goodwood'. Various musical engagements followed before the year closed with a tour of the Irish Republic, including a season at the Theatre Royal in Dublin. The *Dublin Independent* wrote:

---

* The building now houses the Savile Club. The Ball in the Fourth Series of *Downton Abbey* was filmed here. The silver and blue colour scheme was based on that of the exquisite Amalienburg, a small mansion *pavilion de plaisance* in the gardens of the Nymphenburg Palace in Munich.

† This historic house was originally built in red brick by Robert Adam between 1771 and 1778 for Lord Apsley, the Lord Chancellor. In 1817 it was bought by the Duke of Wellington who carried out many renovations. The house was given the popular name 'Number One, London', since it was the first house passed by visitors who travelled from the countryside after the toll gates at Knightsbridge.

> Good music appeals to the Dublin public [...] Mr Brooke is a true lyric singer, has excellent diction and pure tonal qualities. Edward Cahill has fine technique, backed up by expression and interpretation not often found in pianists.

The *Cork Examiner* wrote of George's voice:

> There is magnificent quality in his voice, and he produces his notes without effort. He is full of temperament, and is gifted with absolutely clear enunciation.

Eddie, as the business brains, had by this time decided that this was 'definitely the last time' they would appear in the Variety Theatres. Both had developed far higher musical, social and commercial aspirations. Surviving financially in the London society of the day was a significant challenge that could not be satisfied by the uncertain income of the music halls. Eddie found the other acts on the bill amusing but artistically demeaning. In Dublin they had shared the bill with Ted Waite 'The Lachrymose Comedian', a 'well-formed' girl who 'danced very prettily', a card trickster and 'The Dakotas', a group of rope-spinning and whip-manipulating performers 'from the Wild West ranches.' They had both attended serious music recitals by the great German pianist Wilhelm Backhaus and the spectacular Italian coloratura soprano Amelita Galli-Curci at the Theatre Royal. They realised that additional avenues of serious musicianship could open for them, may even help them survive financially in London, if they applied some serious effort. 'Enough is enough of popular music. No more compromises! Alter course.' From now on, Eddie's address book chronicled a social climber of epic proportions.

* * *

The traditional English country house is arguably one of the finest contributions the nation has made to European art and architecture. The romanticism of woodlands, broad acres of arable or grazing land, a distinguished building and attractive gardens create an aesthetically irresistible ensemble. Many wealthy self-made men of business built new country houses along similar lines.

Eddie and George were invited to stay at Horwood House near the village of Little Horwood in Buckinghamshire. They had already played in the village hall but not at 'the big house'. The mansion had been built in 1911 by the Irish millionaire pork and bacon magnate Sir Frederick Denny and his wife Maude. The motivation at Horwood was decidedly different from their aristocratic forebears. These houses were seldom conceived as a statement of authority, grandeur and power as were the Elizabethan or Palladian prodigy houses of the past. As Vita Sackville-West observed, the new aspired to be 'essentially part of the country, not only *in* the country but part of it, a natural growth.'* As much effort was directed towards varied plantings and inspired garden design as to the house itself. The distinguished gardener Percy Thrower, son of the house gardener Harry Thrower, was born there in 1913.

In a 1923 *Country Life* feature on the house, Christopher Hussey† observed of Horwood: 'the unity is wonderfully complete; the unity is one of genial simplicity.' This emerging class was progressively being absorbed and accepted into the upper classes after the Great War and were increasingly attracted to artistic patronage as an indication of high cultural status. Eddie and George admirably fitted the position of 'musicians in residence' defined for them by the Dennys.

The first glimpse of an English country house by a visitor from abroad is a sight never to be forgotten. In a letter to his sister from Horwood, Eddie relates that one morning in April he was walking beside a formal *étang* or pool between clumps of daffodils and crocus. A stand of tall elms led him to a flagged path past a water-lily pond bordered by weathered brick walls and fruit trees. The path continued to a rugged field newly planted with elegant silver birch and rhododendrons. Beyond, he strolled into a spinney and a wild bog garden over a rickety bridge and stream edged with reeds and spiky iris. Dew glistened on vibrant green fields studded with oaks in the middle distance. He reflected on the extraordinary twist of fate that had brought him to this point

---

* V. Sackville-West, *English Country Houses* (London 1941), p. 7.

† Christopher Hussey (1899–1970) was one of the major authorities on British domestic architecture of his generation and in particular English gardens and landscape. His writings on the ethos and design of the English country house were outstanding and influential. Horwood House is now a conference hotel near Milton Keynes.

in his career in such a short space of time. He wondered how long his good fortune might last.

Frederick Denny had married Maude Marion Quilter (elder sister of the master of the English art song, Roger Quilter) in 1888. Born in 1868 and the eldest of seven children, she had grown up partly in Sydenham near Crystal Palace, the venue for numerous concerts and an area where many eminent English musicians of the time lived. This environment, together with a brother who became a famous composer, had sensitised her to the power of music and musicians. Roger Quilter's biographer Valerie Langfield observed:

> This was a family used to comforts, money, servants, a family that felt it had a reputation to develop and maintain. However, it was above all [her father] William Cuthbert Quilter's autocratic outlook and philosophy that dominated the family.*

Maude's father, Sir William Cuthbert Quilter was a remarkable man: an MP, stockbroker and extraordinarily successful businessman who left an immense fortune when he died in 1911. He had built Bawdsey Manor on the Suffolk coast in 1886, a monumental farrago of architectural eclecticism (Victorian Tudor Revival) where Eddie frequently performed in the late 1920s and early 1930s. Maud's mother Mary Ann Quilter (née Bevington) came from a wealthy Quaker family which had established a leather business in London.

Maude Denny was one of an emerging class of wealthy 'new' hostesses in London. She became Eddie's most loyal patron for the numerous concert tours of England he made between the wars. His idea of musical 'At Home' recitals both in town and country establishments was taken up as a new fashion by many hostesses of the period much to Eddie's financial and social satisfaction. In such country houses they met glamorous and theatrical artistic luminaries such as Dame Clara Butt†, Dame Sybil Thorndike‡,

---

* Valerie Langfield, *Roger Quilter: His Life and Music* (Rochester 2002), p. 6.

† Dame Clara Butt (1872–1936) was an English contralto, recitalist and concert singer. Her voice was unusually powerful and deep fitting the dominant ambience of the British Empire of the time. The Edwardian composer Elgar composed his famous *Land of Hope and Glory* for her.

‡ Dame Sybil Thorndike (1882–1976) was a great British actress who toured internationally in Shakespearean productions. The playwright Bernard Shaw wrote Saint Joan for her in which she starred with great success.

Dame Edith Evans* and Ellen Terry†.

Like many of their patrons in London, Maude had a particular interest in Australia and Australians. She had been close to her exceptionally tall and authoritative brother Arnold Quilter, who had a distinguished military career. He was Rupert Brooke's commanding officer. Quilter was cautioned by the Commander-in-Chief General Sir Ian Hamilton concerning Brooke: 'Mind you take care of him. His loss would be a national loss.' These warnings were to no avail as he was already ill, bitten on the lip in Cairo by the same type of virulent Egyptian mosquito that killed Lord Carnarvon following his discovery of the tomb of Tutankhamun.

Brooke finally succumbed to septicaemia on 23 April, 1915. Arnold Quilter was part of the burial party that made their way to a small olive grove high on the island of Skyros where Brooke was buried in a grave lined with olive branches and aromatic sage. A fortnight later Arnold too lay dead on the grim shores of the Gallipoli peninsula. Her intense grief caused Maude Denny to take a more than a casual interest in matters Australian. She became tireless in the promotion of 'her own two Australian boys' Eddie and George.

* * *

The two musicians had spent Christmas 1924 and New Year 1925 in Paris. The city was an exciting and glamorous revelation. George studied French, corrected his enunciation and increased the many French songs already scattered throughout his programmes. Eddie established contact with one of the most outstanding musicians of the day, the Swiss-French pianist, pedagogue and Chopin interpreter *extraordinaire,* Alfred Cortot‡. This pianist's teaching

* Dame Edith Evans (1888–1976) was an outstanding English stage and film actress. Her stage career spanned sixty years during which she played more than 100 roles. One of the most famous was the haughty Lady Bracknell in Oscar Wilde's *The Importance of Being Earnest.*

† Ellen Terry (1847–1928) was a beautiful English stage actress who became the leading Shakespearean actress in Britain.

‡ Alfred Cortot (1877–1962) was a Swiss-French pianist born at Nyon in the wine-growing district of Vaud on the shores of Lake Geneva. He was one of the most respected and inspiring performers and teachers of Romantic piano music, especially that of Chopin and Schumann. He continues to have an illustrious career even in death as he was among

methods were partly influenced by Tobias Matthay, so Eddie maintained muscular continuity in finger exercises and directives concerning posture. A favourite maxim for Cortot was 'find the right gesture, and the passage will play itself'. He directed Eddie to work on his digital weaknesses using the manuscript of his as yet unpublished book *Rational Principles of Pianoforte Technique.*

Cortot divided instrumental study firstly into psychological factors, which he felt to be a function of personality and taste, and secondly into physiological factors, such as the movement of the arms, hands and fingers. He conceived of the bulk of piano exercises in somewhat hyperbolic language:

> the problem of pianistic technique is seen wearing the terrific aspect of a hundred-headed hydra. My method demonstrates the vulnerability of the monster.*

Although not taken on as a full-time pupil, Eddie took a significant number of lessons from Alfred Cortot in Paris and on the Riviera. He realised that the Cortot Chopin and Schumann interpretations were visionary 'despite the many wrong notes'†.

Eddie and George stayed with the Dennys at Horwood through March and April of 1925, assembling suitable programmes, extending their repertoire and practising. In early May, when the household had moved to London for The Season, Eddie conceived the brilliant idea of hosting their own afternoon 'At Home' using Maud's London residence at 73 Grosvenor Street, Mayfair.‡ Most of the houses in the street were still in private occupation at that time. Eddie was in his element.

'Those clever Australian artists' stood at the head of the heavy oak staircase and welcomed their many distinguished guests. The visitors passed into a double music room, one for the musicians and the other separated by an arch for the audience. George sang a number of duets with the soprano Miss Elsie Treweek. Many in the

---

the last of the great age of 'subjective interpretation'. His controversial support for Vichy France and the Nazis during the Second World War has been forgotten by today's students of the instrument who are fascinated by his individualistic, intuitive and poetic interpretations. Notable pupils of Cortot included Vlado Perlemuter, Halina Czerny-Stefańska, Clara Haskil, Dinu Lipatti, Samson François – and Edward Cahill.

* Alfred Cortot, *Rational Principles of Piano Technique* (Paris 1928), Foreword p. 1.

† Remarked in conversation with the author in Monaco in 1968.

‡ The house is now the London headquarters of Estée Lauder cosmetics.

audience who had not heard Eddie and George for some time were 'delighted with the extension of their repertoire'. It was generally decided the Negro spiritual melodies and Maori songs were the most arresting music on the programme. The Quilter songs, which George had only recently studied, were accompanied by the composer and were also very popular.

Among the guests were the Duchess of St Albans*, the Dowager Marchioness of Dufferin and Ava†, the Dowager Marchioness of Linlithgow, Lady Swaythling‡ (who would become another adoring patron), Lady Weigall, Sir Edward Wallington, the song composer Madame Guy D'Hardelot, Mrs Neville Chamberlain and many other now forgotten members of the aristocracy. The *British Australasian* reported rather trivially

> Tea had previously been served downstairs, and the table decorations of early blossoms conveyed a very refreshing breath of spring. The carnations everywhere, too, were a tribute to the garden at Horwood, Mrs Denny's country house in Buckinghamshire, which is famed for its beauty.

The Sketch in a tone of patrician detachment observed that at the Chelsea Flower Show the 'huge branched *calceolaris* used in the dining room' were now considered acceptable in the best circles 'and don't suggest the semi-detached villa in the least.'§ Society also desperately needed to know that Lady Quilter wore 'a very attractive dress of the new dark powder-blue.' There was no comment on the quality of the music performed. Eddie and George had rather thrust themselves almost exclusively into the midst of the older conservative British upper classes.

---

* Beatrix Beauclerk, Duchess of St Albans, Marchioness of Waterford (1877–1953), born Beatrix Frances Petty-FitzMaurice, was a daughter of the 5th Marquess of Lansdowne and his wife, Maud.

† The Marchioness of Dufferin and Ava (1843–1936) was the wife of Frederick Temple Hamilton-Temple-Blackwood, 1st Marquess of Dufferin and Ava (1826–1902) who was a distinguished Governor General of Canada (1872–78) and an outstanding Viceroy of India (1884–88).

‡ The fabulously wealthy Gladys Helen Rachel Montagu (née Goldsmid) Lady Swaythling (1879–1965) was a member of both the Goldsmith and Rothschild banking families. She was married to Louis Samuel Montagu, 2nd Baron Swaythling (1869–1927) who was a pre-eminent British Jew, financier, and political activist. He was the heir of Samuel Montagu, 1st Baron Swaythling, who had founded the bank Samuel Montagu & Co.

§ *Gastrochilus calceolaris* is a type of orchid endemic to the Philippines.

* * *

Despite the intervening years, the shadows of the Great War had not been dispelled. Eddie and George were well aware of the neglected members of society languishing outside this privileged milieu. Eddie still felt guilty for not fighting in the conflict. As some compensation of conscience they gave a number of concerts for the recently established Not Forgotten Association (NFA), an organisation dedicated 'to provide comfort, cheer and entertainment for the wounded ex-servicemen still in hospital as a result of the Great War.'* It was movingly observed that George Brooke's sympathetic voice made an instant appeal to those cruelly blinded by mustard gas.

Eddie and George only engaged the periphery of that small and notorious Mayfair set, those forty or so publicity-seeking rebels known as the 'Bright Young People' who have passed so sensationally into history as representative of Society. The musicians inhabited the so-called 'Good Set' of birth, power, property and the old school tie, Establishment figures who actually determined significant social and political change. The 'Bad Set' of Bright Young People have been exploited by numerous books and films. Our overview of the period is largely distorted, although vastly entertained, by their exhibitionist activities such dancing the Charleston, the Black Bottom, drugs, alcohol, prostitutes and infatuation with jazz. Despite the wild and occasionally destructive goings-on, these renegades, bored by the formality of their elders and disillusioned with pre-war values, released a great deal of pent-up and brilliant creativity in the arts. Evelyn Waugh satirised their behaviour in his novel *Vile Bodies.*

Noel Coward had two sensational plays running in the West End – *The Vortex* and *Fallen Angels,* both of which Eddie saw and enjoyed immensely. He met the star of *Fallen Angels* Tallulah Bankhead† on

* The NFA continues its good works. The present patron is HRH Princess Anne, the Princess Royal.

† Tallulah Bankhead (1902–68) known as the 'Alabama Tornado' was a wild American stage and screen actress whose gravelly voice, outrageous personality, scandalous sexual behaviour, acidic wit, alcohol and drug taking gave her the reputation of a fascinating and often imitated libertine. 'Good girls keep diaries, bad girls never have the time.' she once noted.

a number of occasions at parties and found her 'an overwhelming personality'. She galvanised London audiences of the day. The uninhibited Americans had arrived. Shocked, he once witnessed her do a knickerless cartwheel in a ballroom. His positive views on the theatre were not shared by the veteran actor Sir Gerald du Maurier, however. 'The public are asking for filth,' he roundly declared. 'The younger generation are knocking at the door of the dustbin.'* In his autobiography, the British sculptor and painter of horses John Skeaping described an incident that graphically illustrates the polarised society of the twenties, so different from the pre-war years

> The twenties were the great era of parties ... I once attended a very grand party, given by the elegant, perfumed Lord Allington and his mother. Her guests were all out of Debrett, while young Allington's friends were from the studio and the theatre. These two factions were drawn up on different sides of the room, when at a lull in the proceedings, Tallulah Bankhead, the gorgeous red-headed film star, suddenly got up and moved across the room to where Lady Cunard was sitting. Grabbing hold of Lady Cunard's dress, a skimpy affair held up on the shoulders by two tiny straps, she ripped it down to the waist, remarking in a loud gin-voice as she did so: 'I always wanted to see your tits. Pandemonium broke out and Bankhead was wafted away, screaming with laughter.'†

* * *

In early June, Eddie and George gave a concert at 39 Upper Brook Street, Mayfair, and later in the month another important concert at Norwich House, Norfolk Street, Park Lane.‡ As ever, Eddie carefully noted in his journal: 'By permission of Mrs Robert Emmet once again in the presence of HRH The Princess Louise, Duchess of Argyll.' The seventy-seven-year-old Princess was the most beautiful and artistically creative fourth daughter of Queen Victoria. She pursued an idiosyncratic marriage with John Campbell, the 9th

* Barrow, *Gossip: A History of High Society from 1920 to 1970*, p. 23.

† John Skeaping, *Drawn from Life: An Autobiography* (London 1977), p. 88.

‡ Norfolk Street no longer exists. It was renamed Dunraven Street by the London County Council in 1939 after the fourth Earl of Dunraven.

Duke of Argyll, known as the Marquess of Lorne.*

No daughter of a sovereign had married a subject of the Crown since 1515, when Charles Brandon, the first Duke of Suffolk married Mary Tudor. Princess Louise and John Campbell lived rather separately. Although sharing an enthusiasm for the arts they failed to have children. Campbell was rumoured to be homosexual which at the time raised a few tentative eyebrows. Princess Louise led an extraordinarily complex and unconventional life. As well as being an able actress, early feminist, pianist and dancer, she was a prolific artist and sculptress. She was also outstandingly talkative, disliked the formality of the court, loved travel and cultivated anonymity. However, by 1925 Louise was often confined to Kensington Palace by poor health and it is surprising she attended this concert at all as she was becoming increasingly reclusive.†

On this occasion Eddie played works by Gluck, Brahms, Mozart, the Finnish composer Palmgren, Schumann, Chopin and Beethoven 'in a masterly fashion'. George gave songs in French by Lully and Massenet, in German by Schubert, Schumann and Brahms, a group of ballads in English by Roger Quilter accompanied by the composer himself. Finally he sang a selection of the ever-popular Negro spirituals which were observed to 'so admirably suit his sympathetic voice.'

The large audience was exclusively made up of duchesses, dowagers, ladies and other female notables such as the beautiful and fashionable Marchesa Malacrida. No gentlemen were present. They clearly preferred the late afternoon male conviviality of their clubs in St James's to musical *soirées*. In attracting such an 'exclusive' group of ladies one can only conclude that Eddie and George must have been possessed of significant and surprising charm and social grace alongside their undoubted musical talents. Certainly it was an opportunity for them to ingratiate themselves with the aristocracy, one of the few roads open to a well-remunerated classical concert career in London.

In July 1925, 18 Carlton House Terrace was 'lent' by the former 1908 Olympic Rackets bronze medallist Major the Hon. John

* John George Campbell, 9th Duke of Argyll (1845–1914), the Marquess of Lorne, was the 4th Governor General of Canada (1878–83).

† Jehanne Wake, *Princess Louise: Queen Victoria's Unconventional Daughter* (London 1988).

Astor and his wife Lady Violet for a further concert in aid of the Southern Irish Loyalists' Relief Association.* Princess Louise was again present, but only for a short time as she was increasingly frail. She had come once more especially to thank Eddie and George 'for so generously giving their services and arranging such a delightful concert.'

* * *

Eddie was always fascinated by the latest developments in science and technology, particularly the gramophone and wireless. The first experimental radio concert broadcast in Britain had been given at 7.10 pm on 15 June 1920, when Dame Nellie Melba's famous trill erupted onto the airwaves from the Marconi Company's New Street Works near Chelmsford, Essex. She sang the *Addio, senza rancor*† from *La Bohème* and two songs by the French composer Herman Bemberg, who had travelled from Paris to accompany her on the piano. The broadcast was received as far away as Madrid, Warsaw and Rome and even a ship at sea off Malta. She had advised Eddie to take advantage of this revolution in music and he was quick to take the opportunity.

One of the first BBC test transmissions was of a boxing commentary on the London station 2LO on 11 May 1922 from the Marconi House studios on the Strand. The British Broadcasting Company ('Company' replaced in 1927 by 'Corporation') had been formed in October 1922 to 'educate, inform and entertain.' Later in its development, in the interests of formality, all announcers were ordered by John Reith, the first General Manager, to wear evening dress to match that of the performers.

The wireless quickly became popular and the number of listeners expanded rapidly. The station was broadcasting for eight

---

* John Jacob Astor V, 1st Baron Astor of Hever (1886–1971) was a son of William Waldorf Astor, the richest man in America who moved to Britain after a family feud in 1891. He was raised on the magnificent and notorious Cliveden estate on the Thames followed by Eton and Oxford. On his father's death in 1919, John Astor inherited Hever castle in Kent where he lived the life of an English country gentleman. In 1916 he married Violet Mary Elliot-Murray-Kynynmound (1889–1965).

† 'Farewell, without bitterness'. Melba was superb in this aria and the words *Addio, senza rancor* were inscribed on her grave.

hours a day by 9 October 1925 when Eddie and George gave their first half-hour afternoon concert at 4.45 pm. Sadly the earliest BBC broadcast recordings to survive only date from the 1930s. As a result of what must have been a favourable reception, Mr Percy Pitt, General Musical Director of the BBC, offered them a wireless contract for the whole of Great Britain.* Eddie was always tremendously enthusiastic about the wireless and its power to disseminate knowledge of classical music. He noticed that after radio became popular, the servants in the great houses following the formal recital would ask him to play Beethoven or Schumann, even Chopin waltzes by title, even by opus number.

As a result of this concert broadcast, they were invited a number of times to country house 'Saturday-to-Mondays' at Rolls Park at Chigwell in the Epping Forest district of Essex. This was the home of one of the best known and admired military men of the Great War, Lieutenant General Sir Francis Lloyd†, who organised many of the defence and recruitment campaigns in London during the conflict. Winston Churchill stayed at 'Rolls' during his 1924 election campaign for the Epping seat in Parliament.

In Australia in 1927 Eddie broadcast a reminiscence of his weekends there

> Sir Francis affected stays, Louis heels, powder and rouge and a complete ignorance of music. At his home I played for fun 'Annie Laurie', Chopin's 'Fantasie Impromptu' and 'God Save the King' and he knew not one from the other. But he said he loved to see me at the piano, because the way I danced up and down the keys was funnier than George Robey. He roared with laughter through the highly complicated opening passages of the 'Fantasie Impromptu' because it was quicker and cleverer than George Robey. He said 'First you pick out a couple of black keys and

* Another forgotten musician of this fertile period. Percy Pitt (1870–1932) was an English organist and conductor. Born in London he studied music at the Leipzig Conservatory before being appointed Chorus Master in 1906 and then the following year Principal Conductor at Covent Garden. In 1908 together with Hans Richter he produced one of the earliest Wagner Ring Cycles in English. Pitt shared the conducting with Richter, who respected his musicianship greatly as did Sir Edward Elgar. Pitt was the first British musician to conduct the Ring in an opera-house. He was Director of the British National Opera Company until 1924 and also a composer of charming light orchestral music.

† Lieutenant General Sir Francis Lloyd (1853–1926) was a British army officer Commanding the Brigade of Guards and General Officer Commanding the London District during the Great War.

catch hold of a couple of whites, then you throw all the black ones down one end and slog into the whites and *La Campanella* sounds like an argument leading up to a battle.'

He told me he never had any idea when 'God Save the King' was being played, and naturally as a soldier he must have heard it hundreds of times. 'Your fingers remind me of little mice running away from the cat!' he exclaimed.

Sir Francis used to give brilliant dinner parties. I have never seen a dinner table look more brilliant and I have seen many great ones. I think Sir Francis and Lady Lloyd must have had one of the best silver dinner services in England. There was always an air of distinction whenever the Lloyds were entertaining a house party. Remember I had a good opportunity of comparing the entertaining in celebrated houses. Lady Lloyd was rather a frail looking little person, but she was always conspicuous by her very gay and youthful dressing. I remember her wearing a very severe white satin dress with a long flowing train and a lot of soft flowing draperies and some lovely diamonds. It seemed to me both these charming people had a flare for wearing very striking clothes.

One thing I remember in connection with the dinner parties which took place at 'Rolls' was that after the meal, the little dog 'Wump' would come into the room and Sir Francis would put 'Wump' on the table. The dog would walk in and out of all the silver things without knocking over anything.

The Countess of Malmesbury once came to dinner at Rolls accompanied by her own little dog named 'Mogul'. She began to discuss the intelligence of this animal.

'He talks to me don't you know. I understand everything he says and he understands everything I say. But of late he has been visiting the servant's hall and has now begun to talk like one of the servants. He is developing a quite frightful accent. I have forbidden my maid to let him go down there again!' Much laughter erupted from Sir Francis at this remark.

In November they were invited to attend the funeral of Queen Alexandra 'in Arctic frost and snow', who had died of a heart attack.* In December in one of their last concerts of the year, George gave a

* Queen Alexandra (1844–1925), Alexandra of Denmark, was Queen of the United Kingdom of Great Britain and Ireland and Empress of India as the wife of King-Emperor Edward VII who died in 1910. She was a dowager queen and the mother of the reigning monarch King George V.

recital of Negro spirituals at the invitation of the Rev. Pennington-Bickford, Rector of St Clement Danes Church. They became close friends as both musicians were 'good Roman Catholics' and fervent supporters of Ecumenism. This church, well over three hundred years old, stands on island in the Strand quite indifferent to the maelstrom of modern traffic that swirls around it. The Rector appropriated the well-known London tune 'Oranges and Lemons' for St Clement's and its famous bells. He established the annual distribution of oranges and lemons to local children.*

* * *

Eddie and George decided to return to Australia in February 1926 for a concert tour. They turned down the broadcasting contract with 2LO. However in the course of a week or so they made twelve recordings for the Colombia Gramophone Company.† Despite all the social and musical success and glamorous engagements, from their letters home it is clear they were missing their families and the familiar environment. They both terribly missed the sun. 'How tired I am of this blasted English climate!' Eddie wrote to his sister. The round of London Society engagements was exhausting. They had been catapulted unprepared into a social world so entirely different to their own that they were suffering a debilitating variety of 'culture shock'.

Among the many farewell dinners in their honour, they gave a recital in late January 1926 at 28 Kensington Court 'lent' by Lord and Lady Swaythling just before they sailed for New York. Among the usual Chopin, Schumann, Liszt and Beethoven, Mme Guy d'Hardelot personally accompanied George in three of her latest songs which he was taking to Australia: *Wings*, *The Quiet Country Places* and *The Great Unknown*. The fabulously wealthy Lady

* Although unconnected with the two musicians, the subsequent tragic and dramatic Second World War history of St Clement's is moving to recall. On 10 May 1941 the Rev. Pennington-Bickford watched the church burn down after the Luftwaffe fire-bombed the building, this church at which he had spent his entire Ministry. A month later, his parishioners considered he was so filled with grief and despair that he took his own life. His wife then leapt from a window three months after that, grief-stricken both at the loss of her husband and the church they both so loved.

† Sadly to date only one recording by George Brooke is traceable, an internet link to which is provided in this book.

Swaythling was to become and would remain one of the staunchest supporters of Eddie throughout his future career in Europe. A number of prominent Americans attended this recital and offered to arrange future engagements in America which Eddie and George enthusiastically accepted.

A feisty character and future patron emerged at this farewell recital. This was Lady Weigall née Grace Emily Blundell Maple, the tremendously affluent daughter of Sir Blundell Maple the furniture magnate.* In 1898 she had married Baron Hermann von Eckardstein, First Secretary of the German Embassy. The Baroness (pet name 'Bunchy') brought an action against her politically notorious husband ('Bear') on the grounds of adultery and cruelty. She had been forced to pay his gambling debts which amounted to some £320,000 during the marriage. A gigantic loss.† After the divorce, in 1910 she married Sir Archibald Weigall. Their interest in Australian artists such as Eddie and George came from their experiences when Sir Archibald had been Governor of South Australia from 1920 to 1922. Both had developed a great love of the country and its people. The Weigalls lived at the recently built 'Tudor to Jacobean' style Petwood House in Lincolnshire, which was filled unsurprisingly with Maple furniture. Here they entertained on a lavish scale.

Once when Eddie was a guest there Nellie Melba was also present and met for the first time the writer Beverley Nichols who was to become her private secretary. His novel *Evensong* published in 1932 presented a 'warts and all' portrait of her in fictional guise as Madame Irela, a famous soprano in decline. The book caused a popular outcry in Australia. In an interview after publication Eddie supported the Nichols portrait.

> When Melba first met Beverley Nichols at Petwood, Lady Weigall's country home near London, she spoke of him to me as the most brilliant young man she had met since Oscar Wilde

* Lady Weigall née Grace Emily Blundell Maple (1876–1950). Her husband Sir Archibald Weigall, 1st Baronet KCMG (1874–1952), was a British Conservative politician who had been Governor of South Australia from 1920 to 1922. Although never explicitly calling for Federation and abolition of the Australian States, he did describe the results of the division of power in Australia as being 'farcical' and 'chaotic', and concluded that 'State Governors and State Legislatures are now anachronisms'.

† Purchasing power of £320,000 in 1910 would be around £29 million in 2015.

> and predicted that he would make a big noise in the world. She also told me later that Nichols was the only man who knew and understood her and could write a book about her. In my opinion Beverley Nichols has very cleverly drawn the character of Melba. He may be a bit severe. His stories about her violent temper and other little things were perfectly drawn.*

Eddie would give a number of future recitals in this historic and attractive house.†

As the boys boarded the MV *Caprera* in Southampton at the beginning of 1926 bound for Fremantle in Western Australia they could not but reflect on three extraordinary years spent in England. By sheer good luck they had begun as variety theatre performers and been launched into the upper echelons of the aristocracy. They planned to return as soon as they had assembled a full diary of future engagements. 'People have been kind beyond our wildest dreams,' Eddie commented to a roving newspaper reporter as they embarked. In a triumph of travel logistics they managed to give a series of concerts in Italy *en route* to Australia performing in Genoa, Florence, Rome and Naples. Despite its fame, they found the Neapolitan opera disappointing with poor soloists but excitedly visited the summit of Mount Vesuvius whilst the volcano was 'in an angry mood.'

---

* *Telegraph* (Brisbane), Thursday, 21 January 1932, p. 1.

† Lincolnshire airfields played a vital role in WWII. Petwood's most notable appearance in wartime history is as the Officers' Mess for the 617 Squadron. It was decided that the 617 'Dambusters Squadron' should be made into a special duties squadron which would work in isolation and secrecy at Petwood and Woodhall airfield. For Officers at war, Petwood was fondly remembered as a 'splendid place' remote from battle. Adapted from *Petwood: The Remarkable story of a famous Lincolnshire Hotel,* Edward Mayor, 2004.

Chapter 6

'See the Conquering Hero Comes'

The long six week voyage home ended when the run-down Italian steamer *Caprera* docked in Fremantle in Western Australia on 3 April 1926. Heading for the Eastern States and Brisbane, they sailed into the Outer Harbour at Adelaide and spent the day there renewing friendships and passing on messages from London. At their farewell London concert Sir Archibald and Lady Weigall had asked them to convey their respects to 'the people of Adelaide' and all the friends they had made there during Sir Archibald's Governorship. The reporter for the *Register* remarked after hearing them enumerate the royals, dowagers and duchesses who had graced their London concerts: 'Australia has reason to be proud of her sons.'

Today it is difficult to appreciate how extraordinary it was in 1926 for any Australian to give a Royal Command Performance. Eddie and George were rewarded with a civic reception in Brisbane Town Hall on 27 April. 'It is wonderful to be back in my own land!' Eddie enthused. 'We needed every penny we saved, despite all the engagements!' he later commented when asked about their financial success. The Mayor of Brisbane congratulated them on their musical triumphs and charity work for the Red Cross. Even Eddie's first music teacher, Mrs Bale, the wife of the Beenleigh milkman, was present and spoke of the day she gave him his first lesson and his rapid progress at the instrument which soon outstripped her own abilities. The well-known Queensland concert pianist and teacher Erich John lavishly praised both their musical and social success abroad. He remarked that they had achieved in three years what it normally took an artist thirty to accomplish, if at all. He paraphrased Schumann's famous remark about Chopin

'Hats off, gentlemen! An Australian artist!'

Eddie in reply spoke of the extraordinarily friendly reception they had received in England with all types of audience and how the English retained a warm spot for Australians*

> You know, I had my first music lesson with Mrs Bale dressed in a suit of red plush and with my hair prepared by curling pins! Quite an outfit for the town that manufactured a powerful rum and had a crack rifle and tough rugby club. Young students will face tremendous difficulties in trying to make a career in London – the Mecca of all artists. You need £1000 of capital to begin a career there.† We were incredibly lucky and Nellie Melba and Lady Stradbroke were tremendously generous with their letters of introduction. The agent we engaged, a Mr L.G. Sharp, also acted for Paderewski. To succeed today you need talent, money, influence and personality – but mostly personality and grit!

He expanded to a newspaper reporter concerning their visit 'home'

> Generally speaking the children of Australia are more musical than the children of Great Britain. In Britain one misses the lovely fresh voices one hears in Australia. As Sybil Thorndike said to Mr Brooke when she heard him sing: 'I know you are an Australian. I can hear and see the sunshine in your voice.'
>
> I think Mr Brooke and myself can attribute our success entirely to the fact that we did not pretend. We went home as Australians and we remained as Australians. The public took a liking to us. They appreciated our efforts and they appreciated us because we were Australians. Others have gone home and have been pleased to pose as British people. But in that they have done wrong. Most English people will like Australians when they go home just because they are Australians. London audiences are marvellous.

Concerning the revolutionary new invention of the wireless.

> The wireless is the greatest event in the history of the art of music. Many of the concert managers in London are opposed to wireless, but many of the foremost artists have already played or sung for the British Broadcasting Company. The company is paying big fees to good artists, fees which are most attractive and which many artists cannot resist accepting. Instrumentalists and orchestral organisations are the most successful broadcasters; wireless has not yet been brought to

* This interview reported in the *Telegraph* (Brisbane), Friday 23 April 1926, p. 5.

† Close to £50,000 in 2015.

> that state of perfection which enabled the human voice to be transmitted without loss of quality by distortion.

Mr Cahill instanced the failure of Tetrazzini as a broadcaster.

> The microphone of the transmitter could not absorb the impressions of her wonderful voice and transmit them with fidelity.

In an interview with the London *Daily Mail* before their departure Eddie had referred to the great changes broadcasting had wrought on the concert world

> Only foremost artists like Paderewski, Galli-Curci, Pachmann and Chaliapine are having good houses. Without a large personal following concert work is not profitable. The work of the conductor Sir Landon Ronald is doing a great deal to revive interest in orchestral concerts at the Palladium.* The only real bright spot! We hope to do more broadcasting on our return to London.

The so-called 'Complimentary Public Welcome' in Beenleigh was scheduled for the evening of 30 April, 1926. On arrival at the School of Arts Eddie passed through a guard of honour formed by local schoolchildren who showered him with confetti. On entering the main hall he made his way to the stage where he occupied the place of honour together with his mother. The Federal Band from South Brisbane struck up 'See the Conquering Hero Comes' from Handel's oratorio *Judas Maccabaeus.* He then received a formal civic welcome from the chairman of the Shire Council. 'The wonderful record obtained by Mr Cahill as a musician is a great advertisement for Queensland and the little town of Beenleigh.' *He's a Jolly Good Fellow* trumpeted out by the band almost lifted the roof.

> I did not realise what Australian blue skies and sunshine meant until I went to England and returned to sunny Queensland! I have never felt so lonely as when I gave my first concert in London.

He also relayed the immense English gratitude for the help and sacrifice of so many young Australian lives in support of England throughout the Great War.

> The doors to Buckingham Palace would never have opened for me had it not been for the letters of introduction from the

* Sir Landon Ronald (1873–1938) was an English conductor, composer, pianist, singing teacher, and administrator. He was a close associate of Dame Nellie Melba and wrote some 200 songs. He was principal conductor of the Royal Albert Hall Orchestra and like Eddie an innovative designer of musical programmes.

former Premier of Queensland, Mr Ted Theodore. For this I am eternally grateful.

He was then presented with a handsome tooled-leather folder with a gold ornamental lyre entwined with his initials. Inside was an encomium in ornate calligraphy from the most distinguished figures in the Beenleigh District. George was also honoured as Eddie's 'musical associate', a fellow Australian but as a native of Melbourne merely considered an 'adopted son of Queensland'. Refreshments, dancing and music was performed by among others his sisters the pianists Lily and Madge Cahill. *God Save the King* concluded the proceedings.

During the 1926–27 Australian concert season Eddie and George gave nine successful concerts in Melbourne, seven in Brisbane, Sydney and Adelaide and made a tour of the J.C. Williamson vaudeville circuit. At the Exhibition Hall in Brisbane Eddie used two instruments: an upright piano for the refined intimacy and elegance of Mozart, Paderewski, Schumann and Chopin and a full-bodied concert grand for the heavier works by Rachmaninoff, Brahms, Liszt and Weber. The improvement in Eddie's technique and depth of interpretation since returning from London was much commented on by critics. 'Mr Cahill has the faculty of intimate interpretation, backed by a formidable technique,' wrote the Brisbane *Telegraph.* George sang a selection of English ballads, German *Lieder* and modern French art songs. His diction and enunciation in all languages was considered outstanding.

In Melbourne they 'imported' the idea they claimed they pioneered in England. The staging of exclusive ticketed 'At Home' recitals for wealthier and more distinguished citizens. Some of the audience were prepared to pay a high price for tickets that would facilitate socialising with the upper echelons of society as well as listening to excellent classical music. 'Versatility and personality are the essentials for success,' Eddie wrote to the wife of the Governor General, Lady Stonehaven.* She, together with a 'Vice-Regal Party' and the Lord Mayor of Melbourne and his wife, attended a number of their sold out concerts at the Assembly Hall in Melbourne. They

* John Lawrence Baird, 1st Viscount Stonehaven, (1874–1941), known as Lord Stonehaven during this period, was a British Conservative politician who served as the eighth Governor-General of Australia (1925–31).

performed the same type of programme that 'mixes the classical and the popular in just the right proportions', a variety of styles which had brought them such success in London. The audience 'found everything to its taste' and recalled them time and again, seeming to respond more favourably to the less demanding popular works.

One rather acerbic commentator put his criticisms obliquely

> The fare provided was all of easy digestion and effectively garnished ... One recognizes that typical drawing-room art is being transferred to the concert hall with results eminently pleasing.

Eddie had arranged the richly flower-decked stage and subdued lighting to evoke the atmosphere of a cultivated nineteenth-century salon. His piano accompaniments to George's songs were regarded as 'discreet and perfect'. Great improvements in both artists were again noted by their friends and those who had heard them perform before their departure for London. Eddie in particular had vastly improved his technique and interpretation under Tobias Matthay and he gratefully acknowledged this immense help. They extended their season by two concerts by popular demand.

* * *

They had only been in Australia for a year before setting off for the extensive tour of America previously arranged in London, which would be followed by a return to the great metropolis. Eddie again began to give his profitable 'farewell recitals', so well attended by virtue of the sweet sentiments of imminent departure. George had been seeing a great deal of an attractive widow, Mrs Thomas Hardman, since his return to Australia and soon they seemed to be becoming romantically involved. Her late husband had been the manager of the Oriental Hotel in Brisbane. George had met her during the musical season in Melbourne and by September the couple had married. Eddie's reaction to this can only be guessed at, but after at least ten years working with George as bachelors a certain psychological and practical adjustment must have been inevitable. However his sunny temperament showed the greatest pleasure in this match for his 'best pal'. The renamed Cahill-Brooke Company would now tour the globe as a trio, apparently without a care in the world.

Their final Australian performances were warmly praised

> These artists did not descend on us meteor-like to surprise us with their brilliance, then to disappear and be forgotten in the blaze of some other luminary. They grew up musically in our midst.

After praising Eddie's performance of Liszt and Paderewski's 'wholly delightful' *Mélodie* and *Minuet* the writer of the review moved into the priceless realms of the visually rhapsodic, perhaps moved by George singing 'Vision Fugitive' from *Hérodiade* by Massenet. The dreary stage of the Theatre Royal in Brisbane came to resemble an altogether different area of exoticism worthy of Salome herself, the designs produced by the clearly gifted Arabian Art Salon

> A priceless Turkish flag, with the crescent flaunted on scarlet satin, hid the horrible old property seat on which countless lovers of Royal melodrama have canoodled. A softly-shaded dusky gold lamp, under which sat a Sphinx-like brass lady, brightened up the foreground, and brass vessels, plaques, candelabra and bowls full of sunset-tinted foliage toned down the vivid flash of colour in the flag [...] Mrs George Brooke wore a lovely frock that appeared as bars of sunlight on old ivory.

And so our trio high in confidence and excitement, basking in the limelight of Australian fame, boarded the SS *Sonoma* on 9 April 1927 for San Francisco on a short concert tour of America. They had been given numerous letters of introduction by the English war poet and playwright Robert Nichols and his wife Norah (née Denny).* The letters to hostesses, various celebrities of the day and movie stars were accompanied by some 'Notes of Explanation' from Norah, which are diverting in themselves:

> *Miss Dolly Green* – very pretty and charming eldest daughter of immensely rich parents who have a big house & garden & swimming pool etc., and who go to N. York & Europe practically

* Robert Nichols (1893–1944) was an officer in the Royal Artillery campaigning during the Great War at Loos and the Somme before he was invalided out suffering from shell shock. His poetry was included together with that of Rupert Brooke and others in the famous collection *Georgian Poetry* 1911–22 edited by Sir Edward 'Eddie' Marsh. He is among sixteen Great War poets commemorated on a slate stone in Poet's Corner at Westminster Abbey. The inscription on his tomb by Wilfrid Owen reads: 'My subject is War, and the pity of War. The Poetry is in the pity.' In 1922 Robert married Norah Denny, the daughter of Eddie's patron, Mrs Frederick Denny of Horwood.

every year. Parents rather dull but know everyone. Daughter exceptionally nice & clever – wants to go on the stage.

Mrs Edgar – one of the greatest hostesses in N. York & used to the very best of everything including music – must be treated with respect – very charming. Knows Robert only.

Douglas Fairbanks – no explanation necessary. He is not musical, but is jolly & kind & friendly – likes to be treated as 'the great man'

Mrs Charles Ray – wife of Charles Ray the movie actor. She is not an actress – gives nice parties – has a lovely house – artistic – knows all the movie people.

The detailed record of this tour is unfortunately sparse, but some high points were recorded in Eddie's scattered notes and cuttings.

The myth of 1920s America, that decade of 'wonderful nonsense', had probably misguided them with illusions. The Treaty of Versailles had been signed for some eight years by the time they arrived. The customary idea of life in the United States was of a giddy release from the stresses of the Great War in the form of jazz, drugs, parties, gangsters and illegal drinking. However on closer examination it was a period of social and institutional upheaval the like of which the country had never before experienced in its history.

> The new society of the 1920s was characterised by vast changes in religion, political philosophy, folkways, moral precepts and uses of leisure time. [...] This was a period of massive cultural conflict focusing on such matters as religion, marriage and moral standards, as well as issues of race, prohibition and immigration.*

Women in particular looked to embrace new and revolutionary sexual freedoms, less restricting and alluring modes of dress as well as the right to drink and smoke in public places. The Charleston was an exuberant expression of feminine individuality and freedom, particularly indulged in by that period sensation, the 'flapper', Defined as follows:

> Two bare knees, two thinner stockings attached to garters, one shorter skirt, two lipsticks, three powder puffs, 132 cigarettes and a long holder, and three boyfriends, with eight flasks be-

* Ronald Allen Goldberg, *America in the Twenties* (New York 2003), pp. 162–3.

tween them. She chewed gum – great wads of it – vigorously and incessantly. Her make-up was as crude as a clown's.*

In many ways this destination seemed an unusual choice for both these increasingly serious classical musicians. With his theatrical temperament Eddie grew particularly fond of the infectious enthusiasm of American girls. However the aesthetic taste of the elite in Society, the stratum they had enjoyed frequenting in England, was being eroded in America and replaced by the taste of the masses. The Europeans who had settled the country carried with them Protestant, even Puritan, values of thrift and hard work that found little place for the social privilege, leisured elegance and self-indulgence of traditional European aristocracy – in many ways the crucible of classical European music. The art of business was increasingly valued above culture. One contemporary writer observed: 'Through business, properly conceived, managed and conducted, the human race is finally to be redeemed.'†

Eddie and George gave an interview to *Musical America* entitled 'Give Your Audiences What They Want Rather Than What You May Like' in which they outlined their general philosophy of concert giving. They pointed out that when their appearances before royalty were advertised in the Court Circular followed by their 'At Homes' in Mayfair, such exposure became an invaluable road to success in London. Such features of their activities, such publicity based on social class, would be infrequent or non-existent in America where society was differently stratified. With gentle irony Eddie observed:

> Naturally that is a condition which could not obtain in a republic, because Presidents of Republics and their First Ladies of the Land do not occupy quite the same place in the affections of the general public, especially the social side of it, as Royalty does.

They then went on to point out the popularity of sentimental 'art songs' as opposed to serious *Lieder*. Eddie, ever the shrewd businessman as well as 'the poet of the piano', continued

> The thing boils down to the question of what you are after. If it is a matter of musical philanthropy, or of educating the public or appealing to the small proportion of highly educated,

---

* Maximillien de Lafayette, *America in the Twenties. Photos and Reports*, vol. 1 (New York 2011), p. 31.

† Goldberg, *America in the Twenties*, p. 84.

highly sophisticated musicians, you had better stick to Brahms, Strauss, Schubert, Schumann, Bach and Handel. But, before you do this, be sure you are well subsidised! If, on the other hand, it is a matter of earning your living and accumulating a bank account, it might be wiser to popularize your programmes to some extent. We often combine both, which seems to work well. Study your public.

In early July 1927 they gave a concert at the Aeolian Hall near Times Square. The famous Aeolian building had been sold some time before to an unlikely but socially representative purchaser, the *Schulte Cigar Stores Company* and was soon to cease hosting classical music concerts altogether. The hall had an illustrious history: Rachmaninoff, Prokofiev, Busoni and Paderewski had all appeared there. George Gershwin's *Rhapsody in Blue* was premiered there one afternoon in February 1924 with Paul Whiteman and the Palais Royal Orchestra. Gershwin entitled the concert 'An Experiment in Modern Music'. This engaging work succinctly expressed the American spirit of the age.

Eddie and George gave their usual programme of Liszt, Chopin, Schubert and Quilter songs together with Negro spirituals (which were surprisingly well received by the educated audience). George had additionally taken a number of lessons from Lawrence Brown on the interpretation of spirituals while in America.* He had become a master of the genre. Just before the concert Eddie had received news of the death in Beenleigh of his eighty-nine-year-old grandmother, Caroline Dauth. This was a particular blow of great poignancy for him, as she had protected him from the displeasure and occasional violence of his publican father when he became a professional musician. He had spent many hours at her house practising in secret and benefited from her wisdom and sympathy.

As I played a couple of Chopin Nocturnes full of sensibility and George sang those sad Negro laments, I cast my mind back to childhood and all those secret assignations at grandmother's

* Lawrence Brown (1893–1972) was the accompanist and arranger for the famous Negro singer Paul Robeson (1898–1976). They were the first to bring spirituals to the concert stage. Robeson later credited Brown for guiding him '... to the beauty of my own folk music and to the music of all other peoples so like our own.' Brown had also worked with the famous gospel singer Roland Hayes who George had also studied under after appearing in concert with him in 1924 before Queen Mary.

> house in Beenleigh. The nostalgia I felt affected my playing in a profound way that night.*

One impression Eddie gained in New York was of the importance of the orchestral section in picture theatres. From his early career Eddie had maintained a great and overriding interest in the cinema. His comments give an interesting insight into the period of transition from the silent cinema to the 'talkies'.

> These orchestras are all so excellent that they almost help you to forget the poor singing that is sometimes heard. I believe that the picture theatre managers in New York are materially assisting in bringing good music to a wider public. These managers now engage star artists. In one of their theatres the other evening I heard the great Mischa Levitzki play a Liszt Piano Concerto with orchestra.†

The excellent press they attracted for their own concerts led to them being offered a season by the famous impresario George Engels, which they were unable to accept owing to previously arranged engagements in England. Although well remunerated it seems fair to assume that they were not sufficiently impressed by 'modernity' to ever seriously consider returning to America. In July 1927 the trio boarded the luxury Cunard liner RMS *Berengaria* that sailed from New York to Southampton via Cherbourg to begin their second and much anticipated tour of England.

---

* Noted by the author in conversation in Monaco 1968.

† Mischa Levitzki (1898–1941) was an outstanding Russian-born American virtuoso concert pianist. He toured the world and gave concerts at Aeolian Hall. He wrote some charming small salon pieces for piano which became immensely popular – *The Enchanted Nymph,* the waltz in A major, the waltz *Tzigane,* and a *Gavotte.*

CHAPTER 7

BROOKLANDS AND THE *COURT CIRCULAR*

Eddie and George had become accustomed to all manner of ships during their Southeast Asian tour but nothing had prepared them for the luxury of the Cunard flagship liner, the stately RMS *Berengaria*. They had been paid well for their American tour and their mutual love of luxury put them in a spending mood. A surprising radiogram wishing them luck arrived on departure from the movie actor Douglas Fairbanks who had hosted one of their American 'At Homes'. Margaret had hardly spent any time at sea and was excited by the fine, spacious cabins, swimming pools of fresh and sea water, tapestry-covered period furniture in the First Class lounge and the wonderful menus in the opulent dining room. For the rich, famous and *nouveaux riches* who sailed on the Cunard trans-Atlantic liners, it was this exclusive social ambience that was their most valuable attribute.

The trio arrived in England after a fast passage of six days from New York for their second concert tour towards the end of July 1927.* Mrs Denny's chauffeur swiftly motored them up to the antler-adorned baronial hall of Horwood in Buckinghamshire. They would stay with her for a few weeks until their first London engagement. They had managed to again rent the spacious flat they occupied at 26 Randolph Crescent Maida Vale. Margaret was anxious to scour the London markets and decorate their temporary home as artistically as she could. She became fascinated with the search for undiscovered treasure among the acres of bric-a-brac at the Friday Caledonian Market in North London.

In the eighteen months they had been away there had been

* In 1927 the *Berengaria* averaged an astonishing 22.54 knots on the New York to Southampton Atlantic crossing. *New York Times*.

some singular events in England, notably the General Strike of May 1926. At the other extreme, the world of fashion had welcomed the 'decadent' Charleston dance craze from America with short skirts scandalously above the knee and shingled hair. The *Daily Mail* commented the dance was 'reminiscent of Negro orgies.' In April 1926 Princess Elizabeth was born to the Duke and Duchess of York, later King George VI and Queen Elizabeth. London's first Director automatic telephone exchange was to open at Holborn in November 1927, which at the time seemed a miracle of technology.

Clearly the hostesses and patrons Eddie and George met on their first tour had been hard at work on arrangements for their return. Invitations to stay at country houses for 'Saturday-to-Mondays' and longer flooded the mantelpiece at Randolph Crescent. Royalty were to be occasional guests on these occasions, which put severe financial pressure on them in sartorial terms. They stayed at Nicholas Hawksmoor's magnificent Easton Neston with Sir Thomas and Lady Hesketh*, Lady Francis Lloyd at Tyringham, Sir Cuthbert and Lady Quilter of Bawdsey Manor, as well as the Earl and Countess of Fingall† at Killeen Castle, a grey Neo-Gothic miniature Windsor, about 20 miles from Dublin.

Speaking of their first seven months in England on this second visit, Eddie commented: 'We have had a wonderful time and been entertained most lavishly.' He was clearly becoming increasingly torn between the seductiveness and quality of upper-class life in England and his emotional ties with Australia. George on the other hand was far less exercised by snobbery and took life as it came. The comparatively provincial nature of Australia had become all too clear after their recent return, however heroically their brows had been crowned with laurels at home.

Their initial London concert engagement after the American tour was on 17 November 1927 at Hill Street Mayfair at the palatial London home of Sir Archibald and Lady Grace Weigall. This concert would be in the presence of HH Princess Marie Louise. The

* Sir Thomas Fermor-Hesketh, later 1st Baron Hesketh (1881–1944) was a peer, soldier and Conservative MP. He married Florence Louise Breckinridge of Kentucky. Thus was another flower added to the bouquet of American hostesses in London who contributed so much of value to the cultural life of the capital.

† Elizabeth Mary Margaret Burke-Plunkett (1866–1944) at 17 married Arthur James Plunkett, 11th Earl of Fingall, 4th Baron Fingall (1859–1929).

song composer Madame Guy D'Hardelot and Mrs F.A. König, an accomplished pianist and Lady in Waiting to Princess Marie Louise, 'kindly agreed to assist'.

Many landed families were feeling the severe financial consequences of the post-war period and were appreciative of 'the economical "At Homes" these handsome young Australians provide!' Houses were often 'lent' by the more generous and more comfortably-off members of Society. Country house owners had not yet been forced to import lions, tigers and rhinos to create safari parks in the Home Counties to retain their mansions and finance costly repairs. The combined effects of high wages, crippling increases in taxation and anachronistic methods of estate management had forced many upper-class members of society into unaccustomed thrift, even penury.

* * *

Eddie had already come up with the idea of charging members of the public to 'rub shoulders with the aristocracy'. The *arriviste* nature of the exercise could be camouflaged by couching it in the setting of an uplifting classical music recital. This idea was irresistible to those of a certain cast of mind in Society or those aspiring to a prestigious place in it. Tickets were available for purchase at fifteen shillings.* The November concert was completely sold out to an audience estimated at five hundred. Lady Weigall's love of music was turning the ballroom of her house in Mayfair into a miniature Queen's Hall. This could well have been the address in Hill Street occupied by the notorious Lord and Lady Metroland that Evelyn Waugh had in mind in *Vile Bodies.* The house may possibly be the location of Mrs Ape's *début.*

> The Bright Young People came popping all together, out of someone's electric brougham like a litter of pigs, and ran squealing up the steps. [...] The ballroom was filled with little gilt chairs and the chairs with people.†

---

* 15/- in 1927 was close to £40 in 2015.

† Evelyn Waugh, *Vile Bodies* (London 1938), pp. 92–6. It is unlikely however that Lady Metroland, who first emerges in Waugh's *Decline and Fall*, was modelled on Lady Weigall although the latter certainly had an extraordinary 'hedonistic secret life' of sexual dalliance. See Carol Henderson & Heather Tovey, *Searching for Grace* (Wellington 2010).

One member of the distinguished audience at Hill Street who became a staunch patron was Hariot Georgina Hamilton-Temple-Blackwood, Marchioness of Dufferin and Ava. Lady Dufferin had established the admirable National Association for Supplying Female Medical Aid to the Women of India. This organisation trained female Indian medical staff to attend women who were not permitted to consult a male doctor. Rudyard Kipling was greatly impressed by the work of Lady Dufferin and wrote a poem of thanks on her departure from India entitled *The Song of the Women.* The Oxford Dictionary of National Biography describes her as 'the most effective diplomatic wife of her generation'.

Other future patrons met at this recital were HH Princess Marie Louise[*] and her sister HH Princess Helena Victoria[†] (known as 'Thora'), granddaughters of Queen Victoria and both highly musical. They were patrons of many concerts at their residence, the Schomberg House at 71 Pall Mall.[‡]

> My sister and I inherited from our mother an intense love and appreciation of music.[§] My sister was a very accomplished pianist; I, alas, could scarcely play a note [...] We were fortunate to enjoy the friendship of most of the celebrated artists, foreign as well as English ...[¶]

Though considered 'frightfully dull' by fashionable society, the princesses became two of Eddie's most loyal patrons. Sir Henry 'Chips' Channon, not a connoisseur of music, wrote rather snootily in his celebrated diary of Princess Helena Victoria after her death in March 1948

> She had once been a bouncing, fat, jolly Princess ... known to her intimates as 'the Snipe'. She was an old maid who may, howev-

* HH Princess Marie Louise of Schleswig-Holstein (1872–1956). In 1891 she married Prince Aribert of Anhalt (1866–1933).The bride's first cousin, the German Emperor Wilhelm II, had influenced the match. The marriage was unhappy and childless as evidenced in her Memoirs.

† HH Princess Helena Victoria of Schleswig-Holstein (1870–1948). She never married and devoted herself to charitable works.

‡ Now the Oxford and Cambridge Club.

§ Her mother, HRH The Princess Helena was the fifth child and third daughter of Queen Victoria and Prince Albert. She controversially married Prince Christian of Schleswig-Holstein. He was her senior by many years but they were devoted to each other and remained very happily married. In her memoirs HH Princess Marie Louise wrote of her mother 'She was very talented: played the piano exquisitely ...'

¶ HH Princess Marie Louise, *My Memories of Six Reigns*, pp. 209–10.

er, have once known love ... She is survived by her even duller sister, Princess Marie Louise ... This female was married in her long-ago youth to a Prince of Anhalt, from which she afterwards got an annulment. When she returned to England, King Edward VII's comment about his niece was: 'Poor Marie Louise. She came back just as she VENT.'*

Eddie had a deeper, less waspish appreciation of their social generosity, musical natures and artistic accomplishments. Performance on a musical instrument of any acceptable standard was rare in royal circles. She and her sister were particularly fascinated by Poland and respected its tragic history of exalted patriotic resistance. This may have been the reason she wished to hear Eddie play as he had a growing reputation within aristocratic circles for playing Chopin idiomatically and sensitively. However for Princess Marie Louise it was the forgotten Russian pianist Nicolai Orloff† who was her favourite Chopin interpreter.

Eddie in full aesthetic flight, noted that the hostess of that afternoon concert, Lady Weigall, had the most beautiful blue eyes and fair complexion he had ever seen. Princess Marie Louise had known her when she was a girl of seventeen and later wrote

> Lady Weigall was the only child of Blundell Maple. [...] She was rather self-willed and, perhaps I may say with all affection, rather spoilt, as no doubt the only child of a multi-millionaire is apt to be. [...] From 1928 to 1946 Gracie was chained to her chair, which she manipulated in the most marvellous manner. For ordinary use she had the usual invalid chair, but in the evening, when she wished to be very smart, she used a gilt chair.‡

The concert was described as 'brilliant' with 'the most distinguished audience London has had for many months' noting the very careful 'thought and study' devoted to programming. Clearly this success augured well for their return to the great metropolis. The importance of this concert was that their names again appeared in the Court Circular which guaranteed a host of further prestigious engagements in most of the fine town-houses in

---

* Robert Rhodes James (ed.), *'Chips': The Diaries of Sir Henry Channon* (London 1967), pp. 422–3.

† Nikolai Andreyevich Orloff (1892–1964). A fine Russian pianist who made only a few recordings that indicate a major player of Chopin.

‡ HH Princess Marie Louise, *My Memories of Six Reigns*, pp. 299–300.

Mayfair until at least Christmas. 'We are made now that we have appeared as favoured artists in the Court Circular!' Eddie wrote triumphantly in his journal.

In his customary flamboyant manner, Eddie followed up this promise of financial success by purchasing a fast four-seater Alvis TG 12/50 Sports Tourer motor car. Motor racing at Brooklands in the 1920s was glamorous and exciting. He took a particularly keen interest in the details of a 'celebrity death' in one of the greatest of sports cars. In September he had read that the 'free dancer' Isadora Duncan was strangled and dragged onto the cobbles by her red silk scarf which had become entangled in the rear wheel of an Amilcar during a drive in Nice.*

* * *

The winter of 1927–28 was particularly severe with one of the heaviest snowfalls of the century. Christmas Day saw blizzards in the Midlands and Wales, which then spread South. In Kent, there was two feet of snow and drifts of twenty feet were measured in the Chilterns and on Salisbury Plain. Eddie and George were snowed in at Horwood, effectively cocooned for the festive season.

A sudden thaw in January combined with heavy rain and freak tidal flows from storms caused the worst flood ever recorded in Central London. Fourteen people died, thousands were made homeless, Milbank needed to be reconstructed, Tube lines were inundated and priceless collections at the Tate Gallery were damaged. The *Guardian* of Saturday 7 January 1928 reported:

> The Thames overflowed at Westminster at 12.45 am this morning, and all trams and buses along the Embankment were interrupted. The flood water flowed into the terraces of the Houses of Parliament …
>
> At the Houses of Parliament the water 'cataracted' over the parapet into the open space at the foot of Big Ben.

The floods and their aftermath dominated drawing room

---

* A controversy continues to rage over whether the car was a Type 35 Bugatti or the more modest Amilcar CGSS. Most evidence points to the latter although the glorious myth embraces the former. Gertrude Stein commented rather uncharitably 'Affectations can be dangerous'.

conversation for many months, a welcome relief from endless talk of fashion and hats. George was prompted to comment to an Australian reporter: 'Tell Australians that I am longing to get back to the Australian sunshine!' Eddie touched upon a dilemma that faces Australian artists to this day: 'I'm drawn between two loves – the love of Australia and the love of London; but I feel the sunshine will win in the end!'

The Russian ballerina Anna Pavlova* was performing in London at this time. She told a reporter that the wild winter reminded her of her childhood in St Petersburg. The effect her dancing had on London aesthetes and balletomanes was galvanic. She had befriended Eddie and George during her successful tour of Australia in 1926 and liked the country a great deal. I found a mysterious note among Eddie's papers concerning an event which involved George and himself. One evening there was a sudden halt during a charity performance Pavlova was giving at the Coliseum. She was raising funds for starving Russian children and distressed Russian dancers. As the silence continued they realised Pavlova needed help and rushed to the stage from their box to fill the gap with some entertainment. He writes of the incident

> When we were playing in London, we received an autographed photograph from Pavlova, and a letter of thanks for rendering such a service for her Russian fund. One thing that still puzzles me is this, that I cannot understand why Chaliapine†, who was also occupying a box at the theatre, did not come forward and help Pavlova from the awkward position she was placed in. The

* Anna Pavlova (1881–1931) at the time was the most famous ballerina in the world. She trained in classical ballet at the St Petersburg Imperial Ballet School. Her origins are rather modest and obscure. Her mother was a washerwoman and her father may have been a serving soldier. Pavlova travelled incessantly around the world (some estimate 400,000 miles before the age of air travel) raising awareness of classical ballet everywhere. She lived at Ivy House in Hampstead, a picturesque suburb of London. Among the exotic animals in her menagerie she kept two white swans on a lake in the gardens of the house. It is believed the study of the movements of these birds inspired her legendary performances of Tchaikovsky's famous ballet Swan Lake. Pavlova died of pleurisy at The Hague on 22 January 1931. She had performed without respite until her death. Her final words were to ask for her Swan costume to be prepared.

† Fyodor Chaliapine (1873–1938) was one of the greatest Russian bass opera singers. He had an enormous international following due to his charismatic personality, musical interpretations and passionate, even brutally robust Russian performances. He toured Australia in 1926 and was lionised. One of the greatest artists of the twentieth century.

> audience was getting restless and it must not be forgotten that hundreds of people had paid a guinea for their seat.* Chaliapine professed friendship for Pavlova.
>
> Had Melba been in Chaliapine's place in his country, and a performance being given in aid of any Australian charity, there would have been a different tale to tell, for I could imagine Melba in her impulsive manner, rushing to the stage to help her countrymen.

* * *

Until the opening of the official London Season in April 1928 Eddie, George and Margaret spent some time settling in and exploring London. Eddie's innate sense of adventure sent him to less frequented galleries and pockets of arcane even dissolute interest. After piano recitals he was fond of walking off his nervous tension alone. Prone to 'nerves' he had a chemist in St James's make up a concoction which was intended to diminish stage fright. He remained prey to debilitating self-consciousness throughout his concert career, although this never seemed to be evident in his extraordinarily charming and energetic disposition on the concert platform.

Although not interested in playing jazz piano, his love of parties meant he could not resist dropping in for late-night cocktails at fashionable smoky haunts in the West End such as the Embassy Club in Bond Street or the Kit-Kat Club in the Haymarket. Being young and strikingly handsome, he was often terribly bored by the society of the ancient dowagers and duchesses who guaranteed his livelihood. Certainly he was never short of young female admirers as dancing partners, but unfortunately the 'young things' had no interest in recitals of serious classical music and soon drifted off. He occasionally drove the Alvis down to Maidenhead at speed for a riotous evening at Murray's, a 'rather spicy club' owned by the dubious Jack May. Cocaine was available there but Eddie's thin wallet could not cope with such expensive stimuli despite its attractions.

The temperament of an artist often contains irreconcilable elements which energise his art. Eddie was no exception to this in

* One guinea in 1927 is the equivalent of £55 in 2015.

his attraction to both the respectable life of the Old Guard lounging in their Mayfair salons and the 'low life' of Soho and bohemia. He became particularly fond of the coffee-stalls that were set up on street corners around Piccadilly Circus. On cold foggy evenings they provided hot coffee, tea, warm snacks and sizzling sausages. These places were often frequented by party-goers in need of fuel in the small hours as they drifted home the worse for wear – a man in silk topper and crumpled white tie, a girl in short dress with shingled hair smoking a cigarette, easing her feet from tight evening shoes, sundry late night workers and then Eddie.

The increasingly rare Hansom cabs he loved still plied the streets of London. Occasionally George and Margaret would leave him on his own in the fog and take a motor taxi home to Maida Vale. Eddie had a fertile romantic imagination and would dream of historical scenes where he would shine like a character in a Balzac novel after playing for the aristocracy in a sumptuous drawing room in Mayfair. The steaming horse clip-clopped along Park Lane, through the deserted streets of Marylebone, past the ghostly white Nash terraces fringing Regent's Park, an occasional window golden lit, home to Randolph Terrace.

* * *

The Antipodean trio launched themselves into the 1928 London Season with a vengeance. In May, despite the atrocious weather with hail as well as rain, Margaret insisted on them going to the Chelsea Flower Show. Eddie, who had a particular love of flowers (he sent them regularly to all his dowagers and duchesses), was overwhelmed by the displays. Also in May, but travelling on his own, he indulged his 'secret vice' and caught the newly electrified Southern Railway train from Waterloo to Brooklands to watch the Essex Motor Club Six-Hour Endurance Race which included factory teams from Alfa Romeo and Bentley. He found the cars becoming airborne over the rough concrete of the member's banking an awe-inspiring sight. The Bentley driven by Tim Birkin, one of the glamorous and daring 'Bentley Boys', covered the greatest distance (considered an important parameter in those days, given the general unreliability of the machines).

In June they played and sang for Lady Jellicoe at a party at their grand residence at 80, Portland Place. Florence Gwendoline Jellicoe (née Cayzer) was the wife of the Admiral of the Fleet John Rushworth Jellicoe, 1st Earl Jellicoe, who commanded the Grand Fleet at the Battle of Jutland in the Great War.* Later in the month the boys donned morning suits and Margaret a fetching cloche hat and a dress with a short hem for Day One of Royal Ascot when the legendary Brown Jack won the Ascot Stakes. One of the highest points of the Season and Ascot Week was an invitation to play 'An Hour of Music' at a garden party in the late afternoon of 14 June at No. 5 Carlton Gardens Pall Mall in the presence of HRH Princess Beatrice.†

The Princess had been the favourite daughter of Queen Victoria. After the death of Prince Albert, when Beatrice was only four, the Queen became claustrophobically possessive of her youngest daughter, even after she married the handsome and dashing Prince Henry of Battenberg.‡ Later she became the Queen's personal secretary and spent some thirty years editing Victoria's personal journals. Beatrice was an accomplished dancer, artist, photographer and actress. Passionate about music, she played the piano to an exceptional standard and was a perceptive and critical judge of pianists. She patronised many of Eddie's recitals.

The house in Carlton Gardens was 'lent' by Mrs Alfred C. Bossom who had only recently taken it over.§ Preceding the concert she gave a 'garden tea' at five o'clock for all ticket holders. However the

---

* Admiral of the Fleet John Rushworth Jellicoe, 1st Earl Jellicoe (1859–1935). His deployment of the fleet at Jutland remains controversial. Churchill described Jellicoe later as 'the only man on either side who could lose the war in an afternoon'.

† HRH Princess Beatrice of Battenberg (1857–1944) was the fifth daughter and youngest child of Queen Victoria and Prince Albert.

‡ Prince Henry of Battenberg (1858–96) yearned to escape the confinement and restrictions of the court for a life of military adventure. Much against the wishes of Queen Victoria, he campaigned in the Anglo–Ashanti War in West Africa and died of malaria in 1896 aboard the cruiser HMS *Blonde* stationed off the coast of Sierra Leone. Princess Beatrice was devastated by his death and as a widow once again became Queen Victoria's 'rock' and emotional support.

§ Yet another American hostess, Emily Bossom (née Bayne), was the daughter of the New York City banker Samuel Bayne. She married Alfred Bossom (1881–1965) in 1910. He was a highly successful English architect who made his fortune designing skyscrapers in Texas. Curiously he also invented a device to prevent people from suffocating if they accidentally got locked in a bank vault.

increasingly frail Princess Beatrice was ill and was unable to attend. This greatly disappointed the flock of elderly female aristocracy who were becoming Eddie and George's most loyal and enthusiastic patrons. The Princess herself was particularly downcast. As she was feeling much improved the following day, she summoned them to Kensington Palace to play a special impromptu concert.

Country house engagements seemed to flower profusely. Classical recitals in London concert halls were not generally well patronised at the time except for those by the decidedly famous, say the violinist of genius Fritz Kreisler. Conservative audiences preferred the 'old composers' Beethoven, Brahms or Schumann. This was evidenced by a cold reception given to Alfred Cortot in London performing modern compositions by Stravinsky and Ravel until enthusiasm erupted during the Chopin section of his programme. In early July Lady Pigott-Brown invited them to perform at Broome Hall in Surrey,* followed by a glorious 'Saturday-to-Monday' at Bawdsey Manor in Suffolk invited by the Hon. Lady Quilter.

Later that week they loaded up the Alvis with exotic provisions from Fortnum & Mason and drove to Henley for a rare brilliantly sunny day at the Royal Regatta. It was the first year of qualifying races. They had a picnic on the grass by the river. Houseboats were ablaze with scarlet geraniums and pink hydrangeas. On the lawns of the riverside clubs and houses girls in floral muslins reclined in deck chairs. 'The Trio' were guests of one of the members of the exclusive Leander Club situated on the right bank just below the Henley Bridge.† Eddie was tremendously amused by the pink hippo, the club's symbol.

This rowing acquaintance enabled them to gain access to the exclusive Stewards Enclosure with its Pimm's, panamas, boaters and school blazers, deckchairs and brightly coloured Japanese parasols almost hiding the spectator boats. Matters on the river were far less controlled than today and in his journal Eddie speaks of jostling,

---

* Lady Pigott-Browne (1886–1964, née Edith Ivy Piggott), eldest daughter and co-heir of Admiral William Harvey Pigott, married Captain Gordon Hargreaves Brown of the Coldstream Guards who was reported missing at Ypres October 1914. Late Victorian Broome Hall was once owned by the roguish actor Oliver Reed. The film director Ken Russell set many scenes from D.H. Lawrence's *Women in Love* at Broome Hall.

† Leander Club is said to have been founded in 1818 and is the third oldest and most prestigious rowing club in the world.

cheering and jovial high-jinks, lounging lethargically, sitting or even standing at climatic moments in comfortably appointed punts. These floated in packed clumps beside the course while the rowers raced by in close proximity to the excited waterborne spectators. Above the carnival atmosphere drifted colourful flights of balloons. It was one of the most successful meetings for years.

Towards the end of July Eddie was invited by the Lord Chamberlain to the Afternoon Party at Buckingham Palace and on this occasion 'caught the eye of the Queen' as she wandered among her more distinguished guests. She asked him how his musical career was progressing in London and tactfully encouraged him to 'continue practising'. Eddie never forgot this flattering recognition of his talent and developed an almost adolescent infatuation with her. Until Queen Mary died in 1953, on every birthday celebration in May, he would despatch to the palace by private courier at fabulous expense, a bouquet of wild Swiss narcissi picked on the slopes of the Alps. His papers contain numerous letters of thanks from her Private Secretary for the flowers he sent. 'Queen Mary loved music although she had little knowledge of its technical arts,' he reminisced later.

In September Eddie was invited by the Viscount and rather forbidding Viscountess Elibank to a country house party at Black Barony Castle in Peeblesshire to once again meet HH Princess Helena Victoria and give a piano recital.* This magnificent castle, also known as Darn Hall, is near the village of Eddleston, seventeen miles south of Edinburgh. The steam locomotive *Flying Scotsman* on which they travelled had begun non-stop services from London to Edinburgh on 1 May.† Eddie was excited about this trip as he

* Gideon Oliphant-Murray, 2nd Viscount Elibank (1877–1951) was a Scottish politician and member of the aristocracy. He had extensive experience of colonial administration including Papua New Guinea, the Transvaal and the Windward Islands.

† These were luxurious trains allowing one to travel in a style and comfort undreamt of today. The first-class compartment coach was sumptuous, as was the first-class restaurant, decorated in Louis XVI style with concealed lighting. All the food was freshly cooked on the train in a kitchen powered by electricity from accumulators. The carriage corridors had illuminated signs as in European Grand Hotel style indicating the Hairdressing Saloon, Ladies' Retiring Room and Cocktail Bar decorated in a ravishingly modern green and silver colour scheme. The revolutionary design of the tender (the section behind the locomotive which carried the coal) had a corridor, which connected it to the adjoining carriage. This enabled a fresh crew to take over without stopping the locomotive, on this route an L.N.E.R. Class A3 Pacific.

had by now developed a deep love of steam trains. At the time it was the longest uninterrupted train journey in the world, lasting a little over eight hours. He was collected at Edinburgh Station and swished off to Black Barony in the Elibank Daimler, his luggage following in another car.

Among the distinguished and aristocratic house guests were Viscount Younger of Leckie,* the somewhat reactionary and puritanical Home Secretary Sir William Joynson-Hicks popularly known as 'Jix',† the American property magnate known as the Duke of Del Monte, and Major-General and Mrs J.B. Seely.‡ Country establishments were not what they had been before the Great War but the atmosphere was far from stuffy. Guests still dressed for dinner and served themselves breakfast from the dining or breakfast room buffet. HH Princess Helena Victoria, although close to sixty, was a lively, ebullient and adventurous personality.

'Jix' was a deeply conservative personality, a Conservative party politician who stood out against the radical social changes that were taking place in the 1920s, particularly among the Bright Young Things. An almost forgotten figure, his period as an authoritarian Home Secretary was seldom without controversy, often of an amusing kind. However he dealt constructively with the profound implications of the General Strike and the imagined fears of Bolshevik conspiracies. He emerged as the *bête noire* of the intelligentsia and became the butt of many of Evelyn Waugh's satirical barbs.

'Jix' suppressed the courageous lesbian novel *The Well of Loneliness* by Radclyffe Hall. A Mr James Douglas wrote in the *Sunday Express* in outrage: 'I would rather give a healthy boy or girl a phial of prussic acid than this book.' He notoriously banned D.H. Lawrence's *Lady Chatterley's Lover*. A close friend, David Lowe the famous cartoonist, mercilessly lampooned him week in and week out and then sent him the original cartoons as Christmas

* George Younger, 1st Viscount Younger of Leckie (1851–1929) chairman of the great Scottish brewing business *Younger*.

† The formidable William Joynson-Hicks, 1st Viscount Brentford (1865–1932) was Home Secretary from 1924–29.

‡ Major-General J.B. Seely, 1st Baron Mottistone (1868–1947) was a Conservative, later Liberal MP and a member of a family of politicians, industrialists and significant land-owners.

presents, getting in exchange a box of cigars signed 'from your admiring victim'.

'Jix' was particularly taken with Eddie's rendering of the Amilcare Zanella arrangement of Liszt's *La Campanella* (The Little Bell). He loved the section of extended and rapidly accelerating trills at the centre of the piece. This was an 'Eddie showpiece' which he brought off in the spectacular manner of the great late nineteenth century virtuosi. At this period many pianists, including Eddie, possessed a unique and exquisite beauty of tone with absolute delicacy and evenness of touch which scarcely any pianist today achieves with the same consistency. Above all, they possessed great sensibility, poetry and charm. He named the section of extended trills in *La Campanella* 'The Jix Thrill' to the great amusement of the Home Secretary. Whenever Sir William subsequently attended one of Eddie's recitals he requested this piece to be on the programme.

While at Black Barony Castle an amusing incident occurred when 'Jix' asked Eddie to demonstrate how loudly a piano could be played. 'Although the house was massive I demonstrated it was not soundproof' Eddie recalled. HH Princess Helena Victoria left the Drawing Room in haste at this suggestion and said she would knock on the floor of her bedroom with her slipper when she felt the sound had become insupportable. Eddie set to work with a vengeance on the Liszt *Marche Hongroise* and not many minutes had elapsed before the princess hammered on the floor of her room. 'At breakfast she complimented me on the completeness of the disturbance.'

HH Princess Helena Victoria and her younger sister HH Princess Marie Louise had become enthusiastic patrons of Eddie and George. During his entire stay he gave a recital every evening at the Princess's request. On another occasion the house party were motoring to Edinburgh to pay a round of social visits. Princess Helena Victoria wanted to know who was going in the various cars and turned to Eddie. 'We cannot afford to let *you* get cold,' she said. 'You must come in the car with me.' He rode with her in the big Rolls-Royce with the foot-warmers.

Curious and eccentric happenings were the order of the day at Black Barony.* The Viscountess Elibank warned Eddie one evening

* In 1940, the castle by then a hotel, became the headquarters of the 10th Armoured Cav-

to beware of the spirits that haunted the castle in the dead of night. She suspected quite rightly he had an interest in the paranormal. She told him in sepulchral tones that in one of the rooms a figure regularly appeared as if sitting in a rocking chair staring at the fireplace. He fades slowly into the ether accompanied by the smell of cigar smoke and brandy. 'I tried and tried but saw nothing!' Eddie lamented the next morning at breakfast. 'I was hoping for at least a cognac and an Havana!'

* * *

Perhaps his most glamorous and spectacular concert audience of 1928 was in London. The audience were made up almost entirely of the severe 'old aristocracy' and his ever loyal Princesses. In early November they assembled to hear Eddie and George at Lady Stradbroke's elegant house at No. 26 Belgrave Square. There was little mention of the actual music in the press but a great deal as ever on the fashions. The formidable Lady Joynson-Hicks wearing red and gold brocade and a diamond tiara was present with her devoted husband 'Jix'. Mrs Wilfrid Ashley[*] wore 'a lovely *robe de style* of bright green tulle embroidered with gold' and carried 'the most enormous green ostrich feather fan.' Other interesting people at this concert were the composer of songs who loved George's voice, Mme Guy D'Hardelot, the famous Australian singer Ada Crossley[†] and the notorious Captain Archibald Maule Ramsay and his wife.[‡]

---

alry Brigade of the Polish Army, under General Stanisław Maczek (1892–1994) and subsequently used as the Polish military staff training college until the end of World War II.

* Her husband Wilfrid William Ashley, 1st Baron Mount Temple (1867–1939) was a Conservative politician and Minister of Transport 1924–29.

† Ada Crossley (1874–1929) was an Australian farmer's daughter born in Tarraville, Victoria. Rather like Eddie, she showed prodigious talent at country shows and studied first in Melbourne. She left Australia for Europe to further her studies and was outstandingly successful, having given a number of command performances before Queen Victoria.

‡ Captain Archibald Maule Ramsay (1894–1955) was a British Army officer who later took up politics and became a Scottish Unionist Member of Parliament. In the late 1930s he also became a rabid anti-Semite, holding the customary vitriolic and imaginative world conspiracy theories concerning the Jews. As the thirties evolved, he appeared to develop some sympathy with the growth of Nazism in Germany and Hitlerite policies. In 1940 he had dealings with a suspected spy at the United States Embassy, which led to his internment under Defence Regulation 18b.

Eddie played several of his own compositions at the special request of the two Princesses. Sadly none of these compositions survive. He considered them minor works for the piano, simply salon miniatures that he did not value unduly and played as encores. Reviews of the day reveal such unassuming titles such as *Élégie, Autumn Leaves* and *The Music Box.* The *Evening Standard* critic was much given to hyperbole in his review of the concert. The sentiments expressed belong to an age of sensibility, even enthusiastic innocence, which had been maintained in certain circles even after the wholesale slaughter of the Great War. This atmosphere would never be recaptured after the even deeper disillusioning horrors of World War II.

> The golden dome lamp's rays shone on gleaming brasses, quaint old tapestries, and bowls of autumn leaves, then lingered on the delicate, sensitive fingers of Mr Cahill seated at the Bechstein Concert Grand piano as he drew from the ivories all the secrets of interpretation. His technique is wonderful; but his power of interpreting either the old or the modern composer is glorious. Mr Brooke sang with ease and fluency through all his numbers – his voice has improved since I last heard it to a marked degree, always it has a sweet quality but now there is added power, and his enunciation is almost perfect. Of the two artists one can only say: What memories! What repertoire! What talents! What joy they give!

Chapter 8

Vienna and *Das Süsse Mädel*

The trio spent the Christmas of 1928 and the New Year of 1929 in Paris as a welcome break from dancing attendance on elderly princesses, dowagers and duchesses. The trio were much younger than their patrons, whose conversation was often suffocatingly dull. Eddie was not married and was a dashing, exuberant personality, a man of the theatre, who still responded to life with youthful energy and *panache.* He always appeared much younger than his years. Paris suited his temperament. There was however a far more serious reason behind the trip.

Eddie had developed a small but worrying nodule on the palm of his left hand, which he had ignored. In time his ring finger seemed to be losing flexibility and he had difficulty straitening it fully. He was alarmed that this condition might worsen and affect his playing. He had consulted a hand surgeon in Harley Street in London and was diagnosed with a mild form of Dupuytren's contracture.* This rare affliction originated in Northern Europe with the Vikings and was genetically inherited among people of Northern European stock. He had been recommended to a surgeon in Paris, who devised a minor corrective operation and exercises. Although he was not suffering from a severe form of the disease, Eddie remained apprehensive. The operation was a success with his hand immobilised for only a couple of weeks.

---

* On 5 December 1831, Baron Guillaume Dupuytren (1777–1835) delivered a lecture on permanent retractions of the flexed fingers, which was published under the title *Leçon sur la rétraction permanente des doigts.* He was acknowledged as the greatest French surgeon of the 19th century, developed surgery to correct this complaint as well as many others and was created a baron by Louis XVIII. Contemporaries thought him 'the greatest of surgeons, the meanest of men'. Anaesthesia was two bottles of wine drunk by the patient before the first incision. He held this post until his death and is mentioned in the fiction of Balzac and Flaubert.

Always searching for professional improvement through further high level lessons which they found difficult to arrange in Paris, Eddie and George decided to travel to Vienna. This would give him time to recuperate. Margaret, being a nurse but from distant Melbourne, hoped to spend some time exploring the advanced medical and nursing aspects of Austrian hospitals.

Eddie wrote of their arrival in economically fraught Vienna

> How can I describe our eventful journey by train to Vienna from Paris? We left Paris on a beautiful day in January 1929, and when we arrived at Munich we encountered a terrific snow storm, perhaps one of the worst for a hundred years. On the following morning we arrived at Vienna at seven o'clock, only to find the city buried in snow, and within a week we were practically isolated. Trains were snow-bound, no coal coming in, and then the government issued very drastic orders as to the amount of coal and water that could be used. Hot baths were quite out of the question, in fact people were threatened with imprisonment if this rule was not adhered to. Only the chestnut vendors roasted their delicious fare over glowing coals.
>
> We were fortunate for we were living in the Dianabad Hotel which is one of the most famous in the world for its baths. Here they had enough coal for at least a year, so we got at least central heating. The Dianabad Hotel has the largest and best baths in the world. It is also called a *Kuranstalt* for treating the cripples and the sick. It has many apartments for the cures with Mud baths, Hot Air treatments, Radium Stations, Inhalation Rooms, Electrographical Examinations of the Heart, Massage and Cosmetics. So one need never go unwashed in Vienna.
>
> [...] I must confess that my first impression of Vienna was not very favourable, as one could not get any idea of what the wonderful buildings or gardens were like. I had quite made up my mind to return to Paris at once, but Brooke was determined to stay, and I can assure you that after a few weeks I felt that I could never leave Vienna. How can I attempt to describe this wonderful and beautiful city? [...] Vienna is a city of romance, and one breathes in music from its very air. Lilac time makes one think they are living in fairyland. Vienna for amusements easily rivals Paris. Opera and concerts surpass Paris. It is regarded as the musical centre of the world [...] the musical season to the visitor appears to be of much more importance to discuss than that of politics. The Staatsoper is really a national institution. The performers are paid by the state and after a number of years are

pensioned for life. The audiences are most discriminating.

At the time Eddie and George visited Austria, the country was still reeling from financial crisis to financial crisis after the dismemberment of the Habsburg Empire following the Paris Conference ten years earlier. The Austrian Jewish writer Stefan Zweig referred to a country which 'showed faintly on the map of Europe as the vague, grey and inert shadow of the former Imperial monarchy […] a mutilated trunk that bled from every vein.'* Crippling reparations and war damage only extended any period of recovery and fuelled an enduring positive feeling towards an *Anschluss* with Germany. Zweig watched the departure of the Emperor Karl and his wife the Empress Zita in 1919 from the train station of Feldkirch on the Austrian border

> The last Emperor of Austria, hero of the Hapsburg dynasty which had ruled for seven hundred years, was forsaking his realm! […] I had seen the old emperor [...] on the staircase at *Schönbrunn*, surrounded by his family and brilliantly uniformed generals, receiving the homage of eighty thousand Viennese schoolchildren, massed on the broad green plain, singing, their thin voices united in touching chorus, Haydn's *Gott erhalte.* I had seen him at the Court Ball, at the *Théâtre Paré* performances in glittering array, and again at Ischl, riding to the hunt in a green Tyrolean hat; I had seen him marching devoutly, with bowed head, in the Corpus Christi procession to the cathedral of St Stephen […]
>
> 'The Kaiser!' From earliest childhood we had learned to pronounce these words reverently for they embodied all of power and wealth and symbolised Austria's imperishability. And now I saw his heir, the last emperor, banished from the country. From century to century the glorious line of Hapsburg had passed the Imperial globe and crown from hand to hand, and this was the minute of its end […] The officials followed it [the departing train] with a respectful gaze, after which, with that air of embarrassment which is observable at funerals, they returned to their respective stations.'†

Soon after their arrival Eddie and George were enthusiastically welcomed into Viennese Society by the *Gräfin* (Countess)

* Stefan Zweig, *The World of Yesterday: An Autobiography by Stefan Zweig* (New York 1943), p. 281.
† Ibid., pp. 283–4.

Coudenhove at a reception at her famous and magnificently decorated salon in her townhouse at 3 Bäckerstrasse in the First District near St Stephen's Cathedral. Here, Franz I, Prince of Lichtenstein, Princess Oettingen, Princess Sophie von Metternich and a multitude of military officers in full dress uniform danced with bejewelled partners to Viennese waltzes under shimmering chandeliers. Champagne seemed to flow endlessly. The famous Moravian soprano Maria Jeritza, who was also a guest on this occasion, dragooned Eddie into accompanying her in arias from Mozart operas. The two Australians could not but be dazzled by this final flourish of the European aristocracy.

Like so many musicians before them, they soon began their pilgrimage to the residences of the great composers who lived or were born in Vienna. Their visit to the Schubert house was a particular joy. They befriended the vicar of the church where Schubert had played and he arranged many remarkable meetings for them with outstanding musicians. Most unusually, they were entertained in a private recital by the *Wiener Männergesang-Verein* (Vienna Male Choral Society), an institution in the capital that had been established for some ninety years. 'To me this night was one of the greatest of my many wonderful nights on the other side of the world,' Eddie later wrote. They were taken to their museum and club where they saw a great many letters and musical manuscripts by Beethoven, Schubert, Brahms and other composers. He read a letter written by the young Brahms in which he described 'trying out' one of his symphonies in the suburbs as he did not feel it was good enough to perform in Vienna itself. A particular thrill was seeing the original manuscript of the Blue Danube Waltz of Johann Strauss II.

An excellent dinner and toasts followed their tour of the museum. The President disconcerted Eddie by speaking of the Great War and what a bitter fight it had been against the Australian troops. This was the first night they had entertained any Australians since that terrible conflict. 'I wondered what he was going to say next!' Eddie wrote. The President however spoke not of hatred but of co-operation, drawing attention to the glowing reception of the Deutsche Staatsoper playing at that time in Covent Garden. He spoke of how royalty had honoured the company on each visit to

London and how it was now their turn to welcome their talented Australian visitors. The lyric soprano Dame Nellie Melba and the magnificent Wagnerian dramatic soprano Florence Austral* had done much to persuade Europe of the glories of the Australian voice. Eddie was forced to make a speech in German (he had learned a little of the language from his mother). The members of the society cheered lustily and rapped on the tables. This was followed by a concert. 'The night will live in my memory forever,' he wrote.

* * *

In February 1929 Eddie made the acquaintance of Sabine Adler, a beautiful blonde Viennese *soubrette* with ice-blue eyes, who was a concert violinist in an orchestra in the provincial monastery town of Melk. He had been inexpressibly moved by the poetic lyricism of her performance in the Brahms violin concerto. Her father was a physician and her mother a pianist and they lived in a beautiful villa in the Wachau Valley near the small picturesque town of Dürnstein with its little ruined castle. From the terrace of the house high above a vineyard cascading down a gentle slope to the Danube, one had a distant view of the burnished cupolas of the great baroque monastery.

Elegantly and expensively dressed in the Italian style, Sabine possessed all the playful, apparently innocent, teasing sexual charm and grace one imagines of the 'typical Viennese'. Despite her serious, intellectual interest in music, she resembled in some ways the type of girl the author Arthur Schnitzler referred to as *das süsse Mädel* or what one might translate as 'the sweet girl'. She was almost fifteen years younger than Eddie so being in her company

---

* Florence Austral (née Florence Mary Wilson, 1892–1968) changed her name as a patriotic gesture. She made her Covent Garden debut on 16 May 1922 as Brünnhilde in Wagner's *Die Walküre*. In 1923, Austral appeared with Dame Nellie Melba who called her 'one of the wonder voices of the world', praising the purity of her tone and the gleaming power of her high notes. She became principal singer with the Berlin State Opera in 1930, but shortly afterwards showed the first symptoms of multiple sclerosis, which appeared while she was actually on stage. The inexorable march of this illness forced her retirement in 1940. Joan Sutherland was inspired by her to become an opera singer. She is unaccountably another forgotten Australian artist of the highest calibre. The sole CD of her astounding flexibility and range of voice in Wagner, Weber, Rossini and Mozart is on *Austro Mechana Historic Recordings* No: 89547.

he likened to a glass of the finest champagne as they dizzily waltzed in the Hofburg Imperial Palace on Carnival Monday at one of Vienna's many masked balls. Throughout his life Eddie appeared younger than his years. She begged him to study the great Schumann piece *Faschingsschwank aus Wien* (Carnival Jests in Vienna), which he played with the greatest élan. Titles in Austria were a social necessity and Sabine soon saw to it that Eddie was referred to as 'Herr Professor Cahill'. Eddie, Sabine, George and Margaret now assembled in Vienna as 'a quartet' rather than 'a trio' and wandered the city together.

So many of the greatest composers the world has seen were born or spent time in Vienna, the lilac city, in spring perfumed by white and mauve blossom. The waltzes of the Strauss family seemed to everywhere. Under the lilac he was captivated by the popular evening dinner of roast pork, new wine and folk music in the *Heurigen.* As summer approached, many charming Mozart concerts and performances of his smaller operas took place in the open air of the Imperial Palace gardens. George felt if this idea were to be adopted in Australia, the venues might turn out to be even more beautiful than Vienna. 'Wishful thinking!' Eddie remarked.

At night Eddie took long romantic walks with Sabine in the Prater. They passionately embraced in a deserted cabin of the *Wiener Riesenrad* (Ferris wheel) as it slowly revolved high above the city. During languid summer picnics they lay in the sun-dappled Vienna Woods, drank fine wine and feasted on excellent bread, cheese, sausage, cake and ripe apricots from the Wachau. A visit to the village of Heiligenstadt near Vienna caused them to reflect on the testament Beethoven wrote there in the summer of 1802 while attempting to come to terms with the horrors of his encroaching deafness. In 1808 in these peaceful, occasionally bucolic surroundings, he was inspired to write Eddie's favourite symphonic work, the *Pastoral* Symphony and the *Ghost* Trio.

> If I approach near to people a hot terror seizes upon me, and I fear being exposed to the danger that my condition might be noticed. [...] But what a humiliation for me when someone standing next to me heard a flute in the distance and I heard nothing, or someone standing next to me heard a shepherd singing and again I

heard nothing. Such incidents drove me almost to despair.*

Numerous cosy cafés such as the *Schubert,* a favourite with musicians, warmed them with the unique Viennese coffee heavy with whipped cream accompanied by a delicious *torte,* particularly at the then glamorous Hotel Sacher. The famous confectioner Demel tempted them with miniature chocolate cakes in gold wrappers, strawberry ices in individual silver bowls, entire trays of cream and spun sugar, baroque sandwiches intricately decorated with salmon paste or *foie gras.* A customer could sit all day in a Viennese coffeehouse over a single cup of coffee or hot chocolate and not be disturbed by an impatient waiter, discuss philosophy at leisure with friends, play chess, write articles, keep up to date on the latest publications and world political events in the magazines and newspapers in many languages, even arrange to receive mail.

Their 'intellectual emotions' as opposed to their more physical desires were satisfied in the hours spent wandering the endless galleries of the Kunsthistorische Museum, marvelling at the paintings. In addition to music, Eddie had wide interests in literature, painting and architecture. He believed that a pianist needed a broad knowledge of the cultural context in which works were created in order to perform them with appropriate style and true conviction.

By day Sabine introduced him to the seductive ultra-sophisticated eroticism of Gustav Klimt's 'Golden Phase' of the *Wiener Sezessionsstil* movement and the frank sexual fierceness pent up in Egon Schiele's passionately tortured figures. At night she revealed a rather low side of modernist Vienna he had never dreamed existed where any sexual fantasy or theatrical wish could be satisfied. The fashionable Viennese theatre, operetta, performing arts and popular press of the time moulded people's exploratory ideas concerning sex, as did the nineteenth century melodramas and silent film. There was a surprisingly straightforward attitude in Vienna between the wars to experiencing pleasure with one's body.

> Whatever her actual presence in Vienna, the New Woman, with her androgynous style, single status, discretionary income, and liberated sexuality was thought to be on the rise [...] Vienna en-

---

* Beethoven, *Heiligenstadt Testament*, 1802, trans. John V. Gilbert.

joyed a leading position within the world of medical sexology.[*] He briefly noted that Vienna was the city where his cultural education 'became airborne'.

This introduction to the world of ultra-sophisticated post-war Viennese decadence was rather a cultural shock for Eddie. After all he was still an unsophisticated Australian country boy at heart. Sabine quickly set about broadening his character. In an access of nostalgia they conjured up the *fin de siècle* Vienna so eloquently expressed in the piano transcriptions of the Strauss waltzes he was studying. His understanding of the waltz was strengthened in performances by the incomparable Erich Kleiber and Clemens Krauss[†] who conducted the Vienna Philharmonic in rhythmically idiomatic renditions of waltzes by Johann Strauss II and Joseph Lanner. They saw the finest performances of *Die Fledermaus* ever staged and wandered streets that even Mozart would have recognized. The architecture of Vienna seemed miraculously suspended in time. Eddie was oddly gratified that he had heard not one note of jazz while in Vienna, yet he was known to entertainingly improvise on popular tunes when 'under the influence'.[‡]

In the *Musikverein* they heard the great violinist Fritz Kreisler, the Polish pianist and statesman Ignacy Jan Paderewski and many of the finest instrumentalists of the day. The spellbinding tone and refined touch of Paderewski's playing in the 1920s captivated Eddie. He greatly admired the Pole's control of the melodic line as if it was being sung. Eddie had a passion for opera as did Chopin

* Britta McEwen, *Sexual Knowledge: Feeling, Fact, and Social Reform in Vienna, 1900–1934* (New York 2012), p. 93.

† Erich Kleiber (1890–1956) was an Austrian conductor, father of the great conductor Carlos Kleiber and respected for his interpretations of the 'standard repertoire' but also championed new works. Disgusted by Fascism in 1939 he moved to Buenos Aires and the Teatro Colón. He never held a permanent post in Europe again. Clemens Krauss (1893–1954) was also an eminent Austrian conductor and opera impresario closely associated with the music of Richard Strauss. He was born into a wealthy banking family and was the first cousin of the vivacious Baroness Mary Vetsera who died in a possible mutual suicide pact with Crown Prince Rudolf at Mayerling. Krauss's relationship with the Nazis remains questionable as he took over many conducting positions that former incumbents such as Wilhelm Furtwängler had abandoned in face of this threat. He was 'rehabilitated' after it was discovered he had saved many Jews from certain death in Vienna during World War II.

‡ Naturally Vienna did not escape the jazz craze that had swept the world at that time but it was not yet common there.

himself when he visited Vienna in 1829. In his teaching Chopin recommended a study of the art of the finest Italian *bel canto* song to develop a beautiful *legato cantabile* at the keyboard. Many in Paris considered the Polish composer *'le Bellini du piano'*. Eddie understood this composer's directive better than many pianists having adored Melba's voice and accompanied George for so many years.

At the conclusion of various Viennese concerts Eddie was amazed to see people rush from their seats in the stalls to the front of the stage to applaud and cheer the artist. This inconvenienced people sitting in the front row, but they seemed to enjoy the display of enthusiasm. At first Eddie thought the stampede meant the concert hall was on fire. One indication of the ostentatious musical culture of Vienna was indicated by members of the audience carefully following the music with the score which could be bought at the door together with the programme.

One evening they heard Richard Strauss conduct the Vienna Opera Orchestra in a production of *Der Rosenkavalier* and on another occasion a voluptuous staging of *Salome* at the imposing Wiener Staatsoper. Over-eager old men, packed as tightly as sardines in the *Stehplatz* (standing room) listened and watched the erotic drama intently. Eddie and George were also privileged to see a new Richard Strauss opera, the magnificent and lavish production of *Die ägyptische Helena* (The Egyptian Helen), again conducted by the composer with Maria Jeritza in the title role he had created for her.* Eddie renewed his acquaintance backstage and she embraced him effusively, saying she would never forget his tasteful accompaniment to her Mozart arias.

George commented later in a press interview

> She was of very fine presence, in magnificent voice and moved regally in the Trojan scenes [...] The Vienna Opera is the finest combination of its sort in the world but it has among its personnel only five great artists: the rest are mediocre.

A personal romantic and musical frontier seemed to be crossed on the night of 6 November 1929 when Sabine and Eddie heard

* The soprano Maria Jeritza (1887–1982) was born Marie Jedličková in Brno, Moravia (now part of the Czech Republic) and was long associated with the Vienna State Opera (1912–35). Her sensational rise to fame and spectacular beauty and personality earned her the nickname 'The Moravian Thunderbolt'.

Wilhelm Furtwängler conduct *Tristan und Isolde* at the Vienna Staatsoper.* The irresistible harmonies of Wagner's sensual music brought their hearts together. The serious cultural atmosphere, gaiety, general *Gemütlichkeit* or charming conviviality of life in the capital meant they fell deeply in love with the city and each other. *Wien,Wien nur du allein!* ('Vienna, Vienna, you alone forever.')

* * *

More seriously, Eddie had begun lessons with Professor Leonie Gombrich (née Hoch or Frau Gombrich as she was known in Vienna), the mother of the great art historian Sir Ernst Gombrich.† She was both an inspiring teacher and a person of the widest culture. Reduced to straightened circumstances during the Great War, she had a large number of applications from Americans prepared to pay high prices for her lessons. It was an honour in itself to be accepted by her as a pupil. As well as being endowed with incomparable technical power and interpretative musical insight, Frau Gombrich possessed the intellectual aura of Vienna in the first decades of the twentieth century, a city that inhabited the pinnacle of European culture. Most of the outstanding artists, writers and musicians in Vienna were Jewish or of Jewish extraction.

Leonie Gombrich had studied with the composer Anton Bruckner as well as being a pupil and later an assistant to the Pole Theodor Leschetizky, arguably the greatest piano pedagogue of the age. He in turn had been a pupil of Beethoven's pupil Carl Czerny and had been the teacher of Artur Schnabel, Ignacy Jan Paderewski, Alexander Brailowsky, Benno Moiseiwitsch, Katharine Goodson, Elly Ney, Ossip Gabrilowitsch, Mark Hambourg, Isabelle Vengerova and other great representatives of the late-nineteenth-century pianistic tradition. She had played with Schoenberg, heard

* Sam H. Shirakawa, *The Devil's Music Master: The Controversial Life and Career of Wilhelm Furtwängler* (Oxford 1992), p. 104 Gunnar Graarud as Tristan, Emil Schipper as Kurwenal, Hélène Wildbrünn as Isolde and Rosette Anday as Brangäne.

† Leonie Gombrich (1873–1968). Elizabeth Powell, the eminent teacher, pianist and pupil of Leonie Gombrich at Oxford assisted my research, writing of Leonie: 'She gave of herself tirelessly with patience, humour, love and generosity as well as her limitless knowledge.' She taught such outstanding pianists as Rudolf Serkin, Martin Isepp and Elizabeth Powell – and Edward Cahill.

Johann Strauss conduct and turned the pages for Brahms. Frequent visitors to the Gombrich home in Vienna included Mahler, Webern, Berg, Adolf Busch, Sigmund Freud and Rudolf Serkin. She was a born teacher, following Leschetizky's principle of framing the individuality of each pupil within a full understanding of the work and absolute soundness of technique. She demonstrated an infinite number of possible dynamics and articulations in the production of a single note on the piano. She often reminded Eddie of Chopin's remark concerning the use of the pedal 'The correct employment of it remains a study for life.'

Eddie was a mature man of forty-four when Leonie Gombrich accepted him for lessons. She was impressed by his technical mastery of the piano and observed that his rather small hands did not hinder him greatly. Gombrich was particularly struck by his breadth of life experience, worldliness, elegant and distinguished appearance, history of royal command performances and the aristocratic milieu in which he was musically active in London and Paris. That she accepted him as a pupil at all with such a 'secular' rather than academic musical background is a testament to his outstanding natural musical gifts and possibly his Irish-Australian charm.

The concept of teaching by the so-called 'Leschetizky Method', a fashionable but misguided portmanteau idea grafted onto the pedagogue by the *cognoscenti*, was not approved of by Frau Gombrich although she had clearly been deeply influenced by her mentor. Following the ideas of 'The Master' she was against standardised interpretations and believed in developing a rich and beautiful *cantabile* tone, seamless legato and the cultivation of a refined touch through relaxation (which she likened to taking a handkerchief off the keys). 'Your soul is expressed in your touch.' She emphasised the employment of a light wrist that allowed enormously varied degrees of staccato execution. Leschetizky's own advice for playing chords was to 'aim every finger' accurately and perpendicularly over the notes before playing them so as to avoid even a slight blurring of the sound. Frau Gombrich told Eddie his favourite question after a pupil had played technically brilliantly but no more than that was 'But where is the *music*?'

Frau Gombrich combined naturalness, simplicity and warmth

and had a great love of Mozart's piano sonatas and concerti, unusual for the time. Eddie was much admired for his Mozart interpretations and the delicate, incandescent tone he brought to this composer. She also concentrated on Chopin, as she was deeply impressed by Eddie's instinctive understanding of what the composer's best pupil Princess Marcelina Czartoryska described as *le climat de Chopin.* She told him that he and the great Russian eccentric Vladimir de Pachmann were among the finest Chopin interpreters she had ever heard. She also considered his interpretation of Beethoven's *Moonlight* Sonata one the finest she had encountered. In addition to serious works, he learnt many of the charming virtuoso arrangements of Viennese waltzes by the Austrian pianist and composer Alfred Grünfeld.* George furthered his studies in *Lieder* interpretation at this time with 'a notable Austrian teacher'.†

In 1930 Vladimir Horowitz commented to the Austrian press '... Vienna, the city said to be the most difficult for a pianist to conquer.'‡ The notoriously severe Viennese critics praised in effusive terms both Eddie and George for the few recitals they gave in the city.

> Young priests from the Temple of the Muses, who have been projected onto the earth to bring comfort unto the hearts of tens of thousands.

Of Eddie, who was acclaimed as playing Strauss waltz transcriptions like an authentic Viennese

> His music brings with it a message of hope and joy that will tend to develop expanding ideas in those privileged to hear it. One leaves the presence of this artist and the music hall in which he plays, but one never entirely leaves the presence of his haunting music, for its essence seems to cling permanently for increased happiness and optimism. If I wanted to do a good turn for anybody I would recommend them to listen to Edward Cahill's

---

* Alfred Grünfeld (1852–1924) was born in Prague and settled in Vienna in 1873. He was appointed pianist to the German Emperor Wilhelm I and from 1897 was a Professor at the Vienna Conservatoire. He was the first renowned pianist to make recordings. His arrangements are today normally tossed off as purely virtuoso display pieces but his own recordings exude an irresistible Viennese charm and refinement. Eddie played in particular the Grünfeld arrangement of the Strauss Soirée de Vienne Op. 56, based on a waltz from *Die Fledermaus* and the Diner-Waltz from the opera *Der Lebermann* (The Man About Town).

† I have unfortunately been unable to discover his name despite intensive research.

‡ Glenn Plaskin, *Horowitz: A Biography* (London 1983), p. 136.

music making, and that as often as possible.

George was deemed by the Viennese press to be 'the greatest singer of German *Lieder* for the 1929 season. The greatest *Lieder* singer in three decades.' This was indeed a magnificent tribute to a singer from Austria, a country abounding in some of the greatest *Lieder* singers.*

Eddie had played many types of piano while on this tour of Europe and became enamoured of what was to become his favourite instrument, the Grotrian-Steinweg, no longer famous on concert stages today. At some time in 1929 he travelled from Vienna to the factory in Braunschweig in Germany and ordered a concert instrument to be made and shipped to Australia for his next concert tour in 1930. This connoisseur's instrument was also the favourite of Clara Schumann, Walter Gieseking and Wilhelm Kempff. Eddie wrote of it later: 'I think it is a wonderful instrument for achieving fine, light singing tones. It is powerful in the bass but lends itself to a haunting, poetical even ethereal delicacy. It suits my light touch.'

* * *

On the return of 'the quartet' to London, Eddie and George gave a number of notable concerts. He described the home of Lord Howard de Walden in Belgrave Square as 'a house crammed from top storey to basement with artistic treasures where the best musicians perform.' They appeared with the largely forgotten but distinguished English stage and screen actor and author George Arliss. This was a benefit concert for the 'distressed actors of London', the music room of the house 'lent' by Lord Howard de Walden. Arliss loved the Roger Quilter songs and was enchanted by the transcriptions of Viennese waltzes that Eddie had mastered and were now included in his repertoire. Eddie had a particular respect for this actor as he had successfully made the transition from the silent cinema to the 'talkies' at the rather advanced age of 61. He played many great historical figures such as Voltaire, Cardinal Richelieu and Wellington. 'We never met a finer nor more intellectual man than Arliss,' Eddie observed.

---

* Vienna reviews are taken from unattributed, undated press cuttings in Edward Cahill's scrap book.

Eddie's final solo recital of note before returning to Australia for the 1930 concert season was in late November again at the palatial home of Sir Archibald and Lady Weigall at 39 Hill Street, Mayfair. George and Margaret had been forced to return to Australia a couple of weeks earlier as George had received the news his mother was seriously ill. Before this recital a farewell luncheon was given in Eddie's honour at Rutland Gate by Mrs F.A. König, whose husband was later to play such a large part in his career. All the Princesses had assembled for this spectacular farewell recital: HH Princess Marie Louise, HH Princess Helena Victoria and HRH Princess Beatrice.

There appeared at this concert a new and fascinating addition to the bevy of acolytes. An alluring woman, Princess Mechtilde Lichnowsky was a writer, painter, composer and lover of the arts from Lower Bavaria.* She was the great-granddaughter of the Habsburg Empress Maria Theresa and in 1904 had married Karl Max, Prince Lichnowsky, who was descended from the German family who had been Mozart and Beethoven's most fervent patrons until the inevitable rifts between artist and patron tore them apart. Her husband Prince Karl Max Lichnowsky had been German Ambassador to the Court of St James at the outbreak of the Great War and was the only German diplomat to strenuously object to the German support of an Austro-Serbian confrontation. His final wire on 29 July to the German Foreign Office stated simply: 'If war breaks out it will be the greatest catastrophe the world has ever seen.' He was ignored at the moment of truth but greatly honoured on his departure from Britain.

In a long, somewhat bizarre letter to Eddie dated 28 November 1929 following this farewell recital, Mechtilde wrote:

> I want to tell you that you have given me a great pleasure yes-

* Mechtilde Lichnowsky (1879–1958) was a close friend of many in the German literary and artistic establishment. Among her close friends were Rainer Maria Rilke, Hugo von Hofmannsthal, Theodor W. Adorno and Oscar Kokoschka. In particular she was a familiar of the famous, even notorious, Viennese writer Karl Kraus with whom she had a long correspondence. She had no sympathy with Hitler and the Nazis, considered them barbarians and in 1939 was placed under house arrest. Her books were burned as she was considered a traitor and forced to report to the Gestapo regularly. After the war she was expelled from Czechoslovakia by the Czech Government and all her properties were confiscated. With tragic irony she and her family were considered Nazi collaborators. Her 18 books are unjustly neglected today.

terday (and I am not easily won!). It was real Music. Take for instance the Schumann, which is known like the Pater Noster: Now you can take the risk of playing it because you can make it sing; others very often let it go like a racing horse. I will tell you one thing which perhaps has not occurred to you:

The musician's soul, as we said before you went, is a very particular kind of soul. You agreed, because you know. Now comes my point: The musician, as I see him must have a sense a keen and very special sense of humour. I have written the little book I'm going to send you, to show what a musician's soul is, should he ever, as my poor hero, be imprisoned within the narrow frame of a tuner. He has a brother who is an opera singer. The World of course thinks he is the musician.

I hope you will have pleasure in reading it, and like the instance of the tuner's dream of the Moonshine [*sic*] Sonata (a walk through endless little rooms, in which tiny chessboards are standing on three legs & with his finger he presses down one corner & the little chessboard moves back to its place – you can see the thing done [small drawing of three-legged 'chessboard' with hand and finger emerging from a sleeve about to press down on it] & in the dream the sounds came [Underlining in the original. Treble Clef drawn on a stave with correct key signature and three opening notes of the *Moonlight* Sonata].

Good luck to you. You can do anything!

[She then mysteriously includes the address of her bank in Berlin as her only correspondence address and the words 'written in a hurry!']

A forgotten example of colonial exotica and a fervent new admirer of music was also present at this recital, the Princess Pauline Melikoff known colloquially as 'the Tassie Princess'. Her colonial story is almost as extraordinary as Eddie's. Born Pauline Curran in Tasmania in 1893 for a time she lived at Eaglehawk Neck, an historically notorious geographical feature of the Van Diemen's Land convict era, once guarded by savage tethered dogs. In May 1924 Pauline was travelling with her mother, preparing to be presented at Court. During this 'Grand Tour' of Europe she met Prince Maximilian Melikoff, the second son of Prince Peter Melikoff and Princess Melikoff (née Baroness D'Osten-Sacken). The lovers became engaged a mere three months after they met, he while working as a chauffeur. They married in Hobart in 1926.*

Two days after this glittering concert, Eddie parked the Alvis in the stables in the safekeeping of Mrs Denny at Harwood. Sabine with his encouragement had decided to return to Austria and take up further advanced studies of the violin in Vienna while he was away. He kissed her perhaps more romantically, certainly more passionately, than he had kissed any woman before and promised he would be back the following year. For perhaps the first time in his life he felt painfully and romantically torn from a close emotional attachment. All too soon Eddie embarked on the P & O liner SS *Chitral* at Southampton bound for Fremantle. They had all planned to return to England in late 1930 for another season after an Australian series of concert engagements.

* Prince Melikoff, who was born in Russia in 1884, had served with distinction with the 13th Hussars Russian Imperial Calvary from 1914 to 1917. A White Russian, he fought against the Bolsheviks from 1918 to 1921 finally to leave the military and join his émigré parents in Nice. Almost destitute after having lost their Russian estates, Maximilian spent the next three years finding work in Europe. Prince Melikoff died in 1950 and the Princess in 1988. Her vast estate was left to benefit Greenpeace, the Tasmanian Government wildlife protection services and Homes for the Aged (Department of Premier and Cabinet, Tasmania).

Main Street in Beenleigh, Queensland, c.1893
– *Stark. W., John Oxley Library, State Library of Queensland*

Cahill's Beenleigh Hotel following extensive remodelling by Edward Cahill Snr. in 1910. The hotel was demolished in 1977 despite a *National Trust of Queensland* Report recommending its preservation. – *Logan City Libraries*

All images are from the Author's Private Collection unless otherwise stated.

Above: The colonial Cahill family of Beenleigh.
Top L-R: James, Elizabeth, Mary, Caroline, Edward
Front L-R: William, Edward Senior, Margaret, Mary Cahill (née Dauth), Lillian

Left: Edward Cahill, aged 35. India and Southeast Asia Tour (1919–1920)
– *State Library of Queensland*

Opposite Right: A letter from the Secretary to the Viscountess Harcourt inviting Edward Cahill Esq. to play for Queen Mary, 1924

The Duke and Duchess of Windsor

request the pleasure of

Mr. Cahill's

company *at dinner*

on *Tuesday - 22nd January*

at *8:30* o'clock

TELEPHONE: MAYFAIR 5702.
TELEGRAMS: HARCOURT, WESDO, LONDON.

69, BROOK STREET,
W.1.

Private. June 7. 1924.

Dear Sir,

The Queen is dining with Viscountess Harcourt on July 1st & has informed her through her Private Secretary that she would like to hear you play. Although Lady Harcourt's programme is already arranged she would be only too pleased

Above: Dinner invitation from the Duke & Duchess of Windsor, 24 Boulevard Suchet, Paris 1946

Above Left: George Brooke and Eddie dressed for London at the time of the Hill Street concert, 1927

Above Right: Edward Cahill during the Vienna sojourn in 1929 when he took lessons from Leonie Gombrich, former pupil of the Polish pedagogue Theodor Leschetizky
– *State Library of Queensland*

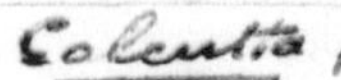

Edward Cahill at the Piano.

Above Left: Edward Cahill in a reflective mood during First British Tour (1923–26)
– *State Library of Queensland*

Above Right: Cartoon in a Calcutta newspaper during the India and Southeast Asia Tour (1919–1920)

Left: The Australian tenor George Brooke (1886–1930) during the period with Edward Branscombe's 'Dandies'. He was Edward Cahill's musical partner for sixteen years (1914–1930)

Above: At 'Stranraer' Warrington Crescent, London 7 July 1937. Recital on a Pleyel *'Grand Modèle de Concert'* during the modern revival of the harpsichord. *Seated direct left:* Sir Leslie Orme Wilson, Governor of Queensland. *Standing:* Mr L.H. Pike, Agent-General of Queensland. – *State Library of Queensland*

Right: Edward Cahill with his most loyal and fervent patron, Helen Sieger. Cape Town, South Africa, 1958

Above Left: Eddie Cahill with a parrot on the Cote d'Azur, 1938

Above Right: Edward Cahill giving a wartime charity recital in the Kursaal Montreux, Switzerland, 1941

Left: After the recital for Eva Perón, Bordighera, Italian Riviera, July 1947

Opposite: Edward Cahill at Clarens on Lake Geneva, while resident at the Clinique La Prairie, prior to his encounter with Wilhelm Furtwängler, Summer 1945

Edward Cahill & 'Noni' the Rhodesian Ridgeback, Somerset West, South Africa, 1955
– *Photograph courtesy of H.V. Morton*

CHAPTER 9

CATASTROPHES

During the long homeward voyage Eddie gave two recitals on board the *Chitral* for the benefit of the Seaman's Mission. Always a man of the theatre, as well as Beethoven sonatas, he performed on the banjo with the ship's cook who played the guitar. Eddie was travelling in far more luxurious conditions than ever before, a reflection of the financial success of the English leg of the second tour. Just before the vessel reached Colombo, Princess Esterházy of Austria (whose family had been patrons of Beethoven and Haydn) presented him with a handsome lizard-skin cigarette case as a token of the passengers' appreciation.

Reporters from the *Telegraph*, the *Courier-Mail* and the *Brisbane Courier* breathlessly besieged him when the ship docked at Fremantle on 31 December 1929. He had been abroad for almost three years giving concerts throughout Europe and America.

> Edward Cahill, of the bright and breezy manner and the mop of musicianly curls, is receiving a great welcome in Queensland, after his tour abroad. Cahill's is a dynamic personality. He is utterly unlike the popular conception of a pianist as dreamy, temperamental, introspective. The man is vital, alert, greedy for life, reaching upward to sensations and translating it into music. Short, stocky, well set up, his speech is jerky as the ideas overtake one another too quickly for smooth running, he gives a vivid impression of packed enthusiasm.

He was questioned on the quayside about the state of music in Europe. These observations form an invaluable first-hand description of his ideas on music and the musical tastes of the 1920s and are quoted in full.

'What is the attitude to modern classical compositions would you say?'

I went to every concert in Vienna while I was there, and I stayed there and in Germany for nine months. Music is flourishing there as it was before the war. Vienna is the art centre of the world and London is the Mecca. Well, in Vienna, concerts where Brahms, Beethoven, Bach or Schumann were being played were always packed to overflowing. Paderewski said to me once on this subject 'The craze for modern music will pass in the same way as the feminine fashion for hobble skirts died a natural death some years ago.' Most modern music, far from beautiful, seems to me to express only a sullen, dyspeptic hatred of things as they are. Art should *console* us for our human plight not rub our noses in the horror of suffering and war – it is bad enough having to experience these things!

'Could you say something about British musical taste?'

In London, German opera packs the theatre. At a Wagner night at the Queen's Hall you can hardly get the people in. And Delius! The Delius Festival was a sensation. Delius is an invalid, but he managed to be present. Beecham was conducting. No one has ever had such a reception as Delius, except the conductor of the Berlin Symphony Orchestra, Furtwängler*, when he visited London.

'And what is actually raising the standard of musical taste? Is it rising?'

Wireless broadcasting! It has done wonders for both music and musicians. Young musicians who would never have been heard of if they had had to rely on concerts, with all their risks, and disappointments and cost, have been popularised over the wireless until they are known everywhere. Curiously enough some great names have been dimmed by broadcasting. Such people as Chaliapine and Tetrazzini, whose extraordinary personalities have helped them when face to face with their audiences, have failed as broadcasters. Their personalities are hidden, and they have been forced to reliance only on their voices.

'And the finest pianists?'

Very much a question of personal taste. Take the mighty Johann Sebastian. The vital core of Bach is the unbroken flow of the spiritual design. The greatest Bach player today and certainly one of the most beautiful of pianists, a woman of tremendous sexual charisma, is Harriet Cohen known to her friends as 'Tania'.

---

* Wilhelm Furtwängler (1886–1954), a German composer and one of the greatest conductors of the 20th century.

Incidentally she was a pupil of Tobias Matthay as I was. She called him 'Uncle Tobs'. Pavlova thought she should have been a ballerina. Myra Hess however is by far the greatest woman pianist. Vladimir de Pachmann is surely the greatest player of Chopin together with the relatively unknown Leff Pouishnoff. And the sublime Moriz Rosenthal ... But for me the greatest living pianist is Vladimir Horowitz. I heard him in Paris and he had a reception that was amazing. I have never witnessed anything like it! Pandemonium!

'And now to Australia ...'

Australia has not had the opportunity of becoming as familiar as people in Europe with great music. It is the reason we explain to the audience the significance of the pieces we are going to perform.

'What with your experience are the possibilities abroad for young Australian talent?'

The extent of the competition is scarcely realised. Plenty of money, a heart of iron and above all, personality are the essential qualities for success.

'Are you pleased to be back in Australia?'

After three years abroad I am thrilled to be back in my own country. I miss the sunshine and the friendliness of Australians. I return with the conviction still deeply rooted in me that there is no place in the world like Australia.

From his youth working as a pianist in the silent cinema Eddie had a broad and particular knowledge of the movies and was asked about his opinion of the new talking pictures.

The 'talkies' have caused remarkable changes in the concert world! Initially the new warm comfortable theatres drew thousands. Far nicer than most concert halls – usually such cold and barren places. However, more recently the 'talkies' are driving people back to the concert halls and legitimate theatres. Talking pictures have come to stay – only for a time in my opinion.

* * *

In March 'an infinitely more cultured' Eddie and George would begin their Australian tour in Brisbane's new City Hall. Eddie performed throughout this tour on his newly commissioned

Grotrian-Steinweg concert instrument. Eddie told a reporter 'This particular instrument is the most wonderful piano I have ever played. Such a responsive touch, it can be both delicate and luminous yet can also express the rich tones of an old cello as well as thunder when required.'

Eddie always visited his mother in Beenleigh as soon as possible on returning to Australia and sent her a telegram from Fremantle. He was soon welcoming family, friends and the press on the Beenleigh railway platform. With great pride he showed his mother the hand-wrought gold fob given him by HH Princess Helena Victoria and HH Princess Marie Louise.

Eddie and George gave a concert in the School of Arts in Beenleigh in mid-March. The happy-faced 'Beenleigh Boy' played a Bechstein Concert Grand and dazzled the audience with his newly acquired Viennese waltz transcriptions. George, equally impressive, had taken lessons in the interpretation of Negro spirituals while on the American tour from Lawrence Brown. Clearly Schubert sung in German was appreciated by many of the Beenleigh settlers who had originally emigrated from Prussia in the nineteenth century

> Saturday proved to music lovers a veritable 'oasis in the desert' and of whose waters one could have remained to drink for interminable hours, enthralled by the exquisite artistry and wonderful touch and brilliant technique of Mr Cahill in his versatile pianoforte program, and captivated with the beauteous charm of Mr Brooke's voice and his delightful personality in his various vocal items which included negro melodies and spirituals, Irish Ballads, an inspiring French chanson and two delightful German folk songs, sung with the *Plattdeutsch* of a native … Recall after recall was made …*

Eddie spent a great deal of time walking, thinking and relaxing in the beautiful setting of rural Beenleigh. One of his favourite philosophical 'dream walks' was beside the banks of the slow flowing Albert River among the mournful eucalypts, racketing cicadas and luminous dragonflies. In the dappled glades where he had captured butterflies as a child he ruminated on his glittering career to date: 'So few of my dreams, my castles in the air have come crashing down! So lucky …'

The day before the tour began, they gave an afternoon 'At Home'

* From Edward Cahill's scrapbook – undated and unattributed.

recital at Government House Brisbane, known as Fernberg, for the Queensland Governor Sir John Goodwin, Lady Goodwin and their guests.* During this concert George developed a severe headache and needed to return to the hotel with Margaret to rest which put rather a dampener on proceedings. Eddie carried the afternoon alone but the frequency of these complaints was causing him to become increasingly concerned about his friend.

* * *

Australia experienced an economic recession in the late 1920s which was to develop into the Depression of the dismal 1930s. The whole country suffered from the Great Depression perhaps more than many others in the Western world. Eddie had built his career in the period of wealth and excess during the 'Roaring Twenties' and had lived life to the full in Europe's most glamorous cities. All that was soon to change. Audiences wanted entertainment and distraction, not profundity.

A number of incidents before the tour reminded Eddie and George that provincialism had not altogether been banished from the Queensland of 1930. They had planned a concert of sacred music on the evening of Good Friday in Ipswich Town Hall. All the permissions, programmes, tickets, billing and advertising had been printed and arranged with the town clerk. At the last moment there was an extraordinary reversion to pre-Monteverdian musical practice in the Venetian Republic. Instrumental music of any type was suddenly considered sacrilegious if performed in the church. The Rev. Patrick Birch 'entered an emphatic protest on the ground that an instrumental concert would offend the religious susceptibilities of many of the citizens of Ipswich.' Eddie and George settled out of court damages with the council of £25† having claimed £100.

The concert on 26 April 1930 in the recently opened new City

* Sir John Goodwin (1871–1960) was a distinguished soldier, medical practitioner and Governor of Queensland from 1927–32. Goodwin was mentioned in despatches three times during the Great War whilst serving in France. He was honorary surgeon to King George V.

† Around £1,100 in 2015 values.

Hall in Brisbane was their first appearance in Australia since 1927. Eddie and George were the first artists to perform there since its official opening. The second incident concerned Eddie's temerity to use a *German* piano for his recitals – his beloved Grotrian-Steinweg. A vociferous correspondence erupted in the columns of the Queensland *Daily Mail*. A certain Mr Holliday, State Secretary of The Returned Sailors and Soldiers Imperial League (RSSIL), in a particularly mean-spirited letter observed of Eddie and George that

> … they could hardly be said to be rendering good service, either to Australia, from whence they receive their money or to the Empire, in deliberately advertising a piano of foreign manufacture.

In his reply Eddie pointed out with unaccustomed acerbity that the instrument had been ordered and *presented* to him *in England* by a German company for his Australian tour, something an Australian firm would be unlikely to do with one of their instruments. He pointed out that almost all the finest pianists in Europe used German instruments

> I have no intention of playing an upright piano in the City Hall or elsewhere [...] Was Mr Holliday upset because Paderewski brought a Steinway piano here with him?

Another correspondent signing himself 'Scales' warned Eddie in rather threatening tones that Mr Holliday

> … has the backing of men who fought for Australia and the Empire. We stand four-square for Empire preference, and it is our aim to inculcate that spirit in the minds of all good Australians.

He concluded that Eddie and George were shirking their responsibilities and were unpatriotic. As a parting broadside he fired off 'Furthermore, Paderewski is not even Australian.'

Although hardly timid in temperament, before the concert Eddie sought police protection as a result of these threats. A letter, purporting to have been written by a group of incensed Anzacs, threatened to kidnap him if he attempted to play the German instrument. 'A large policeman' was posted on duty outside the City Hall before the crowds arrived. To Eddie's great relief no violence erupted. The concert was again attended by Sir John and Lady Goodwin as well as the Lord Mayor of Brisbane, William Alfred Jolly and his wife. Patriotic artists or not, the hall was packed to its capacity of 2,500 seats. Anticipation was so great there were an insufficient number of printed programmes before half the audience had even taken their places. The concert was also one of the first to be broadcast by the radio station 4QG: 'The listeners will discover the balm that so appeased the Viennese.' The remarkable variety of George's songs was rewarded with tremendous enthusiasm.*

Eddie played his pieces in two groups. He began with a couple of sharply contrasted preludes by the forgotten Russian composer Alexander Borowsky†, one entitled *The March of the Convict Women to Siberia* and another inspired by the traditional *Volga Boatman's Song* (a favourite of King George V). This was followed by the Brahms Rhapsody in E-flat major Op. 119 No. 4, a charming minuet by Mozart, the serene yet sensual, even humorous, early Beethoven Sonata in G major Op. 14 No. 2, rounded off with the glittering Grünfeld transcription Soirée de Vienne Concert Paraphrase on Johann Strauss waltzes from Die Fledermaus Op. 56. His second collection was entirely devoted to Chopin – waltzes, mazurkas, studies and impromptus, all performed with unique understanding which utilized his refined, delicate yet brilliant technique and uncanny insight. The critics judged Eddie to have presented 'brilliant passage work' and 'crystalline purity in Mozart' together with, in the Chopin group, 'beautiful shading and nuancing ... glorious resonance ... sureness of touch, perfect legato, brilliant staccato and music that came from within. A poetic piano and its poetic pianist.'

---

* Rare details survive of George Brooke's extraordinarily eclectic choices and unique programming: Burleigh's arrangements of the Negro spiritual *Hard Trials;* the lively *Didn't It Rain* and *I Got a Robe;* the song made famous by Paul Robeson *Go Down Moses* also the Negro convict songs *Water Boy* (Robinson) and the mournful Christian lament *Were You There?* (Thomas). The English group comprised *To Daisies* (Quilter); *The Second Minuet* (Besley); *The Cloths of Heaven* (Dunhill); *Chinese Flower* (Bowers) the words being a translation of a Chinese poem written by Su Tung-po in 1061; the jolly *Waita Poi* (Hill); *To The Children* (Rachmaninoff); *Ay-Ay-Ay* a Spanish ditty by Frevie and *Au Paps* (Holmes). The German group included *Wir Wandelten* (Brahms); *Botschaft* (Brahms); *In Meiner Heimat* (Trunk); *Wohin?* (Schubert); *Zueignung* (Strauss); *Mein* (Gurshman); an old German folk song *Spinner Liedchen* given as an encore and the Negro song *Fat Little Fella With His Mammie's Eyes*. Many of these songs are now completely forgotten and never performed in public concert.

† Alexander Borowsky (1889–1968) was an esteemed Russian-American pianist, a pupil of Annette Essipova, the most brilliant pupil and afterwards wife of the Polish pedagogue Theodor Leschetizky. Eddie probably encountered these works whilst studying in Vienna with Leonie Gombrich, Leschetizky's former pupil.

* * *

Eddie and George now embarked upon an extensive and uncomfortable tour of Queensland by road and train. In addition there were the difficult logistics of transporting the Grotrian-Steinweg concert grand piano around the state. These thirty-eight concerts were clearly an idealistic effort to bring classical piano music and German *Lieder* to Queensland audiences in remote agricultural districts deprived of regular concerts. Eddie always seemed possessed of a 'musical mission' and had the education of the audience as well as their entertainment foremost in mind.

The *Maryborough Chronicle* commented 'Intensive study in the great musical centres of the Continent has widened his vision of instrumental playing'. In one introduction Eddie gave an intriguing account of the musical 'programme' behind Rachmaninoff's famous Prelude in C sharp minor:

> Rachmaninoff told me this story himself during one of his visits to London. In a bizarre episode I remembered it when under the anaesthetic during a serious operation I was having on my left hand in Paris some time ago. I apparently told the surgeon the story behind the C sharp minor Prelude whilst asleep!
>
> The composer related to me how he imagined a man gripped by a seizure who later 'died' in hospital. He had been incarcerated in his coffin but was not truly dead, merely in a coma. He half heard his own funeral mass muffled through the wood but thought he was dreaming. Then suddenly he was fully awake and frantic, the music depicting him beating fruitlessly on the lid in the suffocating darkness. The heavy clods of earth pound on the coffin until he finally succumbs to oblivion and falls victim to the claws of death.
>
> My surgeon found it impossible to continue the operation after this and left it up to his wife to close the wound. She was the assistant surgeon on this occasion.*

Well-received concerts were given in Bundaberg, Rockhampton, Mackay, Townsville, Cairns and as far north as far-flung Atherton. Unsurprisingly this final concert was not well attended but the pleasure the performers gave to 'the happy few' of Atherton in the

* This 'interpretation' gains astonishing credence in Rachmaninoff's own recording of the work.

Shire Hall that evening was highlighted in the hyperbole of the local newspaper

> When listening to the exquisite music of our two Australian artists, Mr Cahill and Mr Brooke, our minds seemed to be steeped in the sweetest of sounds; it was as if the notes took wings, encircling us in an ever-increasing circle of fairy forms; other times we watched aghast the struggles of life and death [...] the world to me became a glorious garden as each note sounded, each flower unfolded, the morning sun awakened and bathed the earth with golden splendour, every petal and leaf rejoiced and trembled in the breeze [...] brooks rippled and danced in the sunlight, larks trilled and sang [...] the whole world danced in a fantasy of delight as Mr Cahill played.

* * *

It was already July when they returned to Brisbane to prepare for a number of important engagements at the City Hall. They were to present a 'more popular programme' even including some 'Red Indian Songs'. Eddie had the mahogany case of the Grotrian-Steinweg painted in an 'elegant ivory and gold', high fashion in the 1930s. However George's health had noticeably declined after the demanding tour of Queensland and unbeknown to the first night audience he had had to rise from his sick bed to take part.

During the first concert Eddie had just finished playing *La Campanella.* The usual tumultuous applause was dying away when George came onto the stage to sing his second group of songs. He began with Schubert and Brahms. Then he suffered a moment that all singers fear like death itself, a lapse of memory for the words. He whispered news of this sudden vocal *horror vacui* to Eddie, who immediately prompted him in an undertone from the piano. Strangely the music did not elude him. Eddie whispered the poetry of the Handel Arcadian love aria 'Where'er You Walk' from *Semele* as he played.

A musical nightmare unfolded for the performers. Often it was only the beginning of a song that needed to be prompted. Outwardly the artists appeared simply to be chatting before each new number and managed to complete the concert without anyone noticing anything awry. In fact, the *Brisbane Standard* noted that George 'won the hearts of his audience completely in a programme that left nothing to be desired. Not only does he use his fine voice with artistic effect, but he infuses into each song the feeling of the people from whom it came.' The Negro spirituals were sung with such ardent devotion that Lady Goodwin was seen wiping away tears.

Eddie was extremely perturbed by this turn of events. Being a highly strung personality, he was thought by many to be simply overwrought when he cancelled a concert in Canberra and hurriedly packed a suitcase. Margaret, George and Eddie caught a train to Melbourne where an emergency appointment with a medical specialist had been made for George. The diagnosis was not encouraging as a dark shadows on a cranial X-ray indicated the possibility that George may have a brain tumour. Whether this was benign or not would need to be investigated by an operation carried out by a neurosurgeon.*

George was immediately admitted to Mount St Evin's Private Hospital where his condition deteriorated by the hour. Emergency medical intervention was to no avail and he slipped away on 2 September 1930 at the age of 44 in the presence of Eddie, Margaret, his mother and brother. Eddie sent a telegram to many of their friends: 'My best pal has passed away. Broken hearted.' They had been performing and travelling the world together for sixteen years.

In Act II Scene III of Handel's opera *Semele,* Jupiter sings a love aria to Semele celebrating Arcadian delights. Eddie found this final Handelian setting that George had sung agonisingly elegiac in the face of his death

Where e'er you walk, cool gales shall fan the glade;
Trees where you sit, shall crowd into a shade
Where'er you tread, the blushing flowers shall rise
And all things flourish where'er you turn your eyes.

Letters, cables and wreaths poured in from all over the world.

---

* In the 1930s such operations were performed mainly with hand drills and surgical chisels with little accurate targeting of tumours and much physical movement of the patient. George consulted the famous Australian physician Sir Richard Stawell (1864–1935), a specialist in nervous diseases and a lifelong lover of music. He was operated on by a Dr A. Newton at Mount St Evin's Hospital, Melbourne.

* * *

Eddie, desolated by George's unexpected death, was advised by his doctors not to give concerts in the immediate future. Characteristically he ignored their advice. He decided to give the first memorial recital informally in the ballroom at Lennons Hotel in Brisbane at the end of October. Sir John Goodwin and Lady Goodwin attended carrying mauve delphiniums tied with a dark ribbon.

Eddie was not without sentiment. A single bowl of crimson roses decorated the stage where George would have stood to sing. He included reflective works bathed in melancholy as well as his customary glittering rendition of *La Campanella* by Liszt and the Józef Wieniawski *Valse de Concert.* His inner turmoil may be gleaned from his choice of the most nostalgic of Chopin nocturnes, preludes and mazurkas, the *Adieu to the piano* attributed by some scholars to Beethoven and a recent work of his own entitled *Elegie.*

The Australian poet Mabel Forrest* read from her George Brooke memorial poem

But somewhere in the hallways of the blue,
Somewhere amid the stars, your song remains
And in the hush of summer silver nights
And in the gentle murmurs of the rain
The wind in the tree tops and the breath of dawn
In all fine, eloquent and lovely things
We shall hear you once more ... remembering.

A festive dance concluded the evening, which had developed in the manner of an Irish musical wake.

* * *

Eddie's personality had more than once teetered on the edge of a nervous breakdown and the pressure of this loss pushed him over the edge once again despite his attempt to continue performing

* Mabel Forrest (1872–1935), writer, was born near Yandilla, Darling Downs, Queensland. She was unkindly considered 'the most industrious versifier in the Commonwealth' and had a mixed reputation. Publishing in the *Australasian*, the *Bulletin*, *Smith's Weekly*, the *Triad* and the *Lone Hand*, she signed herself 'M. Forrest', 'Reca' or 'M. Burkinshaw'.

as normal. A second blow came when he needed an operation for acute appendicitis. In the period of sulphonamides before modern antibiotics, recovery from such major surgery was slow, risky and painful. He filled the abyss of grief and physical discomfort by beginning to write a book chronicling his artistic career with George and their exotic experiences together. Tragically, the manuscript is lost. Not long after this his great mentor Dame Nellie Melba succumbed to paratyphoid in February 1931, possibly caught whilst travelling home to Australia from Munich. Despite his own physical pain Eddie travelled to Melbourne for the funeral and filed past her coffin in Scots' Church. He could scarcely face the burial of a musician he considered had 'the most perfect voice of our time' and who had been so generous towards him.

On the first day of the beautiful spring of 1931, the first anniversary of George Brooke's death, the Australian Wattle League arranged that the famous bass-baritone Peter Dawson plant a Golden Wattle in George's memory at Wattle Park at Burwood, his birthplace in Melbourne. In an emotional speech, Dawson drew attention to George's ability to weave himself into the hearts of his listeners, his charm, and the fine natural voice of 'a man who was indeed a singer of the people'. He felt it a great tragedy that George was struck down at forty-four, so early for a musician that would have soon become a household name in Australia. He could think of no Australian musical artists whose star had risen so quickly as Brooke and Cahill. There were few dry eyes when Eddie spoke of the loss of his 'comrade' of sixteen years. Two months later a memorial plaque was attached to the tree accompanied by moving recitations of Robert Louis Stephenson's *Requiem* and Conrad Aiken's *Music I Heard With You.*

Inevitably Eddie and George's close relationship in this 'masculinist society' became the subject of malicious gossip. Over the years performing together Eddie and George had become close 'pals', mutually dependent on the unique emotional intimacy brought about by such a close musical collaboration. One cruel newspaper article packed with innuendo and prejudice, printed on pink paper wrote

> Ever since the death of his erstwhile friend, George Brooke, Eddie has been more or less at a loose end. Seldom amongst

> men is such an attachment as existed between these two known and these days Eddie finds himself a lonely man. Rumour has it that he has been offered an interest with a leading firm of dress designers in the South, mainly on account of his social qualifications.*

Eddie never married, giving rise to much speculation by the simple minded. Perhaps he was *entre deux lits* or perhaps even a repressed homosexual. A stance impossible to determine and largely irrelevant to his musicianship. There is no reference to his 'sexual orientation' in his letters or private papers which is hardly surprising since homosexuality at the time was considered a serious criminal offence. In time the label 'confirmed bachelor' settled about his shoulders.

Concerts were a way of recuperating from life's reversals for Eddie. His first official public appearance after a fitful recuperation was on 14 November 1931. He gave a well-received account of the Weber Konzertstück in F minor with the Greater Brisbane Orchestra under the German conductor Albert Kaeser in aid of the Returned & Services League. The Overture to *Tannhäuser* and the 1812 Overture were also performed that evening.

* * *

A thread of smoke insinuated itself under the door of the drawing room and wound itself around the leg of the ivory and gold piano and over the cedar bookcase. Soon the valuable tapestry of the Duke Marlborough on horseback at the Battle of Blenheim that was hanging on the wall dissolved in a haze as if engulfed by smoke from distant cannon. A cat fled into the garden through the flap in the kitchen. The Queenslander colonial house of Roscrea, an old Beenleigh landmark belonging to the Cahill family, had caught fire.

On Sunday night 4 December 1932 Eddie and his sister had decided make a social visit to their old friend Mrs Murray on the Tambourine Road, Beenleigh. Shortly after eight o'clock they were told that the family home was ablaze. In alarm they leapt into the Willys Knight Roadster and Eddie drove like a man possessed. They arrived to witness a raging fire engulfing the house and consuming

---

* From Edward Cahill's scrapbook – undated and unattributed.

all their possessions. With no fire-fighting appliances in the town, he and the residents of Beenleigh had to stand by helplessly watching the conflagration. A few pathetic buckets of water were thrown at the blaze, but the wooden house quickly burned to the ground.

Eddie lost everything. All his personal correspondence, a significant amount of cash, tributes and gifts of a diamond pin, diamond cuff links and a diamond studded cigarette case. Rare gifts given him by Indian Maharajahs, the King of Siam and British royalty. He lost two pianos, one being his beloved Grotrian-Steinweg valued at £850*. A particularly significant loss among his recordings and music was a first edition of Percy Grainger's *Country Gardens* marked with fingering and phrasing by the composer for one of his pupils. Eddie spent hours searching the ashes for the treasured solid gold double Albert watch chain and fob given to him by HH Princess Marie Louise. He also lost paintings, French tapestries, all his clothing including his silk top hats and formal dress for concerts and receptions purchased at ruinous expense at the court tailors Ede & Ravenscroft in London.

More tragically, his beloved mother at the age of 68 had died on 24 July only a few months previously. He had been emotionally overwhelmed by this death. She and his grandmother were the only members of the family who seemed to instinctively understand his sensitive, musical nature. Grief had become a constant companion. And now every beloved object associated with his dearest souls and spiritual companions had been consumed by the flames. Eddie remained inconsolable and scarcely sane for months.

With remarkable resilience, he somehow managed to rise above these calamities. No doubt driven by the overwhelming need to stay together psychologically and earn some money after such extensive losses, by April 1933 he had resumed recitals. A newspaper report read: 'Instead of the lovely world-famous piano which was burnt in the fire at Beenleigh, Edward Cahill is to play on a piano which had been practically placed in the junk room at Paling's music store.'

As a solace for grief and a distraction from these tribulations, Eddie allowed another side of his character to flourish. The role of a social butterfly had been hidden away through years of self-discipline. Now he gave this aspect of his personality free reign

* £75,000 in 2015.

and threw himself with almost hysterical abandon into prestigious social events in Brisbane and Sydney. He played at the Farmer's Business Girls' Lunch, accompanied the variety artist 'Burlington Bertie' Ella Shields and gave illustrated talks describing his career among the royals in London on an afternoon radio programme entitled *'Women's Budget' Session.* Most strangely, he was engaged for a season at the Regent Theatre in Brisbane to give solo classical recitals on the same bill as 'B' cinema features such as the sensational Royal Air Force epic *The Lost Squadron.* During this season he also returned to his old stamping ground, the silent cinema, and brilliantly accompanied a re-run of the classic 1919 Australian silent, *The Sentimental Bloke.*

Eddie also actively and rather desperately 'networked' among the many glamorous women attending 'mannequin parades' as they were termed in the 1930s. It was reported that at a fashion parade of 'exquisite pyjama ensembles' Eddie turned to one of the few men present and was heard to remark 'One time the girls seemed to take off things to go to bed, but now they put on four-piece suits – they wear more to bed than they wear anywhere else!' He attended luncheon parties given by the Lady Mayoress of Sydney and 'shared honours' at the Arts Club in the city with Princess Wiki, the Maori singer and granddaughter of a Rotoruan chief. On one memorable evening he borrowed a lavishly decorated flat in a fashionable suburb of Sydney known as Potts Point and threw a party 'where there was quite an Australian De Brett [*sic*] sound about many of the names.' One wonders what may have been passing through his mind concerning his own career when accompanied by Ella Shields he attended a piano recital by the great Ukrainian Benno Moiseiwitsch at His Majesty's Theatre early in July 1932 and was moved by his interpretation of the Chopin *Barcarolle.*

* * *

Eddie had now become a divided man. The social butterfly vied with the serious musician. He profoundly wished to be treated as far more than a society pianist. At 48 he felt age creeping on and being born in Beenleigh was hardly the most advantageous of beginnings for an international concert career. However as a confirmed *bon viveur,* his love of pleasure, good food and wine, beautiful women and fashion temporarily gained the upper hand after these harrowing reversals.

Yet for a period in 1933 he did turn to his serious side and embarked on a taxing series of educational lectures on music at almost one hundred Brisbane schools. He had heard a vague rumour that there was to be a policy to establish mouth organ bands and believed that something more serious should be attempted to cultivate young minds with the best in classical music. He felt all children were singers, potential performers or at the very least might make discriminating concert-goers. He found them eager to learn and at every school complete silence reigned as he talked and played. In this educational effort he was assisted by the great bass-baritone Peter Dawson.

Requesting no fee or expenses for his lectures, Eddie explained the instruments of the orchestra, the nature of melody, the development of the sonata, concerto and symphony in very simple terms. He wittily introduced the instruments as 'the scrapers, the bangers and the blowers', which greatly appealed to their untutored minds. He introduced them to witty and rumbustious Percy Grainger. He commented in an interview:

> Unless children have some preliminary information about the instruments they are going to hear, they cannot keep up a continued interest in concerts. The first and second times, curiosity will sustain them; but, after that, only a minority will want to go again. Also, in Brisbane the second half of the programme was provided by an orchestra of children; and this roused the interest of the juvenile audience to fever heat.
>
> *Sydney Morning Herald,* 30 September 1933

These preliminary talks were given to some 18,000 children at 50 schools. Although he never gave piano lessons, he advocated introducing children to music gradually so that pieces they first heard would be readily appreciated. Then with the establishment of school orchestras and bands they could in time learn to play much of what was already familiar. The whole project was strongly supported by the Queensland Director of Education.

His philosophy of musical education for the young was summed up in a leaflet advertising the first of an outstandingly successful series of children's concerts that followed the school 'lectures' in the Brisbane City Hall. He noticed with delight that the body of the auditorium was filled predominantly with youngsters. Eddie chose his programme carefully to appeal to a younger audience and explained each piece. He performed with the Greater Brisbane Orchestra Liszt's extrovert and spirited *Hungarian Fantasy*. The orchestra also performed the *Overture to Egmont* by Beethoven and Haydn's *Surprise* Symphony.

Eddie in addition played a selection of piano pieces by the Australian pianist and composer Percy Grainger including the ever popular *Mollie on the Shore* and *Country Gardens*. He had recently begun to champion this lively and infectiously charming music. Eddie had mirrored Grainger's pianistic career in London in many ways, sharing the other's charm, graciousness and sense of fun. After the first City Hall concert he attended a reception given in honour of Philip Hargrave, the eleven-year-old child prodigy of the piano. Professors thought Hargrave possessed of great musical genius but this brief comet gave up his concert career to become a doctor after only a few brilliant teenage years.

* * *

All too soon the pendulum of teaching swung away once more from uplifting education to partying. Throughout the remainder of 1933 and much of 1934 Eddie again took up his addiction to the superficial fashionable round and gave recitals at social rather than serious musical venues: the Society of Women Writers luncheon; cocktails in the Lord Mayor's room; concerts in the elegant department store of David Jones in Sydney; places where the hats and gowns, ladies 'wrapped in ermine' or 'rose-red velvet' attracted more column inches than the musical impression he made. He found this musical superficiality depressing compared to his truncated European career but was forced to earn some sort of living from music.

Eddie at some time in the 1930s became acquainted in Sydney with the notorious aesthete William Lygon, 7th Earl of Beauchamp. One can only speculate on its possible significance after discovering a signed photograph of the earl among his papers. This youngest ever Governor of New South Wales had been appointed in 1899 and created a memorable and colourful 'Antipodean Camelot' for two years. His sister Lady Mary had accompanied him to Australia Felix for a few months. She was an excellent pianist and a patron of the English composer Edward Elgar, who actually took up boomerang throwing as a pastime with her lady friends.

On his two-month visit to Australia in 1930, Beauchamp, apart from praising the liberal attitudes of Australian society, failed to conceal he was sharing rather intense sexual pleasures with his valet. He was openly accused of homosexuality by his vengeful brother-in-law Bend'Or, the 2nd Duke of Westminster, and exiled from England. In future William would wander those cities tolerant of homosexuality including 'the clefts in the rocks of Sydney's Botany Bay'. Bend'Or wrote to Beauchamp in a letter 'Dear Bugger-in-Law, You got what you deserved. Yours, Westminster.'* Beauchamp was intelligent, sensitive and particularly fond of music. He had been heartbroken at losing his much loved brother, also named Eddie, to a sniper in the Boer War in South Africa, which may go some way to explaining their mysterious acquaintance.

Despite loving Queensland and having attracted undreamed of success, Eddie felt increasingly impoverished as a musician. Unemployment was high and conditions grim. The limitations of colonial musical life after his experiences in India, Asia and Europe were painfully clear. Besides practical survival, he felt an inner compulsion to continue his pianistic development and above all widen his repertoire. He had remained in much the same rut for far too long.

Eddie felt desperately alone and isolated. Both his parents had died by now and many of his family had been claimed by illness. His sister Lillian had married a fanatical Norwegian military officer with a 'superb soap-waxed moustache', who had fought with distinction in the Boer War and the Great War. He reminisced on battles constantly, played war games and obsessed over his

---

* Quoted in the highly entertaining volume by Jane Mulvagh, *Madresfield: The Real Brideshead* (London 2008), pp. 286–96. The 7th Earl of Beauchamp (1872–1938) was married to the sensual Lettice Grosvenor, sister of Bend'Or. He had an outstandingly distinguished career in public service. The historic and distinguished Lygon family and their country seat Madresfield were the inspiration for Evelyn Waugh's *Brideshead Revisited*. Lord Marchmain was modelled on the 7th Earl of Beauchamp. The 2nd Duke of Westminster was named 'Bend'Or' because of his possession of a shock of chestnut hair.

Australian specialist stamp collection. Another sister, Bessie, a fine operatic soprano, had married the latest owner of Cahill's Hotel in Beenleigh, Ted Moran. The family home Roscrea had burnt to the ground. His musical partner George had been cut down by a brain tumour. The silver voice of his mentor Dame Nellie Melba had been stilled in 1931. It had been a horrible four years. No, there was not a great deal to hold him in Australia.

Like many Australians of the time Eddie felt correctly that he had begun his serious musical studies rather too late in life. Many of the glamorous hostesses in London who had regarded Eddie as their 'pet pianist' were continually pressing him to return to England. He had resumed his correspondence with the woman he came closest to loving, the Austrian violinist Sabine Adler. She was pressing him to meet her again in Europe. After four years apart their letters had become understandably fitful. Eddie had engaged in some passing romantic affairs in Australia (and possibly Sabine had also been tempted in Austria), but this relationship remained important for both of them. Sabine was attempting to arrange some concerts in Austria and Germany where they could play Bach, Brahms and Beethoven together. He had always suspected that this glamorous creature would by now have become embroiled with a young dashing Austrian cavalry officer or in his more pessimistic moods, a Nazi *Gauleiter*. But as far as he could tell from her ardent letters, she seemed to have remained unattached and anxious to meet him again.

Chapter 10

High Society and *Le Train Bleu*

Towards the end of 1934 Eddie Cahill, an inveterate traveller for some 20 years, decided to leave Australia on another tour of England. He agreed to give a series of concerts at the invitation of the ever loyal Mrs Denny in Buckinghamshire. However on this occasion he would be performing as a soloist and judged entirely on his own merits. With his limited funds he was forced to taking passage to England on the cargo liner SS *Stuart Star.* In October he boarded as the first and only passenger on the newly inaugurated Blue Star Line Brisbane to Southampton route. On the day he sailed his sister Bessie, an outstanding *mezzo soprano,* laid on a farewell tea at the cottage in the grounds of the Belle Vue Hotel in Brisbane. He played some Chopin and appropriately the melancholic *Adieu* for piano attributed to Beethoven. Eddie would never see Australia again.

On the long voyage he gave a number of concerts on an old upright piano which were much appreciated by the crew. Being alone gave him the opportunity to work up additions to his repertoire for his new programmes for London and the concerts Sabine had arranged in Germany. He practised Liszt's virtuosic *Hungarian Fantasy* for two pianos, a challenge for a pianist with such small hands. He was also able to learn the piano part of the sonatas he would perform with Sabine – Beethoven's magnificent *Kreutzer* and *Spring* sonatas for violin and piano as well as Bach's Sonata No. 3 in E major, BMV 1016 for violin and harpsichord.

* * *

In the warm Queensland sun, Eddie had not considered the living conditions and social problems of the England he was approaching in the 1930s. He thought conditions for classical musicians could not be worse than in Australia. Eddie possessed an established reputation and promises of lucrative engagements in London that only lay in hibernation. He was brimming with optimism.

The inclement winter climate and unhealthy air of the British Isles checked this mood. Fog in the English Channel, among the worst in living memory, delayed the boat from docking for fifty-eight hours. While waiting on board a friendly radiogram arrived from Mrs Denny at Horwood: 'Welcome home. All waiting for your arrival.' which lifted his spirits. Grey light and smog lay oppressively over London as he chugged past the grim urban brick dwellings on the steam train from Southampton. Millions of smoking chimneys rather than white Pacific beaches filled the narrow window of the carriage.

The economy of England had been at least as affected by the Wall Street debacle as that of Australia. An economic blizzard was howling through the land. 'Times, we all thought, had never been worse or England closer to the abyss.'* The style of life, social status and political power of many in the milieu of peers Eddie had frequented in the 1920s had continued its inexorable decline during his absence. The profound upheavals resulting from the deaths in the Great War of perhaps two generations of a single family continued unabated. Crippling rises in taxes and punitive death duties, the depression of agricultural revenues and the lure of overseas investments in the United States or the South American railways meant that the secure predictability of Edwardian upper-class life was slowly leaching away.

Numerous historic seats were sold or demolished during the interwar years. All the great estates in the entire county of Middlesex, except for a number of parks, were subsumed under brick and concrete. Broad acres were broken up and sold off piecemeal for sterile modern housing developments. Some great houses were simply abandoned and fell into irreversible disrepair.† In 1933 Duff Cooper writes in his diary of a party he attended at the later notorious Londonderry House with the 'most beautiful

---

* Diana Cooper, *The Light of Common Day* (London 1959), p. 102.

† John Martin Robinson, *Felling the Ancient Oaks: How England Lost its Great Country Estates* (London 2011), p. 31.

woman in England', his wife Diana. The tone is rather revealing of upper-class attitudes and the savage differences remaining within society.

> It was an exceptionally delightful party. Young and old admirably mixed. [...] It is of course true that nowhere else in the world nowadays, and not often in England, are there parties where statesmen, ambassadors and debutantes meet. We didn't get home till past three. [...] We went to Breccles for the weekend. Just before luncheon the butler blew his brains out, which was rather distressing.[*]

However the decline of the powerful and privileged in society was all but invisible to the majority. The elite seemed to float effortlessly above strife, always mindful of keeping up appearances. Fun and games were still pursued with a vengeance by some members of the upper classes during the thirties

> Treasure-hunts were dangerous and scandalous, but there was no sport to touch them ... A clue might lead to a darkened city court, there to find a lady in distress, with a dead duellist at her feet, who would hand the next clue through her tears. This might lead to a plague-spot where a smallpoxed ghost would whisper a conundrum that took you to a mare's nest in Kensington Gardens, and thence to a Chinese puzzle in Whitechapel. Quick thought, luck and unscrupulous driving might bring you first to the coveted prize.[†]

There is no finer description of the favoured circles Eddie moved within than the entries from the diaries of Harold Nicolson and Sir Henry 'Chips' Channon[‡], who in 1934 lived in some splendour at 5 Belgrave Square in a house next door to the notorious Prince George, Duke of Kent. Harold Nicolson describes Channon's house:

> All Regency upstairs with very carefully draped curtains and Madame Récamier sofas and wall paintings. Then the dining-room is entered through an orange lobby and discloses itself suddenly as a copy of the blue room at the Amalienburg near Munich – baroque and rococo and what-ho and oh-no-no and

* John Julius Norwich (ed.), *The Duff Cooper Diaries 1915–1951* (London 2005), pp. 222, 225.

† Cooper, *The Light of Common Day*, pp. 112–3.

‡ Sir Henry 'Chips' Channon (1897–1958) was an American-born wealthy Conservative politician, author and famous diarist.

all that. Very fine indeed.*

Some inheritors of great wealth persisted in fecklessly gambling entire fortunes away in extravagant and mindless pleasures, sinking vast sums into the world of horses or falling victim to their own financial incompetence. Eddie's royal patrons were scarcely affected by anything during the decade.

Lower down the social scale, the middle classes during this decade experienced a significant expansion in suburban housing. This satisfied the English desire for a self-contained house with a small garden where one might pleasantly occupy snatched hours of leisure. The intractable problem of long-term unemployment among the working class in the industrial North remained. An average of twenty-two per cent of men were 'on the tramp' (searching for work) during the decade.

> … groups of idle sullen-looking young men stood at the street corners … Everything had the look of a Sunday that had lasted many years … a disused, slovenly, everlasting Sunday.†

Eddie took up residence at 7a Manchester Street, Westminster.‡ Scarcely venturing outside Mayfair and Belgravia and attending the fashionable dinners hosted by his well-insulated patrons, he would have been only vaguely aware of 'actual hunger – hunger gnawing at the stomach, hunger making one dizzy and weak, hunger destroying one's body and destroying one's mind.'§

Thy mother is crying
Thy dad's on the dole:
Two shillings a week is the price of a soul

A Carol, C. Day Lewis

His Australian relations and friends accused him of becoming an arrant snob and social climber in London. However in such a brutal economic climate one can scarcely criticise him for the career he valiantly set out to carve for himself among the English

---

* Harold Nicolson (1886–1968), *Diaries and Letters 1930–39* (London 1966), p. 244. Nicolson was a diplomat, politician, author and famous diarist also the husband of the writer Vita Sackville-West. In the 1930s they moved to magnificent Sissinghurst Castle in Kent.

† The poet Edwin Muir quoted in Juliet Gardiner, *The Thirties: An Intimate History* (London 2010), p. 34.

‡ Destroyed by bombing during the Blitz.

§ Fenner Brockway, *Hungry England* (1932) quoted in ibid., p. 61.

upper classes through his contacts, talent and charm. In the arena of fashion and privilege, Eddie Cahill was merely a society pianist (albeit a brilliant one) forced to earn a living entertaining the *haut ton* who were passing through, as Lady Swaythling put it, 'most wearisome economic times'.

* * *

Eleven years had passed since Eddie as a raw colonial witnessed his first royal wedding in 1923. By coincidence he had arrived back in England just in time to witness the marriage of the controversial, privately scandalous figure of Prince George, Duke of Kent, the fourth son of George V and Mary of Teck.* He was to marry Marina, the beautiful daughter of Prince Nicholas of Greece and Denmark and Elena Vladimirovna, Grand Duchess of Russia (a granddaughter of Tsar Alexander II). It was to be the last marriage between the son of a British sovereign and a member of a foreign royal house.

The 29th of November 1934 dawned romantically foggy. Eddie felt that the misty haloes surrounding the gas mantles along the route created the atmosphere of an hallucinatory dream. He saw the opulent state carriages with postilions in royal livery wearing tricorn hats, black Rolls-Royce Phantoms, Daimler limousines and the mounted regiments of the Life Guards moving like disembodied ghosts. London was in festival mood, with Bond Street decorated in waxed paper flowers and the Greek and British flags. This was the first royal wedding to be broadcast on the wireless. Previously the Westminster Abbey Dean and Chapter had refused this technology fearing that disrespectful people 'might hear the service, perhaps some of them even sitting in public houses, with their hats on.' Two days before the marriage there had been a ball at Buckingham Palace. Among some eight hundred guests were a Mr and Mrs Ernest Simpson, friends of the Prince of Wales. The Prince introduced Mrs Simpson to his parents. 'It was the briefest

---

* Prince George, Duke of Kent (1902–42) was a strong advocate of the policy of appeasement and was immensely popular with the public. He died in the mysterious crash of a Short Sunderland flying boat in Scotland in August 1942. He was a colourful and sexually scandalous member of the royal family.

of encounters. A perfunctory greeting, an exchange of meaningless pleasantries and we moved away,' she wrote later.*

Marina was a favourite royal with Eddie and he closely followed her activities for much of his future life. After the ceremony at Westminster Abbey, the 'dazzling pair' drove back to Buckingham Palace to appear on the balcony before the multitudes who were waving white handkerchiefs. Eddie noted the scene was 'like foam on a wind-tossed sea'. A Greek Orthodox ceremony took place immediately after this balcony appearance. They set off for their long honeymoon from Paddington Station in the midst of huge cheering crowds.†

Eddie was requested to play at the farewell party given for the handsome, exiled King George II of Greece‡, who was leaving for Paris shortly after the royal wedding. The King had been living at Brown's Hotel in London and would be restored to the Greek throne in November 1935. Diana Cooper wrote of him:

> His life, they say, is a very sad one. He has not one man he can trust or take advice from, and not one personal friend. He's made himself more or less of a dictator, he says, though disapproving of dictators ...§

Eddie felt the familiar elation 'bordering on vertigo', the damp palms, that particular inspiration that electrified his nerves when playing for a royal audience.

* * *

Eddie spent Christmas 1934 with the large house party at Horwood House in Buckinghamshire as a 'performing guest' of Maude and Frederick Denny. It appeared to him as if nothing had changed for him socially and professionally as he began to take up the threads of his life and altered career. Time to renew old friendships. His fears of performing in London alone without the moral support of George were set at rest. The greatest musical shock the Dennys

* Quoted in Barrow, *Gossip: A History of High Society from 1920 to 1970*, p. 73.

† Description of the wedding taken from Edward's notebook and Alison Weir, Kate Williams, Sarah Gristwood and Tracy Borman, *The Ring and the Crown: A History of Royal Weddings 1066–2011* (London 2011), pp. 110–15.

‡ King George II of Greece (1890–1947) reigned from 1922 to 1924 and from 1935 to 1947.

§ Cooper, *The Light of Common Day*, p. 182.

provided for Eddie were the astounding new recordings of Liszt by the virtuoso Russian pianist Simon Barere.* Early in the New Year of 1935 he drove the sixty miles to London for the Musicians' Fund Dinner given in honour of Maude's brother, the English art song composer Roger Quilter. He started the Alvis without difficulty, negotiating the narrow, snowy English lanes at speed, wildly sliding the car just for the amusement of it.

Before her marriage to the poet Robert Nichols, the Dennys' daughter Norah had been taught music by a musical friend of the Quilters, the Australian composer and virtuoso pianist Percy Grainger. Eddie loved the originality, the relative lack of intellectual complication of much of Grainger's piano music. He admired his eccentric athleticism, his entertaining personality and his complete eschewal of atonalism in his compositions. They both wore their Australian heritage as a badge of pride.†

* * *

At the recital for King George of Greece, Eddie had made the acquaintance of the largely forgotten sculptor Felix Weiss de Weldon, who was considered in his day 'the Michelangelo of American sculpture'‡. He was commissioned by governments, presidents, royalty, artists and religious leaders, but would only sculpt figures he considered outstanding in their fields. He

---

* Simon Barere (1896–1951) was born in Odessa. In a similar way to Edward Cahill he began his astounding virtuoso career playing for the silent cinema in order to support his family. He first studied at the Odessa Imperial Musical Academy with Benno Moiseiwitsch as a fellow student and then with Annette Essipova (one of the most brilliant pupils of Leschetizky) and Felix Blumenfeld (who taught Neuhaus and Horowitz). On 2 April 1951, Barere suffered a cerebral haemorrhage during a performance of Grieg's Piano Concerto at Carnegie Hall. Eugene Ormandy was conducting the Philadelphia Orchestra. Barere collapsed and died shortly afterwards in the artist's green room.His 'supercharged virtuosity' is once again being recognised through historic recordings.

† Percy Grainger (1882–1961) was a highly original Australian composer, arranger and concert pianist. Known to Eddie who championed his work, he shared rather similar aristocratic audiences for concerts in London but somewhat earlier than Cahill. A fine interpreter of Chopin.

‡ The Austrian sculptor Felix Weiss de Weldon (1907–2003) created more than 1,200 public monuments including busts of Elvis Presley, Harry S. Truman, John F. Kennedy and Simon Bolivar. He is the only artist in the world with a masterpiece on all seven continents, including one of Richard Byrd at McMurdo Sound in Antarctica.

asked Eddie to sit for him. The fragile plaster head survived the bombing of Central London during the Second World War stored in a hatbox. Eddie had put it under the bed of 'a certain lady'. Her house was severely damaged, almost completely destroyed, but the head survived. Eddie always subsequently referred to it as 'The Royal Head'.

* * *

Following the death of George and the house fire, Eddie practised the Roman Catholic religion more fervently than ever. As an altar boy, the aesthetic theatre of the Tridentine Mass had appealed to him perhaps above the spiritual content. He had always dreamed of visiting Rome. Before sailing to England he made strenuous efforts to realise his fantasy of meeting Pope Pius XI. During his work in musical education in Brisbane he had befriended the legendary Irishman Sir James Duhig, Archbishop of Queensland.*

Before sailing for England the Archbishop had written Eddie two letters of introduction to influential priests in Rome and the Vatican. An audience and brief recital were arranged for 24 February 1935. Before this 'pilgrimage' he had spent much of January practising in the deserted London residence in South Street, Mayfair of Lady Gwynedd Quilter, the wife of Roger Quilter's eldest brother Eley. She wrote to him: 'Use the flat to your heart's content if you would not mind the furniture being covered up.'

Travelling to Rome by train from London was an adventure in 1935. From the reports by his friends who raced cars at Brooklands, Eddie knew of the famous Blue Train Races and was particularly excited at the prospect of this journey. He took his reserved seat in the Pullman car of the boat train from Victoria Station to Dover. Not being a particularly good sailor, he had organised a private cabin on the boat for the Channel crossing to Calais. He had booked a sleeping compartment as far as Menton in the exclusively first class,

* Sir James Duhig (1871–1965) was Archbishop of Queensland for almost sixty years – the longest-serving bishop in the Roman Catholic Church. Known as 'Duhig the Builder', in fifty years he added over 400 major buildings to the Brisbane cityscape – religious, educational and charitable institutions, as well as hospitals. (T.P. Boland, *Australian Dictionary of Biography.*)

chic and luxurious *Le Train Bleu* (the steel 'Grand Luxe' carriages of the Compagnie Internationale des Wagons-Lits were painted cream and dark blue). Passengers on 'the millionaires' train' had the advantage of avoiding French customs delays at Calais before the 750 mile onward journey to Paris, Nice and the Côte d'Azur.

The train set off from the Gare du Nord for Nice in the early evening. Shortly after departure from the Gare de Lyon a great ringing of bells announced that dinner had been served. The long hours until bedtime were eased by a meal in the sumptuous *haute cuisine* restaurant followed by a leisurely coffee, cognac and a cigar in the mahogany-panelled salon bar. During dinner he had made the acquaintance of a mysterious young Russian, the 'Countess Maria Z __' who was much taken with his playing of Chopin Nocturnes on the upright Bechstein that stood in one corner of the lounge. A romantic intimacy became quickly established between them. This was often the case with women when the handsome concert pianist played Chopin. On returning to his compartment he noticed the attendant had already turned down his bed. Soon after retiring there was a gentle knock on the door and to his surprise the Countess appeared dressed in a spectacular creation by Schiaparelli, her throat adorned with Cartier jewellery and carrying a Pekinese. He spent an unexpectedly erotic night with her as the train haltingly made its way south.*

After a fitful sleep of broken rhythms he awoke the next morning to the dazzling sunshine of the Côte d'Azur. Palm trees and a riot of yellow mimosa lined the shore of the glittering Mediterranean as he poured coffee from the chased silver pot and broke open the feather-light croissants. The Countess had silently quit his compartment during the night and he never saw her again. Eddie felt something almost deliciously sinful in this encounter as he journeyed towards the Vatican and his audience with the Pope. At Ventimiglia he changed trains to board the majestic *Rome Express* which travelled along the picturesque Ligurian coast across Tuscany to Florence and finally down to Rome.†

* Eddie often did not note or even remember the names of his 'acquaintances of the night', a phrase he used when describing such brief encounters to the author during conversations later in Monaco in 1968.

† The Blue Train inspired many writers and artists. In 1924, it inspired Serge Diaghilev and the Ballets Russes to create a ballet entitled *Le Train Bleu*. The train is featured in the

* * *

Eddie wrote an account of the Papal audience on 25 February 1935 published in the Australian *Women's Weekly.* The description by 'Mr Cahill, who has played before almost every crowned head of Europe' was breathily introduced as being 'as exciting as any film story or a novel of the sixteenth century.'

'The Glory That Is Rome!'

by Edward Cahill

> All this glory seems to be concentrated in that one vast and palatial dwelling - the Vatican. The special suite where the Pope holds audience is a dream of splendour. One enormous salon leading into another. The public reception salon, the Throne Room, and the more exclusive and smaller Thronetta where the private audiences are usually held and where I was privileged to have a personal conversation with His Holiness.
>
> Massive bronze doors, decorated with beautifully wrought panelling lead from one room to the other, and the rich claret-coloured carpet tones with the purples and wine-shades of the tapestries which cover the walls, and the brocade covering the massive gold furniture. Pomp and ceremony are everywhere. The young noblemen who form the special Papal Guard are sumptuously attired in papal blue and gold with dazzling brass helmets and long swords. It is a special honour to be appointed to the Throne Room guard, and the highest born of the young Roman nobles vie for the honour.
>
> While I waited in the Throne Room I saw the guard being changed, and a very impressive sight it was. All the ladies present who were awaiting the ordinary public audiences wore the customary veils and high-necked dresses. I wore full evening dress, tails and a white tie, which is the correct attire, although it was only one o'clock in the afternoon. I was received by Father P. Murray, Superintendent General of the Redemptorists, who a couple of years ago came out to Australia and was the guest of Archbishop Duhig of Brisbane. Archbishop Duhig had written to them. That was how I was able to have the honour of *un'udienza speciale.*

Agatha Christie's novel *The Mystery of the Blue Train* (1928). The Blue Train Races were a series of record-breaking attempts between cars and trains in the late 1920s and early 1930s. It saw a number of motorists and their own or sponsored automobiles race against *'le train bleu'*. The Blue Train Bentleys (two Speed Six Bentleys) owned by the dashing 'Bentley Boy' Woolf Barnato took part in these races.

> I must confess to feeling more excited here than I have ever felt when faced with my greatest concert audiences. The Pope is a majestic figure although, apart from the enormous emerald ring on His Holiness' first finger, he was dressed in great simplicity. The Pope talked with me in German, as he doesn't speak any English. He showed me the gold watch which he always wears, and told me it was presented to him by His Grace the Archbishop Duhig, of Brisbane and the pupils of All Hallows Convent. He pointed out that it was made of Australian gold. He sent his blessing and good wishes through me to all Australian musicians.

After the *udienza speciale* Eddie lunched with Father Murray at the *Redentoristi* and afterwards in the concert hall gave a piano recital to over 100 priests, one of them an Australian. He continues

> I was still feeling the reaction of this rich, emotional experience as I descended the noble marble staircase and made my way out to the piazza. Suddenly I heard my name called, and turned to find a young friend from the Scandinavian Embassy. I felt, and probably looked, somewhat unusual, bareheaded and in formal evening clothes on the clear winter afternoon. Besides I was in a hurry to get to the opera.
>
> Glancing at the clock I realised how little time there was, and calling good-bye to my friend I started to dash down the street. Suddenly I felt a grip on my shoulder. I was under arrest. Mussolini was to pass that way in a few minutes. There had been a warning that a dangerous character was around and I was a suspect.
>
> 'Where are your papers?'
>
> 'Why are you glancing at the Vatican clock so furtively?'
>
> 'Who are you?'
>
> I searched for my papers. Of course, I had left them at the hotel when I changed into my dress clothes for the audience. I was taken to the police-station, and kept there for some hours until my identity was proved. Of course, I missed the opera.
>
> Even so, my adventures were not over. My train, the *Rome Express,* was the ill-fated train which just missed a terrible avalanche. All the passengers had to get out and drive through the Alps by car to connect with another train.*

Eddie remained in Rome for a week or so, attending the opera and

* *Australian Women's Weekly,* Saturday 30 March 1935.

sightseeing. Early in March 1935 Sabine had agreed to meet him in Berlin to begin their short concert tour of Germany. The inveterate traveller made his way back to Cannes once more on the *Rome Express* and then joined the luxury *Riviera Express* to Berlin. After the loss of George he was greatly looking forward to performing once again with a sympathetic and talented musical partner, quite apart from the fact she had once been a distant *inamorata.* The Russian Countess was already a distant memory.

Chapter 11

Into the Jungle of Germany

The growing might of a rejuvenated Germany was clear from the train as Eddie approached the city. The line passed through forests, cut past lakes, numerous smallholdings and passed through the heavily industrialised outskirts of the capital before steaming into the imposing Lehrter Bahnhof adjacent to a bend in the River Spree. The weather in early March 1935 was still cruelly variable, bleak winds cut across the city with occasional flurries of snow.

Eddie had wanted to visit Germany for a number of reasons. His mother's side of the family were all German. He was curious about the source of his musical gifts as well as unravelling aspects of his 'difficult' personality, the obsessive attention to detail, intense concentration and almost insane perfectionism. He also wanted to replace the Grotrian-Steinweg piano destroyed in the Roscrea fire. Berlin was an important centre of piano manufacture at the time. He intended to visit the C. Bechstein factory. Before the war their grand pianos were considered to be the *sine qua non* of instruments by many great pianists. Wilhelm Backhaus, Wilhelm Kempff, Dinu Lipatti, Artur Schnabel and the composers Scriabin and Liszt all owned and admired these instruments. Sabine enthused constantly of things German and Austrian and spoke glowingly of the changes Hitler had wrought. She insisted Eddie must come and see 'the transformation of the country!' He agreed. Intellectual curiosity and love of travel were two of his most positive character traits.

Sabine was not the only enthusiast for Nazism that he had encountered in his life. Eddie was not particularly interested in politics, preoccupied as he always was with practising for concert engagements. However his Mayfair audiences were mainly conservative and some held extreme right-wing views. Most of the aristocracy he had met in the 1920s had by the middle of the following decade, under financial and social pressure, developed quite a different outlook on their lives. Democracy was called into question as an acceptable form of government by those whose education and lineage had given them a sense of entitlement. The middle and working classes were also losing faith in traditional values as the Empire seemed to be coming increasingly under duress. Unemployment was a rising threat. But the overriding fear was of creeping Bolshevism, not the Nazis. Some believed more in the dangers posed by a Judaeo-Masonic world conspiracy and practised what might be conveniently termed 'parlour anti-Semitism.'

'Uncle Matthew' in Nancy Mitford's *Love in a Cold Climate* (a caricature of her father David, Lord Redesdale) thought 'abroad is unutterably bloody and foreigners are fiends!' or he may have used his favourite term 'sewers' for undesirables, remarking 'wogs begin at Calais'. In real life Lord Redesdale was temperamentally 'one of Nature's Fascists'. The family visited Germany, where 'They were lent a chauffeur-driven Mercedes-Benz and shown all the gaudy trappings of the new regime and they returned full of praise for what they had seen.'* Redesdale, who defended Hitler as 'a right-thinking man of irreproachable sincerity and honesty', was a member of the Anglo-German Fellowship, the Right Club and the notorious pro-Nazi organisation known as The Link founded by Admiral Sir Barry Domvile. By June 1939 it had a membership of 4,300 pro-German advocates of various social classes including Gallipoli veterans and the Duke of Westminster.† Domvile, a former Director of Naval Intelligence, on a visit to Germany in 1935 praised the freedom of motorists on the autobahns and found Heinrich Himmler 'a charming personality who wears glasses and in appearance might be a benevolent professor'. Various small 'patriotic societies' of an almost 'Boy's Own' variety existed during the thirties such as the English Array, the English Mistery and the Imperial Fascist League.

There was also surprising sympathy for Italian Fascism and respect for Mussolini's social achievements. More theatrical than

---

* Jessica Mitford, *Hons and Rebels* (London 1960), p. 63.

† Richard Griffiths, *Fellow Travellers of the Right: British Enthusiasts for Nazi Germany, 1933–1939* (London 1980), p. 308.

threatening were Oswald Mosley's British Union of Fascists, whose increasingly thuggish and militaristic appearance was derided by observers. 'They look like Nazi jackboots' was one comment which attracted the rejoinder 'More like King Zog's Imperial Dismounted Hussars'.* Mosley himself was known as 'the Rudolph Valentino of Fascism'. Hitler was considered a clown by some but envied as a statesman by others. They believed he had revolutionised living conditions for the average German and was attempting to restore a deserved degree of national pride after the Great War and the disproportionate punishments of Versailles. Many at this time thought Britain should be allied with Hitler and Mussolini against Stalin.

'There is no doubt that, from an early date, the European dictatorships had an aura of glamour for certain members of London's high society. Two of London's great hostesses, Lady Cunard and Mrs Ronnie Greville, were bowled over by Nazism ...'† Nancy Astor and the Cliveden set were influential in this regard although they were never seriously engaged in the 'spiritual' metaphysics of Nazi ideology. The hostess Mrs Ronnie Greville attended the 1934 Nazi *Parteitag* in Nuremberg and returned full of such enthusiasm that her report became the talk of London. Socialites found visiting Germany as a tourist destination 'frightfully exciting'; the Nazis added a dramaturgic and dangerous spice to the Baedeker tour. More serious admirers considered Germany and Britain shared a great deal of 'common sense'.

> The Third Reich was energised from top to bottom by people who wanted to whistle a recognizable tune after a concert, who liked to be able to tell at a distance whether a painting was hung the right way up or not, and who longed for the architecture of pointed roofs, vernacular ruralism, and the Doric order.‡

Over elegant dinners hostesses, dowagers and eccentrics electrified their listeners with ebullient accounts of their travels. Sir Henry 'Chips' Channon writes in July 1936: 'George Gage lunched, and was enthralling about his visit to Germany last year when he

* Quoted in Mary S. Lovell, *The Mitford Girls: The Biography of an Extraordinary Family* (London 2001), p. 195.

† Griffiths, *Fellow Travellers of the Right*, pp. 168–9.

‡ Gerwin Strobl, *The Germanic Isle*, quoted in Robin Saikia (ed.) *The Red Book: The Membership List of the Right Club – 1939* (London 2010), p. 19.

was received by Ribbentrop, Hitler, and escorted everywhere by Storm Troopers. Honor [his wife, Lady Guinness] and I can now hardly wait to go.'* Harold Nicolson wrote angrily in his Diary on 10 April 1939 'The harm which these silly selfish hostesses give is immense. They convey to foreign envoys that policy is decided in their own drawing-rooms [...] the whole thing is a mere flatulence of the spirit.' Unity and Diana Mitford spent much time in Munich together and attended the Nuremberg Rallies. Hitler took great pleasure as he said 'in the light-hearted company of these typical young Englishwomen of today'.†

* * *

How did the rather insignificant society pianist Eddie Cahill fit into this incestuous hothouse? Quite unwittingly, Eddie had entertained many figures who would later became thorns in the side of reasonable men as war inexorably approached. Hastings Russell, the Marquess of Tavistock, 12th Duke of Bedford, was an eccentric and lonely creature in private life but liked classical music and often invited Eddie to give recitals at Woburn Abbey. His much put upon son John (known as 'Ian'), the 13th Duke, was to befriend Eddie in South Africa long after the war. 'My father had no political judgement whatsoever,' he wrote.‡

An unsavoury character, Captain Archibald Maule Ramsay, had attended one of Eddie's recitals on his second London concert tour in November 1928 at the home of Lady Stradbroke in Belgrave Square. This Eton and Sandhurst-educated Scot, valiant soldier and Member of Parliament, became increasingly inflammatory and rabidly anti-Semitic as war drew nearer. He founded the infamous Right Club in May 1939. The names of members were entered in a Bramah-locked leather-bound ledger known as 'The Red Book' and included Lord Galloway, Lord Redesdale, the Duke of Wellington, William Joyce (Lord Haw-Haw) and the spy Anna Wolkoff.§ Ramsay believed that the coming war was

* Robert Rhodes James (ed.), *'Chips': The Diaries of Sir Henry Channon* (London 1967), 8 July p. 69.

† Quoted in George Ward Price, *I Know These Dictators* (London 1937), p. 37.

‡ John, Duke of Bedford, *A Silver-Plated Spoon* (London 1959), p. 155.

§ Saikia (ed.). *The Red Book*, members of the Right Club are listed pp. 97–132.

entirely 'the work of Jewish intrigue centred in New York'. He wrote anti-Semitic verses with such derisory titles as 'Land of Dope and Jewry'. Churchill interned him under the notorious Defence Regulation 18b at the outbreak of war. The sultry and provocative Princess Mary Brenda de Chimay (née Hamilton) was also a member of the Right Club and had attended many of Eddie's Mayfair 'At Homes' and knew him well.* Much had changed in England since the innocent days of those early recitals in the fun-filled 1920s.

* * *

The Prince of Wales was the patron of the British Legion. Eddie was to play often for the Duke and Duchess of Windsor in their Parisian exile. The naive Prince made a highly controversial speech at the British Legion conference in June 1935 which gave a propaganda coup to the Nazis. In it he praised the idea of a British Legion visit to Germany and observed

> I feel that there could be no more suitable body or organisation of men to stretch forth the hand of friendship to the Germans than we ex-Servicemen who fought them in the Great War and have now forgotten all about it.

Members of the Legion often visited Germany and on one occasion were treated to a 'quiet family supper with Herr Himmler'. They found him 'an unassuming man anxious to do the best for his country.'† Some felt respectful of their 'very gallant enemy', especially the Great War ace pilots of the *Deutsche Luftstreitkräfte* (German Imperial Air Service) such as Hermann Göring. They felt an emotional need of 'justice for Germany'. This sympathy for Germany before the Second World War often came from the enthusiastic forays to the country by English tourists keen to explore the rich museums and art galleries of Dresden and Berlin. Mountaineering and hiking in the Bavarian Alps or the Black Forest were highly popular outdoor activities with the English upper classes. There was a desperate and compelling desire to avoid another war.

---

* Saikia (ed.), *The Red Book*, p. 105.

† Quoted in Griffiths, *Fellow Travellers of the Right*, p. 130.

An artist and apolitical creature, Eddie was often privy to heated, even seditious, conversations and arguments across the dinner tables of great houses following his recitals. The social order was changing and as an artist he was rarely consigned to the kitchens and tradesman's entrance. After dinner in the mansions he frequented in Mayfair, hushed but forceful masculine conversation often dealt with inflammable material concerning the policy of appeasement of the Nazis over fine cognac and cigars. Eddie was a musician, often a respected dinner guest, even a close friend of many of his hosts. But essentially he performed for them like any other 'artist of the evening' and was to all intents considered blind, deaf and invisible. Such extreme points of view as he overheard caused him some disquiet but never sufficient to compel him to report these radical opinions. When on one occasion over the port he revealed his maternal Teutonic roots he was enthusiastically encouraged by his hosts to travel to Germany 'to see for yourself'. Eddie felt a strong pro-German change of attitude taking place in Britain in 1935. Certainly his curiosity about the country had been greatly aroused.

* * *

Sabine was anxiously waiting to meet him on the platform in Berlin. They both felt rather awkward after so many years apart and both being attractive had naturally had brief affairs. They caught a taxi to the imposing Hotel Adlon on the majestic boulevard Unter den Linden opposite the Brandenburg Gate, the hotel where Charlie Chaplin, Louise Brookes (Eddie's favourite actress) and Marlene Dietrich had once stayed. Most of the afternoon and evening was spent exchanging news and attempting to plan for an increasingly uncertain social future. Playing music together thawed their initial emotional stiffness and intimate relations were soon resumed.

They danced many nights away in some of Berlin's most opulent hotels and visited bohemian nightclubs which offered entertainment for the daring. The School for Physical Culture in Grunewald displayed almost naked young people performing athletic exercises in the spirit of ancient Greece, the perfect Aryan body of Nazi ideology on display. 'Nudity, light, fresh air, sunshine, worship of living, bodily perfection, sensuousness without either false shame or prudishness.'*

Berlin at this time appeared full of energy, charm and friendliness, as if Hitler had rekindled the German spirit. Its citizens felt the country had been reborn and their pride renewed after the impotent years of the Weimar Republic. Nazism would protect them against the creeping wrath of Communism. There was much anticipation of the Olympic Games to come in 1936 and the country rejoiced in a rejuvenated national spirit, a moral strength and a feeling of growing excitement in the new and promising future. A British diplomat wrote: 'In the *Tiergarten* the little lamps flicker among the little trees and the grass is starred with the fireflies of a thousand cigarettes'.†

In stark contrast to London, Eddie noticed with disgust the ubiquitous militaristic spirit that pervaded the capital with groups of marching, goose-stepping soldiers of the freshly named *Wehrmacht* accompanied by brass bands. Laughing and singing groups of young boys of the *Hitler-Jugend* (HJ) played in controlled tasks in the Tiergarten among the elegant horse riders. Hitler had declared 1935 to be *Ein Jahr der körperlichen Ertüchtigung* or 'A Year of Physical Fitness'. Physical strength was to be considered more important in the new Germany than educational excellence.

Crude and brutal Brown Shirts were everywhere. Nazi swastikas and banners in red and black hung from public buildings that Eddie thought looked like 'washing hanging out on the line'. Cafés were packed with fashionable diners while expensive cars jockeyed with bright yellow trams and horse-drawn carriages carrying tourists.

Eddie began to feel deep disillusionment with the way the traditional German culture was disintegrating. Discrimination against Jews (albeit low key owing to the increasing international publicity for the imminent Olympic Games) bothered him greatly. He witnessed summary brutal beatings in the streets and saw a number of Jewish businesses daubed with Stars of David and crude slogans. The most ill-situated seats in the *Tiergarten* were designated for Jews and painted yellow. An unremitting and

* *Berlin in Lights: The Diaries of Count Harry Kessler (1918–1937)*, trans. & ed. Charles Kessler (London 1971), p. 395.

† Quoted in Erik Larson, *In the Garden of the Beasts* (New York 2011), p. 50.

steadily increasing process of persecution was underway.

This potential threat did not seem to worry Sabine, who felt her own Jewish origins were remote enough and her blonde Aryan appearance attractive enough to make her invulnerable. Perhaps surprisingly, along with many of her countrymen, she felt more pride in being Austrian than in her distant Jewish heritage. Her family considered themselves perfectly assimilated and even looked down upon orthodox Jews with their 'long curls and grubby kaftans'. She knew nothing of the tough anti-Semitic Nuremberg Laws then in the planning, which sought to racially define a Jew and which would condemn her entire family to an uncertain future of 'resettlement' if their origins were revealed.* Like many Austrians, she secretly hoped Germany and Austria would eventually be united in an *Anschluss* 'once more after the Second Reich, Bismarck and the Prussians'.

* * *

The English classical music world of 1935 seemed not unduly worried by the racial discrimination taking place within the great German musical institutions and orchestras. Musical life was in a ferment in Germany at the time of Eddie's visit. Orchestral appointments were becoming inextricably linked to the Nazi party's political control and 'cultural philosophy'. Otto Klemperer, Bruno Walter, Artur Schnabel and Arnold Schoenberg had already been driven out of the country and the tactically apolitical Richard Strauss would soon be dismissed as *Reichsmusikkammer* President for supporting his librettist, the Austrian Jewish writer Stefan Zweig.

---

* On 14 November 1935 the Nazis issued the following detailed definition of a Jew: 'Anyone with three Jewish grandparents; someone with two Jewish grandparents who belonged to the Jewish community on 15 September 1935, or joined thereafter; was married to a Jew or Jewess on 15 September 1935, or married one thereafter; was the offspring of a marriage or extramarital liaison with a Jew on or after 15 September 1935'. Those who were not classified as Jews but who had some Jewish blood were categorized as *Mischlinge* (hybrids) and were divided into two groups: *Mischlinge* of the first degree – those with two Jewish grandparents; *Mischlinge* of the second degree – those with one Jewish grandparent. During the second world war first-degree *Mischlinge* were incarcerated in concentration camps and ultimately deported to death camps. Sabine was a First-degree *Mischling.* (Jewish Virtual Library.)

Eddie and Sabine both greatly looked forward to hearing the charismatic Wilhelm Furtwängler conduct the Berlin Philharmonic Orchestra. On his American tour Eddie had witnessed the partisan rivalry that had erupted in New York between the high seriousness of the German conductor and the white-heat intensity and almost painful precision of the Italian Arturo Toscanini. They had never forgotten the first time they heard Furtwängler together when he conducted *Tristan und Isolde* at the Vienna Opera in 1929. Both adored the hypnotic passion and the weight of 'flowing' *legato* orchestral sound this conductor was able to produce.

However, in early December 1934, not long before their arrival in Berlin, the charismatic conductor had been fearlessly championing Paul Hindemith in the press. Furtwängler considered this musician the greatest modern German composer, but his music was deemed by the Nazis to be 'degenerate' and the composer himself an 'atonal noisemaker'. One of the main reasons behind the Nazi proscription however 'was Hitler's prudish response on seeing the 'naked' Laura in the bathtub scene of Hindemith's opera *Neues vom Tage*.'*

Furtwängler had been cunningly inveigled into 'resigning' from both the Berlin Philharmonic Orchestra and the Staatsoper for championing music 'unsuited for the movement's task of cultural reconstruction'.† He had always considered the world of politics and musical culture entirely separate, a distinction he upheld to the bitter end against all Nazi protestations. It was a belief that would cause him endless grief. His passport had been withdrawn. Hitler intended to break him 'once and for all' but declarations of loyalty poured in. International condemnation and domestic uproar followed with a wholesale return of season tickets, much to Goebbels' financial discomfort. A potentially profitable and prestigious English tour by the orchestra was cancelled. A series of guest conductors took over Furtwängler's planned concerts but they attracted little public support.

On 11 March 1935 Eddie and Sabine, deeply disappointed, attended the last occasion on which the Berlin Philharmonic's programme contained Jewish music. The virtuoso violinist Georg

* Fred K. Prieberg, *Trial of Strength: Wilhelm Furtwängler and the Third Reich* (London 1991), n. 62, pp. 349–50.
† Ibid., p. 140.

Kulenkampff performed Mendelssohn's violin concerto under Max Fiedler.* The concert was reviewed in *Der Angriff* but the concerto and Kulenkampff's sublime performance were simply omitted from the critical account, his heart-rending *portamenti* unremarked.

Germany's plans for war seemed incontrovertible to Eddie when a few days later he witnessed a full 'air-raid rehearsal' in Berlin. Göring had been planning this 'realistic experience' for six weeks. Junkers three-engined monoplane bombers and Messerschmitt fighters flew over the city in arrow formation at treetop level, lights in houses and vehicles were dimmed, fire engines roared through the deserted streets, gas mains and incendiary bombs were seen to 'explode', house windows were masked and the police checked all instructions and the issue of gas masks.

Early in April, less violently but with similar operatic melodrama, Eddie and Sabine, standing hand in hand, were among the wildly excited crowd who witnessed the spectacular state wedding of Hermann Göring to the actress Emmy Sonneman†. Looking at the infatuated crowd Eddie felt that National Socialism had infected the German people with a dangerous variety of delirium that would inevitably lead to catastrophe. Faced with a wedding one wonders what was coursing through their minds concerning the future of their own romance.

It was a sunny day. As the bridal couple drove in a massive open Mercedes limousine through the lines of some thirty-three thousand paramilitaries and Nazi storm troopers towards the cathedral, a squadron of the latest German warplanes (forbidden by the Treaty of Versailles) thundered overhead. The British ambassador, the acerbic Sir Eric Phipps, commented in a dispatch to the Foreign Office:

> A visitor to Berlin might well have thought that the monarchy had been restored and that he had stumbled upon the preparations for a royal wedding ... [in the cathedral] the German ladies

---

* Georg Kulenkampff (1898–1948) was one of the finest 20th century concert violinists and one of the best-known German virtuosi of the 1930s and 1940s. His recording career coincided with the Nazi period. This, together with his early death, means this brilliant violinist is now virtually forgotten apart from the violin competition dedicated to him. Max Fiedler (1859–1939) was a German conductor and composer and a noted interpreter of Brahms.

† Emmy Sonneman (1893–1973) was a German actress who after marriage to Hermann Göring served as hostess for Hitler on many state occasions earning the title 'First Lady of the Reich'.

> wore evening dresses and diamonds, the men wore uniform or dress clothes with decorations [...] two boys of the Hitler *Jugend* held her train.*

After the wedding Göring spent an hour alone beside his late wife Karin's grave at his monumental and ostentatious home, Karinhall.

* * *

At the end of April 1935 Furtwängler was offered a guest engagement conducting the Berlin Philharmonic for two *Winterhilfe* (Winter Assistance) concerts for the poor, prompted by pressure from the unhappy public and the Party's concern for their international reputation. His first concert was instantly sold out, ovations erupted in the street as the lanky conductor was forced to scuttle through a side door of the *Philharmonie*. Cars arriving were jammed solid. People without money even attempted to pay for tickets with pieces of Meissen porcelain or black-market cigarettes.

Thunderous applause, clearly an expression of dissent, made it difficult for Furtwängler to begin. He turned directly to the orchestra without the obligatory Nazi salute. At the end of the concert the applause lasted an hour and he was recalled to the stage seventeen times. However by agreeing to conduct this concert he was generally judged by his many critics abroad to have 'knuckled under after all'. Yet his fervent belief was to preserve the true spirit of German music which he felt was under threat. Believing passionately in the separation of culture and politics, throughout the war he was to tread the finest of cultural lines and the most skilful of moral compromises with Hitler and the Nazi leadership.

Eddie and Sabine had their wish finally fulfilled on 3 May at the second *Winterhilfe* concert when they heard Furtwängler conduct the Berlin Philharmonic in Beethoven's *Egmont*, the Symphony No. 5 and the *Pastoral* Symphony. Much to Furtwängler's annoyance (in a rage he had ripped the wooden covering off the radiator in his dressing room), Hitler, Göring and Goebbels attended this concert. On their entering the hall the audience stood to give the Nazi salute.

---

* Quoted in a full account of the wedding described in Leonard Mosley, *The Reich Marshal* (London 1974), pp. 246–8.

The conductor avoided giving this so-called 'German greeting' by turning immediately to the orchestra.

At the end, Hitler approached the podium to shake Furtwängler's hand and give him a bunch of roses. A notorious photograph of the conductor bowing to the audience, which included the grim-faced Nazi leadership, flashed around the world and indelibly stained his reputation.* The Nazis were not blind to the power of cultural propaganda and in the future would attempt to use him for this purpose and exploit his possibly naive underestimation of their political intentions.

Eddie always said this all-Beethoven concert was one of the greatest musical experiences of his life. He felt the incidental music to the play *Egmont* by Goethe captured to perfection the power, drama and heroism of the sixteenth-century Dutch nobleman, Lamoral d'Egmont. Furtwängler's approach to the 5th Symphony seemed to contain an uncanny, even fierce, anger against the Nazi regime and the *Pastoral* Symphony seemed full of that extraordinary love of nature possessed by the composer.

Furtwängler is considered a demi-God among conductors by classical musicians. Musically, Eddie felt his conducting was a lesson in complete emotional commitment. With the awkward, almost disjointed, movements of his entire body he appeared unlike any other conductor he had ever seen, the 'puppet on a string' effect, as one English orchestral violinist commented later. The beat of his baton seemed impossible to follow, but Eddie noted afterwards that this fluidity of what appeared to be improvised rhythm preserved an extraordinary precision. Furtwängler utilised tempi and attack that made him seem possessed by the spirit of the composer, especially Beethoven, Brahms, Bruckner and Wagner. It was as if there was a telepathic communication between conductor, music and orchestra.

This concert was Eddie's only glimpse of the Nazi high command. He did not at all like what he saw of the *Führer*. 'Not one distinguished feature in his entire body, frozen in such a severe expression. And that frightful hair and moustache!' he told me in

* Shirakawa, *The Devil's Music Master*, pp. 195–6 for a full account of this notorious concert and at http://www.furtwangler.net/inmemoriam/data/conce_en.htm Also Cahill's reminiscence in conversation with the author in Monaco 1968.

Monaco. Many among the English aristocracy such as Nancy Astor and the so-called 'Cliveden set' appeared fascinated by the cosmetic attractions of the Nazi uniform. The infatuated Unity Mitford waited patiently daily for Hitler's arrival at the Osteria Bavaria in Munich. When 'the greatest man of all time' finally noticed and spoke to her on 9 February 1935, she described the day as 'the most wonderful and beautiful of my life'.* Later she was to plead with him to come to an agreement with her country. Shortly after the declaration of war, she attempted to shoot herself in Munich's *Englischer Garten* with the pearl-handled pistol given to her by the Führer.

Not all visitors to Germany were impressed with the Nazis, particularly the Duff Coopers. In complete contrast, Eddie's patron Diana Cooper, perhaps with the benefit of editorial hindsight, vividly and with deliciously ill-concealed venom describes the German Chancellor in unflattering terms at the 1933 Nuremberg *Parteitag*

> At Nuremberg the beautiful town had an extra million Nazis in possession. The organisation impressed us. [...] It was not long before thunderous acclamation announced the Chancellor's advent, but it was a very long time before we heard his guttural, discordant, scrannel-speech. He passed, alone and slowly, two feet away from me [...] I found him unusually repellent and should have done so, I am quite sure, had he been a harmless little man. He was in a khaki uniform with a leather belt buckled tightly over a quite protuberant paunch, and his figure generally was unknit and flabby. His dank complexion had a fungoid quality, and the famous hypnotic eyes that met mine seemed glazed and without life – dead colourless eyes. The silly *mèche* of hair I was prepared for. The smallness of his occiput was unexpected. His physique on the whole was ignoble. Slowly he took up his position on the platform alone, while we listened to forty delightful minutes of Wagner [Duff and Diana left fifteen minutes after the oration began 'We crept out, not unnoticed. Trouble came'].†

In Germany itself in 1935 only a few perceptive intellectuals such as the writers Thomas Mann and Hermann Broch had misgivings and fears for the future. The Nazis manipulated the irrational through their fertile amalgam of music, mystical dreams, theatrical

* Quoted in Lovell, *The Mitford Girls*, pp. 181–3.

† Cooper, *The Light of Common Day*, pp. 147–8.

demonstrations of power, the occult and Norse mythology. Seductive ideas of poetic truth were fatally woven into the fabric of political truth. The perceptive, courageous and charismatic Claus von Stauffenberg, soon to recognise the madness of this demagogue and attempt his assassination, thought Hitler 'capable of inspiring the mass of the people to devotion and self-sacrifice, even though to their own disadvantage'.*

* * *

Eddie and Sabine's own concert was given not in Berlin but in the exquisite palace of Sanssouci in Potsdam. They spent the spring afternoon like many lovers wandering in the sun through the monumental park laid out by Frederick the Great, King of Prussia. The ensemble is an unsurpassed marriage of landscape and architecture created by this cultured, rather private figure of the Enlightenment. Hitler idolised Frederick and even hung a portrait of the benevolent monarch above his desk. Characteristic of the man, Frederick is now buried beside his hounds in the gardens just outside the palace in a simple grave plot without decoration. Admirers place potatoes rather than flowers upon it to indicate his lack of pretension. The architecturally modest yet sumptuously decorated palace interior delighted them especially the Rococo Music Room where they (and formerly J.S. Bach) performed.

Eddie felt a singular sympathy with Frederick the Great†. The king had been treated cruelly by his father, the obsessively militaristic Frederick William I. His son wanted to study music and learn to play the transverse flute. Dr Charles Burney, the urbane yet critical English music historian, had a high opinion of his playing when he heard him in Berlin in 1772. He wrote 'his *embouchure* was clear and even, his finger brilliant, and his taste pure and simple'. The paternal accusations directed at Frederick of betraying 'effeminate, dissolute and unmasculine preoccupations' had a painfully familiar ring for Eddie. Of course his father did not beat him in public with a

* Joachim Kramarz, *Stauffenberg: The Life and Death of an Officer* trans. Richard Barry (London 1967), p. 44.

† Frederick II (1712–86) or Frederick the Great was King of Prussia from 1740 until 1786. Apart from military victories he was a great patron of the Arts and the Enlightenment in Prussia.

cane or force him to watch the beheading by sword of his best friend as did Frederick's psychotic militarist father Frederick William.

This recital was also Eddie's first encounter with the harpsichord, albeit a heavily constructed modern Pleyel instrument with numerous pedals. He fell in love with it. In this concert with Sabine he performed a Bach Sonata for violin and harpsichord as well as various sonatas for flute and harpsichord by Frederick the Great himself and his teacher Joachim Quantz. Performing in this enchanting fairytale palace with its intimations of eighteenth century high European civilisation was an intensely romantic moment for both Sabine and Eddie.

* * *

They visited the C. Bechstein showroom Haus am Zoo in a fashionable part of Berlin. The 1930s were a particularly bad time for C. Bechstein sales. Many potential buyers disappeared in the ruthless expulsion and murder of wealthy Jewish citizens by the Nazis. Having a Bechstein pianoforte in the home of any educated Jewish bourgeois was a sign of both affluence and taste. With such low production figures the company were anxious to sell Eddie an instrument and made him most welcome.

The director, Edwin Bechstein, had died in Berchtesgaden in September 1934. On the occasion of Eddie's visit in the spring of 1935 his widow Helene Bechstein was by chance visiting the showroom and heard him trying out various instruments. She was particularly impressed with his performance of Bach and Beethoven. She learnt with enthusiasm of their forthcoming concert tour through Southern Germany with his partner, the beautiful blonde Austrian violinist who happened to be standing nearby. She persuaded them to give an extra recital at the Villa Bechstein in Obersalzberg, a mountain resort just above the farming town of Berchtesgaden. This concert would follow their performance in Munich. Eddie accepted with some reluctance but he was curious to see Hitler's secondary residence and the Nazi ruling echelon at close quarters. Sabine thought the idea quite brilliant and seemed flushed with excitement at the possibility of performing before 'those splendid young Nazi officers'.

The repertoire for their German tour included Beethoven's *Kreutzer* and *Spring* Sonatas. The concerts in Nuremberg and Weimar had been a great success. At the spa of Baden-Baden they performed in a private villa once owned by the Russian writer Ivan Turgenev. In 1865 Dostoevsky, an inveterate punter, dictated the amusing yet tragic story *The Gambler* here to his 19-year-old amanuensis Anna Grigoryevna whom he eventually married.

> With what avidity do I look at the gaming table on which are scattered *louis d'or, friedrichs d'or* and *thalers*, at the little piles of gold as they fall from the croupier's shovel in heaps of burning fire ...*

Eddie and Sabine risked a little at the tables one evening, more for romantic excitement than in the hope of winning riches. They strolled in a lovers' reverie along the picturesque Lichtentaler Allee beside the diminutive River Oos, admiring the thousands of glorious tulips and flowering magnolias. On a longer excursion to the resort of Lichtental, they passed the Brahms house where the composer had rented rooms to be close to his unrequited love, Clara Schumann. He had spent summers here from 1865 to 1874 where he completed large parts of the *Deutsches Requiem* and the First Symphony, the draft of the Second Symphony as well as many chamber works. When they tired of walking, the lovers bathed naked (separately due to Nazi prudishness) in the many pools of the grandiose Renaissance style thermal baths known as Friedrichsbad. In his journal Eddie wrote that bathing naked in such opulent surroundings was one the most sensual experiences he had ever had, 'an unaccustomed feeling of being one of Nature's children.'

In Munich they gave a recital in the *Schönheitengalerie* (Gallery of Beauties)† situated then in the *Festsaalbau der Münchner Residenz*, the monumental seat of the Wittelsbachs.‡ They played surrounded

* Dostoevsky, *The Gambler*, Chapter 17, trans. Ronald Meyer (London 2010). There is a large bronze statue of Dostoevsky in one of the Baden-Baden parks commemorating his stay and the story.

† This extraordinary collection of portraits of outstandingly beautiful women of the day was assembled by Ludwig I without consideration of birth or background. Portraits of Archduchesses, Alexandra the King's daughter, Lady Spencer and Lady Jane Ellenborough (better known as the notorious Jane Digby) were hung beside those of a beautiful butcher's or cobbler's daughter.

‡ The powerful Wittelsbach family was the ruling dynasty of Bavaria from 1180 to 1918 and of the Electorate of the Palatinate from 1214 until 1805 providing many German

by the unique collection of paintings of the most beautiful women of the epoch assembled by King Ludwig I of Bavaria. Eddie was particularly attracted by the portrait of Maria Dolores Elisa Gilbert, 'the most scandalous woman in the world', better known as Lola Montez. 'A feverish illness of the senses would take possession of some men at the very sight of her.'* She had been Liszt's lover and they lived together in Dresden during a short and violent affair. She ended up impoverished, tragically acting out the story of her own life in a circus.

* * *

Unknown to Eddie but perhaps not to Sabine, Helene Bechstein had been an admirer and patron of Adolf Hitler from as early as 1921. She is quoted as saying 'I wish he were my son' and had found his youthful shyness and naïveté rather affecting. Through her infatuation, Hitler gained access to the highest society of wealthy German industrialists. She may even have bought him a luxury red Mercedes-Benz motor car. Helene also gave him a dinner suit and patent leather shoes so he might appear well in society.

Eddie was intrigued to learn from Helene that Hitler had a favourite pianist. As she described him, he was clearly not an artist of the calibre of the immortals, but had studied with Bernhard Stavenhagen, Liszt's last pupil. He was the eccentric and visually arresting Ernst 'Putzi' Hanfstaengl, who was a member of a family of upper-class Bavarians who were fine art publishers. His mother had American roots, his wife was American and he himself was a graduate of Harvard.

Hanfstaengl's first impression of Hitler was not overwhelming. He later wrote: 'Hitler looked like a suburban hairdresser on his day off'.† The young Adolf Hitler was a frequent visitor to the family home and it was through the Hanfstaengls that Hitler had first met Helene Bechstein. 'Putzi' helped him escape in his car after the Beer

Kings and Holy Roman Emperors.

* Henry Channon, *The Ludwigs of Bavaria* (London 1952), p. 46. This delightful book is almost unknown, eclipsed by the great *Diaries*. In 1955 the film director of genius Max Ophüls made one of the masterpieces of the cinema based on the life of Lola Montez simply entitled *Lola Montez*.

† Ernst Hanfstaengl, *Unheard Witness* (Philadelphia 1957), p. 22.

Hall Putsch in 1923 and later the family supported him through the difficult Weimar years.

At the piano 'Putzi' was mainly admired for his loudness and stamina, useful attributes when performing endless accounts of Liszt's Wagner transcriptions. Hitler was put into a state of high excitement by Putzi's first performance of the overture to *Die Meistersinger von Nürnberg*. '"You must play for me often," he said. "There is nothing like that to get me into tune before I have to face the public." [...] Hitler would literally yell with delight as Putzi played "with Lisztian *fioritura* and fine romantic verve."'* He also adored the Overture and *Liebestod* from *Tristan und Isolde*, demanding it be played hundreds of times. However Putzi's playing did not impress the feisty Martha Dodd, daughter of the straight-laced and frugal American ambassador of the day, William E. Dodd. 'He always left the piano crumpled and exhausted, not to mention himself and his listeners. The rooms of the embassy reverberated with sound for days afterward.'†

Putzi became Hitler's foreign press secretary, but finally became disenchanted with a regime 'run by that Gangster clique' and fled to the United States to escape 'the last mad throw of the political desperado'.‡ He described his own life as a 'melancholic revue' and summed up his career later: 'It is a terrible thing when you think you got on a bandwagon and it turns out to be a dustcart'.§

* * *

A degree of elation had taken possession of Eddie and Sabine as the train pulled into the small station at Berchtesgaden in late May 1935. They almost felt a sense of privilege. The town was flooded with Nazi soldiers and officers as they booked into the Berchtesgadener Hof. Later that afternoon they were driven in a huge black Mercedes between fields dotted with spring flowers up to the mountain

---

* Quoted in Peter Conradi, *Hitler's Piano Player: The Rise and Fall of Ernst Hanfstaengl, Confidant of Hitler, Ally of FDR* (London 2005), p. 50. A fascinating and highly entertaining biography of a largely forgotten figure of the Third Reich, packed with striking and diverting Hitlerian anecdotes of the bizarre psychological variety.

† Quoted in ibid., p. 131.

‡ Quoted in ibid., p. 276.

§ Quoted in ibid., p. 325.

retreat of Obersalzberg and the Villa Bechstein. Eddie thought the snow-capped Untersberg massif of the Berchtesgaden Alps thrust in spectacularly Wagnerian fashion into the sky, a vista wrought by Nature to stimulate Hitler's grandiose imaginings.

Helene and her husband had completed the villa in 1927. In the early thirties it was used as a guesthouse by high-ranking Nazi officials such as Martin Bormann and Joseph Goebbels until acquired from the Bechsteins by the Party. The nearby Haus Wachenfeld was a picturesque and quiet Bavarian guest house in which Hitler used to rent rooms. He eventually purchased it outright from the enormous royalties earned from *Mein Kampf*. Gazing admirers of all ages passed by on tours. At the time of Eddie's visit the area was still an idyllic rural retreat for successful Bavarian families. These local families were to be summarily ejected, some murdered, farms hundreds of years old forcibly purchased. The superb landscape was finally commandeered by *Reichsleiter* Martin Bormann for the establishment of Hitler's headquarters known as the Berghof.

Hitler and the highest-ranking Nazis were absent from the resort at the time of the concert but a few members of the German aristocracy were holidaying in the region and had been invited to the evening by Helene. The elegant social life of the élites and nobility had been hardly affected by Nazism. 'Essentially the old aristocracy felt at ease under a regime that respected it, preserved its dignity, and drew it into an ideological adventure whose bases it shared.'* Many German aristocrats loathed the 'lack of breeding' of the new government though they wisely kept this opinion to themselves.

The audience in the villa's music room were a potpourri of glamorous women in evening gowns leaning on the arms of men afflicted with ram-rod posture and attired in *Der klassische Smoking*. They were clearly some variety of 'the aristocratic class'. They sat together with a scattering of young Nazi officers in black SS Mess Dress jackets with the *Totenkopf* (Death's head) pin, black bow tie and red Swastika armband. Eddie reflected later that he felt 'most uncomfortable and foreign among these horrifyingly handsome uniformed types'. Helene Bechstein played the perfect hostess organising the serving of the champagne, large diamonds glittering

* Fabrice d'Almeida, *High Society in the Third Reich* (Cambridge 2008) p. 235.

on her fingers. Concerts of classical music were always considered special occasions for 'the more cultured Nazis', almost mystical events.

Eddie noticed a curious light shining in Sabine's eyes as he sat at the mahogany C. Bechstein grand, something he recalled never having seen before. She turned to the predominantly military audience, lifted her violin and bow, glanced towards Eddie and the gloriously lyrical opening theme of Beethoven's *Spring* Sonata emerged like a flower. This performance was a great success and the listeners were particularly appreciative. There followed a break with further drinks and surprisingly civilised conversation. Eddie was restricted to English with a smattering of German, while Sabine carried on animated and surprisingly flirtatious conversations with various unattached Nazi officers.

She was clearly flushed and elated when they resumed the concert and confidently launched into the highly virtuosic and powerfully sensual violin opening of the first movement of the *Kreutzer* Sonata. This piece had always been a source of the deepest erotic emotions between them, a merging of like musical minds that had by now developed into a passionate personal relationship. However on this particular night Eddie felt an invisible barrier had been erected between them like a pane of frosted glass. His heart filled with premonitions and anxiety. 'There seemed to be an emotional disconnect between us during *this* Kreutzer,' he reflected later.

Encores were enthusiastically demanded and Eddie played as a solo the Alfred Grünfeld arrangement of the Johann Strauss Soirée de Vienne based on a waltz from Der Fledermaus and in addition his arrangement of the *ultra charmant* and fashionable Diner-Waltz from his operetta *Der Lebermann* (The Man About Town). These were hugely popular and Sabine joined him in their final flourish of encores: a Sarasate arrangement for violin and piano of a Chopin waltz followed by the splendidly virtuosic Henryk Wieniawski *Scherzo-tarantelle.* They concluded with the *Caprice viennois* by the great Austrian violinist Fritz Kreisler which almost reduced the Nazis to tears. The Austrian encores gave both the audience and Sabine enormous pleasure. Eddie reflected later there was clearly no recognition of Kreisler having had a Jewish father.

The successful concert concluded with a light supper. *Natürlich,* blonde blue-eyed Sabine shone before the officers. Her youthful elegant figure sheathed in her favourite close-fitting black chiffon gown enhanced by a single jewel was particularly appreciated. Eddie wrote how self-conscious he felt of his small stature in this company. Sabine was elated to be in the mountains. 'I so love the wild mountains! Eddie, you love silent films. Have you ever seen *Der heilige Berg,* The Holy Mountain, starring Leni Riefenstahl?' Eddie had to confess he knew nothing of it. 'Oh! She plays the dancer Diotima who falls in love. Her lover is a tough mountain climber played by Luis Trenker, the handsome German actor. Face like a sculpture and so athletic!'* As an Austrian she felt that mountain climbing expressed everything that was heroic, mystical and an expression of physical superiority.

Back at the hotel Sabine appeared rather detached as they emerged from the big black Mercedes. She seemed curiously uninvolved in their lovemaking that night under a cheap reproduction of the *Führer* draped in swastikas that had been nailed above the bed head. For the first time he detected something decadent about Sabine, a curious feeling of appropriateness when he envisioned her as the mistress of a Nazi officer. 'Is anything wrong?' Eddie asked but received no answer apart from a tossed off remark: 'I am so pleased you are at least half German, Eddie!'

Years before, Nellie Melba had sung for Leo Tolstoy and had recommended that Eddie read the novella *The Kreutzer Sonata* before studying the Beethoven work. In this story Tolstoy had observed: 'Under the influence of music, it seems that I feel what I do not really feel, that I understand what I do not understand, that I do what I cannot do.' Unpleasant thoughts and apprehensions coursed through Eddie's mind and kept him awake much of that night. He had begun to feel his age and her comparative youth.

---

* Leni Riefenstahl (1902–2003) was a German film director, producer, screenwriter, editor, photographer, actress and dancer widely known for directing *Triumph of the Will,* a Nazi propaganda film. *Der heilige Berg: Ein Heldenlied aus ragender Höhenwelt* (The Holy Mountain. An Heroic Song from a Towering World of Heights) was directed by Dr Arnold Fanck (1889–1974).This silent film with orchestral accompaniment was released in December 1926. Now overlooked, it belongs to the German Expressionist genre of the *Bergfilme* (mountain films). The visual power and atmosphere of the film is striking. The indestructible Riefenstahl was still scuba-diving at the age of ninety.

They travelled back to Vienna and for a period in June continued to perform together. Eddie resumed his studies with Frau Gombrich. These lessons were more intense than the first series. In helping Eddie to discover and explore his own individuality as a pianist, she introduced him to an illuminating poem written by Theodor Leschetizky* that enshrined his principles (referring to him as 'Lesche')

No life without art
No art without life
One does not win people's hearts
Only with runs of scales and thirds
But rather with a noble singing style
Clear and powerful, gentle and soft

According to Paderewski, Leschetizky's pupils 'all had a singing tone. That was very, very important'. Hans von Bülow pedantically stated: 'Anyone who cannot sing – with a lovely or unlovely voice – should not play the piano.'† This obsession with the production of a beautiful tone, a 'noble, singing melody', preoccupied Eddie as a direct result of the lessons with Leonie Gombrich. His exquisite tone was often commented upon, combined with his fine *cantabile,* a true *Fingerfertigkeit* (finger dexterity) of velvet fullness, whilst retaining delicacy, velocity and evenness of touch. She compelled Eddie to project the *meaning* of music through poetry and sensibility. She trained him in the subtle use of the displacement of rhythm, arpeggiation and achronicity.

> The base tone and the melody note need not always be taken together with rhythmic precision. [...] the melody rings out more clearly and sounds softer.‡

This affecting manner of playing was common in a subtle form among the greatest pianists before the Second World War such as Ignacy Jan Paderewski, Leopold Godowsky, Josef Hofmann, Vladimir Horowitz, Moritz Rosenthal, Vladimir de Pachmann and occasionally by Eddie himself. It has now been completely

* Theodor Leschetizky (1830–1915).

† Quoted in Kenneth Hamilton, *After the Golden Age: Romantic Pianism and Modern Performance* (Oxford 2008), pp. 139–40.

‡ Malwine Brée, *The Leschetizky Method: A Guide to Fine and Correct Piano Playing* (Original, Mainz 1902; this edition New York 1997), pp. 55–6.

abandoned. The effect Eddie created was as if 'the audience did not know what was happening, but they knew they felt something, and were experiencing something great and profound.'*

* * *

Something sacred seemed to have broken between the lovers at Obersaltzberg. Did Sabine love him in the way he loved her? It seems unlikely. Eddie's innocent and exclusive first love rather late in life appears to have shattered beneath Hitler's huge portrait that hung on the wall of the Bechstein villa. After returning briefly to Berlin for a concert, Sabine became increasingly involved with the Nazis, their 'handsome masculinity', the rising might and self-confidence of Germany. Eddie was not in the slightest sympathetic to their regime after having witnessed at first hand their brutality and militarism in Nuremberg. His fear of a future war was confirmed even more strongly when on Sabine's recommendation he went to see *Triumph of the Will* by Leni Riefenstahl. He liked the intimate scenes of medieval Nuremberg at dawn, the half-timbered houses, brooding castle, canals and wood fires. The rest he found 'indigestible propaganda that frightens me.'

The generally positive attitude of the Austrian population to the rise of the Nazis and a possible future *Anschluss* with Germany worried him. Eddie had never considered Sabine as anything other than Austrian and so quite different to the Germans.

> His Germanness [of Austrians], loyal and faithful as he feels towards it, has, through the mixture of many bloods in his veins and though historical experiences, become less single-minded, less harsh, more conciliatory, more cosmopolitan, more European.†

He warned Sabine that her distant Semitic background would eventually be revealed 'such is the thoroughness of the Teutonic mind'. She laughed gaily and told him not to be 'such a fearful old woman'.

Throughout this German concert tour Eddie had remained in

---

* Jonathan Summers, Curator of Classical Music at the British Library, on great pianists of the past.

† Anton Wildgans quoted in George Clare, *Last Waltz in Vienna: The Destruction of a Family 1842–1942* (London 1981), p. 134.

contact with his English patrons. Mrs Denny had written to him of the possibility of arranging more concerts in London and was impatient for his return from 'the heart of the enemy'. She favoured the idea of him giving a 'Jubilee Concert'*. At all events he had reached the end of his tether with the hyperactive military enthusiasm lying like an ominous cloud over German society. Towards the end of June Sabine decided to stay in Berlin, which only served to confirm his suspicions and deepen the corrosive jealousy that had been aroused in Obersaltzberg. There were tears at the station, promised letters and telephone calls, but both recognised subconsciously that the bloom of their love, if that is what it was, had been somehow blighted, perhaps forever.

*1935 was the Silver Jubilee (1910–1935) of King George V.

Chapter 12

Lost in the Darkness of Change

Eddie returned to London submerged in melancholy thoughts. His labile temperament, inability to sleep and uncontrollable surges of jealously seemed to indicate he was once again approaching the edge of a nervous breakdown. Having lost George, he now seemed to be about to lose Sabine. The exhausting train journey from Berlin had given him far too much time to ruminate on the seductive power of the booted and muscular Fascist male. It seemed an impossible concept. His feelings towards Sabine and German culture had been distorted on the tour. 'When I hear the word "culture" ... I release the safety on my Browning!'*

England was the scene of much public rejoicing in 1935, King George V's Silver Jubilee year. He had seen them through the greatest conflagration in history, the Great War. Eddie with his passionate attachment to Queen Mary was disappointed that he had missed the spectacular State Drive of their Majesties for the Thanksgiving Service at St Paul's Cathedral in May. 'Other anxieties may be in store,' the King warned, scarcely realising the prescience of this observation.

Eddie again rented the flat at 7a Manchester Street, intent on taking up the social threads of his concert life. His finances were in their usual parlous state, not assisted by the sombre economic blizzard. Being an opportunist and something of a social snob, he had no intention of allowing himself to be forced into the financial extremity

* Declared by Friedrich Thiemann, a character in the play *Schlageter* by Hanns Johst devoted to Nazi ideology through the martyr Albert Schlageter (1894–1923). He was a German saboteur executed by the French in 1923, a hero martyr of the Nazis and mentioned in *Mein Kampf.* This famous line is often misattributed, sometimes to Hermann Göring, Joseph Goebbels and sometimes to Heinrich Himmler. Jean-Luc Godard in his 1963 film *Le Mépris* has a producer say to Fritz Lang: 'Whenever I hear the word culture, I bring out my chequebook.'

of trying his luck in the north of England. He did not want to slip into the disinherited world of 'impotence and despair', the world of George Orwell's *The Road to Wigan Pier.* In Mayfair, the ladies seemed to regard him as some sort of 'pet' and cared for him with the extravagance and emotional attachment elderly women expend on their Siamese cats or King Charles Spaniels. He did not object to this treatment, but often felt smothered and financially beholden to them.

He had frequently performed for the Dowager Viscountess Harcourt and her friends at Nuneham Court, her country house in Oxfordshire. She had arranged his first valuable recital before Queen Mary in 1926 and the initial prized mention in the Court Circular. His fine playing had not been forgotten and his undoubted charisma maintained its power. The generous fees enabled him to survive in some degree of comfort but not to save. He attended parties given by the Duchess of Devonshire at St James's Palace in honour of the Duchess of York and another given by the Marchioness of Londonderry at glamorous Londonderry house, the very heart of Society and a fulcrum of power. Eddie also renewed his acquaintance with the Dowager Lady Swaythling for whom he had first played at Kensington Court in 1926.

The Dowager was becoming a close friend and staunch patron. On 8 May she was hostess at a large dinner party given in honour of the Prime Minister of Australia Mr A.J. Lyons and Mrs Lyons. She planned that he give his 'Jubilee Concert' there on the evening of June 30. Eddie's loyal patron of long-standing HH Princess Marie Louise signified her intention to attend and invited him to luncheon. The ex-King and Queen of Siam (Thailand), Field Marshall Lord Allenby* and Lady Allenby and that conspicuous exile, Milo Petrović-Njegoš, Prince Milo of Montenegro, would also attend the concert. Supper would be provided for the aristocratic audience after the recital which was soon subscribed at one guinea each for the marginally less distinguished of the sixty guests.

Prince Milo of Montenegro was a quite extraordinary character who had been educated at the élite Corps des Pages Military Academy in St Petersburg. His cousins Miliza and Anastasia had been invited

---

* Edmund Allenby, 1st Viscount Allenby (1861–1936), commander of T.E. Lawrence ('Lawrence of Arabia') in the Sinai and Palestine Campaign of World War I. One of the greatest British generals.

by Czar Alexander III to be educated at the Smolny Institute, a school for the female nobility in the same city. Both sisters were socially influential at the Russian imperial court. They dabbled in the occult and fatally introduced Rasputin to the imperial family. Prince Milo had spoken often to Czar Nicholas II and knew the younger members of the ill-fated family well, spending holidays with them in the Crimea. The tortuous history of his oft-betrayed country meant much of his life was spent wandering in exile. While in Shanghai staying at the Hotel Astor in 1924 he had a diverting dinner with a flirtatious but painfully thin US naval pilot officer's wife named Wallis Spencer soon to become the infamous Wallis Simpson.*

In an amusing divertissement, on July 3 Eddie gave a 'Viennese' charity recital of Strauss waltzes in the ballroom of Lady Dance's home in Regent's Park for HRH Princess Alice, Countess of Athlone. In 'beergarden' style all the guests at midnight sat 'informally' on the floor to eat supper, save the characterful Princess who stood regally by the piano admiring his musicianship. Eddie gave her a huge bunch of Tiger Lilies.

***

Princess Marie Louise had been interested in Eddie's career ever since she had first heard him and George perform in Mayfair in 1927. She had been greatly saddened by news of George's death and endeavoured to bolster Eddie's spirits whenever she could. Apart from her passion for music, she was a keen tennis follower, rarely missed a day's play during Wimbledon and often presented the prizes. Eddie shared her interest in tennis, having played a great deal at club level as a young man in Australia.

In perfect weather she attended the exciting Men's Singles Final of this championship on 5 July 1935 between the great English player Fred Perry† and the German aristocrat Baron Gottfried von

* The full romantic story of the gallant Prince Milo of Montenegro (1889–1978) written by his daughter is contained in *My Father, the Prince*, Milena Petrovic-Njegoš Thompson (Xlibris, Bloomington, 2000).

† The legendary Fred Perry (1909–95) was a championship-winning English tennis and table tennis player who won 10 Majors including eight Grand Slams and two Pro Slams. Perry won three consecutive Wimbledon Championships between 1934 and 1936 and was World No. 1 for four consecutive years.

Cramm.[*] Eddie's close friendship with the great Australian tennis player Sir Norman Brookes[†] and his own interest in the game often led him to attend prestigious matches.

Gottfried von Cramm was admired for his remarkably handsome 'Aryan' looks, his charm and refinement as well as for his fine sense of sportsmanship. 'Like a comet a new star fell from the tennis heavens,' wrote one French newspaper. 'If he plays tennis as well as he looks,' remarked a female member of his tennis club, 'he'll be world champion'. It was reported that he practised 'like a professor of mathematics for five hours a day'. The legendary Australian coach Harry Hopman observed: 'Gottfried was the most fluent and best-looking stroke maker I have seen in my fifty years of international tennis.' His first serve was good but his second serve was even better, 'a loathsome thing'.

However, von Cramm was homosexual and had befriended a Jewish transvestite actor Manasse Herbst at the notorious Eldorado nightclub in Berlin. This meant initially at the very least the possibility of a Nazi jail sentence, more likely execution. He led a perilous existence. Von Cramm was defeated by Perry in the Wimbledon final 6–2, 6–4, 6–4, which actually put his entire life and career in jeopardy. The British correspondent Alistair Cooke commented: 'Every year that von Cramm steps onto the Centre Court at Wimbledon a few hundred young women sit straighter and forget about their escorts.'

Sir Norman Brookes invited Princess Marie Louise and Eddie to a small dinner party he and his wife had arranged in Eaton Square after the championship. Several of the leading tennis players of the day had been invited to meet her. Walter Pate, the US Davis Cup captain, the British player Reginald Bessemer-Clark, Gottfried von Cramm and the man who would be his next opponent in an immortal Davis Cup match in 1937, the 'ugly' young American tennis virtuoso Donald Budge. Eddie had promised to play the piano informally after dinner and received unusually intense

* Gottfried von Cramm (1909–76) was a German amateur tennis champion and twice French open champion (1934, 1936).

† Sir Norman Brookes (1877–1968) was an Australian tennis champion, World No. 1 in 1907 and President of the Lawn Tennis Association of Australia. Brookes was the first non-Briton to win the men's singles at Wimbledon. He won the men's singles twice, in 1907 and 1914. He was a major figure in establishing the Australian Open, which he won in 1911.

approbation from both sportsmen and royalty.

* * *

Eddie did not hesitate to accept the invitation from the Lord Chamberlain to attend the Jubilee Afternoon Party in the grounds of Buckingham Palace on Thursday 25 July 1935 from 4 to 6.30 pm Morning Dress (Weather permitting). He would be able to renew many useful acquaintances. The weather turned out to be gloriously sunny with a huge Empire crowd of some ten thousand ambling about the tents and marquees, listening to the military bands, drinking tea and nibbling tiny cucumber sandwiches laid out on tables decorated with vibrant pink carnations. At exactly 4 pm King George V and Queen Mary emerged from a side entrance to the palace. She was dressed in beige lace and carried a pink parasol while other ladies wore long dresses with elbow-length gloves also carrying parasols. The King together with the other men were dressed in dove grey morning suits and grey top hats. They mingled with the many high Indian officials and their wives who added vibrantly coloured silks to the splendour of the occasion. Many were presented to Their Majesties under the Durbar canopy.

As Eddie circulated in the gardens, Queen Mary again briefly engaged him in conversation with her usual succinct phrases of encouragement: 'Keep up the practice!' After attending this socially inclusive gesture on the part of royalty, Eddie with the greatest relief felt he was now back 'in the swim' of London Society and his worries drifted away like a summer cloud. In August he holidayed at Elcot, the Dowager Lady Swaythling's country house on the Suffolk coast. Eddie wrote of her 'enormous enthusiasm' for Australia and Australians.

* * *

The excitement of speed had always acted like a drug on this eccentric pianist. Fast driving 'at the limit' created a wonderful elevation of the spirit. It distracted him completely from his customary destructive 'neurotic introspection and dwelling'. Eddie found he was missing the pleasure of driving the Alvis. Bowling along through English country lanes at speed in summer, wind in his hair, deep breathing the scents of nature, sometimes hearing the birdsong, gave him a similar exhilaration to playing *La Campanella a tempo* at the very limits of his piano technique. The August Bank Holiday race meeting at Brooklands promised a duel between two impossibly glamorous lady drivers: the beautiful and diminutive Kay Petre in her V12 Delage and Gwenda Stewart in the Derby-Miller. Kay won the race with a lap of 134.25 mph and both were given the coveted 130mph badge held by very few Brooklands drivers, male or female.

Since his concert tour of Siam (Thailand) in 1920 and his recital at the Royal Palace, Eddie had taken a close interest in that country and its royal family. At this time the famous Siamese driver Prince Bira* was driving at Brooklands for White Mouse Racing, supervised by his cousin Prince Chula.† In the Siam Trophy race Prince Bira came second in an ERA. Eddie wrote in detail to his cinder-track motorbike-obsessed sister Bessie in Australia about these intoxicating speed events at Brooklands. He described the British Racing Drivers' Club meeting when the legendary John Cobb and Tim Rose-Richards raced the formidable Napier-Railton. Cobb went on to win despite being hit in the face with a lump of concrete as the Members' Banking began to break up.‡ Many of Eddie's wealthy young aristocratic friends in the Paddock ('The Right Crowd and No Crowding') enthusiastically shared with him

---

* Prince Birabongse Bhanutej Bhanubandh (1914–85) was known as Prince Bira of Siam (Thailand) or by his *nom de course* B. Bira. He was a well known Formula One and Grand Prix motor racing driver competing for the Maserati, Gordini and Connaught teams among others. Two days before Christmas 1985, the impoverished Prince Bira was found dead from a heart attack in an empty railway carriage at Baron's Court Underground Station in London, an abject end to a glamorous life.

† Prince Chula Chakrabongse of Siam (1908–63) was also a member of the Siamese (Thai) Royal Family. When Prince Chula's cousin Prince Bira went to England in 1927 to complete his education at Eton, Chula was supervising a car racing team called White Mouse Racing. Prince Bira decided to drive for him in 1935. Bira's partnership with Prince Chula ended in late 1948.

‡ The Members' Banking at Brooklands was one of two built-up sections of track designed to accommodate cars racing at high speed. The other was called the Byfleet Banking. The Members' Banking was a dangerous, rough and tremendously exciting portion of the circuit where many dramas occurred. Cars became airborne or flew off the top of the banking, the drivers usually killed and their cars wrecked. Sections of the banking have been restored for nostalgic and rather safer forays into the past history of motor racing.

what was considered a 'noisy and brutal passion' by the dowagers and duchesses. They felt he should 'stick to the refinement of Mozart'. But he knew these interests to be not incompatible.

* * *

Severe gales in September and serious flooding throughout the country in November meant his patrons were more preoccupied with erecting defences and repairing destruction at their country houses than holding classical concerts. As Christmas approached and the trains began to run again Eddie decided to head for Rome where he gave a number of recitals returning to England via the relative warmth of the Italian and French Rivieras. He hoped to renew the patronage of his many acquaintances wintering at Menton. Earning a living as a society concert pianist was a fickle affair depending on the vagaries of fashion, the changeable weather and the cultivation of whimsical society women.

The year 1936 opened with unprecedented political upheavals. It would be one of the most significant and turbulent years of the decade. At home in November 1935 the National Government had been elected under the Conservative Stanley Baldwin as Prime Minister. Malcolm Muggeridge wrote of Baldwin 'His talent for making mistakes and being inconsistent without diminishing the esteem in which he is held, is unique.'[*] Europe was transfixed by the looming crisis in Abyssinia (Ethiopia), which had erupted into full-blown war when Italy invaded the country in October 1935. The word 'peace' and pleas for peace tumbled desperately from the lips of most European statesman. No one wanted another war and most politicians were prepared to sacrifice almost anything to avoid it. Muggeridge wrote 'Rats, when they find a carcass, take watchful bites at its extremities; then prudently withdraw to see whether any ill consequences follow before attacking the main portions.'[†] Mussolini's 'triumph of Fascism' in Abyssinia – guns, tanks and planes against spears and antiquated firearms – had exposed the impotence of the League of Nations. The Emperor of Ethiopia Haile Selassie, or more ironically, 'the Lion of Judah', sought refuge in Bath.

* Malcolm Muggeridge, *The Thirties 1930–1940 in Great Britain* (London 1940), p. 208.

† Ibid., p. 163.

Adolf Hitler too was to follow the example set by the rat. The paralysis of the League gave him the confidence to exploit unopposed aggression. He began to treat the terms of the Versailles Treaty in a cavalier fashion. The *Führer* and his fantastic aspirations were initially regarded as the antics of a clown, then observed with incredulity followed by that grim fascination the insane inspire loping about their asylum, finally raw fear. Trivially amusing, an English publican advertised his brew as having 'put the hit in Hitler'. Churchill remained a lone voice in the wilderness calling for rearmament and warning against the expansion of the German *Luftwaffe*.

The first signs of that dark year are revealed in Eddie's correspondence. A letter from Sabine gave an enthusiastic account of a spectacular ball she had attended in Berlin early in January to celebrate the forty-third birthday of the Minister for Air, Hermann Göring. She had been accompanied by the same young Nazi officer she had befriended in Obersaltzberg during the recital at Villa Bechstein. She told Eddie that many said it was the most spectacular celebration since the days of the Kaiser: 'There were such wonderful jewels! The Nazis certainly throw a good party! Reinhard loves music and I danced a lot. But don't worry, we are only good friends.' she assured him. He did not believe it for a moment.

Concerning parties Eddie Cahill was at heart as much of a *bon viveur* as Arthur Rubinstein. His battered address book was jammed to bursting with aristocratic names, addresses and phone numbers. Famous London restaurants of the day are also listed alongside his detailed views on food and price. He was also a connoisseur of wine. He patronised the renowned Berry Bros. of St James's and became a good friend of the director Francis Berry, 'a gentleman in every sense of that word.' Very much his own man, Francis Berry thought it an excellent idea to begin the day's work at 4 pm much to the dismay of his staff. He was famous for his hospitality and generosity. On one occasion after dinner at his Wimbledon home, following a performance of some Mendelssohn *Caprices* and *Songs Without Words*, Eddie was presented with a valuable drypoint of the wine merchant by the famous artist Muirhead Bone*. Berry is

* Muirhead Bone (1876–1953) was born in Glasgow, and trained originally as an architect.

depicted standing in the shop in St James's before a burbling gas fire, the walls hung with cartoons by 'Spy'.*

* * *

Letters and envelopes from Eddie's English patrons edged in deepest black soon began to fall into the cage on the front door.

Duff Cooper opens his 1936 journal with the title 'Diary of the New Reign':

> I was talking about claret and burgundy to Mr Berry in his wine shop at the bottom of St James's Street on Friday afternoon, January 17, when he suddenly pointed to the street and exclaimed 'I don't like that'. It was a poster with the words 'The King – A Cold'.†

The king had been suffering from long-term bronchial problems. On the evening of 20 January, only three days after the news of his contraction of 'a cold', it was announced by the royal physicians that 'the king's life is moving peacefully towards its close'. This famous observation was drafted by Queen Mary herself.

Eddie sat by the radio unable to do anything constructive, the message being repeated every fifteen minutes. At five minutes before midnight on 20 January 1936 it was announced the king was dead. We now know that at Sandringham the royal physician Lord Dawson eased his passing in a manner unacceptable today

> At about 11 o'clock it was evident that the last stage might endure for many hours, unknown to the patient but little comporting with the dignity and serenity which he so richly merited and which demanded a brief final scene. Hours of waiting just for the mechanical end when all that is really life has departed only exhausts the onlookers and keeps them so strained that they cannot avail themselves of the solace of thought, communion or prayer. I therefore decided to determine the end and injected

---

He began making prints in 1898, without any formal training. Although his first known print was a lithograph, he is better known for his etchings and drypoints, usually produced in relatively small editions. He was appointed the first Official War Artist, serving with the Allied Forces on the Western Front in the First World War, and served again as a war artist in the Second World War. He was knighted in 1937.

* Biographical material on Francis Lawrence Berry (1876–1936) from Berry Bros & Rudd house journal *Number Three*, Autumn 1976, pp. 19–24.

† Norwich (ed.), *The Duff Cooper Diaries 1915–1951*, p. 225.

(myself) morphia gr. 3/4 and shortly afterwards cocaine gr. 1 into the distended jugular vein.*

Even the time of the King's death had to follow a protocol. It had been decided that if the hour of the demise was controlled, notices could appear 'in the morning papers rather than the less appropriate evening journals'. Universally popular, King George V was a sovereign of apparently simple tastes whose mind, character and devotion to public service was deeply respected by all his subjects. The court went into mourning and Mrs Ernest Simpson wore black stockings in a rare gesture of social empathy. Play at the Casino in Monte Carlo was suspended for a minute's silence.

A few days later the body was brought to King's Cross by special train from Wolferton station. Eddie watched the coffin taken in procession to the lying-in-state in Westminster Hall. The cortege turned into New Palace Yard, the gun carriage having been followed two miles on foot by the former Prince of Wales, now King Edward VIII. Suddenly the cross from the Imperial State Crown perched on the coffin fell off into the gutter. 'Christ, what will happen next!' Edward was heard to mutter as a soldier retrieved the jewel. It was noticed that the Prince's gait following the procession seemed curiously lacking in pride and determination.

On 23 January a short service was held in the Hall in the presence of the Royal family. The lying-in-state lasted five days and Eddie along with a quarter of a million others filed past the dead sovereign. A staunch monarchist, on a damp and foggy 28 January, Eddie stood by as the king's coffin on a gun carriage was taken in ceremonial procession drawn by a Royal naval gun crew to Paddington Station whence it was conveyed to St George's Chapel Windsor for burial.

Eddie experienced a deep fit of depression whenever news of a prominent death came to his notice. His favourite author Rudyard Kipling had died only two days before the king on 18 January. He had read Kipling stories with great enjoyment during his concert tour of India in 1920. Eddie noted gloomily in his journal that with his own recurrent illnesses and romantic trials, he too had begun to feel the cold draught of the reaper upon his neck.

---

* From the published clinical notes of Bertrand Edward Dawson, 1st Viscount Dawson of Penn (1864–1945).

* * *

Eddie was not greatly interested in politics or events outside his immediate social circle. His preoccupation was how to survive financially in London at the expensive social level he had chosen to inhabit. He spent a great deal of time drumming up concert engagements through the good offices of his duchesses and dowagers and using his own social adroitness. At this time he was living hand to mouth and desperate for engagements. He was feeling wretched about Sabine's apparent coldness and her flirtation with the Nazis. Telephone calls to Berlin had become an addictive nightmare. As an attempt to distract himself after one concert, Eddie invited to dinner the highly sexed and darkly alluring brilliant pianist Harriet Cohen ('Tania') who happened to be briefly in London. They danced and played duets at a few *soirées*, but this definite 'opportunity for a sensual alternative' was wasted on him. His deeper emotions were engaged elsewhere in Berlin.

More immediate was the preparation and practice for an important recital at Australia House at the beginning of July under the patronage of HRH Princess Beatrice and HH Princess Helena Victoria. Unfortunately, no programmes or reviews of this concert survive. However a letter from the Dowager Lady Swaythling enthused: 'Dear Edward, I have never heard you play better. It was splendid. 1000 congratulations.'

When the Spanish Civil War broke out in July 1936 Eddie's invitation to the annual Afternoon Party given by King Edward VIII seemed infinitely more important than General Franco battling the Republicans or the recruitment of idealistic men for the International Brigades. In vain he had been trying to persuade Sabine to come to London to accompany him for tea in the palace gardens. She seemed increasingly evasive and cold on the expensive trunk calls. 'I am not sure you will have enough money for me, Eddie. There are things I want to do.' A male voice occasionally answered the phone in stentorian tones which caused Eddie to hang up immediately.

The Afternoon Party on 21 July was the first social gathering to be held at Buckingham Palace since the death of King George V. Queen Mary had by now adopted full mourning and was absent. To receive the debutantes King Edward VIII was seated on a crimson and gold chair of state under an Indian Durbar tent. It began to rain heavily and the debutante ceremony was temporarily abandoned. Eddie, perhaps because he was an Australian, liked and greatly respected the 'modern outlook' of Edward VIII. His informal, even fashionable stance, did not endear the king to the Establishment who were fearful of any perceived threat to the status quo and their dominance of society.

* * *

During July 1936 a generally unknown but distinctly ominous event took place when Ernest Simpson moved to his club and out of the home he shared with his wife Wallis. He soon set in motion the divorce proceedings both desired by spending a compromising night at the Hotel de Paris at Bray with a lady intriguingly named Buttercup Kennedy. Special Branch referred to him as being 'of the bounder type' and Mrs Simpson as being 'very partial to coloured men'. None of these findings surfaced in the public domain.[*]

Eddie followed the progress of the developing affair with his usual close attention, following at least the limited revelations in the press and the gossip among his patrons. In August Wallis had embarked *toute seule* on a yachting cruise along the Dalmatian coast, through the Greek islands, the Aegean and the Bosphorus aboard the luxury twelve-bathroom steam-yacht *Nahlin* belonging to Lady Yule, chartered by the king. Duff Cooper wrote in his diary on 20 January 1936 before the cruise: 'I think she is a nice woman and a sensible woman – but she is as hard as nails and she doesn't love him.'[†] Speculation over the king's relationship to Wallis Simpson reached fever pitch. Close observation of the couple ensued. 'Chips' Channon in his diary considered that 'The Mediterranean cruise was a Press disaster'[‡] and further that 'The King is insane about Wallis, insane'.[§] The Minister 'Shakes' Morrison thought the king had behaved 'like a petulant lunatic, and there is nothing to

* Gardiner, *The Thirties: An Intimate History* (London 2010), p. 545.

† Norwich (ed.), *The Duff Cooper Diaries 1915–1951*, p. 228.

‡ James (ed.), *'Chips': The Diaries of Sir Henry Channon*, p. 79.

§ Ibid., p. 84.

be done to save him from himself. He must go'. Eddie overheard many indiscreet conversations over dinner in great houses after his concerts in his unusual role of 'friend and classical pianist'. The notion of abdication remained unthinkable, even among the well-connected in society.

More personal matters were on Eddie's mind such as the direction of his musical and pianistic career. His unrequited love for Sabine continued to blight his moods. He knew she was free to attend many events during the summer Olympic Games in Berlin that August. He tortured himself wondering which Nazi officer might have facilitated her invitations and possibly afterwards accompanied her to exotic nightclubs catering to who knows what questionable sexual tastes.

Eddie distracted himself from his financial plight, the gathering clouds of another war and his private emotional agonies by visiting the theatres in Shaftesbury Avenue. Much of his youth had been spent playing the piano in the silent cinema and vaudeville so the lively London theatre scene attracted him enormously. In October he was reduced to tears by Robert Morley in one of his first acting roles in the play *Oscar Wilde* by Leslie and Sewell Stokes.* Eddie had written in a note on the performance, perhaps enigmatically 'Ah! The terrible dangers of following one's heart in that way.' James Agate, who had favourably reviewed Eddie and George in 1923, wrote in his own baroque style that Robert Morley, who played 'O.W.'

> differentiated very cleverly between the overblown peony which was Oscar in the witness box and the bedraggled rhododendron he became in the dock. I shall long remember that Awful Face ... the play's total gesture is to point the peculiar tragedy of the homosexual, which is that of the tight-rope walker preserving his balance by prodigies of skill and poise and knowing that the rope may snap at any moment.†

---

* Sewell Stokes (1902–79) was a well-known English novelist, biographer, playwright, screenwriter and broadcaster. For many years he lived with his brother Leslie Stokes opposite the British Museum.

† James Agate, *The Selective Ego: The Diaries of James Agate* Tim Beaumont (ed.) (London 1976), p. 48. These highly entertaining, unjustly neglected diaries give a fine and colourful period portrait of the London theatre scene before the outbreak of war.

* * *

On the night of 30 November 1936 Eddie received an emotional phone call from the composer Roger Quilter who was visiting a musician friend living near Sydenham. He hurried over to the house and watched in horror as the dark skies over London turned a desperate and feverish orange. He knew fires. The great Victorian structure of glass and steel known as the Crystal Palace was ablaze.

This remarkable building designed for the Great Exhibition in 1851 was a venue in the 1930s for numerous concerts. The area became a part of London where many eminent musicians lived. Eddie watched in dismay as the great central transept of glass and steel collapsed in a rumbling inferno like a scene from *Götterdämmerung*. He remembered the horror of watching his own house in Beenleigh burn to the ground reducing everything he valued to ashes. 'The fire raged for the entire night, windows and metal liquefying in the intense heat fanned by the wind', he wrote in his journal. Only the two great water towers designed by Isambard Kingdom Brunel remained as a bleak testimony to the genius of Victorian engineering. In hindsight the fire came to be seen as an omen for the conflagration and upheavals to come.

In early December the newspapers broke their self-imposed silence and the world suddenly learnt that Edward VIII was deeply in love and wanted to marry 'that woman', the divorcee Mrs Simpson. Harold Nicolson thought Society minded her being an American rather than divorced, while the bulk of the country considered her being divorced far more serious than being American. After the initial eruption of horror, the lava of personal invective wound its fiery way through the capital. The Prime Minister Stanley Baldwin refused to countenance a morganatic marriage.[*] He thought the Cabinet would certainly resign over the issue and the Dominions reject the idea. This gave the king an invidious choice – renounce Wallis or abdicate.

London was divided in its sympathies. 'Chips' Channon

---

* A morganatic marriage is a legally valid marriage between a male member of a sovereign, princely, or noble house and a woman of lesser birth or rank, with the provision that she shall not thereby accede to his rank and that the children of the marriage shall not succeed to their father's hereditary dignities, fiefs, and entailed property (*Encyclopaedia Britannica*).

separated the camps into Cavaliers and Roundheads. In the deprived North, the handsome and charming Prince of Wales was extremely popular. He had supported the downtrodden with true and unaccustomed warmth of feeling. 'Something must be done' he was heard to say. Mrs Simpson's windows were broken in Cumberland Terrace. She fled secretly to Cannes by chauffeur-driven car together with a detective and spent interminable hours and wretched days on the telephone to the king.

> The Abdication in December 1936 was a personal tragedy for those involved. Edward VIII departed in a state Queen Mary described as 'absolutely unhinged'. Although he professed never to have regretted his decision, one look at his eyes told a sadder story. [...] the Abdication is not one of the great romances of the twentieth century, it is one of the great tragedies.*

Harold Nicolson in a letter to Vita Sackville-West on 7 December relates that after a long final desperate meeting between the Prime Minister Stanley Baldwin and the king, both were walking in the garden of David's beloved Fort Belvedere. They returned at length to the library. Baldwin raised a glass of whiskey and soda and declared in the form of a toast: 'Well, Sir, whatever happens, my Mrs and I wish you happiness to the depths of our souls'. On hearing this, the king burst into tears and Baldwin too then fell to weeping, both of them seated on the sofa, 'blubbering'. A bizarre moment indeed.†

Wallis certainly did not want Edward to abdicate. He personally bears most responsibility for the final decision. Lord Brownlow the peer, courtier and friend of the Prince of Wales, saw Wallis 'moaning and sobbing while King Edward gave his farewell broadcast'. She was cowering under a rug 'with my hands over my eyes, trying to hide my tears' at the Villa Lou Viei at Cannes. The Instrument of Abdication was signed on 10 December. 'I have never known in any assemblage such accumulation of pity and terror', wrote Harold Nicolson of the mood in the House of Commons that day. Lady Nancy Astor sang out to 'Chips' Channon in the Chamber 'People

---

* Hugo Vickers, *Behind Closed Doors: The Tragic Untold Story of the Duchess of Windsor* (London 2011), p. 288. An extraordinarily moving book full of sympathy for the plight of all the protagonists. A tale worthy of Balzac.

† Nicolson, *Diaries and Letters 1930–39*, pp. 282–3.

who have been licking Mrs Simpson's boots should be shot'.[*]

Eddie wrote in a letter to his sister 'The country will fall apart. Everyone I know is rather vicious towards them but I like them both! Oh dear me ...' Virginia Woolf wandering down Whitehall felt 'slightly yet perceptibly humiliated ... I thought what a Kingdom! England! And to put it down the sink ... Not a very rational feeling. Still it is what the Nation feels'.[†] Eddie moved in upper class circles where wildly differing opinions of the abdication were forthrightly expressed. 'What a bloody shit! Now we are going to get a republic,' exclaimed Baroness Rothschild when she heard of Edward VIII's abdication.[‡] Queen Mary lamented his lack of spine. 'It seemed inconceivable to those who had made such sacrifices during the war that you, as their king, refused a lesser sacrifice.'[§] Lady Ottoline Morrell put the entire relationship down to a unique sexual affinity: 'I believe really that the poor little fellow has found at last a woman with whom he could be sexually happy & think this has never happened before'. Unity Mitford was heard to whisper to her companion: 'Oh, Hitler will be terribly unhappy about this. He wanted Edward to stay king'.[¶] Finally Harold Nicolson wrote laconically in his Diary on 11th December: 'Thus ends the reign of Edward VIII. Back to my steak-and-kidney pie. Down to Sissinghurst.'[**]

* James (ed.), *'Chips': The Diaries of Sir Henry Channon*, p. 99.

† Quoted Gardiner, *The Thirties: An Intimate History*, p. 468.

‡ Quoted in Gardiner, *The Thirties: An Intimate History*, p. 478.

§ Quoted inVickers, *Behind Closed Doors*, p. 289.

¶ Quoted in Barrow, *Gossip: A History of High Society from 1920 to 1970*, p. 86.

** Nicolson, *Diaries and Letters 1930–39*, p. 287.

CHAPTER 13

'SKELETONS COPULATING ON A TIN ROOF'

The year 1937 was considered by Harold Nicolson politically to be the 'year of no surprises'*, though for Eddie Cahill it was an excellent year full of musical wonders. The Prime Minister Stanley Baldwin resigned in May and was succeeded by Neville Chamberlain, who would play a pivotal role in the future destiny of Britain. Industrial output was improving and motor car production increased. There was even a boom in the housing industry. Abroad, Nazi Germany continued its insidious propaganda campaign and demanded the return of her colonies. The status quo seemed to be being maintained in Italy. The ferocity of the Spanish Civil War increased. In April the bombing of the small town of Guernica in the Basque province of Vizcaya was universally regarded in Europe as an atrocity.† In May, short of funds and hoping to meet Sabine, Eddie with grave reservations agreed to another short concert tour of France and Germany. Sabine failed to contact him.

British diplomatic policy remained rather static through the year, underpinned by the belief that peace was still possible. War was to be avoided *at all costs*, although the pace of rearmament continued to increase. The perpetual background threat of conflict was like the distant hum of a massive machine, unceasing but not particularly worrying. The threat was emphasised by the government announcement that gas masks were to be ordered for every Briton. On 6 May, in hindsight what could be seen as a premonition of the coming catastrophe, the great German airship

* Nicolson, *Diaries and Letters 1930–39*, p. 310.

† On 26 April 1937 the Basque government reported some 1,654 people were killed and 889 wounded. These figures are disputed and revised down by various Spanish studies. Nazi Germany denied responsibility.

Hindenburg crashed in flames in Lakehurst, New Jersey.

London Society was engrossed in the preparations for the coronation of King George VI and Queen Elizabeth on 12 May (the planned date for the coronation of Edward VIII). Prince Albert had only reluctantly taken over the kingship from his brother in mid-December 1936 but he felt himself a naval man and completely ill-equipped for the role of King. Eddie remained a fierce monarchist and with his talent for connections made sure he achieved a superb view of the glittering coronation procession. He was seated on the balcony of Mrs Harding's apartment overlooking the former East Carriage Drive near Marble Arch. The magnificence of the day reflected a continuing statement of undiluted imperial power.

The entire route from Buckingham Palace to Westminster Abbey was lined with guardsmen, naval cadets, midshipmen and other servicemen and women. The eighteenth-century Gold State Coach in which the King and Queen rode, an opulent and grandiose carved object weighing four tons, was drawn by eight Windsor Greys with one mounted and one ambulant postillion per pair. In addition to the mounted Life Guards, burnished and resplendent, the Yeomen of the Guard proceeded on foot. The mounted King's Escort from the Indian Army gave additional and extraordinary exoticism to the event. Eddie even managed to distinguish himself in this vast throng as he was included in the panoramic photograph published in the *Daily Telegraph* the following day.

The Duke of Windsor and Wallis Simpson were married on 3 June 1937 at the Château de Candé, Monts, Indre-et-Loire in the pastoral surroundings of Touraine lent by the American businessman Charles Bedaux. Completely ostracised by the Royal Family and aristocracy, a few close friends nevertheless braved censure and attended the modest ceremony. Their union was blessed by the obscure 'Kensite', agnostic and dissenter cleric, the Rev. R.A. Jardine of the Durham Diocese, a 'large-nosed, bulgy-eyed, red-faced little man.'* Possibly the worst disappointment for them both, particularly Edward, was that Wallis was to be deprived of the title 'Her Royal Highness'. Lady Alexandra ('Baba') Metcalfe, the wife of the Duke's old friend 'Fruity' Metcalfe, perceptively confided to her diary

* Kensites were puritans who devolved from the High Church, deeming it idolatrous. Lady Alexandra ('Baba') Metcalfe's diary quoted above, Vickers, *Behind Closed Doors*, p. 318.

The effect is of an older woman, unmoved by the infatuated love of a younger man.

The simple menu for the wedding reception comprised a cold course (York ham, crayfish, *foie gras,* caviar, Russian salad) two hot courses (lamb and vegetable casserole and pullet fricassee and chicken) and for the sweet, pastries and fresh fruit salad.* They left Candé to enjoy the hospitality of Count Paul Munster's Schloss Wasserleonburg in Carinthia in Austria the very next day.

Perhaps the reception of news of the wedding in aristocratic London is most succinctly expressed in a letter written by Niall Campbell, the 10th Duke of Argyll to the Rev. Bartholomew Hack, reporting the view of the Brazilian Ambassadress: 'how utterly that odious woman seemed to have mesmerised that nitwit.'† Eddie was however to come to a quite different opinion of them both when playing Mozart and Chopin at their home in Paris in 1945.

* * *

The clearest evidence of pro-German sentiment running through upper-class society was at the Interzone Final of the Davis Cup at Wimbledon in July between the American Don Budge and the German Baron Gottfried von Cramm: the number one in the world pitted against the number two, America against Nazi Germany (despite the fact Cramm was anti-Nazi), democracy against fascism. This match achieved the reputation of being 'the greatest match ever played.' The stands were packed to capacity, as was the Royal Box.‡

HH Princess Marie Louise had made sure Eddie received privileged tickets for the match and he watched intently from the stands. Queen Mary was present, other members of the Royal family and prominent politicians. Hollywood was represented by Paul Lukas, Ed Sullivan and Jack Benny. Budge, the homespun son of a Scottish immigrant laundry truck driver, was performing against the aristocratic grace of Baron von Cramm, who was risking

---

* Menu discovered during the author's research visit to the Château de Candé in 2012.

† Vickers, *Behind Closed Doors*, p. 319.

‡ A full account of this legendary match is given in Marshall Jon Fisher, *A Terrible Splendour: Three Extraordinary Men, a World Poised for War, and the Greatest Tennis Match Ever Played* (New York 2009), pp. 208–24.

everything on the outcome of the match: 'I am playing for my life' he coolly observed. Homosexuals were being rounded up and brutally murdered in Nazi Germany. An apocryphal story says Cramm received a telephone call from Hitler wishing him luck just as he was walking from the dressing rooms towards Centre Court. Cramm received tremendous spectator support as the match progressed and his win seemed inevitable. He won the first two sets 6–8, 5–7 however the contest began to turn in the American's favour. By 'grim and reckless determination' Budge won the next three sets 6–4, 6–2, 8–6 and the two and half hour match.* James Thurber thought the match 'something close to art'. Merely a year later Baron Gottfried von Cramm was languishing in a Gestapo prison, a damp and gloomy dungeon, charged with 'moral delinquency'. After the war he was briefly married to the fabulously wealthy heiress Barbara Hutton and died in a car accident in 1976.

* * *

Eddie's love of theatre often took him to the West End. Although certainly no socialist, he had been 'terribly moved' by the play *Love on the Dole*.† Although a snob, his temperament was at base that of an egalitarian Australian, not prey to the corrosive nature of the English class system. He well remembered the endless days of drudgery as a youth working long hours in the drapery and his father's hotel.

A vignette of his life as a pianist is instructive of his egalitarian attitudes. He had been engaged to play by a wealthy American hostess, a rather less grand personage than his customary dowagers and duchesses. On his arrival at the appropriate time, he was ushered into the servant's quarters and told to wait in the housekeeper's room. In keeping with the changing times, in the houses of the aristocracy he was more often respectfully invited to mingle with the guests before a performance. 'Are you sure there

* *Chicago Daily Tribune*, 31 July 1937.

† *Love on the Dole* was a novel (1933) by Walter Greenwood (1903–74) adapted for the stage in 1934 by the dramatist Ronald Gow (1897–1993). The work dealt with working class poverty and unemployment in the North of England (Salford) in the 1930s. The drama critic of *The Times* wrote: 'Being conceived in suffering and written in blood, it profoundly moves its audience.'

isn't some mistake?' he asked politely of the butler. He waited for some time for 'the summons' becoming increasingly impatient as time passed.

Impulsively he asked the housekeeper to gather together those servants who were not occupied in the servant's hall. During his career Eddie had often been surprised by the increasingly detailed classical musical knowledge of servants in the grand houses he performed in. He felt this to be a result of the new recordings and the advent of wireless broadcasts.* Musical education always remained uppermost in his mind. He would often address the audience directly, explaining his programme and the logic of his choice of pieces. Surprisingly the servants would often whisper a request for a specific piece. Bearing this in mind he played the entire programme for the staff on a modest upright piano in the basement. An hour had passed before the hostess eventually sent for him saying she was now ready to hear him play. He went upstairs and to her embarrassment declared 'There must be some mistake, Madam. I arrived at the stated time and have already played. Good evening to you.' And then he left. He received his cheque.

* * *

For Eddie Cahill 1937 was predominantly the year of the harpsichord. He was always alert to historical discoveries and the opportunity to offer his audience variety and novelty. 'Keeps the men awake!' he once joked. The fate of an unemployed musician in London living in lodgings was all too dreadful for him to contemplate. He had seen the beggars on the streets of the capital and the homeless sleeping underneath the arches at Charing Cross. He wanted to avoid this all too common fate and fulfilment of his father's prophesy of musicians ending up in the gutter.

One evening at dinner with the Dennys at Horwood, he made the acquaintance of a Major George Henry Benton-Fletcher. This

* The BBC considered their mission was to broadcast opera, symphonies and chamber music so that 'the shepherd on the downs, or the lonely crofter in the farthest Hebrides and, what is equally important the labourer in his squalid tenement in our all too familiar slums, or the lonely invalid on her monotonous couch, may all, in spirit, sit side by side with the patron of the stalls and hear some of the best performances in the world.' Quoted in Gardiner, *The Thirties: An Intimate History*, p. 513.

interesting character had served in the Boer War, was a social worker in south London and had excavated with Flinders Petrie on archaeological sites in Egypt. A strongly patriotic man, he was not a musician but intensely devoted to the preservation of significant works of English art, furniture and artefacts. 'Ancient' music, old instruments and ancient monuments fascinated him.

As a collector he was impressed by the cabinet craftsmanship and rich sound of the magnificent English harpsichords of Jakob Kirckman and Burkat Schudi. The Major certainly did not share Sir Thomas Beecham's acidic observation: 'The sound of a harpsichord? Two skeletons copulating on a tin roof in a thunderstorm.' Benton-Fletcher began to collect these instruments and also historical English spinets and virginals at a time when interest in such things was considered the height of eccentricity. To provide the harpsichords with an appropriate setting he purchased the run-down aristocratic seventeenth-century residence of Old Devonshire House in Bloomsbury in London.

Benton-Fletcher restored the house and in 1937 gave it and its entire contents to the recently founded National Trust. 'It is not to be a dead museum of glass cases, but a living institution with performances of music & lectures upon kindred subjects,' he wrote in a letter to the Friends of Music Society.* Eddie arranged to visit the collection and play the instruments. He had been interested in the harpsichord ever since playing at the Sanssouci Palace in Potsdam with Sabine in 1935. He was captivated by the baroque and early classical repertoire performed on these authentic instruments.† At the outbreak of the World War II, the Major rusticated his instruments. The beautiful aristocratic residence he had restored from a ruin was bombed in the Blitz, destroying not only the lovely old building in Bloomsbury but also an entire ancient music library, his collection of valuable paintings and the precious original harpsichord stands.

* Quoted in Mimi S. Waitzman, *The Benton Fletcher Collection at Fenton House: Early Keyboard Instruments* (London 2003), p. 94.

† Before beginning this quest I had left the piano for a time and taken up the harpsichord. An extraordinary wave of emotion passed over me when I discovered quite by chance browsing through the newspaper clippings in the trunk that Eddie had also taken up the harpsichord in London. As so many parallels in our very different lives began to fall into place, similarities of musical outlook unearthed, similar character traits revealed, I became at once elated and yet unsettled.

* * *

Eddie had long been an admirer of the great Polish harpsichordist Wanda Landowska but in her far lesser-known guise of concert pianist. He thought highly of her recent recording in London of the Mozart Piano Concerto No. 26 in D major K 537 with the London Philharmonic Orchestra under Walter Goehr. 'A great artist as opposed to simply a great instrumentalist,' Eddie observed. This recording of the concerto, popularly known as the *Coronation,* was released in celebration of the Coronation of King George VI. The intimacy of her tone, elegance, refinement and lightness of touch which she had developed playing *fortepianos* spoke directly to him. His own style of playing Mozart on the piano had a similar radiant delicacy. 'Mozart and Bach are the greatest of composers!' he often exclaimed. Mozart solo keyboard works or the Bach *Das Wohltemperierte Klavier* were not then popular in recital programmes.

He knew that Landowska had caused a musical revolution with her revival of the harpsichord. She had made a legendary visit to Russia in 1907, first to Moscow and then later (with her harpsichord perched precariously on a sled) to play for Leo Tolstoy at Yasnaya Polyana. 'Tolstoy was the most musical being I have ever met,' she commented later.*

At this time Eddie was very much in a *humeur ancienne.* On a recent short concert tour of France he had played at a concert arranged by Marie de Faucigny-Lucinge at the Château Vaux-le-Penil at Melun near Paris and at her palatial home at 2 Rue Rude in the XVI arrondissement.† The interior decoration of both buildings was strongly redolent of eighteenth-century France, the world of Jean-Antoine Watteau and his delicious depictions of lovelorn *fêtes galantes.* All he needed was period harpsichord music to complete

* Wanda Landowska (1879–1959) is little known as a pianist but her Mozart recordings are surely some of the finest in existence. She had always loved the piano and regretfully abandoned it for the harpsichord. She encountered and further refined the modern Pleyel harpsichord with its large tone and pedal-controlled registration but mistakenly felt it could compete with the volume of the piano in large halls. She was a vital pioneer in the revival of the instrument. The present dominant aesthetic to construct harpsichords on accurate historical principles had not yet been established.

† Marie Juliette Elizabeth Amélie (née May Ephrussi) Princess de Faucigny-Lucinge (1880–1964) was the second wife of the unapproachably named Ferdinand Marie Gaspard François Charles Robert Louis, Prince de Faucigny-Lucinge et Coligny (1868–1928).

this imaginative and seductive picture. Also as the modern 'man about town' he had attended the glamorous nocturnal horse racing at Longchamps. The course was floodlit, the aristocratic race-goers dressed in white tie and tails the ladies in long gowns and fur stoles. With his usual interest in fashion, Eddie wrote in a letter home

> What struck me most in daytime were the skimpy skirts showing a slit with lots of leg and the enormous sleeves which would have served for skirts. With these freaks the ladies wore funny little straw hats with ribbon chinstraps and some had enormous lapels on coats and a buttonhole of exotic flowers in each lapel.

The spectacular dinner was served in huge marquees under a full moon accompanied by chilled champagne and concluding with a lavish firework display. His desire and enthusiasm for everything French was in full flight.

On an impulse he decided one morning to take the little train from Paris and briefly visit Landowska's Temple de la Musique Ancienne at Saint-Leu-la-Forêt just outside the city. After the death of her husband in a road accident in 1919 Landowska had conceived this idea in collaboration with the famous French architect Jean-Charles Moreaux. By 1927 they had established a Concert Hall and Gardens. She had quite precise ideas concerning the acoustic, audience capacity, construction materials (a glass roof flooded the hall with radiant natural light) and had laid out fine gardens. She wanted to carry on the methodical teaching of historical performance practice. To support these ideas she utilised her many original historical instruments, a priceless music library and a valuable collection of historical musical scores, letters and manuscripts.

Le Temple is the only building of its type ever planned in detail by a musician of international reputation. This 'sacred domain' attracted many connoisseurs and professional musicians. Composers such as Arthur Honegger, Georges Auric, Jacques Ibert and Francois Poulenc; the pianist Vladimir Horowitz; the writers Paul Valéry and Edith Wharton; naturally her own harpsichord pupils who included Ralph Kirkpatrick (their two egos clashed and he did not enjoy his lessons), Jose Iturbi, Ruggero Gerlin and Isabelle Nef.*

---

* Information on Le Temple de la Musique gleaned from the informative booklet written

After war broke out Landowska was urged by her friends to flee the Nazis. She postponed her flight till the last moment and like a pathetic refugee finally left Saint-Leu-la-Forêt for Paris with just two suitcases. Being a Jewess, her priceless possessions were deemed by the Nazis to be 'ownerless' and not French cultural property. Before she eventually fled the city, she made a recording of Scarlatti sonatas where falling bombs and artillery can distinctly be heard in the background.*

Landowska had been deeply involved in the evolution of the Pleyel concert harpsichord. The concert harpsichord known as the 'Grand Modèle de Concert' was finally conceived and constructed in 1912 according to her specification. Musical tastes and tonal aspirations for the harpsichord have changed and her modern design philosophy has fallen from favour.† Although never a pupil of Landowska, Eddie heard her play Bach (the *Goldberg Variations*) at one of her famous Sunday concerts at Le Temple on her Pleyel. He was quite overwhelmed. Like her, he believed that one should 'play with all your heart and all your intensity'. Six years older than Eddie she cultivated the demeanour of a 'high priestess who presided over her acolytes with the omnipotence of the Delphic oracle', albeit with the attitude of a charming intellectual. She always presented herself theatrically. At the beginning of concerts she appeared to mysteriously 'materialise' at the instrument. He felt drawn to the authenticity of the harpsichord for much the same reasons as Landowska.

Eddie also greatly admired the forgotten English harpsichordist Violet Gordon Woodhouse whom he considered a 'musical genius'. He heard an extraordinary performance at a private recital at her home, Nether Lipiatt Manor in Gloucestershire. Violet had been influenced by the Arnold Dolmetsch early music revolution

---

by the fine harpsichordist Skip Sempé accompanying the Landowska 1933 Bach recordings re-mastered for the Paradizo label combined CD and DVD PA0009.

* Landowska's own Pleyel instrument was found in Bavaria in the day room of a Nazi Officers' Club under empty wine bottles and other detritus.

† I am indebted to the article *The Pleyel Harpsichord* by J.A. Richard from *The Harpsichord Magazine*, Vol. 2, No. 5, for the history of the Pleyel instrument. Oddly but perhaps inevitably, there is a movement to perform historically relevant music on restored examples of these instruments. There is a growing nostalgia for the sound of the Pleyel 'Grand Modèle de Concert'.

and that evening played one of his harpsichords and a Tom Goff clavichord. She had abandoned public performance in 1926 when her life was financially transformed after the bizarre double murder of her husband's sisters by their deranged butler.*

* * *

Eddie was fascinated by the instrument and determined on his return to London to search out a Pleyel and give recitals on it. He was attracted by the 'marvellous effects' unobtainable on the piano. There was only one instrument in use in London in 1937. Demand by the few performers was high and he had to battle for practice time. When asked in an interview if such a delicate-toned instrument would have sufficient volume to fill a concert hall he commented:

> Yes, its high and quick vibrations give it an amazing carrying quality, the sound is sustained at least in a salon ... close by it is rather organ-like and the music itself seems to retain its original simplicity. I have not played it in a large hall. Your finger-work must be absolutely faultless – touch even a fraction of a note ever so lightly and it strikes. Actually, my hours with the harpsichord have improved my piano-playing immensely in terms of accuracy.

There was high excitement in London upon the arrival of this instrument. The conductor Arturo Toscanini demanded it for concerts at the Queen's Hall and at Covent Garden. The Pleyel was heard on the radio and even appeared on early television.

Eddie had an enthusiastic letter from a Mrs Pugh Jones who was in charge of the Pleyel & Cie. piano showroom in Gloucester Place who felt he had a great concert future playing the instrument. In July 1937 he gave the first of two recitals in the private chapel of 'Stranraer' in Warrington Crescent, Maida Vale. This Regency house, built by the Earl of Stranraer was originally situated in wooded parkland.† The chapel had a notorious reputation for black magic and Eddie thought the interior 'darkly intriguing'. The capacity audience of 130 listened to Mozart, Handel and Bach and the

* Jessica Douglas-Home, *Violet – The Life and Loves of Violet Gordon Woodhouse* (London 1996) gives the full account of her remarkable life.

† A Scottish title belonging to Earldom of Stair. Stranraer is a town and parish at the head of Loch Ryan in Wigtownshire in Scotland.

Concerto in D major by Haydn. The orchestral part was performed on the piano by a Mrs Davies Reynolds. He also played several pieces by François Couperin, who was becoming his favourite composer for the instrument. He explained to the audience the nobility of the *Livres de Clavecin* and how they conjure up a bitter-sweet aristocratic melancholia of love. He also indicated similarities between the French composer's sensibility and that of Fryderyk Chopin, an original observation for the time. In Manchester Street he lived close to the Wallace Collection in Manchester Square which enabled him to become familiar with the social and aesthetic context of this music – the furniture, paintings and porcelain of the French Baroque and Rococo.

As was customary at such social events, there was scarcely any informed musical comment or criticism concerning the recital itself apart from one writer noticing the 'wonderful colour in tonal effects from the seven pedals of the harpsichord'. Many years later after a recital in Paris the respected music critic Mario Facchinetti wrote perceptively of a Cahill recital in *The Musical Week*

> The second part, dedicated to Corelli, Scarlatti, Beethoven, Mozart and Bach proved an excellent understanding of classical music and a clever manner of treating the modern piano with the lightness of the harpsichord.

* * *

Christmas 1937 was spent as usual with Fred and Maud Denny at Horwood with music and festive cheer. But as the weather became increasingly gloomy and the mists descended, Eddie crossed the Channel on a ferry. He once more boarded *Le Train Bleu* at Calais following the majority of his wealthy patrons to Menton and the relatively warm shores of the Mediterranean. In recent years the journey had become somewhat less glamorous with the rise of the Popular Front government in France and the imminent nationalisation of the railways. The road to war had begun. But for the moment at least the train journey preserved its opulent refinement. The marvellous *haute cuisine* of the dining car remained intact.

Previously Eddie had only passed through the French Riviera *en route* to his Papal audience early in 1935. He was full of anticipation to properly explore this legendary place at the height of its glamour and allure. His 'confectionary imagination' revelled in the glamorous, slightly misleading, almost clichéd image held by many who had never visited those shores. From the train he could see an azure morning rising over the sparkling Mediterranean. Curving capes, bays, inlets, wooded hills and webs of land stretched between fingers of rock, the slopes speckled with white villas, tall hotels and palm-filled gardens. Despite it being winter he recalled Scott Fitzgerald's phrase from *Tender is the Night*: 'the diffused magic of the hot, sweet South'[*]. He would discover many different levels of society, some that particularly suited his rather whimsical temperament. The Riviera was ever the perennial refuge of writers, painters even composers who inhabited quite different worlds to the aged dowagers, hypochondriacs and wealthy Americans who migrated to Menton each year. In winter they drifted from the grey north like birds, those elderly folk who were his indispensible patrons. He needed to follow them.

Eddie arrived in Monaco in perfect weather at the end of January, the same time as the 1938 XVII Rallye Automobile Monte Carlo concluded. Moving up and down the Riviera like a musical butterfly, he alighted here and there to give recitals and engage in a series of flirtations. The debonair *bon viveur* Arthur Rubinstein spoke of Chopin as being a perfect composer for the purposes of seduction. The consequence of both the intrigues and the travelling was that money became a constant requirement.

* * *

In the wider world Eddie did not follow politics in England closely but being robustly Australian in surprising ways, even more significantly as a Queenslander, he was not an advocate of appeasement as a policy. He had already seen too much of dictators. He agreed with Winston Churchill concerning this notorious policy

> this great country nosing from door to door like a cow that has lost its calf, mooing dolefully now in Berlin and now in Rome – when all the time the tiger and the alligator wait for its undoing.[†]

---

* F. Scott Fitzgerald, *Tender is the Night* (New York 1934), Book 1, p. 43.

† Quoted in Nicolson, *Diaries and Letters 1930–39*, p. 328.

Eddie's already overwrought mood was only heightened when he learned on 14 March that Hitler's troops were marching along the Ringstrasse in Vienna. The romantic problems resulting from his separation from Sabine seemed to have reached a climax in the perverse Nazi consensual rape of Austria. The invasion appeared to him the 'symbolic sexual consummation' of all he had feared from the first moments of seeing her in Berchtesgaden in company with 'that Nazi officer' Reinhard. The author George Clare wrote graphically of Vienna

> The whole city behaved like an aroused woman, vibrating, writhing, moaning and sighing lustfully for orgasm and release. This is not purple writing. It is an exact description of what Vienna was and felt like on Monday, 14 March 1938, as Hitler entered her. As the Führer's motorcade passed through the streets of the old Hapsburg city, lined by hundreds of thousands waving jubilating Viennese, its church bells rang out their own obscene *jubilate.* [...] but I also know that there were many thousands, by no means only Jews, who stayed away behind tightly closed windows in order not to hear the frenzy of the streets.*

Sabine even sent Eddie a telegram expressing her joy at the so-called *Anschluss.* An Austrian-Jewish cellist who had fled the city and whom he met later in the year after a chamber concert in Cannes told him that the Jews of Vienna were being shamefully treated by the Nazis. The resulting wave of suicides had been appalling. Eddie instinctively felt the Jewish roots of Sabine's family would eventually be revealed with dire consequences for her. He was surprised at himself that in his heart and despite his many brief romantic dalliances he still appeared to care.

Towards the middle of March he gave a recital in the Casino Municipal in Monte Carlo. The high point of this concert was his meeting with the great Austrian-Jewish violinist Fritz Kreisler who had attended his recital. Kreisler 'did nothing but praise Monsieur Cahill and further the Australian public for their attention during his own performances'. Many music lovers travelled from Monaco and other parts of the Riviera later in the month for Eddie's 'musical party' at the Château de Saint Laurent owned by Lady Wilmot near the exquisite *village perché* of Eze. The *Daily Mail* reported in a tone reminiscent of a more civilised age

* Clare, *Last Waltz in Vienna*, pp. 195–6.

> Before the recital, the guests spent some time on the terraces and in the gardens which were a blaze of colour. The music room was lovely with the delicate spring tints of irises and daffodils. Tea was served and later champagne. Mr Cahill was at the height of his form. His playing is charged with life. His Scarlatti, Mozart and Handel sonatas had a gemlike quality of clarity and brilliance and his Chopin, Chaminade, Debussy, Schumann and other composers were interpreted with a fine understanding and a splendid technique. He also included some of his own compositions among them a beautiful setting of *Londonderry Air* and a charming *Musical Box.**

Through his talent and charm Eddie evolved all manner of social safety nets. In an attempt to lay the ghost of Sabine who had ignored all his invitations to join him on the Riviera, he began to frequent the less salubrious side of the Côte d'Azur. In his address book and notes there is mention of the Zanzi Bar. This former garage is possibly the oldest gay bar in Cannes, established in 1885. Jean Cocteau use to frequent it, but tracing its clientele has proven an elusive task. One can only speculate about what Eddie may have been doing or who he may have been meeting there.

Although honoured by the attentions of the aristocracy, he needed increasingly to escape the cloying atmosphere of 'sanatorium Menton', that picturesque refuge of the geriatric English. Menton was also a warm nest for that incestuous international set of writers afflicted by diseases of the lung or mind seeking therapeutic winter sun. Place names now redolent with the accumulated connotations of bohemian excess, conspicuous vulgarity, industrial cupidity and sublime creative hedonism drew him increasingly – Nice, Cannes, Cagnes-sur-Mer, Antibes, Juan-le-Pins, the casino tables of Monte Carlo, even the sexual *qui-vive* of Somerset Maugham's extravagant Villa Mauresque parties at Cap Ferrat. The spirit of 'a sunny place for shady people' infected his very blood. He found Chopin a reliable aid to the more civilised of his seductions.

By this time Eddie could manipulate with ease his reputation within the English upper classes. His colonial background was a distinct advantage. Being Australian placed him outside the strictures of the cruel and exclusive English class system. He

* Apart from Lady Wilmot, the customary line-up of aristocratic guests was present at this recital including interestingly Princess Giulia Ottoboni, related to Cardinal Ottoboni, patron of the composer Domenico Scarlatti.

never bothered to conceal his Queenslander accent, having full confidence in the power of his musical personality. He always had the ability to communicate directly with his audience by having 'something to say' in his interpretations. He often cited his pianistic idol, Vladimir de Pachmann, who referred to the image of the pianist as 'an expression of the informing spirit'. Eddie also valued the rare quality of 'being natural', akin to an unaffected child. His rare ability to interpret Chopin in an affecting yet unsentimental manner created a group of fiercely loyal patrons and listeners who would travel long distances to hear him.

In Menton he renewed acquaintance with Frederick Adolphus König, a prominent American banker who was married to Gerda von Chappuis, an accomplished pianist and Lady in Waiting to Princess Marie Louise.* Eddie had first met her at a recital patronised by the Princess in London in 1927. He regularly gave recitals in their Temple of Music pavilion in the gardens of Tyringham, their country house in Buckinghamshire. Designed by Sir John Soane, the house was remodelled in part by Sir Edwin Lutyens after its acquisition by Frederick Adolphus. Lutyens added a bathing pavilion and built the Temple of Music where Eddie used to perform. Princess Marie Louise would often attend these recitals and afterwards Eddie might dine with the Princess and Mrs König at the Savoy and then go on to the Russian ballet at Drury Lane.

Frederick Adolphus's brother, Hans-Heinrich ('Henri') König, was also a banker who in 1906 had built and lived in palatial Ardenrun Place at Blindley Heath in Surrey. The house was that extraordinary phenomenon, a new country house constructed in the William and Mary style.† Of particular interest to Eddie, the house

* Frederick Adolphus König and his brother Hans-Heinrich ('Henri') König were American bankers from New York. The family fortune originated with their father who had patented a process for hardening rubber. The Königs moved to Britain around 1890 as one of the first of a 'veritable invasion of rich Americans'. His wife, Gertrude von Chappuis, is one of those credited with the idea of Queen Mary's Dolls' House at Windsor. In 1910 a striking portrait of her and her greyhound was painted by the Irish artist Sir John Lavery RA (1856–1941). Sold at Christies in 2006 for £96,000.

† Ardenrun Place was designed by the English architect Ernest Newton (1856–1922), who was President of Royal Institute of British Architects. 'His eminence as an architect of unexcelled skill in a class of work that constitutes England's chief or sole claim to supremacy – the capture and apt embodiment of the very spirit of the home ...' Obituary in the *Architect's Journal*, 1 February 1922, p. 187. Demolished in 1933 after a fire.

had been purchased in 1921 together with 1,000 acres of surrounding farmland by the 'Bentley Boy', Woolf Barnato. The property was reached down a long drive from Tandridge Lane. In racing parlance 'the straight' leading to Moat Farm was approximately half a mile long. This is where the 'Bentley Boys' used to race their cars against the clock. On one occasion Ettore Bugatti, who was a great friend of Woolf Barnato, brought several of his cars to Ardenrun Place. The guests raced from the house to Tandridge Lane and back. Eddie excitedly combined wild parties and piano recitals with his interest in motor racing on various occasions here.

In 1923 'Henri' König had purchased the elegant Villa Maria-Serena at Menton-Garavan on the Côte d'Azur.* Eddie would stay at this villa often for long periods before and after the war and gave regular recitals there which were well received. Villa Maria-Serena has a collection of rare palms. Entire walls of vibrant purple bougainvillea line the drive, a Chinese dragon bowl graces the centre of a lily pond. A spectacular panorama of the Mediterranean and Menton is laid out before one from the breezy portico. Wild overgrown paths behind the house lead down to the sea from towering granite rocks. These picturesque natural treasures inspired Eddie to excel when practising his French repertoire of Chaminade, Poulenc and Debussy. He felt at home in what amounted to almost tropical surroundings.

After one recital at the villa Eddie met the formidable Swiss society hostess Helen Sieger, who lived with her husband Arthur at the magnificent Villa Sieger at Bordighera. She was passionate about music and the couple were to offer Eddie a measure of financial stability during the tortuous war years and beyond. She was the extraordinarily wealthy daughter of a Hatton Garden diamond jeweller in London. She would exclaim in exasperation whenever the lack of 'indispensible' servants was discussed 'My dear, I have never done my own hair in my entire life!' Her German husband owned immensely profitable sisal mills in Tanganyika (Tanzania) in former German East Africa. Eddie's meeting with them was to prove a watershed in his life although this was not at all clear in 1938.

* The Villa Maria-Serena was constructed in 1886 by Charles Garnier (architect of the Paris Opera and Monte Carlo Opera) and owned by the de Lesseps family of Suez Canal fame. The villa was sold in 1923 by the daughter of Ferdinand de Lesseps, Giselle de Lesseps, Baronne la Caze to the American banker 'Henri' König.

* * *

'All done in the tying of a cravat' Sir Percy had declared to his clique of admirers.

We seek him here, we seek him there,
Those Frenchies seek him everywhere.
Is he in heaven?—Is he in hell?
That demmed, elusive Pimpernel

Sir Percy's *bon mot* doggerel had gone the round of brilliant reception-rooms.

It was at Monaco in 1938 that Eddie met for the first time a curious figure who combined both the aristocratic and the bohemian temperaments, the Hungarian writer Baroness 'Emmuska' Orczy, the remarkable author of *The Scarlet Pimpernel.** She had been born in Transylvania in the vast 'ugly' mansion of Tarna-Örs built on the River Tarna by her maternal grandfather, Count Wass. She also spent her childhood on extensive and picturesque agricultural lands surrounding a manor house at Tisza-Abád on the River Theisz. Following a machine-breaking peasant revolt in July 1870 that put fire to their lands and killed their livestock, the disinherited family wandered Europe for years before finally settling in London.

The Baroness was a great lover of music and an excellent critic, although not a performer. Her father, Baron Felix Orczy, was a talented musician, composer and pianist. He became a great friend of Franz Liszt during his studies at Weimar where Liszt had established a renowned music school. The great virtuoso considered Baron Orczy 'the finest amateur musician in Europe', who 'made the piano sing'.† When in London the Abbé Liszt would often play for them at their home in Wimpole Street. Her father assisted the great conductor Hans Richter in his rise to fame and the family knew the pianists Ignacy Jan Paderewski and Anton Rubinstein as well as the composers Grieg and Gounod. The family moved in the highest aristocratic circles in Edwardian London, Hungarian gypsy music and culture being quite the rage before the outbreak of the Great War.

* Baroness 'Emmuska' Orczy (1865–1947). The pimpernel is a flower of the primrose family. A plant of bare ground and waste places, it is symbolically an appropriate choice for Sir Peter Blakeney who conducts his business on the bleak field of the French Revolution.

† Baroness Orczy, *Links in the Chain of Life: The Autobiography of Baroness Orczy* (London 1947), p. 21.

Baroness Orczy began her own career as a painter but found it an unsatisfactory profession. However during her studies at Heatherley's School of Fine Art in Chelsea she met and married the English painter Montague Barstow. They spent some time living in Paris and the marriage was to be a long, supportive, and artistically creative relationship. The couple travelled a good deal and after a delightful short holiday in Monte Carlo in 1915, the painter and writer found themselves charmed by the undeveloped environment of the French Riviera. Despite having lost her inherited fortune following the Armistice in 1918 they decided to buy, sight unseen, the modest Villa Bijou in an area that was eventually to become 'the Mayfair of Monte Carlo'. Her description of those far-off days is scarcely believable in view of the airless, claustrophobic agglomeration of structures that today choke the Principality

> There were a few streets – one important one which was the direct tram road to Nice – there were one or two unpretentious hotels, there was a tennis court on which only the local people played, and there was the port; as for the rest, there were olive trees isolated or in groups through which a few palm trees raised their melancholy heads.*

Over the years the house and gardens were transformed. In February 1938 at Villa Bijou Eddie gave his first recital of what was to become an annual musical engagement and they became close friends. 'She is quite the reverse of wealthy and lives in very moderate comfort in an unpretentious villa' he noted. At the time he met her she was staging a performance in Monte Carlo of the play she had originally based on the Scarlet Pimpernel book. The Baroness had encountered great difficulty getting the original story published until as a play it was staged to great acclaim at the Theatre Royal in Nottingham in 1903.† The book itself was finally successfully published in 1905.

She told Eddie how she had conceived of the character of Sir Peter Blakeney and wrote her own account of the unprepossessing moment in her entertaining autobiography. Sometime in 1901 while standing on the platform of London's Temple Underground Station

* Ibid., p. 158.

† The famous actor Fred Terry played the part of Sir Peter Blakeney and Julia Neilson that of Marguerite. Many in the audience were so enthusiastic they missed their trains, an unheard of occurrence.

while waiting for a Circle Line train he appeared in her mind's eye

> It was foggy too, and smelly and cold. But I give you my word that as I was sitting there, I saw – yes, I saw – Sir Peter Blakeney just as you know him now. I saw him in his exquisite clothes, his slender hands holding up his spy-glass: I heard his lazy drawling speech, his quaint laugh … it was a mental vision of course.[*]

Her father had taught Baroness Orczy to respect music and musicians. She felt that

> music is the most absorbing of all the arts. It absorbs the mind of the artist, whether creator or executants, to the exclusion of every other consideration outside his immediate necessities or desires. It is essentially a selfish art … he must first and foremost think of his own worth, his own success or failure.[†]

During their meetings they exchanged many stories of the London Society and musical life they shared. He played for her and her friends on a number of occasions, which in time became much anticipated annual events. He wrote to friends in Australia

> One meets all the famous people of the world in Monte Carlo. For every day brings two or three cocktail parties attended by the most celebrated authors, musical, and movie stars. During the season there I met Vesta Tilley[‡] (now Lady de Frece) who was the original male impersonator, Claudette Colbert[§] and the one time famous Edna May[¶], who still looks wonderful despite her age and of course, many of the exiled kings and queens and most of the Russian aristocracy.

* * *

In May 1938 Eddie remained in the South of France and so missed the Empire Exhibition in Scotland which validated the sustained

* Baroness Orczy, *Links in the Chain of Life*, p. 97

† Ibid., p. 35.

‡ Matilda Alice Powles (1864–1952), was an English music hall performer who at the age of 11 adopted the stage name Vesta Tilley and became one of the most famous male impersonators of the day.

§ Claudette Colbert (1903–96) was a famous French-born American actress, and a leading lady for two decades. She was one the greatest female stars of the classic Hollywood era.

¶ Edna May Pettie (1878–1948) was known on stage as Edna May. She was a ravishingly beautiful American actress and singer famous for her leading roles in Edwardian musical comedies.

power of Empire. In July there was a royal visit to France, which among the many glittering social events of that year attempted to cement the solidarity of democracy against the rise of the dictators. The month of September witnessed events in Europe of the greatest magnitude. The crisis over ethnic Germans in the Sudetenland grew in intensity. Neville Chamberlain emerged as a champion of peace with his visits to Hitler at Berchtesgaden and Bad Godesberg. 'European peace is what I am aiming at and I hope that this journey may open the way to get it.' Chamberlain was desperate to avoid war.

Many in the United Kingdom believed that the 'one great function of this country is to maintain the moral standards of Europe, not to make friends with people whose conduct is demonstrably evil'.* Although Chamberlain was widely adored in the House for his peace initiative, after the Munich Conference Churchill declared 'we have sustained a total and unmitigated defeat'. The RMS *Queen Elizabeth* was launched by King George VI who addressed the crowd

> Be of good cheer despite the dark clouds hanging over [you] and indeed over the whole world. The launching of a ship is like all great human enterprises – an act of faith. We cannot foretell the future.

A newspaper poster urged the populace to 'Keep Calm and Dig'. Eddie kept calm and played for the Baroness Orczy.

On 2 January 1939 Eddie travelled to Cannes and attended a recital given at the Théâtre du Casino Municipal by one of his musical idols, the great Swiss-French pianist and Chopin specialist, Alfred Cortot. Eddie had taken lessons from him in Paris in 1925 and managed to speak to him after the concert. He invited Cortot to his own recital at the Casino in Menton the following Thursday under the patronage of HRH the Princess of Belgium (Madame la Duchesse de Vendôme). He played Beethoven, Schumann, Brahms, Chopin and arrangements of waltzes by Johann Strauss II. Cortot was particularly impressed with his gemlike tone, delicacy of touch and beautiful *bel canto,* which were the touchstones of Eddie's playing. He felt he had much improved over the last fourteen years. On the Riviera Eddie took a number of further lessons with the

* Nicolson, *Diaries and Letters 1930–39*, p. 354.

master as Cortot was not returning immediately to Paris.

The French pianist's later support of Vichy naturally did not sit well with the Australian. He tried to ignore the master's apparent political affiliations and sympathies, but found it difficult. However throughout his career Eddie remained inordinately proud to tell anyone who would appreciate it 'Of course, I have been privileged to study with Cortot in Paris, the Riviera and Switzerland.' Resemblances in their approach to performing Chopin and Schumann are marked. Eddie noted that in lessons, always assuming the pupil had a complete technique, Cortot emphasised the uniquely poetic, the inspirational, the narcotic and magical effect of music always searching for spiritual depth. He was rarely 'normal' in his approach to any score. The conductor and pianist Daniel Barenboim has spoken perceptively of Cortot as continually 'searching for the opium in music'.

CHAPTER 14

NOSTALGIE POUR LA PATRIE

While giving concerts on the Côte d'Azur Eddie often took the train to Bordighera on the Italian Riviera to stay with his new patrons, the Siegers, at their palatial villa overlooking the bay and shingle shore at Madonna della Ruota (Madonna of the Wheel).* In February 1939 the British Consul-General at Nice, Major James Hugh Dodds, invited him to give a recital at an afternoon tea party in nearby Menton to celebrate the imminent completion of a memorial to Queen Victoria. The concert was intended to raise funds for the needy and strengthen Franco-British relations.†

Queen Victoria had been immensely fond of her holidays on the Riviera. In March 1882 she set off for Menton for the first time, travelling incognito as 'The Countess Balmoral' with Princess Beatrice and 160 servants. The royal train took some 30 hours from Windsor to the temporary station erected near her accommodation, the 'very prettily situated' Châlet des Rosiers. It was reported she ate macaroons continually. The Queen had come not for leisure but for medical reasons to see her beloved son, Prince Leopold, Duke of Albany. His doctors thought the salubrious winter climate of Menton might benefit his painful inflamed joints, a complication of his inherited haemophilia. The treatment ultimately failed and he was to die two years later in Cannes. Despite her grief, the Queen's first visit had created great affection for the Riviera and she returned in 1887. And so began the popular English leisure activity of wintering in Nice or Menton. Economically the area had been chronically

* Bordighera is a town on the Italian Riviera famous in the last century and before for the salubrious climate, flora (particularly palms) and lovely gardens which attracted many predominantly English visitors during winter months. It was still a glamorous destination before the Second World War but suffered greatly during the conflict, particularly the gardens and magnificent villas which were pillaged and severely damaged by Fascist troops.

† The 'statue' was officially unveiled on 10 April 1939.

depressed until the Queen began her regular visits. The memorial indicated French gratitude for her transformation of their economy.*

The Paris edition of the *Daily Mail* wrote of Eddie's concert in Menton:

> Edward Cahill was at the top of his form. His playing is charged with life. His Mozart had a gem-like quality of clarity and brilliance, and other composers were interpreted with a fine understanding and splendid technique. He is certainly a pianist who makes one 'sit up'.

* * *

In Monaco however it was the strain between the French and Italian population that exercised Eddie's mind. English residents were ordered by the local authorities to dismiss their Italian employees. Baroness Orczy ignored this directive with her customary panache and 'did nothing of the sort'. She observed that the Principality at the conclusion of 1938 was 'in a state resembling panic'. There was consternation and fear on the Côte d'Azur when at the end of November Mussolini demanded that France cede territories to Italy including Nice, Tunisia, Corsica and Djibouti.

On a more personal front, Eddie's love of fast driving again landed him in trouble while practising for the final historic 6.3 km La Turbie hill climb.† The winding unsealed route cut through austere white limestone and red porphyry fringed by precipitous drops of a thousand metres. The narrow-streeted villages with wandering chickens gave him a singular sense of excitement and challenge. He was energetically driving a borrowed 1936 Talbot Lago T120 Baby Sport owned by a wealthy couturier in Monte Carlo. He swerved to avoid a dog in the road just before reaching the Roman monument at La Turbie known as the *Trophée des Alpes*. The car skidded in the wet and slammed into a rock face. No serious injury, the coachwork only superficially damaged but the jarring of the steering wheel sprained his wrist. A French doctor strapped it in an elastic bandage and suggested he refrain from giving concerts

* Nelson, Michael, *Queen Victoria and the Discovery of the Riviera* (London 2001), pp. 20–36. A fascinating volume.

† This was the very first hill climb competition in motoring established in 1897 and remained in competitive use until 1939.

for some weeks. This was to become a great personal and financial frustration.

* * *

Around the time of this incident he also began to have trouble with his hearing. He developed a persistent earache which, allied with his hand injury, made practice even more difficult. The fear of such an incapacity turned him irritable and morose, the dark shadows of mortality gathered in his imagination. Naturally he thought of Beethoven and his terrible suffering. Acute nervous anxiety was an affliction Eddie was forced to fight all his life. Baroness Orczy suggested he return to England for immediate medical attention as he began to question his future as a pianist. In late February 1939 he once more boarded *Le Train Bleu* at Monte Carlo for Calais. His return to London was rather mournful and introspective. He missed the Côte d'Azur, the balmy weather and its social delights the moment he left the Mediterranean.

In London while waiting for a consultation with an orthopaedic hand specialist in Harley Street, Eddie picked up a newspaper and read a curious article entitled 'The Fallacy of the Piano' by the distinguished English physicist, astronomer and mathematician Sir James Jeans.* With the subtitle 'A Scientist Looks at Music' it addressed the Music Teachers' Association to examine whether a pianist could put any emotion he wished into a note by the way he struck the key. Sir James concluded that

> ... as far as single notes are concerned, it does not matter how the pupil strikes the key [...] If he strikes it with the requisite degree of force, the tone quality will be the same whether he strikes it with his fingers, or even the end of his umbrella. For successions of notes he concluded it was merely a question of achieving the right hand position. This is all there is in the much debated problem of piano touch.

* Sir James Jeans (1877–1946) taught at both Cambridge and Princeton. He was deeply concerned with music and published *Science and Music* in 1938. The article may have followed publication of this well-respected book. He was the first to propose that matter is continuously created throughout the universe. Possibly his most famous quote is 'The universe begins to look more like a great thought than a great machine.' (*The Mysterious Universe*, London 1930.)

When Eddie read this he became incensed, impulsively left the consulting room, returned to Maida Vale and immediately wrote a rebuttal. His refined touch at the piano was always favourably commented upon as distinctive by all his listeners and patrons. He had worked all his life at the instrument to achieve his marvellous luminosity of tone. These remarks are his only statement on record concerning this vital aspect of piano playing

> In direct antithesis to what Sir James Jeans says I maintain that *everything, everything* mark you depends on the way that the key is struck. It is a matter of 'approach', of delicacy and refinement of touch – the way in which the key is pressed after the finger has touched it. *On this depends the colour of the note.* I myself feel every note by a kind of emotion in the muscles of my fingers and hands *before* I play it.
>
> Sir James is a very eminent scientist – let him stick to his science. *This is a matter of art.* Delicacy of touch is all a matter of muscular control in which the fingers, hands, wrists, arms and the whole body play a part. It is impossible to get this delicacy of touch other than through the fingers.

The hand specialist eventually diagnosed bruising from the accident but also a worrying return of Dupuytren's contracture, which might necessitate another operation. He was further depressed after a letter from Sabine in Austria informing him that she was now quite happy living 'under the Nazis'.

* * *

Unfortunately, in addition to the problem with his hands, Eddie was shocked one evening after a bath to discover a lump behind his ear. His chronic earache had become increasingly severe. He was diagnosed with *otitis media* or middle-ear infection. Antibiotic treatments apart from sulphonamides were not available in the late 1930s. The purification and chemistry of penicillin was still in the experimental phase. The infection unfortunately developed into mastoiditis, indicating the bacteria were in danger of spreading to the brain which could result in death.

The problem necessitated an operation to remove infected tissue from the air spaces behind the ear drum. There were few precision surgical instruments then and bone drills were primitive. This was a particularly nerve-wracking time for the concert pianist as his highly strung personality did not deal with the notion of deafness (or possible death) with equanimity. He was assured by surgeons that his hearing would return to normal, but he did not share their confidence.

A clinical curiosity today, the complex mastoidectomy operation was carried out in London in early March 1939 and his recovery was slow. He had fits of dizziness and periods of tinnitus. The infection lingered on and off almost until the end of 1942 causing him severe pain and constant apprehension of death. While recovering he heard of a soldier who had died following a second operation for the same complaint.

* * *

Before the Second World War broke out in September 1939 Eddie was already resident in Switzerland giving charity concerts for the British Red Cross. After being discharged from St George's Hospital, Hyde Park, London following two weeks as a patient, he decided to convalesce in Switzerland. The digging of trenches in Green Park, the issuing a of gas masks to every citizen and the testing of barrage balloons convinced him to leave England. He managed to take one of the last Imperial Airways flights before Geneva airport was officially closed for the course of the war.

Eddie had no idea how long his convalescence might remove him from professional concert life. How would he survive financially? His friends the Siegers who had also sought what they hoped would be temporary refuge in Switzerland would at least insulate him from the worst which was to come. Their home was to become a haven of peace for the sick man. However although his psychological strength to remain optimistic in the face of adversity usually pushed him through most barriers he was often on the edge of a nervous collapse. The shadow of death haunted him throughout the war.

He took up residence in the Hôtel Helvétie et des Familles in Montreux in April 1939. This beautiful old hotel on the shores of Lac Léman (Lake Geneva) was constructed in the French style with a mansard roof, spacious high-ceilinged rooms and opulent staterooms. The hotel enjoyed an uninterrupted view over the lake. During his enforced rest, Eddie spent a great deal of time exploring Old Montreux above the hotel and the villages dotted about the hills. He also read many of his favourite authors who had wandered the shores of Lake Geneva – Scott Fitzgerald, Somerset Maugham, Rousseau – and Byron, whose poetry he had come to love through performing the music of Liszt. He also read the Voynich translation of Chopin's correspondence which he believed gave him an invaluable insight into the composer's *espaces imaginaires*.

Temperamentally, Eddie could not remain musically inactive for long and courageously, in view of his fragile mental health, began what was to become a long series of charity concerts in Montreux during the war years. He simply ignored the lingering symptoms of his ear operation and the pain in his wrist. The first, in May, was for the British Red Cross not long after his arrival. He raised well over a thousand Swiss francs.*

Eddie gave two well-received recitals in Montreux at the hotel. By the time of this first concert he had added Chopin's *Andante Spianato and Grande Polonaise Brillante* to his repertoire. The *Journal de Montreux* published an enthusiastic review of the concert in its *Chronique musicale* column on 5 May 1939:

> The charming Salle de Concert of the Hôtel Helvétie generously offered by Mlle. Krähenbühl was almost full on Friday the 5th at 5 pm. A sizeable audience composed mostly of foreigners had come to applaud the great pianist Edward Cahill. Where we consider the English to be tall, M. Edward Cahill is slight, white-haired with an expressive and 'sympathetic' head. But with what vigour, what virtuosity this master plays the piano! This white-haired gentleman performs like a youth with a soul full of boundless enthusiasm for his art. I have learned that due to an accident Mr Cahill has not given a concert for a year. To hear him one would never have believed it. As a matter of fact Mr Cahill gave proof of his astonishing virtuosity especially in Schumann and several pieces by Chopin, amongst others the *Grande Polonaise* as well as the Hungarian Rhapsody of Liszt. Here he was truly amazing as much in his technique as his interpretation.
>
> The features which I particularly admired in his playing and which one seldom finds to such a rare degree is the velvety

* Well over £2,500 in 2015.

smoothness, the finesse and the perfection of tone (nuances). Under M. Cahill's fingers the piano literally sings whether he plays *piano, mezzo-forte, forte* or *fortissimo*. The melody is never sacrificed and it is this which most impressed me in the performance of this artist.

The first works played were his own compositions. One of these in particular stood out, one in the treble register which the artist called *Les Clochettes* (The Bells). The manner in which the artist brought out the poetry and harmony of this piece was a rare treat. We may say the same of another English melody of which Mr Cahill is the composer and also his admirable execution of Schumann, Schubert and Chopin. Our sincere congratulations to the sympathetic and generous artist with the wish to hear him again soon. This fine concert has brought a substantial contribution to the British Red Cross Fund.*

Unfortunately Eddie's excitable and adventurous Irish nature often got the better of him, particularly if motor cars were involved. A few months after this concert he had been taken on a rather reckless drive by a friend around the shores of Lake Geneva towards beautiful Évian-les-Bains in a Type 57 Bugatti. He was greatly missing his Alvis, stored in England with Mrs Denny at Horwood and continued to harbour a passion for the adrenalin of fast cars and fast driving. They took a corner too fast near the border village of Saint-Gingolph and left the road. Fortunately it was not on the section above the lake but in a flat forested area.

Neither was badly injured, but the car was heavily damaged and Eddie severely strained three fingers on his right hand, neatly reversing the healing that had already taken place after the hill-climb incident. The local Swiss and French people of the nearby village of Saint-Gingolph were immensely helpful and sympathetic after the accident. Eddie never forgot their assistance and was able express his gratitude some time later when they in turn suffered reversals.

He was not fit to perform again until December 1939. He compensated somewhat by living a rich and varied social life. In Montreux he met one of the greatest of all violinists, the Pole Bronisław Huberman,† who was resting at his country home

* My translation. Sadly no original compositions by Eddie survived his peripatetic lifestyle.

† Bronisław Huberman (1882–1947) was a great Jewish Polish violinist.

in Switzerland when war was declared on 3 September. By coincidence, he was recovering in Switzerland from severe trauma to both his hands as a result of an aeroplane crash in Sumatra on 6 October during a tour of Indonesia. He counted himself fortunate as four of the nine passengers had been killed. However by the time he met Eddie he had begun to play well again and was in an ebullient mood.

He was delighted to discover Eddie was Australian and told him an amusing story which Eddie often repeated over dinner. At the conclusion of his Australian tour in August 1937, Huberman was to have begun a similar concert tour of Southeast Asia to the one Eddie and George had undertaken in 1920. He decided to fly to Darwin, which took four days rather than the two weeks by boat from Fremantle. Refuelling to cover such a vast distance was necessary and on one occasion the plane landed in the remote Gibson Desert. Huberman decided to take a walk and was unexpectedly greeted on the parched red earth by his Polish compatriot and friend Arthur Rubinstein with the words 'Dr Huberman, I presume?' Neither knew the other was coming to Australia to perform and both were astounded at the coincidence.

Both Eddie and Huberman volunteered their services in Swiss concerts for the benefit of the Red Cross and other charities, including the Polish Fund. Eddie thought this Polish Jewish musician performed Bach with unsurpassed sensibility that moved the listener to tears. He also loved his interpretations of Henryk Wieniawski and his arrangements of Chopin for violin, particularly the Waltz in C sharp minor, Op. 64 No. 2. Violinists of the 1930s played with a far greater degree of *portamento* (sliding from one note to another) expressing an emotive sensibility than the more 'motoric, factual interpretative style of our times'*.

* * *

Despite his success, Eddie's depressed state of mind worsened as the war progressed. Early in 1940 he took the risk of travelling back to the comparative heat of the Italian and French Riviera. Europe was on the verge of catastrophe and travel hazardous. The Siegers

* A comment by the great German violin virtuoso Georg Kulenkampff.

had also returned to the warmth of their villa at Bordighera where they had a fine Blüthner concert grand on which Eddie could do some desultory practice. He languished in their opulent, sun-dappled gardens. He explored this beautiful region which had inspired Claude Monet with 'this brilliance, this magical light' when the artist was resident in 1884.

Eddie gave a number of concerts at the archaeological Museo Bicknell in the town in February 1940 and also at the superb Villa Etelinda.* *L'Eco della Riviera* wrote of this concert

> The room was crowded with a cosmopolitan audience ... the programme brought to a brilliant conclusion by Mr Cahill, who displayed remarkable technique as well as musical culture of the very first rank … the pianist has a most remarkable musical memory and great sensitiveness.

The lotus-eaters of the Riviera were becoming increasingly worried about the growing belligerence of Fascist Italy and the likelihood of an alliance with Hitler. In March 1940, still resident on the Côte d'Azur despite stern advice to quit from the mayor, Eddie managed to give a charity recital at the Théatre du Casino Municipal de Cannes for the benefit of Bon Pasteur (the Convent of the Good Shepherd). This orphanage was increasingly in need of funds during wartime and was dedicated to the moral and practical education of deprived children and the rehabilitation young 'abandoned' women†. The car accident and his damaged hand forced him to reduce the number of pieces he performed, but he managed a demanding programme which included Schumann, Chopin, and the Brahms Rhapsody Op. 119 No. 4 together with the elegant and popular Brahms-Glück Gavotte from the opera *Iphigénie en Aulide*. With the well-known French pianist Rachel Blanquer he also played Liszt's second Hungarian Rhapsody and the *Hungarian Fantasy* arranged for two pianos by Hans von Bülow. This was to be

* Villa Etelinda was designed by Charles Garnier (architect of the Paris Opera) in 1914 and purchased by Queen Margherita of Savoy who died there in 1926. The Bicknell Museum and Library and English garden contains prehistoric rock engravings from the Valle delle Meraviglie (Vallée des Merveilles). The museum was founded by the Rev. Clarence Bicknell (1842–1918) in 1886–88.

† The Sisters of Our Lady of Charity of the Good Shepherd is a Roman Catholic order. They take the customary vows of poverty, chastity, and obedience but are also dedicated to the care, rehabilitation, and education of girls and young women of dissolute habits, who wish to do penance and lead a Christian life.

his last recital on the Riviera until after the war.

In June 1940, in the words of Franklin D. Roosevelt, 'the hand that held the dagger has struck it into the back of its neighbour'. Italy invaded France. The woefully inadequate Italian forces only penetrated as far as Menton along the Mediterranean coast, a paltry six miles before being halted. The Siegers with Eddie aboard immediately fled Bordighera for Switzerland in their plum-coloured Isotta Fraschini.

* * *

In July Eddie gave a recital at the Helvétie hotel for the Montreux Section of the Swiss Red Cross. This had been arranged by the British Women's Wartime Work, which had offices at 9, Avenue de La Prairie in Vevey, a picturesque town on the lake shore near Montreux. The British and Australian internees and residents benefited greatly from his generosity. There was a chronic shortage of currency in Swiss Francs in the British community owing to the restrictions imposed by the Swiss National Bank. The heightened emotions aroused by war resulted in many personal letters of thanks to Eddie couched in the most effusive terms. On 17 August 1940, after a British Red Cross concert in the presence of David Kelly, the British Minister at Berne, his wife Marie-Noële de Jourda de Vaux, Lady Kelly wrote: 'Words are useless to express the gratitude I feel for all that you have done for us & for the intense pleasure of your exquisite music which moved one to tears'.

The British community in Switzerland comprised mainly retired folk who, if they relied on income from Britain, were on short commons owing to British exchange control. However they were very anxious to engage in work to assist the war effort. In addition there were British refugees from Italy and France. David Kelly, the highly capable British Minister at the Legation in Berne, was a substantial individual and great traveller.* Temperamentally

* Sir David Kelly (1891–1959), highly capable diplomatist and writer, was born on 14 September 1891 in Adelaide, South Australia, the only child of David Frederick Kelly (1847–94), Professor of Classics at the University of Adelaide and Sophie Armstrong (d. 1933) daughter of the Revd Ignatius George Abeitshauer d'Arenberg of Trinity College Dublin. Both his parents were Irish.

he was inclined to seeking peace terms with Germany rather than confrontation. Upon arrival in Berne he was particularly surprised at the Swiss ignorance of English life, character and history, considering the long relationship that had existed between the two countries. He referred to the English refugees he encountered as

> typical specimens of the *déraciné** flotsam and jetsam, which before the war had floated perpetually between Deauville, the French Riviera and the Venetian Lido, with Paris as a winter quarter. They spent the war propping up the bars in Lausanne or Geneva and, when not pro-German, in accusing each other to anyone who would listen, of being German spies.†

He was particularly critical of what he saw as the 'defeatism' of the French and the low morale of the French diplomatic community in Berne, except for the 'old school' Ambassador Monsieur Charles Alphand. Kelly was also a party to what he termed Hitler's intriguing 'peace feelers' in the person of the envoy Prince Max Eugen zu Hohenlohe-Langenburg.‡ His response to these overtures did not always chime with that of his superiors in London including Churchill.

Eddie and David got on well, both being from Irish stock and both fervent Catholics. They even shared disasters, having lost all their personal possessions in house fires. In his memoirs entitled *The Ruling Few,* David Kelly mentions Eddie, albeit briefly

> On a visit to Montreux, when I addressed perhaps two hundred courageous but very depressed elderly British subjects, after a piano recital for charities by Mr Cahill, the Australian pianist …§

At the outbreak of war, Switzerland found herself surrounded by hostile powers.

---

* Rootless

† David Kelly, *The Ruling Few* or *The Human Background to Diplomacy: The Memoirs of Sir David Kelly G.C.M.G., M.C.* (London 1952), pp. 71–2. This volume gives an informative and entertaining anecdotal 'insider's view' by the British Minister at Berne during the early stages of the Second World War in Switzerland, 1940–2. The book presciently points up his view of the importance of the media and shows an acute knowledge of economic and financial considerations on the part of diplomatists long before such factors became common currency.

‡ These meetings and their outcomes and responses were presented erroneously as a confrontation between the German Foreign Minister Joachim von Ribbentrop and Sir David Kelly in the classic war film *The Battle of Britain* (1969).

§ Ibid., p. 269–70.

> The presence of Kelly's small legation in Bern kept the union flag flying in the heart of Nazi Europe, and enabled Britain to organize espionage and smuggling activities which proved invaluable to Britain's beleaguered war effort.*

His work for the intelligence services meant the German High Command planned to have Kelly assassinated. As a result he found life as a minister in Bern 'more exciting than depressing'.

Matters did not always proceed well in the modest and restricted world of charity concerts as money was in such short supply. Significant friction in the small, tightly knit British community arose as the British Red Cross felt that humanitarian concerns were a priority and that funds from all Eddie's concerts should be raised for them alone. However he wished to remit a proportion to the Legation in Berne for the comfort of soldiers at the local internment camps at Büren and Münchenbuchsee.

An 'unpleasant atmosphere seems to prevail in Montreux', which prevented the British Minister and his beautiful aristocratic second wife, Marie-Noële Kelly, from attending Eddie's recitals.† Political in-fighting seemed to have entered even the mounting of charity concerts. Marie-Noële was a close friend of Rebecca West and Freya Stark and was a great traveller, photographer, writer of literary travel books and hostess. She became platonically enamoured of Eddie and they became very close during her husband's posting during the early course of the war. The vivaciousness and élan of both was palpable when together. When David Kelly was unexpectedly transferred to Argentina as ambassador in 1942, it was another blow to Eddie's psychological stability and further increased his sense of isolation. The British community was by now cut off from nearly all avenues of personal and national news on the progress of the war. A growing sense of abandonment and insecurity began to take hold of this frail collection of patriots.

---

* *Oxford Dictionary of National Biography*, 'Sir David Kelly', entry by Neville Wylie.

† (Renée Octavie Ghislaine) Marie-Noële Kelly (née Jourda de Vaux), Lady Kelly (1901–95). One of her ancestors on her father's side her ancestors was the Maréchal Charles Noël de Jourda, Comte de Vaux, who conquered Corsica for Louis XV.

* * *

Eddie was free to live in Switzerland but felt imprisoned. He was a constant reader of Byron and took a deep interest in the poet's visit to Lake Geneva and the history of the area. Although no intellectual, he was a cultured man and drawn to sentimental eighteenth-century French literature and heroic nineteenth-century English poetry, novels and travel writing. He made various literary and musical pilgrimages from Montreux. On one visit to Lausanne in 1940 he called on his friend Ignacy Jan Paderewski who had been very ill. The great pianist would never play in public again but had not lost his sense of humour. At his villa in Morges Eddie recalled 'He told me he had been advised as a young man to give up the piano and study the trombone!'

Eddie wandered the streets of the historic city of Geneva, making the long climb to Villa Diodati at Cologny. In 1816 Byron had fled the opprobrium in England that followed accusations of incest and sodomy. He stayed there with Percy and Mary Shelley, his physician, the 'handsomely saturnine' Dr John Polidori, as well as his sometime pregnant lover Claire Clairmont*. Here these brilliant young people competed to invent ghost stories, the most famous of which, *Frankenstein*, was conceived by seventeen-year-old Mary Shelley.

Switzerland was an integral part of the intellectual and cultural Grand Tour taken by many young English aristocrats in the eighteenth century. Throughout history the Swiss Alps have drawn English mountaineers, artists such as Turner, writers such as Dickens, Wordsworth and Coleridge and other travellers in awe of the alpine scenery. In a letter to Walter Savage Landor in 1848, Dickens wrote perceptively of the Swiss:

> They are the thorn in the side of European despots, and a good wholesome people to live near Jesuit-ridden kings on the brighter side of the mountains. My hat shall ever be ready to be thrown up, and my glove ever ready to be thrown down for Switzerland.

On a boating excursion Byron and Shelley had almost sunk in

* Claire Clairmont was the mother of Byron's daughter Allegra whom, out of convenience, he placed in a Capuchin convent in Italy where she died from typhus at the age of 5.

a storm just off the village of Saint-Gingolph. Byron had become fascinated by the story of François Bonivard, the libertarian Prior of St Victor's Monastery. In 1530 Bonivard was imprisoned in the dungeon of Chillon castle by the Duke of Savoy and chained to a stone pillar for six years. While the two poets were staying at the Hôtel de l'Ancre at Ouchy, Byron – according to Shelley, 'as mad as the winds' – wrote his famous poem *The Prisoner of Chillon* in just a few days.

The poem is both a celebration of freedom and a pessimistic meditation on the spiritually crippling effect of imprisonment. Somewhat self-indulgently Eddie drew parallels with his recent psychological and physical reversals while reading the poem. He wandered in a dismal mood through the damp and dark dungeons of Chillon, one of the last tourists before the castle was closed due to the hostilities. In his copy of Byron's great poem he had heavily scored the lines

Among the stones I stood a stone,
And was, scarce conscious what I wist,
As shrubless crags within the mist;
For all was blank, and bleak, and grey;

Eddie by now received no replies to his letters to Sabine. The days of romantic passion in the balmy evenings wandering Vienna's Prater seemed a distant memory, the charming days of lovemaking in the sunny glades of the Vienna Woods a faded recollection.

* * *

Christmas 1940 was fast approaching for six thousand Polish officers and men interned in Switzerland. Snow and ice lay heavy on the ground. When in the midsummer of 1940 General Guderian's Panzer divisions had pinned the French 45th Army Corps commanded by General Darius Daille against the Swiss frontier, the Swiss Federal Council rapidly granted refuge to the beleaguered French and Polish troops who had put up fierce resistance. The 45th Army Corps included some twelve thousand men of the Polish 2nd Rifle Division (2DSP *Dywizja Strzelców Pieszych* under General Prugar-Ketling). They were among the valiant Poles who had joined the French to continue the fight for their homeland after the brutal

German conquest of their country.

Unlike the French soldiers who were sent home in January 1941, the Poles now found themselves homeless. The Polish state had once again been erased from the map of Europe. Under international law, the Swiss were now forced to finance their detention. To facilitate this and simultaneously defuse political tension with Nazi Germany (which had planned to invade Switzerland in Operation Tannenbaum prior to the outbreak of war) a Polish mass detention camp housing some six thousand men was established near the picturesque medieval village of Büren an der Aare near Berne. It was completed by the winter of 1940. Up to that time the Poles had been billeted in scattered villages where they had become rather too popular with the female population in the absence of Swiss men gamely manning the frontiers and fortresses.

Their abrupt imprisonment at Büren led the Poles to suspect the Swiss were acting on German instructions. Morale fell. The Swiss tightened discipline. Anger erupted into revolt in December 1940. Shots were fired and a number of Polish soldiers were wounded. Following the revolt, the Poles were permitted to work for the princely sum of one franc per day in field, forest and factory, producing badly needed food. The results of this work more than repaid the costs of their internment, to the great satisfaction of the Nazi-encircled Swiss.

* * *

> The cold on 15th December 1940 was Siberian in its intensity.* The new arrivals at the little village station of Büren had crossed the grey winter-wasted plains at the foot of the first range of the Jura mountains by train. Swiss families of soldiers billeted in the village were overjoyed to see their loved ones and thronged the platform. However, among the passengers were a number of Polish internees who descended from the train under watchful eyes, their heads covered by forage caps like common prisoners. They were forbidden to acknowledge any civilians who

* For the following rare first-hand poetic description of a concert by Eddie in wartime I am indebted to the then 29-year-old Colette Muret who wrote a fine, if rather 'purple' review in French (which I have translated and paraphrased) for *La Revue de Lausanne* sometime in December 1940. Muret, '*la doyenne* of Vaud journalists', died in 2009 at the age of 98.

had come to gawp. They saw no-one, watched nothing except the little train returning to civilisation on its meandering course and disappearing into the distance. They watched as one might watch a ship slowly pass over the horizon with no hope of return. In the streets of the old town above the great medieval covered wooden bridge that spanned the River Aare, their comrades sauntered in the village streets in small groups dressed warmly in heavy brown overcoats and Basque berets. They vaguely gazed into the windows of the Gothic-fronted boutiques, windows already too familiar and jammed with naive and rarely changed arrangements of fashion and antiques.

This Sunday was unlike any other. Today the celebrated Australian pianist Edward Cahill would give a concert in the 13th century Evangelical Reform church in the village. This was a rare gift of God for such innate musicians as the Poles. Well before the appointed time, the church was filled to bursting with men sitting erect, wearing sombre expressions on faces weathered to the colour of Spanish leather. Officials brusquely turned back any civilians who tried to enter. The same veto applied to any journalist from Berne who lacked official authorisation to attend the concert. Polish and Swiss officers sat in the gallery while the soldiers sat closely packed around the grand piano placed in the centre of the choir. Then, Edward Cahill, who is small, slender and quick had to thread his way through the rows of soldiers to get to his instrument. He began with two impromptus by Schubert followed by the famous *Minuet in G* by Paderewski. He gave such an exquisite interpretation a tremor passed through the audience.

The first notes of the Chopin 'Heroic' polonaise reverberated through the church. Edward played works by the Polish master for more than an hour. Many present had never known a more moving moment in their lives, occurring as it did in the middle of a bloody conflict and desperate dispossession. In the darkened church an immense atmosphere of self-communion or meditation descended over the assembled refugees, the magnificent white hair of Edward Cahill seeming to softly glow above the keyboard of the black instrument in the choir.

Before long, these toughened soldiers had closed their eyes. Some had buried their heads in their arms, unable to stop their shoulders shaking with sobs. On the Polish officers' handsome faces, all military stiffness of expression had disappeared to be replaced by an inexpressible nostalgia for their motherland that sang from the piano. Next to Cahill one Polish soldier had stood as immobile as a statue throughout the performance, his arms crossed. When the music ceased, he relaxed. He seemed to lose the fierce resistance to his emotions, a painfully maintained self-control, and collapsed within as he groped blindly for a seat to support him.

Edward stopped playing and, exhausted by his efforts, waited for a few moments in the silence that descended over the company. He did not dare to separate them from their patriotic dreams. He understood that he must allow these tough men time to collect themselves before finally launched into a ravishing *Carillon de Noël* of his own composition. He concluded the concert with a dazzling interpretation of another impromptu by Schubert, lifting the gloom into the realm of renewed hope.

Silence reigned once more, the faces of the soldiers and officers again froze into stoic immobility as the Polish internees left the church and plunged into the clammy mist and ice that enshrouded their camp. They carried in their hearts a seemingly interminable depression.

The morality of the neutral stance taken by Switzerland during the Second World War has been discussed at length but it enabled Eddie and many others to carry out vital humanitarian tasks which would otherwise have been impossible if the country had been occupied by the Nazis. In addition to giving the piano recital described above, he selflessly despatched three cases of supplies to the camp at Büren which contained a precious radio for the canteen, over a thousand packets of cigarettes, Swiss chocolates, tens of pairs of slippers, dozens of razors, razor blades, bars of shaving soap, toothbrushes and toothpaste, bootlaces, socks, handkerchiefs, sponges and combs.

Later the same evening he repeated the concert for the small number of British and Australian interned troops. The following evening, he performed the programme again at the British Legation in Berne for Sir David and Lady Kelly and the diplomatic community. Eddie's courage, charm and generosity seemed to override his poor health. His strength of resolve impressed all who met him. Marie-Noële wrote after the concert

My dear Edward, Your precious and magnificent envelope reached me this morning and I was quite flabbergasted when I opened it and it revealed such a large sum of money. It is an

> incredible sum, and my husband and I think you are quite extraordinary as your drive and your talent have worked a miracle amongst the people living in Montreux. Really it is amazing what you have done.
>
> Marie-Noële Kelly

Another moving letter of appreciation after this concert came from the municipality of Lyss charmingly addressed to Monsieur Edward Cahill – Virtuoso, Hôtel Helvétie, Montreux from Capitaine Cuénod de Châteauvieux of the E.M. Région Seeland Int. It reads in part

> How great and sublime your interpretations were. I would have wished to show my enthusiasm by wild applause but unfortunately the sacred place we found ourselves in could not allow this, but believe me, *Cher Maitre,* all hearts vibrated in sympathy while hearing you play. ... hearing the immortal works, interpreted by such an artist as you, is of great comfort to us during the painful times we are living through.

Throughout 1941 Eddie gave many concerts in the Kursaal in Montreux which were always enthusiastically and gratefully received by the critics and of course the funds welcomed by the charities involved. However his health continued to decline as is evidenced from the many caring letters from Marie-Noële Kelly in Berne asking after his well-being. He was greatly saddened when he learned of the death of his greatest musical champion, Ignacy Jan Padrewski, in June 1941. In some compensation he was 'quite overwhelmed' by the playing of the Polish pianist Józef Turczyński whom he heard play a 'truly beautiful *Polish* Chopin with superb colour, poetry and tone' to a similar group of interned troops.*

Eddie had made many friends among the soldiers at the camps in Büren and Münchenbuchsee as a result of his concerts. He found their company a welcome contrast to his previous life in Mayfair. From the correspondence he received, it is clear that he came emotionally close to many of them in their shared isolation. The Swiss authorities had a policy of providing courses of study or manual work for selected soldiers from such internment camps.

* The great Polish pianist and pedagogue Józef Turczyński (1884–1953) had studied the piano under Annette Essipova-Leschetizky in St Petersburg. The essential qualities of his art were familiar to Eddie who had studied in Vienna under Frau Gombrich, a former Leschetizky pupil and auxiliary assistant.

As a result of Eddie's good offices, a few soldiers had been sent for training to the famed Ecole Hôtelière in Lausanne. During the entire course of the war he sent the troops continuous but modest supplies of money gathered from his Montreux recitals as well as winter clothing, shoe coupons and spare suitcases.

Towards the end of 1941 some of the men were packing up with other students at the hotel school to depart for the winter season at the resort of Les Avants, a few kilometres north-east of Montreux. Others were travelling to camps further away. A soldier friend, Arthur Cox, attending the school wrote to him in October

> Although everyone has been very good to us & we really have found some jolly good friends in this part of the country, I consider that you have been really and truly our 'best friend' in every sense of the phrase. The time is rapidly getting close for our departure & I did want you to know that I have & still do appreciate every small action. I suppose it is perhaps because I have done most of the writing to you on behalf of the boys ...

But the communication that gave him the greatest pride was a telegram from the then Prime Minster of Australia, Sir Robert Menzies, which read:

> Congratulations on your good work.
>
> Menzies, Prime Minister, Australia. 27 March 1941

An increasingly neurasthenic Eddie had moved by this time from the busy downtown Hôtel Helvétie et des Familles to the blissfully quiet Hôtel Victoria at Glion, a picturesque village above Montreux. On top of everything else he had begun suffering from a throat infection and asthma attacks under stress. He hoped the peace and quiet would help (asthma was considered a psychosomatic illness in the early 1940s). However his Swiss doctor was well informed for the time and relieved these attacks with aminophylline injections that dilated his bronchial tubes. Courageously ignoring this illness, he hoped to give another concert in Büren at Christmas 1941 but could not obtain anything definite from the Office of the British Military Attaché at the British Legation. For some unexplained reason the Swiss authorities were undecided as to whether they would permit the men to assemble for Christmas as they had the year before. With utmost dismay he learned of the Japanese attack on Pearl Harbour bringing the United States into the war.

Eddie's mental health was becoming progressively frail as a result of the lingering ear infection allied to the threat to his hearing, the asthma attacks and the silence from Sabine. The Adler family had decided not to emigrate before war broke out although many of their Jewish friends had done so. Rumours had percolated through the internment camps in Switzerland via reports from fleeing Allied soldiers of what was happening to Jews in Germany and Austria, the draconian and increasingly bizarre methods of establishing Jewish ancestry. The Adlers however had believed 'the Jewish taint' could never be traced back through so many generations. Sabine relied for protection on her remarkably Aryan appearance with her aquiline features, natural blonde hair and blue eyes. Eddie knew that thousands of Jews or Austrians of Jewish descent had by now disappeared or had their synagogues, homes and businesses burnt down, looted or appropriated.* Musicians seemed to be under particular suspicion owing to the Jewish genius for the art of music.

* By 1938 there were some 185,000 Austrian Jews living in Vienna. Following the terror unleashed after the *Anschluss* by May 1939 some 130,000 had emigrated with scarcely any possessions. More than 65,000 Viennese Jews were deported to concentration camps in Poland, Czechoslovakia or Austria itself. Only 2,000 survived. Around 800 Austrian Jews were left in Vienna at the end of the war. (Jewish Virtual Library.)

CHAPTER 15

CHEATING THE DANCE OF DEATH

Early in 1942, David Kelly, the British Minister at Berne, was replaced by Clifford Norton and his wife Noel Evelyn (née Hughes).* At a stroke in the midst of his own tribulations Eddie lost two more good friends, one being an important emotional relationship. For much of 1942 he rested, except in December when he gave a single recital in Montreux for The British Legation Fund for Soldiers.

Following this 'bereavement', Eddie ceased to give recitals altogether. As he put it 'I floated around' spending time reading his favourite authors, brooding on his present state as an exile of war and taking precautions with his health. Eddie visited the chateau at Coppet on the northern shore of the Lake Geneva, once home to the formidable writer Mme de Staël, daughter of the Swiss banker Jacques Necker, Finance Minister to Louis XVI. This domain had once been the intellectual focus of Europe.† Byron once remarked of Madame de Staël 'Her profile is as frightful as a precipice'. He also travelled to Voltaire's house at Ferney, a town that from 1759 to 1778 was home to the great French writer and philosopher. Meeting Voltaire at Ferney was obligatory for Europe's eighteenth century intellectual elite.

Psychologically rudderless at this time, Eddie wandered the shores of Lake Geneva, strolled around the villages of Clarens, Vevey and the city of Montreux, occasionally hiking through the Alpine landscapes, forests and flower-filled meadows of the Rhône

* Sir Clifford Norton (1891–1990), diplomat, was the son of the Revd. George Norton. He was educated at Rugby School and Queen's College, Oxford. He served on the Gallipoli Peninsula and in Palestine and entered the Foreign Office in May 1921.

† Anne-Louise-Germaine Necker, Baronne de Staël-Holstein, known more widely as Madame de Staël (1766–1817), was a French-Swiss woman of letters, political propagandist, and conversationalist who personified contemporary European culture. She connects the history of ideas from Neoclassicism to Romanticism and cultivated a famous intellectual salon, writing in a wide number of literary genres.

valley. Time was spent ambling around Old Montreux and the steep village streets of Caux and Glion. Eddie spent many hours watching the sun set over Lake Geneva from the terraces of the Hôtel Victoria where he lived for some weeks. Lord Byron had stayed at Glion and sensed the Romantic atmosphere that Jean-Jacques Rousseau had described half a century earlier in *Julie ou La nouvelle Héloïse.* At Vevey Eddie boarded one of the antique steamers that plied the lake and crossed the waters for a day spent in France at picturesque Meillerie. Provincial wine festivals in this charming town lifted his spirits. He even managed to enjoy the old excitements of alpine butterfly hunting.

His patrons the Siegers supported him financially through this difficult period, financing a course of injections at Professor Paul Niehans' famed cell regeneration centre, the Clinique La Prairie at Clarens. Eddie looked so youthful and behaved so energetically that when in health he successfully misled people as to his real age. He took a course of the Niehans controversial foetal sheep cell injections which seemed to have a positive outcome on his mood and asthma attacks.

At Raffles Hotel in Singapore during his 1920s tour of Asia he had met the charismatic and notorious pioneer of gland therapy, the Franco-Russian Dr Serge Voronoff. The doctor had been married to the daughter of Ferdinand de Lesseps who designed the Suez Canal. He was later married to Evelyn, Countess de Périgny, née Bostwick, the daughter of Jabez Abel Bostwick, an early American oil pioneer and business partner of John D. Rockefeller of Standard Oil. Voronoff pioneered the grafting of monkey glands (thyroid and testicles) into humans in pursuit of the secret of reversing or slowing the process of ageing. Voronoff and Eddie were later to become friends. Owing to the difficulty of imports and high demand for testicles, Voronoff was forced to breed monkeys in the gardens of Villa Voronoff (Château Grimaldi) on the Italian Riviera for his experiments. They regularly escaped and caused havoc along the *Riviera dei Fiori.*

After Evelyn's death in 1921 at the age of 48, the doctor had come into a vast fortune which funded his work. Crude gain did not drive his audacious experiments. 'Possession of active genital glands constitutes the best possible assurance of a long life. [...] Great lovers are the only ones who reach advanced ages ... Longevity depends upon the action of the endocrine glands.' This remark comes from his extraordinary book *The Sources of Life*. Among many astonishing case studies he presents a number of photographs purporting to be of a four-year-old 'myxoedematic idiot' possessing 'null intelligence' transformed after monkey thyroid gland grafts into an 'intelligent, vigorous, active' man of 40 resembling a cavalry officer.

He cites the case of one Thomas Parr who lived in 17th century London to the age of a hundred and fifty two and who remarried at one hundred and nineteen. Examined after death by the English doctor William Harvey, physician to Charles I, he reported that the genital glands were 'heavy and voluminous'.* Prolonging the virility of wealthy men past their prime had attracted the attention of the growing eugenics movement in the 1920s and the wrath of anti-vivisectionists. Gland therapy and Voronoff had become the 'secret' subject of hushed conversations in upper-class European drawing rooms and at dinner parties. Some elderly magnates even pounded their chests during banquets to demonstrate their regained virility after undergoing expensive *greffes testiculaires*.

Voronoff's work soon found its way into popular culture. In 1913 Irving Berlin had written a song entitled *Monkey-Doodle-Doo*. A version of this song in a different key was featured by the Marx Brothers in a Broadway musical called *The Cocoanuts* in 1925 but with different lyrics incorporating the Voronoff monkeys. The song also appeared in one of the first Marx Brothers 'talkies' in 1929. One verse contains the lines

Let me take you by the hand
Over to the jungle band
If you're too old for dancing
Get yourself a monkey gland

In Parisian cafés, novelty ashtrays depicting monkeys protecting their private parts had printed on them '*Non, Voronoff, tu ne m'auras pas!*' ('No, Voronoff, you won't get mine!'). Even a 'Monkey Gland Cocktail' was created in the 1920s by Harry MacElhone, owner of Harry's New York Bar in Paris. Wildly popular at the time, the drink was red, forbidden, dangerous and

* Serge Voronoff, *The Sources of Life* (Toronto 1943), see pp. 39–41 and p. 120.

had sexual connotations. It contained an explosive mixture of gin, fresh orange juice, grenadine and absinthe.

Voronoff inspired the rare genre of 'rejuvenation novels' stimulated by his monkey gland grafting. The blurb of *The Gland Stealers* by Bertram Gayton (London 1922) reads

> Gran'pa is ninety-five, possessed of 100,000 pounds sterling, a fertile imagination, and a good physique. He sees in the papers accounts of Professor Voronoff's theory of rejuvenation by means of gland-grafting. How he puts back the clock (and that of his lover, a lady of seventy-five) by means of glands borrowed from a gorilla, and how he collected old men and went to Africa in search of gorillas. A comedy of today, to which the gorilla-hunting scenes give a note of tense drama.

The most famous literary product was the satirical novella featuring the creation of 'Homo Sovieticus' entitled *The Heart of the Dog* by Mikhail Bulgakov. Sir Arthur Conan Doyle also wrote a Sherlock Holmes story called *The Creeping Man* in which the protagonist experiments with monkey extracts with dire results.

* * *

One of Eddie's favourite authors was Jean-Jacques Rousseau. In a melancholic frame of mind brought on by what now seemed a permanent separation from his Austrian lover, he turned once again to *Julie ou La nouvelle Héloïse: Lettres de deux amans, Habitans d'une petite ville au pied des Alpes* (Julie or the New Héloïse: Letters of Two Lovers who live in a small town at the foot of the Alps). He spoke and read French fluently and was living in the vicinity of Vevey where many scenes in this elegant exercise in sensibility take place. Eddie could not resist perusing it once again seated by the shore of the lake. His eye would encounter yachts floating past, their sails 'like rose petals in the breeze'. He readily identified with the sufferings of Peter arising from letters that have been delayed or not received from Julie. In his French edition he had marked

> *'A hundred times have I when reading Novels laughed at lovers' cold moanings over absence. Ah I did not know then how unbearable yours would be one day!'* (Letter XIX from Peter to Julie)*

* This epistolary novel by Jean-Jacques Rousseau was immensely popular and influential when first published in 1761. The story follows the passionate destinies of two lovers, Julie

After strenuous walking in the mountains

> *'where the air is pure and subtle, one breathes more freely, one feels lighter in body, more serene of mind … there one is content to be and to think …'* (Letter XXIII from Peter to Julie)*

* * *

In December 1942 Eddie made a tentative return to society. With his passion for the cinema overcoming daunting obstacles, he obtained and arranged the screening of a 35 mm print of the multiple Academy Award winning film *Mrs Miniver* at the Château Petit Sully near the lakeside village of La Tour-de-Peilz near Clarens.† He overcame his reluctance in the face of fragile health and depression to give a short piano recital after the film. Here he met for the first time Queen Ena of Spain‡. She was a beauty in her youth and had been an avant-garde fashion icon in the 1920s often wearing fabulous jewellery and dresses whose revealing cut teetered on the edge of 'scandalous'. Forced into exile by the Spanish Republicans in 1931, she lived in the Swiss chateau known as the Vieille-Fontaine in Lausanne. She maintained a fine sense of duty to the poor during the war and is considered 'the mother of the Spanish Red Cross'.

Her Lady in Waiting, Mrs Margaret Houghton, wrote a charming letter of appreciation of Eddie's efforts on 1 December 1942

> How glad I am that coming out the other afternoon did you no harm and I am delighted indeed that you made that enormous sum through your own unceasing effort which must have been a considerable one in your present condition of health.

---

d'Étange and Peter Saint-Preux, chronicled in the cultural context of eighteenth-century France. Jean-Jacques Rousseau, *Julie or the New Héloïse: Letters of Two Lovers who live in a small town at the foot of the Alps,* translated and annotated by Philip Stewart and Jean Vaché (Hanover, New England 1997), pp. 57–8.

* Ibid., p. 64.

† *Mrs Miniver* (1942) based on the novel by Jan Struther was the winner of six Academy Awards and starred Greer Garson and Walter Pidgeon. It was directed by William Wyler and produced by Sidney Franklin.

‡ Princess Victoria Eugenie of Battenberg (Victoria Eugenie Julia Ena 1887–1969) was queen consort of the Spanish King Alfonso XIII. Her father was Prince Henry of Battenberg and her mother Princess Beatrice, fifth daughter and youngest child of Queen Victoria. She was the first cousin of George V, Empress Alexandra Feodorovna of Russia, Queen Marie of Romania and Kaiser Wilhelm II of Germany. King Juan Carlos of Spain is her grandson. Born in Scotland, she was known to her family and the affectionate British public simply as 'Ena'.

> The Queen and all of us thought the film *Mrs Miniver* was wonderful, the best I have seen in a very long time, bringing us a fuller realisation, although quietly and without ostentation, of those particular qualities in the English character that do not find their counterpart in any other nationality whatever good traits they may possess.
>
> Queen Ena enjoyed meeting you very much and appreciated your charming thought and gift of those beautiful carnations.
>
> Hoping that when you are quite well again that I may have the pleasure of seeing you here some time.

The final words of the vicar's powerful sermon delivered in the ruins of the parish church during the closing final scene affected Eddie so profoundly he wrote them down: 'This is the People's War. It is our war. We are the fighters. Fight it then. Fight it with all that is in us. And may God defend the right.'

* * *

Early in the Second World War a pilot returning from a raid on Italy glanced below him and described Switzerland as 'a fairy land of bright neutrality in a pool of ink'. However Switzerland was not immune to physical disturbance during those terrible years and the political stance of 'permanent neutrality' did not protect the country from the effects of war.

The Swiss government considered overflights by the Royal Air Force on bombing missions to Germany a violation of Swiss airspace and neutrality. This uncompromising line almost led to a breakdown in relations between the two countries in December 1940 when by accident some bombs fell on Geneva, Basel, and Zurich killing citizens and destroying property. Eddie became aware of a sudden unaccustomed social frostiness. Air Marshall Arthur 'Bomber' Harris, who was by 1942 Commander-in Chief of Bomber Command, following criticism by the British Cabinet, wrote in a minute of January 1943: 'Brief the crews accordingly. They will still transgress. Who cares?'* He considered the use of aircraft in war not subject to international law, believing passionately in the

---

* Quoted in Neville Wylie, *Britain, Switzerland and the Second World War* (Oxford 2003), p. 215.

'freedom of the air' during both war and peace. However historical respect for the Swiss was such that some minimal restrictions were imposed on bombing missions.

On the night of 12/13 July 1943 two tragic accidents struck Bomber Command on a sortie over Turin. Lancaster ED412/EM-Q of 207 Squadron based at RAF Langar in Nottinghamshire was one of 13 aircraft lost of the 295 which attacked Turin that night. Switzerland by this time was blacked out in a 'symbolic retaliation' for the overflying. Some marker flares were to be dropped over Lake Annecy to keep the bombers clear of neutral Swiss territory. They were then to fly over the Alps with Mont Blanc on their left before descending into Italy and on to Turin. However, over France the bombers ran into severe weather. Electrical storms and heavy cloud made navigation problematic. Over one hundred Lancaster bombers found themselves entering Swiss territory. The Swiss fired an estimated 400 shells from their flak batteries at the intruders – considerably more than simple warning shots.

ED412 was hit and broke cloud cover over Vevey trailing black smoke and losing height before crashing into Le Grammont, a mountain above the town of Le Bouveret at the eastern end of Lake Geneva. There was a tremendous flash and explosion, the forested slopes above the town catching fire. All seven crew, one of whom was Australian, were killed. In Vevey three large windows of the Hôtel des Trois Couronnes were smashed. The Aga Khan, one of the hotel guests, was hit in the head by flying glass. Eddie too was awoken in his room at the Hôtel Victoria at Glion, but had no idea what had happened.* Another Lancaster from 467 Squadron from RAF Bottesford in Lincolnshire on the same raid (ED531 PO-T) was forced down by Swiss flak and flew into high-tension cables at Thyon on the western side of the Val d'Hérémence in the Lower Valais, killing all on board. Five of this seven-man crew were Australian.†

Eddie attended the funeral of these fourteen airman at St Martin's Cemetery at Vevey. Almost half the dead were his Australian

* 207 Squadron Royal Air Force History, http://www.207squadron.rafinfo.org.uk/lebouveret/

† Australian War Memorial and the National Archives of Australia. 467 Squadron RAAF Second World War Fatalities by Alan Storr, p. 22.

compatriots. Hundreds of wreaths from British expatriates and the Swiss lay over the coffins. A battalion brass band played Beethoven's Funeral March from the *Eroica* Symphony, which brought Eddie close to tears. 'I cannot bear this war. How much longer?' he wrote in his journal. One cannot help but feel he could have been a great deal worse off during the course of the war than living in a comfortable hotel in neutral Switzerland with wealthy patrons to assist him. The ceremony was attended by the British Minister Clifford Norton, many high ranking officials and military attachés, RAF Air Commodores, British internees, and representatives of the Greek, Belgian, Dutch and Yugoslav colonies in Switzerland, the Aga Khan and many civilians. Three salvos from a Swiss military detachment were fired as handfuls of earth fell on the coffins.

* * *

This tragic incident brought the war close to Eddie, shocked him out of his depression, reignited his sense of duty and he almost immediately resumed his charity concerts. Mrs Clifford Norton, the wife of the British Minister, gave him every assistance. This remarkable woman had a passion for abstract and surrealist art, was known as 'Peter' to her friends and was one of the founders of the Institute of Contemporary Arts. Her husband Clifford Norton had a rather easier time of it as British Minister than Sir David Kelly. Sympathy for the British continued to grow in Switzerland over the duration of the war. Norton felt that Britain owed the Swiss 'an enormous debt [...] for all they are doing and will have to do'.

By August 1943 Eddie was resident with the internees at the Grand Hotel Regina at Caux, some way up the mountain above Glion. The story of this luxury hotel is worthy of a film. Over a period of two years the Caux-Palace was built with difficulty on an impossibly difficult slope and opened its grand salons in 1902 to cater for a sophisticated and wealthy clientele. In the summer of 1905 the young Polish pianist Arthur Rubinstein stayed for some months. He had recently left the Roman town of Orange in Provence and an extravagant champagne, women-filled and caviar-enriched period in the company of his friend the great Russian bass Feodor Chaliapine. Rubinstein wrote a fine description of the hotel. For fun, he mounted an amateur production of Oscar Wilde's *Salome* in German. The hotel officially closed to paying guests at the outbreak of war in 1939. The Great War had severely wounded the tradition of grand hotels, but the Second World War destroyed it for good.

Rubinstein writes

> The Caux Palace was a five-story building of vast proportions, perched on a protruding cliff above the lake. A balustrade, on the edge of a precipice and following its outline, offered a perfect panorama of the entire lake and its guardians the snow-covered Alps. A truly majestic view!
>
> Inside the building, the discreet elegance and meticulous order so typical of Swiss hotels exuded a pleasant feeling of comfort. A wide, carpeted marble staircase led from the entrance hall to the first-floor lobby, a large place with tall bay windows. Here the hotel guests would get together, play cards, sip their coffee, or just gossip. The adjoining dining room, in white and gold, had an open balcony, where, on clear days, one could eat and enjoy the sun. The food was excellent.*

The Crèche Pouponnière Jardin D'Enfants et Entr'aide Montreux, an institution dedicated to orphaned children, benefited from this first new series of Eddie's charity recitals. However his most important concert of the year was in November 1943 in the Grande Salle Paroissiale in Avenue Nestlé for Les Familles pauvres (Catholique de Montreux). The two concerts raised almost 800 Swiss francs.† Professor Bosset writing in the *Journal de Montreux* of 14 November was effusive

> That a musician meets the challenge of filling a concert hall twice within eight days in Montreux in these difficult times is in itself almost a miracle. Well that miracle is Eddie Cahill the Australian pianist [...] Amongst the crowded audience were noticed her majesty the Queen of Spain and the wife of the Dutch Minister at Berne. Her majesty came especially from Lausanne to hear Mr Cahill and show her esteem for this great Australian pianist [...] Mr Cahill gave a second concert (the twentieth altogether so far). We must mention this last recital was one of the most transcendent that Mr Cahill has ever given in Montreux. The four waltzes of Chopin were played with unsurpassable finesse. This concert

* Arthur Rubinstein, *My Young Years* (London 1973). For the full account of his highly entertaining stay, see pp. 159–64.

† Approximately £1,700 in 2015.

was assuredly one of the musical feasts of the winter season here in Montreux. [My translation.]

On 15 November following the recital Eddie received the following typed letter in English from the Lady in Waiting to H.M. Queen Ena of Spain

Château Petit Sully, Tour-de-Peilz, 15/11/1943

Dear Mr Cahill

My trusted fountain pen, alas, after many years of wear and tear has just struck. It probably needs cleaning and so I have to resort to this inglorious machine as I dislike an ordinary pen so much and can only use it for a signature. I had a little talk with the Queen about your beautiful concert and she was so enthusiastic about your great talent, interpretation and the choice of pieces you put on your programme. This is so important and she feels, as I do, that programme making is an art in itself and one is surprised over and over again that musicians of great repute seem to lack the taste in the happy and varied selection that should go with any musical gift. She principally adored your way of playing the Chopin Waltzes, the Scherzo and she found *La Campanella* marvellously played and interpreted in a way that was truly *renversant* [astounding].

In putting forward these particular pieces, in quoting the Queen, it doesn't mean that she didn't enjoy the others tremendously too, for she often looked at me nodding appreciatively in other parts of the programme. These only happen to be her favourite pieces and which she has often heard, as we all have, rendered unsatisfactorily. It is such a disappointment when one is looking forward to some special number.

For my part, I want to add how enchanted I was by the first Mozart, a lovely thing exquisitely played. I did not know it. Neither had I ever heard Noveletten No. 2 by Schumann. Your beautiful tone and shading made of it a very moving piece, there is something so profound in the nature of the feeling and it was splendid to be able to bring it out as you did

We are all so grateful to you for all you have done and to have used your talent so generously for others.

All many thanks for this great musical treat which took us far away for a while from the depressing factors which more or less beset all our lives at present.

However it was not all plain sailing despite the adulation of queens and ambassadors. At the Caux-Palace, which had by now become a military internment camp, Eddie was treated in an off-hand and dismissive manner by a Colonel Batterscomb when he suggested giving a classical concert to raise funds for the internees. Eddie had befriended many of them and had arranged tea parties and other entertainments while resident at the hotel. They were extremely grateful for these 'splendid efforts for the boys' as wrote Private Douglas Holzkamp, a South African, on 18 July 1944. In the same letter he apologised for 'the breach of manners by Colonel B' and thanked Eddie for a Saturday party that was 'the best time we had in years and your kindness will never be forgotten by us'.

* * *

In addition to raising funds for war work, Eddie and the Siegers entertained fifty or more Australians every week at their villa in Montreux. No Australian was forgotten and Eddie made sure of the specific arrangements for each. The Australian Prime Minister John Curtin sent him cable in May 1944 during the first British Commonwealth Prime Ministers' Conference in London congratulating him on this work and sending greetings to all Australians in Switzerland.

Eddie was gratified to receive numerous private thank-you letters from interned troops for his charitable work. Many revealed aspects of life that an internee seldom recorded. From the Civil Prison in Vevey he received the following note from an interned prisoner, one W. Morgan

> I want to thank you for the cakes, cigarettes and all the other things you sent us here. All the boys imprisoned here with me send their thanks. The five of us sat up and looked when the parcel arrived and then when the lid was lifted we fell upon it like hungry wolves.

One disturbing undated letter in 1944 from Private A.D. Curtis of the 2/28th Battalion Australian Imperial Force dealt with incidents of torture and ill-treatment when he was incarcerated in an Italian prisoner of war camp. He clearly hoped Eddie would disseminate this information abroad. 'Mr E Cahill is at liberty to show this letter to any persons he may wish, or to use it during any talks he may give.' Eddie with his talent for empathy lent a sympathetic ear to these troubles and became emotionally committed to the destinies of many soldiers. A classical concert for men who had survived such experiences was like a breath from heaven. The pressure and compulsion he felt to assist the internees may have led to his second nervous collapse, described as 'the agitated state of mind you have been in lately' by one of his correspondents.

* * *

On 14 July 1944 many French citizens living in Montreux and along the Swiss Riviera celebrated the storming of the Bastille and the beginning of the French Revolution. The Marseillaise was to be heard in the air and the tricolour flew from windows quite against Swiss regulations. However everyone knew where their real sympathies lay and no 'official reports' were made. For Eddie, Sunday 23 July began like any other with attendance at the old church in Glion followed by his customary informal morning tea concert in the elegant salon of the Hôtel Victoria. Little has changed in the *Belle Epoque* atmosphere of its salons now decorated with Art Nouveau and Vienna Secession art and ornaments, fresh roses in Sévres vases, tall pink and apricot gladioli. The beautiful gardens retain the bronze sculptures of deer. (During my own stay at the hotel I placed Eddie's own music on the music stand and nostalgically played some Chopin on the *Erard* grand piano in the salon.)

At one afternoon tea at the Victoria Eddie was playing Liszt's tender impressionistic tone poem *Au Lac de Wallenstadt,* a piece from the *Anneés de Pèlerinage: Première Année – Suisse.* Marie d'Agoult described the piece as 'the sighing of the waves' with the 'rhythm of the oar strokes'. He had marked the quotation Liszt had taken from Byron's *Childe Harold's Pilgrimage* written at Villa Diodati where the poet describes Lake Geneva. The verses are printed above the music

Clear, placid Léman! thy contrasted lake,
With the wild world I dwelt in, is a thing
Which warns me, with its stillness, to forsake
Earth's troubled waters for a purer spring.

Childe Harold's Pilgrimage Canto the Third LXXXV

Eddie looked up from the keyboard gazing in a reverie past the steeple of the Temple de Glion out over Lake Geneva far below. The clink of silver against the finest bone china punctuated by desultory, *sotto voce* conversation formed a civilised background.

He vaguely noticed smoke rising from the far shore of the lake behind the border village of Saint-Gingolph but thought nothing of it. After the concert he strolled, as was now his habit, on the sunny terrace of the gardens of the hotel and sat in the shade. It had been rather a hot day. Elderly Swiss gentlemen and ladies passed and complimented him on his playing. He seemed to be coming to terms with his nerves and felt he may well be able to resume normal concert life in Montreux. The smoke he noticed had now become a rather denser haze spreading along the further shore. As there had been little rain recently he surmised a forest fire must have broken out.

By the following Wednesday everyone in Clarens, Vevy and Montreux was speaking of nothing but the brutal reprisal burning of Saint-Gingolph. The picturesque village was divided by the tumbling river Morge, which formed the border between Switzerland and France. It lay on the road to the glamorous French spa town of Évian-les-Bains. On 22 July members of the Free French Resistance from the town of Thonon-les-Bains (the Maquis de Glières of the Haute-Savoie) also known as the *Francs-tireurs et partisans* were ordered to attack German positions along the shores of Lake Geneva*. They enthusiastically agreed 'to harass and attack the enemy wherever they could', having been frustrated in this intention for years.

Around midday most of the German soldiers and officers were having a quiet lunch on the lakeside terrace of the Hôtel de France when a small German patrol in the town was suddenly attacked by the guerrillas. The scene soon became a bloody battle and many Germans, some civilians and a guerrilla were killed. By the evening the resistance fighters had retreated and the customary German reprisals were now greatly feared. The mayor of the Swiss part of the village, André Chaperon, tried to talk to the German Commanding Officer but was told by another German officer in hysterical tones

* FTP or Partisan irregular riflemen were established in 1941 as the military branch of the French Communist Party.

that he had been ordered to raze the entire village to the ground. Panic set in and many French residents fled through the now open customs barrier into Switzerland, welcomed by their courageous Swiss neighbours. Some three hundred were able to seek asylum in the area of the Valais and Vaud. Trains were organised to evacuate some inhabitants to Vevey and Montreux.

By midday on Sunday, SS reinforcements equipped with flame-throwers had arrived in Saint-Gingolph. Eight civilians from the French part of town including the parish priest and a thirteen year-old girl were taken hostage and locked in the customs house. As the fierce flames devoured some eighty houses and barns these hostages were summarily shot in the courtyard of the *gendarmerie.* At the height of the conflagration the mayor and one brave Swiss officer, Brigadier Schwarz, pointed out to the SS officer that the church belonged to *entire* parish of Saint-Gingolph and not only to the French. Further that it was sheltering Swiss women and children. If the Germans attacked it, he would be forced to respond with force of arms, which would constitute an act of war. On hearing this a German soldier grabbed one of the few fire-fighting hoses and doused the church. He was later acquitted of war crimes when this unique case came to trial. The Swiss half of the village was ultimately saved and the French part rebuilt after the war.

When Eddie heard these details of the incident he made immediate preparations to give some charity recitals in Montreux to raise funds for the victims and refugees of Saint-Gingolph. He had never forgotten the assistance its inhabitants had given him when he and his friend crashed their Bugatti on the outskirts in 1939. At the Kursaal in Montreux he performed his usual programme of Liszt, Brahms, Schumann and Chopin. The many letters of thanks and commendation he received always mentioned the Chopin *Marche funèbre* from the B-flat minor Sonata as being the most appropriate and moving of pieces in these hellish circumstances.

Marius Moutet was a remarkable French Member of Parliament and Minister for Colonies. He was a committed, tireless and deeply patriotic Socialist and distinguished himself during the Great War and fought doggedly for the political rights of the indigenous populations under French colonial rule. A fervent pacifist, he voted alongside eighty French parliamentarians against the delegation of powers to Marshal Pétain. Arrested by the Vichy regime for his pains, he was interned with his son at Val-les-Bains in the Ardèche, but escaped to Montreux, where he remained until the end of the war. He gave an eloquent speech at the Kursaal in Montreux after one of Eddie's charity concerts for the Saint-Gingolph refugees

> Montreux 5 August 1944
>
> We should not have done our duty if at the end of Edward Cahill's concert tonight a voice from France had not made itself heard. We wish to thank him for his generous gesture and for the magnificent way in which he acquitted himself in this task. In view of the intimate character of this gathering I take it upon myself to express in all simplicity to our friend here, our deep gratitude for giving so generously of himself and suffering compatriots in Saint-Gingolph, Haute-Savoie. He was able to give the right tone to this evening so appropriate to the sad circumstances for which this concert was given. Through his talent he increased those emotions which were stirred when we think of the victims and martyrs who suffered under the abuses of force and brutality.
>
> Through the sad tones of Chopin's *Marche funèbre* offered to the memory of our countrymen fallen under the blows of the enemy, he united all our grief in this manifestation of the most heart-rending musical evocation of tragic love. With this high artistic and moral attitude he made a victory of this concert, a revenge of the spirit so to speak. This master of the keyboard gave us all the resources of his heart and art. He has thanked us on other occasions for having responded to his appeal. But on this occasion on him alone lie the honour and responsibility, the honour of an artist. I feel this spontaneous initiative speaks so well of the habitual generosity we know so well. We also highly appreciate the fraternal value of his action, which goes to show how close are the bonds that unite all the Allies in the defence of the same ideal and the same cause, that of liberties, that of liberty itself.

Eddie raised almost 1300 Swiss francs for the Aide aux Réfugiés de St-Gingolph.* The courageous mayor André Chaperon wrote in a letter acknowledging his gift 'we will never forget this magnificent gesture'.

As the war drew to an end Eddie continued giving piano recitals

* Approximately £6,300 in 2015.

but talked of leaving Switzerland for Paris with the Siegers as soon as was feasible. The German surrender took place in late April and early May of 1945. However his increasingly fragile nervous condition created paralyzing indecision. He constantly postponed his departure. The social contacts he had made during those years sustained him in Montreux on and off until at least Christmas 1948. Mrs Noel Norton hosted various recitals and he continued loyally entertaining the remaining internees. By this time the billet at Caux had been augmented by escaped prisoners of war. He was awarded an ornate certificate by the British Legation in Berne acknowledging his war work.

Signaller L.V. Leith spoke for so many who heard Eddie over those war years and gained vital succour from his rare musical powers. In a letter dated 22 September 1944 Leith wrote eloquently from the military camp at Caux-sur-Montreux

> This war is full of surprises. Its biggest surprise, as far as I am concerned, will always be the occasion when I had the privilege of attending a private recital by an artist of such as your calibre [...] What was a mere incident in your life will remain a memorable occasion in ours.

CHAPTER 16

BRIDESHEAD NOT REVISITED

For myself I am one of the most convincing proofs that the real Germany is alive and well and will remain alive. The will to live and work in me is, however critically I view myself, that of a completely unbroken nation.

Wilhelm Furtwängler*

As the war staggered to an end, Eddie at the age of sixty faced agonising choices. The tensions and uncertainties of the conflict had exacted a high psychological price. He found sleep difficult and although usually not seeking comfort in alcohol, he had begun to drink excessively. The many stories of suffering, torture and death he had heard from the officers and men had accumulated in his mind. The poor food, the repetitive nature of his concerts, his suffering over unrequited love and the fatigue of endless charity work had drained his energy. And then by the middle of 1945 it was all over and a strange sense of anti-climax descended over him. This rather intense and exacting life had suddenly become a dead blank. With no more charity concerts to give, he felt he no longer had a purpose. Was there any compelling reason to remain in Switzerland?

The Swiss Alps under snow remained a symbol of freedom in a devastated continent. Berlin and all the major German cities had been pulverised. His beloved Vienna had lost some ninety thousand apartments and the infrastructure of bridges, sewers, gas and water pipes had suffered severe damage. He learned from an interned Polish officer that only some 80kms from Sabine's home of Melk the immense Mauthausen slave labour complex had been established

* Wilhelm Furtwängler, *Notebooks 1924–1954*, trans. Shaun Whiteside, ed. Michael Tanner (London 1989), p. 151.

with around ten thousand inmates. The camp was mostly used for extermination through labour of the intelligentia and educated middle classes. Conditions were so exceptionally brutal and severe it was known colloquially as the *Knochenmühle* or 'bone-grinder'. The possible destiny of the Adler family in such a place was all too terrible to contemplate.

Switzerland and much of Britain had avoided the disastrous physical destruction of many major continental cities. Having escaped invasion and occupation, both countries would also avoid the immense displacement of human populations that were soon to come, especially in the East. Concerning the relations between the two nations, Clifford Norton, the British Minister in Berne, claimed 'the British flag flies higher than any other in this small country'.* Swiss manufacturing during the war years had been weighted in favour of the Axis powers. Yet Switzerland, a self-styled observer, had remained a constitutional, democratic and federal state. London, unlike the United States, remained well-disposed to 'neutral' Switzerland throughout the conflict. British officials often turned a tolerant eye on the disagreeable Swiss refugee policies and misdemeanours concerning the sale of German plunder and spoils. Churchill wrote to Roosevelt early in 1944 'if Switzerland did not exist it would need to be invented'. He remarked in a Personal Minute to Anthony Eden that autumn

> Of all Neutrals Switzerland has the greatest right to distinction. She has been the sole international force linking the hideously sundered nations and ourselves. What does it matter whether she has been able to give us the commercial advantage we desire or has given too many to the Germans, to keep herself alive? She has been a democratic state, standing for freedom in self-defence among her mountains, and in thought, in spite of race, largely on our side.

Switzerland in 1945 remained a horn of plenty compared to the rest of the continent. As the country was outside the Sterling Area, British residents were subject to exchange controls, which severely restricted movement abroad. If Eddie was to make Switzerland his home, he would have been unable to transfer sufficient money from England and would need to extend his residence permit

---

* Quoted Wylie, *Britain, Switzerland and the Second World War*, p. 333.

indefinitely. In the meantime he remained a guest of his wealthy patrons Mr and Mrs Arthur Sieger in Montreux. In many ways he had become financially trapped by them, his future determined by their decisions. Yet he was happy enough. He would often sit in the garden of their villa at Pré-Choisi above Clarens dreaming whilst gazing over Lake Geneva to the distant Savoy Alps and the Dents du Midi, the elegant steam ferries scything soundlessly through the still waters. The possibility of earning a decent living through giving classical piano recitals at this turbulent time seemed a lost illusion.

Eddie began at last to receive correspondence from friends and patrons in England. Having at one point seriously decided to return to London, his initial attempts to find accommodation proved fruitless. On celebratory VE Day, amid the shambles of the bombing, the photographer Cecil Beaton found Kensington 'as quiet as a Sunday' and added 'There is no general feeling of rejoicing. Victory does not bring with it a sense of triumph – rather a dull numbness of relief that the blood-letting is over'. But from The Mall all the way to the gates of Buckingham Palace a sea of closely packed people waited patiently for the appearance of the Royal Family on the balcony. In the West End an excitable WAAF wrote

> There was wild excitement in Trafalgar Square, half London seemed to be floodlit – so much unexpected light was quite unreal. There were people dancing like crazy, jumping in the fountains and climbing lamp-posts.

July 1945 had seen a landslide victory for Clement Atlee leading a Labour Government. No one wanted a return to the glaring social inequalities, mass unemployment and poverty of the thirties. Here was a chance to rebuild a better Britain. Churchill was universally admired but little liked according to a melancholic 'Chips' Channon who after the election was 'shocked by the country's treachery' when he was not elected. The former Prime Minister remained as sanguine and jovial as ever.

Domestically, rationing of almost everything seemed endless – meat, butter, margarine, sugar, tea, cheese, jam, eggs, sweets, soap, clothes, petrol and coal were all in short supply. Silk stockings were as prized as gold and a shop in Holborn sold dead crows as food.

> Piccadilly is crawling with life, but equally repellent in its different way. The summer murk, stagnant and tepid, is eddying with the aimless movement of British and American soldiers and the deteriorated London tarts that circulate slowly or clot in groups.*

Mayfair residences had been bombed, country estates despoiled and across Britain two and a half million ordinary homes had been destroyed or damaged. Great country houses had been requisitioned by civil service diktat for military purposes. Avenues of ancient trees had been lopped for unused airfield runways, concrete roads had been built willy-nilly, picturesque landscaped parks had been designated for assault courses, mortar ranges and tank training with live rounds. Some three hundred Rolls-Royce cars had been commandeered or loaned for military use, some converted into Armoured Cars. Superb interiors had become brigade headquarters or boarding schools. Even open-cast mining for low grade coal took place on some estates, destroying forever the sublime landscape garden creations of a Capability Brown or Humphrey Repton.†

In his novel *Brideshead Revisited,* Evelyn Waugh nostalgically describes in an eloquent symbol the destruction of art and culture that even the Luftwaffe had failed to achieve

> That fountain is rather a tender spot with our landlady; the young officers used to lark about in it on guest nights and it was looking a bit the worse for wear, so I wired it in and turned the water off. Looks a bit untidy now; all the drivers throw their cigarette-ends and the remains of sandwiches there, and you can't get to it to clean it up, since I put wire around it. Florid great thing isn't it?‡

Matters were exacerbated by crippling death duties and supertax imposed by the Labour government. Eddie would never recover those halcyon days of visiting princesses in their town houses, the leisured country house 'Saturday-to-Monday' music parties, servants at beck and call and rambles in the deer park mentally rehearsing a Chopin programme. The era of privilege and cultivated

---

* Edmund Wilson, *Europe Without Baedeker* (London 1948), p. 177.

† Nearly one thousand country houses were demolished as a result of war damage between 1945 and 1955. Some estates that were sold became golf clubs or hotels and some were even transformed into prisons in which guise they remain to this day.

‡ Evelyn Waugh, *Brideshead Revisited* (London 1945), p. 273.

taste that he had loved so dearly had been swept away forever.

On occasion his thoughts turned wistfully to another of his familiar haunts, the French Riviera, the source of so many of his past sensual pleasures, that 'eternal Carnival by the Sea'.* By August 1939 Cap Ferrat had become a designated military area with machine guns and anti-aircraft emplacements. Roads clogged with refugees and fleeing expatriates heading north collided with soldiers marching south. *Le Train Bleu* was booked solid. When Italy entered the war in June 1940 just before Hitler marched into Paris, there was tumult on the Côte d'Azur as the British population of Menton and Monaco began to flee. John Taylor, the British Consul in Nice, had requisitioned two stinking colliers to repatriate British nationals and thousands of others. All classes of society fled together. Luxury cars were abandoned on the quayside, the keys thrown ostentatiously into the local crowd; the English film director Guy Hamilton drove his Rolls-Royce into the Mediterranean rather than have the Italians purloin it.

Somerset Maugham abandoned his beloved Villa Mauresque and his lover Gerald Haxton, who stayed on as a temporary caretaker. He boarded the filthy MV *Saltersgate* at Cannes where he had been allocated a small space in the hold. There were no cabins and no sanitary facilities save for that of the crew. Three unspeakable weeks elapsed before the mouth of the Mersey appeared through the smog.† Eddie and his patrons the Siegers had already fled in their Isotta Fraschini to Switzerland and the safe haven of their mansion at Pré-Choisi overlooking the Île de Salagnon at Clarens near Montreux.

They had simply abandoned their villa at Bordighera after secreting valuables and paintings with their Italian friends. Fraught discussions now took place on the shores of Lake Geneva as to whether they should return to contemplate 'the ruins of the Riviera'. St Tropez had been bombarded and Eddie's favourite town, 'martyred Mentone', occupied by the Nazis.‡ Life there could barely be carried on at all. It was the last town to be liberated as

* F. Scott-Fitzgerald essay 'Early Success' in *The Crack Up* (New York 1945).

† For a full gruelling account of Somerset Maugham's flight see Selina Hastings, *The Secret Lives of Somerset Maugham* (London 2009), pp. 445–9.

‡ 'Menton' in French and 'Mentone' in Italian is situated on the Franco-Italian frontier.

late as April 1945 with atrocities and reprisals perpetrated by the desperate SS following destruction from allied shelling. All avenues for a return there also seemed closed.

Further along the coast at Monaco the Baroness Orczy had remained in fitful contact with Eddie. When he could, he would send her month-old English newspapers and food parcels (bacon, a cheese, tinned peas), which she greatly appreciated. Monaco had remained defiantly neutral at the outbreak of war but most of the English and American colony were frantically trying to escape the inevitable. The Italians had been stopped in their advance at Mentone. The Baroness and her ill husband were desperately short of cash. Monaco was not in the Sterling Area and they were subject to severe exchange controls; transfers were limited to £25 per year.* They were forced to sell items of jewellery at a significant loss. Throughout the war the numbers of 'collaborationists' grew alongside hatred of the British by the Vichy French. The baroness was advised not to speak English in the streets.

> But how intolerable was the sensation of living and constantly rubbing shoulders with those who hated us and our country so virulently, and wrote and published such abominable lies.†

Italy occupied the Principality in November 1942, a popular move as many of the residents were Italian. 'They strutted about like turkey cocks in a farmyard,' observed the baroness. In addition 'under pressure from Germany one could suppose – [Italy] suddenly developed anti-Semitic tendencies'.‡ Prince Louis II issued many of the three hundred resident Jews of Monaco with false papers, but the intervention of the Vichy Government and the Gestapo meant some eighty souls were transported to an inevitable fate at Auschwitz.§

The Fascists soon ordered all British nationals to leave the Riviera. Some fled to Grenoble, others were sent to Vence or into *résidence forcée* in the hinterland of the Mediterranean, some ended up in

* Around £940 in 2015 values. The Sterling Area was a wartime emergency measure that involved cooperation in complex exchange control regulations between a selected group of countries, mostly Commonwealth dominions and colonies.

† Baroness Orczy, *Links in the Chain of Life: The Autobiography of Baroness Orczy* (London 1947), p. 209.

‡ Ibid., p. 214.

§ Conclusions of the Jewish Cultural Association of Monaco.

prison camps. The Germans finally occupied the Principality in September 1943 after Mussolini's collapse. They enjoyed their stay immensely, gambling and indulging in other sybaritic recreations.

> The young women – heaven forgive them – were only too ready to bring about this friendly *entente* with the German soldiers as they had been with the Italians and learned to say *Guten Tag* with as broad a smile as they said *Buon Giorno* before.*

The Allies systematically bombed the French Riviera and Monaco harbour in the early summer of 1944 causing considerable damage to the port area, narrowly missing the baroness herself when a bomb exploded on the roof of her home. Many civilian deaths resulted in towns along the coast. The Principality was finally liberated on 3 September when a US Army jeep finally sped into the casino square. Most of Eddie's friends had by then abandoned Monaco and he felt not the slightest inclination to return to a social desert struggling to recover from a horrifying war.

As for a return to his homeland, scarcely any passenger ships other than military vessels were sailing from Europe to Australia in 1946 so soon after the end of hostilities. At any event he had by now been well and truly 'spoiled by European culture' as he put it and no longer had any wish to return to his colonial roots. Having ruled out Australia, he thought about the haven of the US, by now harbouring in exile many of the most brilliant Jewish European musicians and intellectuals. However his brief concert tour of the United States had not been a particularly happy one. Unlike Arthur Rubinstein who left his Paris home before the war, Eddie had no family responsibilities weighing him down or emotional attachments to protect. He did not feel like a refugee and did not wish to face the bureaucracy of settlement in America or the idea of possibly surrendering his Australian citizenship.

Marooned in Switzerland what was he to do? And where was he to go?

* * *

Eddie's mental and physical health was giving rise to increasing concern among his friends. The Siegers insisted he again consult the

* Orczy, *Links in the Chain of Life*, p. 218.

debonair Professor Niehans at the Clinique La Prairie at Clarens. They would settle the exorbitant fees. He could recuperate at the clinic and take a course of the famed cell regeneration therapy at their expense. This charismatic professor had inherited the mantle of the gland grafter Dr Serge Voronoff whom Eddie had first met at Raffles Hotel in Singapore in 1920. By this time however Voronoff had been comprehensively discredited by the medical establishment. 'His error was simply self-deception and this defect he shared with many scientists before and after him.'*

A charlatan American businessman, 'Dr' John R. Brinkley, followed Voronoff in originating the catchy marketing slogan 'You are only as old as your glands'. His particular preference was to graft goat glands and not monkey testicles. A journalist who was grafted by Brinkley brightly reported that now he

> could work long hours day after day with no sense of mental fatigue but a certain gaiety of heart as if life was rather a lark, he being accurately introspective and not easily deceived into optimistic conclusions.†

He had deceived himself. Modern science has proven that tissue rejection from animal to man would have taken place within hours if not minutes. In a foot race, seventy year-old John Pearson, an inmate of San Quentin prison, reputedly came a good second carrying an extra grafted testicle, beating several younger inmates restricted to the more usual two.

Professor Paul Niehans was a remarkable character. Possibly descended from an illegitimate daughter of the liberal Hohenzollern German Emperor, King Frederick III of Prussia, he unlike Brinkley, had a distinguished academic career of precocious brilliance. As a young man he was an excellent horseman, mountaineer and pistol shot. 'He breaks hearts and tosses off champagne at six in the morning on the shores of the Danube.'‡ By the age of thirty-three he had become a doctor of both theology and medicine, distinguishing himself particularly by treating wounded soldiers in Serbia during

* David Hamilton, *The Monkey Gland Affair* (London 1986), p. 145. This excellent and highly entertaining volume written by a trained transplant surgeon is the best short introduction to Dr Voronoff and his fellow gland grafters.

† Ibid., p. 43.

‡ Gilles Lambert, *The Conquest of Age: The Extraordinary Story of Dr Paul Niehans* (New York 1959), p. 49.

the Great War. By 1925 he had become the most renowned glandular surgeon in Europe.

Music played an important part in his life, which may account for his accepting Eddie as a patient. Niehans recalled that the function of the hypothalamus gland came to him during a performance of the Beethoven *Coriolanus Overture* conducted by Karl Münchinger. Following a famous emergency incident in 1931 when Niehans successfully injected a patient with macerated parathyroid glands from a steer, he abandoned his own early gland grafting experiments and took to injecting the foetal cells of hand-reared lambs directly into his distinguished celebrity clientele. One of the first was the Maharajah of Darbhanga, 'supine on precious silks, among the rarest furs, he remains plunged in a kind of definitive torpor ... Nothing can awaken a flicker of interest in his weary eyes'.* Niehans diagnosed the improbable and fascinating complaint 'neuro-vegetative dystonia', a disease unique to '*those who have everything.* There is nothing left to desire, even life itself'.† After an injection of foetal sheep cells, the Maharaja slowly recovered his appetite for food and *continued to live.*

Gland therapy had by now become an ultra-fashionable topic of conversation among the seriously rich. Somerset Maugham, Gloria Swanson, Marlene Dietrich, Noël Coward all took rejuvenation treatments at Clarens. Charlie Chaplain, Aristotle Onassis and even the Duchess of Windsor were rumoured to have attended the clinic. Konrad Adenauer, Winston Churchill and many other prominent people who made the journey to Clinique La Prairie swore by the efficacy of the treatment.

To maintain anonymity, rather theatrical admission procedures prevailed. After waiting weeks for an appointment, famous clients would arrive at the clinic by night and gain admission through use of a secret headlight signal from the taxi driver. Did their positive outcomes come from the placebo effect, the puritan health regime or simple embarrassment at the fabulous amounts of money misspent?

Paul Niehans' sense of style, the world fame of his patients, his careful choice of only the elite as worthy of treatment (he rejected

---

* Ibid., p. 80.

† Ibid., p. 81.

Stravinsky) and the cloak-and-dagger secrecy attendant on his procedures meant he was always in demand and handsomely rewarded. At his Renaissance villa at nearby Burier, approached by a grand *allée* of cypresses, Dutch and Italian Old Master paintings adorned the walls, the floors and walls warmed by Abusson carpets and Gobelin tapestries once owned by Napoleon.

The treatments at the Clinique La Prairie remain controversial to this day, despite modern medical opinion being much modified by substantiated contemporary scientific research into the nature of human embryonic stem cells, their replication and use in cancer and other treatments. Some respected gerontologists are now returning to the original early findings and possible blind alleys of Alexis Carrel, Serge Voronoff and Paul Niehans, those pioneering sleepwalkers in the science of senescence. The Clinique La Prairie remains a well-kept secret. 'Youth is the one thing worth having', Lord Henry told Dorian Gray in Oscar Wilde's novel *The Picture of Dorian Gray*. 'It [beauty] is one of the great facts of the world, like sunlight or springtime. [...] It cannot be questioned. It has its own right of sovereignty. It makes princes of those who have it.'

The clinic was located almost at the water's edge. In the early morning Eddie would be given his treatments. After a healthy breakfast he would take the sun on the veranda of the alpine villa under a striped awning, reading or writing in his journal until lunch. His afternoon walk by the lake offered one of his favourite opportunities to wander and dream. The air is soft and pure. A solitary fisherman in a straw hat can lend an almost oriental immobility to the scene. Eddie's imagination did not need to range far to conceive Rousseau's 'bower at Clarens' from *La Nouvelle Héloïse* where Julie's rosy lips first alighted on those of Saint-Preux, a first kiss that drove him 'raving mad'. This enchanted place seems miraculously to inspire thoughts of new loves, fictional loves or a nostalgia for lost loves.

Many famous musicians and writers are associated with the village of Clarens. Most famously, in 1816 Byron and Shelley sailed across the lake from Geneva in search of the 'visionary woods' of Rousseau only to find them obliterated by development and local ignorance. Nevertheless

> At Clarens, his 'sweet Clarens', Byron found every aspect of Nature charged with the 'breath of passionate thought'; it is the home of Love, 'who here ascends a throne, to which the steps are mountains.'*

Tchaikovsky took a rest cure there for various periods between 1877 and 1879 and worked on the operas *Eugene Onegin* and *The Maid of Orleans.* He also wrote the D major Violin Concerto inspired by his love for the violinist Iosif Kotek, who stayed with him. 'It goes without saying that I would have been able to do nothing without him. He plays it marvellously.'† Tolstoy, a great admirer of Rousseau, resided in the 'Village de Julie' in the spring of 1857. He wrote in his diary

> I was at Clarens for two months, and every time when in the morning, and especially after dinner towards evening I opened the shutters on which the shadows were already falling, and glanced at the lake and the distant blue of the mountains reflected in it, the beauty blinded me and acted on me with the force of a surprise.‡

In October 1910 Igor Stravinsky left his home in Ustilug in Ukraine for the pure air of Clarens in search of a cure for his beloved wife, who was suffering from tuberculosis. During the winter of 1911–12 in a small furnished room a mere eight foot square with a piano, a table and two chairs, he completed the sketch of the revolutionary score of the Russian ballet of ecstatic pagan love, *Le Sacre du Printemps*. More recently, the Russian writer Vladimir Nabokov took up residence with his wife and muse Vera in a suite of rooms at the nearby Montreux Palace Hotel in 1961 to write short stories, poetry, lectures, *Speak Memory* (his 'Autobiography Revisited') and novels. Nabokov died in 1977 and is buried together with his wife Vera in the cemetery at Clarens.

* * *

One morning in the summer of 1945 Eddie was reading as usual in the garden of the clinic in this enchanted place and noticed a tall

* Charles I. Elton, *An Account of Shelley's Visits to France, Switzerland and Savoy in the Years 1814 and 1816* (London 1894), Introduction, p. 5.

† Quoted in David Brown, *Tchaikovsky: The Crisis Years, 1874–1878* (New York 1983), p. 261.

‡ Aylmer Maude, *The Life of Tolstoy: The First Fifty Years* (London 1917), p. 170.

figure in hat and long coat walking briskly towards the path by the lake. With a start he felt sure he recognized the great German conductor Wilhelm Furtwängler. How could it possibly be that the greatest conductor of the day was wandering here? Had he somehow escaped the Nazis and the conflagration in Berlin? The following day he managed to arrest him in mid-stride and modestly introduced himself. The extraordinary history of Wilhelm Furtwängler during the war years should be considered in some detail as it is the source of Eddie's enduring and deep respect for this conductor both as a man and musician.

Despite their general philistinism, the Nazis clearly had a pathological relationship with music and employed it on every possible public occasion. They also utilized the unwitting and arguably naive Furtwängler and 'his' Berlin Philharmonic Orchestra as a formidable cultural propaganda weapon and showpiece. He had taken over the role of principal conductor from Arthur Nikisch in 1922. Since the Berlin Philharmonic was privately financed and facing bankruptcy, by the 1930s it had fallen under the Goebbels Ministry. Some Jewish orchestral musicians soon fled or were expelled despite Furtwängler's efforts to retain them.

The Mendelssohn medallion was removed from the pantheon of German composers dotted around the frieze in the Philharmonic Hall. Yet only sixteen orchestral players actually joined the Party (one played in full uniform when they performed in Germany) far fewer than in the Vienna Philharmonic. Furtwängler and his players were a very privileged group being particularly well paid. They were offered such perks as opportunities to buy real coffee ('like diamonds') on overseas tours which could be exchanged for food or cash on return to Germany. Remarkably, Hitler insisted on the players being exempted from military service. However near the end of the war Goebbels ordered that the musicians were to be drafted into the *Volkssturm* or German national militia.

With great skill Albert Speer, Nazi Minister of Armaments and War Production, managed to delay this military draft. A little over two weeks before Hitler's suicide on 30 April he requested at their final concert on 12 April 1945 they perform Beethoven's Violin Concerto.* Also, rather morbidly in view of subsequent

* With the German violinist Gerhard Taschner as soloist.

events, Brünnhilde's last aria and the finale from *Götterdämmerung* as well as Bruckner's *Romantic* Symphony. The concert was conducted by Robert Heger. Speer wrote later: '"When Bruckner's *Romantic* Symphony is played, it will mean the end is upon us," I told my friends.'* It was reported to be an unforgettable concert in the unheated Beethoven-Saal inexplicably still standing among the ruins, the audience 'huddled in overcoats'. The historic old *Philharmonie* had already been reduced to ashes with the loss of priceless scores and instruments. Baskets containing cyanide capsules were proffered to the audience at the exit by child members of the Hitler Youth. Speer was horrified.†

The members of the Berlin Philharmonic had seldom considered the political implications of their playing. 'We are artists not politicians.' As the final death throes of the Reich took hold, the orchestra performed in the dark when the electricity failed and paused only briefly during air raids. In the abandoned Olympic Village converted to a Wehrmacht hospital, they played for the amputees as the Russians inexorably advanced on the capital.

Throughout the conflict, the Nazis considered Furtwängler to be directing what the authorities pretentiously termed 'the intellectual war' running in tandem with their military campaigns. The Russians fought for Berlin from 16 April until 2 May. On 1 May it was announced that Hitler had committed suicide in his Berlin bunker. As part of the 'memorial address' on the radio given by Admiral Karl Dönitz, a recording was broadcast of the *Adagio* from Bruckner's Seventh Symphony with Furtwängler conducting. The orchestral players who courageously remained in Berlin to 'face the music', were reunited as soon as 16 May and gave their first concert on 26 May 1945, astonishingly soon after hostilities ceased. The Berlin Philharmonic under Leo Borchard made sure they included Mendelssohn's overture to *A Midsummer Night's Dream* in the programme.

Unlike conductors such as Herbert von Karajan, Oswald Kabasta and Hermann Abendroth, Furtwängler never joined the Nazi party, never made the 'German greeting' and refused to conduct the

---

* Albert Speer, *Inside the Third Reich: Memoirs by Albert Speer*, trans. Richard and Clara Winston (London 1970) p. 463.

† Gitta Sereny, *Albert Speer: His Battle with Truth* (London 1995), p. 507.

Berlin Philharmonic on tour in any occupied country. He avoided conducting at the opening ceremonies of the *Parteitag* in Nuremberg and never signed his correspondence or concluded conversations with Goebbels or any other Nazi using the words 'Heil Hitler'. To the best of his ability, he assisted and saved the lives of many Jewish musicians and even Jews not involved in the musical world, terrible risks at the time. Just as the National Socialists claimed Beethoven and Wagner for propaganda purposes, so they used Wilhelm Furtwängler to spin a web of cultured illusion. He was in fact finally fully exonerated in December 1946 after two de-Nazification trials, one in Vienna and the other in Berlin. He was permitted to begin conducting the Berlin Philharmonic again in May 1947 and resumed his punishing schedule at the Lucerne and Salzburg festivals shortly after.

Envy and professional fear of his musical genius played their part in making him a musical pariah in the United States. He never performed there again. The Jewish violinist Yehudi Menuhin was one of the few musicians of international renown who supported him throughout his trials and never believed in his anti-Semitism. Menhuin recorded a renowned interpretation of the Beethoven Violin Concerto under the conductor with the Lucerne Festival Orchestra during the Lucerne Festival of 1947. 'Furtwängler, the aristocrat of conductors, embodied the noblest of the great German musical tradition. He was really, truly the servant of the music.'*

The details of Furtwängler's flight from Germany, although unknown to Eddie at the time, emerged during his de-Nazification trial in December 1946†

> In October 1944, Mrs Himmler's personal doctor [Frau Dr Richter] came to see me and told me of Himmler's and the SS intentions. From the start Himmler personally considered me an enemy of the State, this lady confirmed to me. She came back in November. In January 1945, when I was in Berlin for the last time, she came suddenly early one morning, and told me: 'Mr

---

* Commentary on Furtwängler by Menuhin in *The Art of Conducting: Legendary Conductors of Golden Era*, Teldec Video 0927 42668 2.

† At the Potsdam Conference July–August 1945 the Allies decreed that 'all members of the Nazi party who have been more than nominal participants … are to be removed from public or semi-public office and from positions of responsibility in important private undertakings.'

> Furtwängler, nobody is to know that I have come to see you. Let me inform you that the SS are talking of putting you in quarantine. No Nazi is supposed to talk to you anymore. Everything you do, all your telephone calls are under surveillance. You are accused of having participated in the attack against Hitler [the Claus von Stauffenberg assassination attempt at Wolf's Lair in July 1944]. It's up to you to draw your own conclusions'. Then she left. I decided I should not go back to Berlin after my concerts in Vienna and so I hid out for three days near the Swiss border.*

Götterdämmerung was fast approaching for these less-than-Gods. The Nazi upper echelons despite their professed fervour for the sublime pantheon of German composers actually preferred beer halls and cafés. Hitler would listen to Wagner's music as if in a trance, the vast conceptions working on his megalomania like a drug. He commented 'there is no more glorious expression of the German spirit than the immortal works of the Master'.† Hitler absorbed the stagecraft and operatic gestures of Wagnerian singers and possibly the conducting style of Mahler for his harangues at the Nuremberg rallies.

During the interval of a Berlin concert in December 1944 Albert Speer had been invited to the great conductor's room backstage.

> With disarming unworldliness he [Furtwängler] asked me straight out whether we had any prospect of winning the war. When I replied that the end was imminent, Furtwängler nodded; he had come to the same conclusion. I advised him not to return from an impending concert tour in Switzerland. 'But what is going to became of my orchestra?' he exclaimed.‡

Taking advantage of the Swiss concerts that had been planned earlier, Furtwängler crossed the Swiss border uneventfully on 7 February 1945 to join his wife Elizabeth and baby son Andreas in Zurich. Later the conductor and his family settled at Clarens with his friend Professor Niehans at the Clinique La Prairie, where he stayed until June 1947. This was where he met Eddie.

---

* From trial transcripts in the Wilhelm Furtwängler Archives, Zurich.

† Quoted in Alex Ross, *The Rest is Noise* (London 2008), p. 315.

‡ Speer, *Inside the Third Reich*, p. 462–3.

* * *

The diminutive Irish Australian and tall German seemed to hit it off astonishingly well. The two musicians built a brief friendship during their time together at Clarens.* Eddie knew little of the detail of Furtwängler's escape from Germany but was well aware of the critical anti-Nazi storm, a type of press 'civil war' which had broken over the conductor's head upon his arrival in Switzerland. Many Swiss musicians rallied behind his 'intellectual self-determination' but there were also violent demonstrations. At Winterthur the police were forced to deal with stink bombs and even resorted to water cannon to disperse an angry crowd.

Both musicians were supremely apolitical creatures and found much to discuss concerning art, composers and interpretation. Furtwängler himself was a fine pianist.† Eddie was bubbling over with enthusiasm for a concert he had attended in Lausanne on February 12, where Furtwängler conducted Beethoven's First Symphony, the Leonore Overture No. 2 as well as the Second Symphony of Brahms with the Orchestre de la Suisse Romande. He felt the conductor to be a deeply religious person who was magically able to elevate performances, especially of Beethoven, into the realms of an 'inevitable spiritual universality'.

Both were fond of walking. The lake shore at Clarens gave them ample opportunities for long discussions *en marchant*. Occasionally they would breakfast or dine together and Eddie found Furtwängler's wife Elizabeth to be a 'wonderfully passionate and lively person, full of intelligence and charm'.‡ He reflected later they were clearly 'deeply in love'. The two musicians shared a passion for Beethoven, Wagner and Brahms. As a 'Chopin specialist', Eddie was surprised to discover that Furtwängler greatly admired the music of the Polish composer and considered him a master of sonata form. On

---

* Much of the meeting with Wilhelm Furtwängler at Clarens was recalled by Edward Cahill in conversation with the author in Monaco during his extended stay in 1968.

† He made a fine recording of Schubert and Wolf *Lieder* with Elizabeth Schwarzkopf at the 1953 Salzburg Festival (EMI Classics).

‡ Elizabeth Furtwängler (1910–2013). After Furtwängler's death in 1954 she lived in their beautiful villa at Clarens until the end of her long life sadly dying shortly before the author arranged to meet her. She was one of the only surviving people who may have remembered Eddie Cahill in Switzerland.

an upright C. Bechstein piano at the clinic Eddie played Chopin for Furtwängler, who admired his delicacy and refinement and then the conductor played for him. 'A very fine pianist too!' Eddie observed in surprise. Both were experienced at accompanying singers and felt the phrasing and breathing of the natural voice was a vital base to musical understanding. Furtwängler completed his second symphony and began his third at Clarens while preparing for his 1946 de-Nazification trials in Vienna in February and Berlin in December.*

On fine mornings they might meander along the shores of Lake Geneva by the Port du Basset, sitting in silence on a bench gazing over the still blue water to the Île de Salagnon with its Florentine villa and beyond to the crystalline clarity of the Savoy Alps. Furtwängler considered music-making by composer or interpreter as an act of love. He felt Beethoven had clearly 'loved humanity' when composing the Ninth Symphony. This message of brotherhood and goodness was so strong that to conduct a performance for him was a type of rare sacrament, particularly during the war when the German people needed spiritual strength. They both believed that after this terrible conflict unconditional moral values had disappeared from life and with them any deeper appreciation of what a work of musical art is, should or might be.

For Furtwängler, musical interpretation was both complicated and uncomplicated, like any aspect of life involving significant love. Eddie had always been deeply impressed by the 'high seriousness' of Furtwängler's approach to music. He had been impressed too by the uncanny feeling that in some mysterious way the conclusion of any work under Furtwängler's baton was prefigured in the beginning – destinies fulfilled, something bordering 'the divine' in his conducting that miraculously transformed music into a confession of faith. He embodied the past ideal of the 'productive' and the 'reproductive' musician.

Eddie spoke with Furtwängler of what he felt was the destructive nature of the current fascination with the interpreter rather than the essence of the music. Performance had now become a question

* Unlike many conductors, Daniel Barenboim is particularly fond of performing Furtwängler's symphonies and has been influenced by his musical philosophy and conducting style.

of who performed the music rather than the music itself; the vanity of the virtuoso, the shallow emphasis on technique rather than an individualistic, 'subjective' and above all spontaneous *recreation* of the work, the feeling of improvisation. 'I never want to be a dinosaur set in my ways! Each performance is different … I hope!' Eddie exclaimed. The notes on the stave were simply an indication, a starting point for the real work of the interpretative musician. Furtwängler thought every great conductor extracted his own characteristic sound from an orchestra. Above all a control of *legato* was of prime importance, one sound must lead to another with a feeling of absolute inevitability. He then made a remark which Eddie never forgot and wrote down: 'A great work of art is a king standing before us. One must permit the time to be addressed by him.'

'I could not abandon Germany, this Germany ruled by Nazis. I could not forsake my people at this most sinister time. I am a German artist. I felt I could do more for them by staying on during the reign of terror. Even Schoenberg agreed with me. I worked against them! I wanted to save the soul of German music!' The conductor had become unexpectedly emotional, passionate and spoke suddenly very loudly, almost shouting. Passers-by stared. Germany signed the instrument of unconditional surrender in May 1945. 'All forces under German control to cease active operations at 2301 hours Central European Time on May 8, 1945.'* Eddie broke down in tears at the news. The great conductor and society pianist embraced in the garden of a Swiss clinic.

* * *

Many fine artists had visited Switzerland to give concerts during the war years, among them the pianists Wilhelm Backhaus, Walter Gieseking (the pianist Eddie much resembled in refinement of tone), Edwin Fischer and the great Norwegian soprano Kirsten Flagstad. On one afternoon stroll, Furtwängler told him the tragic story of the brilliant young German-Dutch concert pianist Karlrobert Kreiten, an outstanding pupil of Claudio Arrau and informally his protégé.† Eddie was deeply shocked.

* German surrender documents ending the Second World War.

† The Chilean master pianist Claudio Arrau commented: 'Karlrobert Kreiten was one

Not only Jewish musicians were subject to brutal treatment under the Nazis. Karlrobert made some emotional, unguarded remarks during a family dinner criticising Hitler as sick and insane. He thought that after the debacle of Stalingrad, Germany would certainly lose the war. A so-called 'family friend' reported this twenty-seven-year-old musician to the Ministry of Propaganda for 'endangering the final victory'. Kreiten was arrested by the Gestapo hours before a piano recital he was to have given in Heidelberg in May 1943. Thrown into prison with thieves and murders he was accused of aiding the enemy and 'demoralizing the nation'. He was finally condemned to death by a vengeful court prosecutor. Owing to an electrical failure he was hanged by candlelight. 'I learned with horror of his fate. He was totally non-political.' Furtwängler commented. His family were later sent not his body but a detailed invoice for the cost of the execution.

* * *

During their time together Furtwängler gave Eddie a carbon copy of the English translation of a detailed ten page document he had submitted to the Swiss Government in 1945 explaining and justifying his position during the war. Eddie wrote on it in ink 'Given to me personally by Furtwängler October 1945 in Clinique Prairie Montreux.'

Concerning accusations of anti-Semitism

> At first no one dared to take any action against me. [...] not one Jewish member of the Orchestra can claim to have been dismissed because of his race. [...] Even up to the very end of the régime, contrary to all other orchestras in Germany, half-Jews and members with Jewish wives remained unmolested in the Berlin Philharmonic Orchestra, in spite of my being continually attacked by the Party on their account.*

The final paragraph of this document reads

> Besides, I could not be expected to see my main duty in fighting against the Nazi spirit, although circumstances often compelled me to do so. First of all I was an artist. It was my main task to

of the greatest piano talents that I have met personally ... one of the greatest German pianists. He was the lost generation that would have been able to follow in the series after Kempff and Gieseking.'

* P. 1 of the document.

> keep my art pure, to preserve and represent for my people the great masterpieces of German musical art. This was the task for which everything else was but a preliminary condition and to which every other interest had to be subordinated![*]

At Clinique La Prairie on 5 November 1945 Furtwängler gave Eddie a charming signed photograph of himself clasping his baby son Andreas.

* P. 10 of the document.

CHAPTER 17

ROOM 855, LE GRAND HÔTEL, BOULEVARD DES CAPUCINES, PARIS

Eddie had planned to spend Christmas 1945 with the Siegers at their villa in Bordighera despite the ruination of the estate. He had obtained his Allied Force Permit to travel 'on a single journey to Italy and return to Switzerland'. As the year drew to a close and Eddie prepared to leave Switzerland and Clinique La Prairie, he received an invitation to give a series of concerts from a most unlikely source. The Parisian socialite Lady Michelham invited him to give a number of recitals for parties she was holding in her suite at the Ritz.* His name had been given to her by Lady Diana Cooper.

In many ways the agony of indecision concerning his next move in life was removed with this invitation. It would be an entertaining distraction and usefully paid. He had been living in Montreux for almost six years and although he found the Swiss-French charming, he was tired of the restrictive and often petty nature of the small English community that had been isolated there during the war. Despite the luxuries and ease available in this 'neutral' domain, a rare place in Europe without serious shortages of food, he was unhappy socially and not in the slightest artistically stimulated. Many of his 'elderly ladies' were leaving for England, so in the future he would simply be 'rattling around' the shores of Lake Geneva. Exchange control regulations meant his English friends could not easily visit him. His brief sexual liaisons gave him physical release but little emotional succour. Although a 'well preserved' sixty, attractive women were no longer queuing at the stage door.

* Lady Michelham was born Bertha Capel (1883– ?) daughter of the wealthy 'general merchant' Arthur J. Capel (1849– ?) and his wife Bertha (1856– ?). Arthur 'Boy' Capel (1881–1919) the onetime lover of Coco Chanel was almost certainly their son, although a few doubts exist.

Owing to the post-conflict transportation chaos, he had to take the tortuously slow train to Paris from Geneva clutching various bureaucratic permits to travel. The journey took a week. Ever since his recitals in France in the twenties and thirties, Paris had attracted the side of Eddie that eschewed scholarship. Here he indulgently avoided the effort of extending his repertoire that would have catapulted him into the first rank of concert pianists. In Paris performing his highly successful standard programme, he could embrace the hedonism and unashamed lifestyle of the natural *bon viveur.*

The French capital had finally been liberated in August 1944 with much rejoicing and dancing in the streets despite the dangers of sniper fire from German soldiers. De Gaulle proclaimed victory from the main window of the Hôtel de Ville. Ernest Hemingway, in the guise a war reporter but now 'commanding' a group of *fifi* irregulars, screeched to halt in a jeep outside the Ritz.* This 'rough crew' drank a few martinis, sat down to a superb dinner and are forever credited with liberating the Ritz Bar 'on the Cambon side'. A reporter from *Le Figaro* described the contemporary Parisian street scene

> As soon as I left the Hôtel de Ville, I was stopped, submerged by an enormous crowd that was everywhere, on the streets, the quays, the avenues, the passageways. They applauded. They shouted. They stamped their feet. They cried. On one of the tanks, surrounded by the din of motors and smoke, a cat, a minuscule little cat, calmly sat surveying the scene. The crowd roared their approval. That was what this unique day was like: one part exuberant celebration, exalted, delirious, an incredible light-heartedness that poured out in song, kisses and unbounded joy; the other part, a climate of civil war.†

Despite the Führer's orders to raze the city to the ground (explosive charges had been laid), a compassionate Nazi officer spared Paris the destruction meted out to Warsaw.

Paris knew none of this scale of destruction. There were some

* *'Les Fifis'* was the name given by Coco Chanel to the *Forces Françaises de l'Intérieur* (French Forces of the Interior), the formal name given by General Charles de Gaulle to the French Resistance fighters who at this time were being amalgamated into the French regular forces.

† Quoted in Rosemary Wakeman, *The Heroic City: Paris 1945–1958* (Chicago, 2009), p. 25.

traces of combat, but that's all. And the most celebrated, legendary places, the Concorde, the Invalides, the Latin Quarter, the Luxembourg, the Étoile: they were free and safe.*

Socially the country was divided between the Vichy *collaborateurs* on one side and the Resistance and *non-collaborateurs* on the other. By early December 1945 when Eddie arrived, optimism had risen like a party balloon and some of the old street gaiety had been restored. A mood of reconstruction was sweeping France, but the reality of daily life was rather different. In the immediate post-war period the struggle for food and coping with black market exploitation dominated most people's thoughts. Severe rationing followed the war. Supplies of water and electricity remained sporadic. Deliveries of coal for heating were limited and many people appeared haggard and gaunt, exhausted by their struggles to adapt to the Occupation.

In many ways the city offered the keen observer the face of Janus. One aspect still gazed towards the legendary and seductive Ville Lumière, the Right Bank, the city of culture, *lieux de plaisir*, refinement, romance, cuisine and sophistication, where for some even the very air seemed finer. As early as March 1945 the French fashion houses had launched their collections at the Louvre in miniature, using dolls as models. The other face turned a stern glance towards the altogether larger Paris of misery, neglect and deprivation. The real heart of Paris was the populous working class in the bleak eastern and northern industrial districts of the Antoine, Charonne, Belleville, Buttes-Chaumont and La Villette, those areas of 'the civilisation of the Resistance'.†

The city was attempting to return to its glittering past when Eddie checked into Room 855 at the Le Grand Hôtel overlooking the Place de L'Opéra. On his first evening he sat in the opulent Second Empire Baroque salon sipping tea and contemplating his alternatives. He concluded after some thought that the grim effects of the war throughout Europe meant he needed to grasp at any musical opportunity that presented itself in order to survive. Would he be satisfied with mere survival as a jobbing society pianist after the adulation of the aristocratic *glitterati* he had experienced between the wars? At least he was now able to furnish an impressive address

---

* Ibid., p. 21.

† A phrase coined by the French historian Patrick Fridenson.

when Lady Michelham or Lady Diana Cooper contacted him.*

Finding a decent place to live in the capital in 1945 posed seemingly insurmountable problems. Many affordable apartments were without lavatory, baths or even heat. Eddie could not fund a long stay at a fine Paris hotel but certainly did not want to rent a cheap, uncomfortable mansard apartment without a piano. Even worse, he feared he might end up penniless in a slum, dying in one of the dreaded *îlots insalubres*. Often finding himself at a loose end, Eddie indulged his perennial passion for the cinema. He saw the newly released *Les Enfants du Paradis*† and emerged overwhelmed by its joy and street spectacle. In many ways the artistic atmosphere of Paris immediately following the war was reminiscent of the greasepaint world of raucous theatres, music hall, vaudeville and silent cinema of his Australian youth.

* * *

Lady Michelham was an exotic creature much the same age as Eddie. She was the sister of the charming and notorious Englishman Arthur 'Boy' Capel. He rejoiced in being the one true love of Gabrielle 'Coco' Chanel. Theirs was a tumultuous affair. He usefully created around himself a cloudy background of 'mysteriously obscure' origins with the tantalising whiff of illegitimate aristocracy. This contrasted greatly with the far more likely background of middle-class trade. However in Paris his background was quite overlooked as he was an intellectual, an excellent polo player, a wealthy coal-shipping magnate and to cap it all a flamboyant playboy who left broken hearts in his wake. Chanel had met him in 1908 and was mesmerised by his love of horses, the physical delights of country pursuits and his English wardrobe. He had 'inherited' her as a mistress from his close friend Étienne Balsan, a wealthy former cavalry officer, horse breeder and socialite.

---

* This hotel was frequented by many society figures who were loath to pay the exorbitant rates at the Ritz. Harold Nicolson went to Paris at the end of July 1946 to broadcast for the BBC and remained at the hotel until October when the Peace Conference concluded.

† The wonderful *Les Enfants du Paradis* (The Children of Paradise) was released in 1945. It is the story of the theatrical life of a beautiful courtesan and the four men who love her. Directed by Marcel Carné, the scenario and dialogue was by the French poet Jacques Prévert and starred Arletty, Jean-Louis Barrault and Pierre Brasseur.

'Boy' encouraged Chanel's first craft activity in Paris, that of a milliner, by lending her the money to buy a shop at 21 Rue Cambon. However after the gaiety of the initial lovemaking and partying, the joy had faded and she reluctantly adopted the role of one of his *irrégulières*. He continued to be supportive and helped her finance a shop in the fashionable resort of Deauville during the Great War and then a full *maison de couture* in Biarritz before she moved permanently to Paris at 31 Rue Cambon. Here she remained until her death in 1971. To her despair in 1918 he announced that he had decided to marry into the English aristocracy, the beautiful young widow the Honourable Diana Wyndham (née Lister). However, late in December 1919 motoring *en route* to Cannes to meet his young wife for the Christmas festivities, a tyre burst on his car. It left the road and he was instantly killed and his mechanic Mansfield seriously injured.*

Before the funeral, Chanel's friend Bertha (later Lady Michelham) offered the devastated Gabrielle a bed in her hotel suite in Cannes but 'the lean peasant woman' faithful to the mores of her class sat bolt upright in a chair throughout the night. She refused to attend the funeral. Coco did not cry bitter tears but did insist on visiting the site of the accident. At this spot, seated on a milestone beside the wreckage of the burnt-out car, she finally broke down and wept uncontrollably for hours.†

Bertha had adored her brother 'Boy' and revelled in being a free, attractive and very wealthy woman able to indulge her whims, one of which was to engage Eddie to play at her parties. So successful were her separate marital arrangements that some forty years later husband and wife happened to both be sitting around the same roulette table in Monte Carlo but failed to recognise each other. 'That face rings a bell,' Baron Herman Stern whispered to the *maître d'hôtel*.‡ 'Who is that old woman?' The servitor replied, 'That is Milady, Milord,' which intelligence caused Lord Michelham to 'back away from the baize-topped table and take

---

* Another version of this story is that he was on his way to meet Chanel clandestinely. Chanel's biographers can be notoriously inaccurate and the truth is clouded with cumulus.

† According to Edmonde Charles-Roux, *Chanel*, trans. Nancy Amphoux (London 1976) p. 180. This book is an entertaining but occasionally over-imaginative, possibly inaccurate and controversial account of the life of Chanel.

‡ Herman Alfred Stern, 2nd Baron Michelham (1900–84).

his leave as precipitously as propriety would permit.'*

* * *

The Ritz hotel is actually two buildings linked by a long corridor known as 'Temptation Walk' lined with display cases of irresistibly luxurious items. The building that faces the Place Vendôme was originally the residence of the Duc de Lauzun; the other faces the Rue Cambon. At the time Eddie performed there, the hotel was the most admired in the world, the *ne plus ultra* of luxury, elegance and chic. From its opening in 1898 it attracted royalty, heads of state, artists, musicians, actors and writers of the calibre of Proust, Audrey Hepburn, Cole Porter, Hemingway and the Scott Fitzgeralds; they were followed by society leaders, couturiers, captains of industry and business tycoons. The list appears endless: King Edward VII, the Shah of Iran, Rudolph Valentino, Charlie Chaplin, Greta Garbo, Marlene Dietrich, Orson Welles, Maurice Chevalier, even the existentialist philosopher Jean-Paul Sartre.

Bizarre stories of the behaviour of the fabulously wealthy abound. Georges Scheuer spent four decades working at Le Grand Bar, the hotel's main bar on the Cambon side and reminisced when pressed about the eccentricities of the rich and famous. The Marquesa Casati needed to be provided with live rabbits for her pet boa constrictor. 'Wooly' Donahue of the Woolworth riches wandered the hotel and bar with a puma on a leash, where 'everyone greeted him as usual, trying not to make him self-conscious'. King Alfonso of Spain regularly drank a quart of Dom Perignon 'liberally laced with Cognac' while consuming dozens of strawberries. The Duchess of Windsor invariably had cocktails with the playboy Jimmy Donahue and then went off to join the Duke for dinner. The Duchess would often appear for lunch the following day but without the Duke, who had not yet recovered from the night's revels remarking 'I married David for better, for worse, but not for lunch.' One guest ordered elephant's feet to be prepared for his twenty dining companions. These were sourced from a recent pachyderm death at the Paris zoo and were reported to taste 'like something between sponge and flannelette'.

* Charles-Roux, *Chanel*, p. 173.

The hotel had operated more or less normally during the war. However unbeknown to the resident Nazi officer corps, it was a hotbed of Resistance activity. The Nazi officer class had curiously been somewhat in awe of the establishment and astonishingly agreed to many restrictions on their activities by the management. Excepting of course Hermann Goering, that pagan 'monstrous, jewel-encrusted hippopotamus of the Third Reich'.* Powdered and rouged, he had taken the Imperial Suite. In the palatial drawing room overlooking the Napoleonic column commemorating the Battle of Austerlitz, he triumphantly wandered about wearing silk dresses and lipstick, exhibiting red lacquered nails, jewelled sandals, gowns trimmed in ermine and mink, emerald brooches and diamond earrings. He was seen to fondle bowls of emeralds, black pearls and rubies which sat beside a crystal bowl of morphine tablets which he consumed by the hundreds.† 'Twelve good years!' he commented nostalgically at Nuremberg after the fall of Germany.

For many celebrities such as Coco Chanel, the Ritz was their permanent address. Noel Coward observed that her gas mask, ceremonially placed on a cushion, was brought to the air-raid shelter by an attendant. She had a smallish room on the Rue Cambon side throughout the war and a German officer lover for which she paid a high price: upon Liberation she had to briefly flee Paris accused of collaboration. After the conflict, Lady Michelham (together with her nineteen yards of pearls) had also taken a suite, not long vacated by a high-ranking Nazi officer. As might be imagined Eddie was 'quite overcome by her glamorous summons' to this remarkable place.

On the evening of his recitals, he would clamber out of a taxi before the noble entrance in the Place Vendôme, climb the famous filigree wrought-iron staircase and pass along a richly carpeted but bare corridor painted in pastel shades approaching two tall doors furnished with gleaming brasses. The high-ceilinged room that opened before him was decorated in gold and ivory with crystal chandeliers, the furniture in Louis XV style, tapestry-covered armchairs and oriental bowls of orchids. The flames of the ormolu

* Simon Schama, *Landscape and Memory* (London 1995), p. 67.

† Stories of the rich and famous quoted from the article *A Legend as Big as the Ritz* by A.E. Hochner in *Vanity Fair*, July 2012.

candelabra gently flickered in a faint breeze coming through the French doors to a balcony, the shutters slightly ajar in the English fashion for 'bracing air', even in winter. The piano sat in one corner beneath a French Impressionist painting surrounded by two rows of antique chairs. The only way he could discern that the room was a hotel suite rather than the salon of a palace was a glimpse through a partly open door of a brass bedstead covered with a silk coverlet.

A gentle murmur of conversation, the glint of jewels and clink of crystal champagne glasses floated around the salon. Eddie was greeted effusively by Lady Michelham and introduced to her guests. He failed to recognise the names of most of the French aristocracy but was taken aback when introduced to the Duke and Duchess of Windsor and happily renewed his old acquaintance with Lady Diana Cooper. Bertha's old friend Gabrielle Chanel was always 'expected' but the dark, diminutive figure attended only once. The Chopin, Schumann and Liszt were the most successful pieces together with the virtuoso arrangements of Viennese waltzes. The Duchess of Windsor exclaimed '*Oh! J'aime tant quand vous interprétez Mozart … il est si élégant!*' As with his 'Royal' beginnings in London, he emerged from this recital massively relieved with many lucrative future engagements.

* * *

Eddie was immediately invited to dinner with the Windsors, despite 'David' having being bored with Chopin performed by Arthur Rubinstein at a London dinner party given by Sybil Colefax. The Duke of Windsor had spent the war years as Governor of the Bahamas. The Duchess had written to Walter Monkton in 1940 of this posting 'The place is too small for the Duke … a man who has been Prince of Wales and King of England cannot be governor of a tiny place.' The couple were still battling with King George VI and the British Government over questions of monies to be regularly paid to HRH the Duke following the abdication. At the end of October 1938 they had taken a lease on an eighteenth-century town house in Paris at 24 Boulevard Suchet in the fashionable 16th arrondissement near the Bois de Boulogne. It was built in 1929 in Louis XVI style and had twenty rooms and six bathrooms. The mansion housed the couple themselves, three secretaries, two detectives, two chauffeurs and nine other servants. The property included a small garden. Both of them spent a great deal of time, money and talent, lavishly filling it with period French furniture that they had fossicked out in *antiquaires.* The building itself had been spared by the Nazis during the Occupation and its aftermath.

What with the increased political tensions in the city, the reprisals, the pillorying and head-shaving of women accused of *collaboration horizontale,* the shortages of food and the unpredictability of power supplies, the Windsors found little to divert themselves socially among 'the Quality'. During the Occupation, superficially dashing Nazi officers were much admired by gay *Parisiennes* deprived of male company. Now conditions in the capital for glamorous social engagements were rather dismal and could be unpleasantly retributional. They invited French, British and American military guests to dinner as well as British friends such as the Duff Coopers. Afterwards they might amuse themselves with cabaret artists and entertainers like Maurice Chevalier if they were not playing cards. The Duchess had written to her Aunt Bessie Merryman 'We have no Xmas plans and with cost it seems hardly worthwhile to make an effort for a party for there is no-one exciting …'* The Windsors were bored and rather lost in the post-war chaos of Europe. Eddie was a welcome distraction.

Mainly out of vanity, he kept all the numerous affectionate short letters, dinner invitations, thank-you notes and telegrams from the Duchess. The first time they invited him to dinner, shortly before Christmas 1945, the electricity had failed as it was prone to do but in compensation the house was beautifully lit with candles. Eddie found the Windsors painfully thin but in good general spirits. The house was stiflingly overheated, unlike most of the freezing apartments in Paris, including Le Grand Hotel, which was as cold as a tomb. They would soon be packing to move as the house had been unexpectedly sold.

Their French chef M. Pinaudier was always able to source the rarest in foods (particularly venison), champagne and whisky, despite the general famine blighting the city. Eddie regularly organised the despatch of boxes of lemons and oranges to the Duchess from

* Quoted in Michael Bloch, *The Secret File of the Duke of Windsor* (London 1988), p. 222.

'the land of plenty' as the Riviera was then considered. Fresh fruit was scarce and greatly appreciated. In January 1946 the Duke returned from London after learning that he was still not wanted as a resident in England. He hoped he would be offered a 'position' of some consequence if he went to live in the United States. Now he simply waited restlessly. Eddie recalled a scene concerning the Duke of Windsor, whom he calls 'A One-Fingered Musician'.

> Indeed, if I played for many crowned heads, I may also say that one day, a Sovereign who had reigned over an immense Empire, played for me. This happened at Boulevard Suchet in His Royal Highness the Duke of Windsor's mansion. His Royal Highness the Duke and the Duchess, who adore music, had asked me to come to dinner and play Chopin for them. When I had finished, I had an opportunity, while exchanging a few words with His Royal Highness the Duke, to tell him that I knew that he had himself, in the past, composed a piece especially for Scottish bagpipe players.
>
> 'I am surprised that you should know about it!' replied the Duke. 'But this is correct and I can still play the tune for you.'
>
> Upon which, with one finger only, he played this piece which he had composed himself and which is played by the bag-pipers, not always knowing that its composer is one of the most eminent figures in England. In the time-honoured fashion of Johann Sebastian and Frederick the Great, I improvised a few variations on it which delighted them both.*
>
> I find the Duchess of Windsor a most refined and dignified woman with great artistic flair, particularly in clothes and interior decoration. She is always the perfect hostess and I may say perfectly charming. A perfectionist and a very independent and strong personality. They do play a lot of card games after dinner, which I am not so keen on but Paris is in such a state just now! The Duke may go to America but wants some official status there. Why did he abdicate if he still yearns for public office? He once possessed the greatest office possible, that of King. Anyway I have never believed the Duke of Windsor ever really wanted to be a King at all!
>
> I could never understand fully the dislike of the Duchess that seemed all too common during the traumatic Abdication, but then unlike many people I actually know her. On one occasion when the Duchess was staying at the Ritz in 1946, I was walking

* The piece is still played and known as *'Mallorca'*.

> in the Faubourg St Honoré with Lady A. who was rather critical of the Duchess referring to her in a derogatory fashion as a grasping *femme fatale.* 'I am sorry but I completely disagree!' I replied. 'Do you know her?' she asked me. At that very moment a chauffeured car drew up and the Duchess appeared at the passenger window. 'Dear Mr Cahill! Fancy seeing you! Thank you so much for the lovely roses. We are so looking forward to hearing you play once again.' The car glided away and Lady A fell silent. A wonderful moment!*

A quite different opinion of the Duchess was given by the British Ambassador Duff Cooper in his diary entry of June 7, 1946

> A dull reception at the Chamber of Commerce followed by a call on the Windsors – in a small apartment at the Ritz. Wallis was looking strikingly plain. It is sad to think that he gave up the position of King-Emperor not to live in an Island of the Hesperides with the Queen of Beauty but to share an apartment on the third floor of the Ritz with this harsh-voiced ageing woman who was never even very pretty.†

* From loose leaf notes left in Edward Cahill's scrapbook.

† Norwich (ed.), *The Duff Cooper Diaries 1915–1951*, p. 412.

Chapter 18

Grand'Uff. Eddie Cahill Contemplates the Ruin of Europe

Eddie left Paris in May 1946 on the recently re-instated *Calais-Méditerranée-Express* to join the Siegers who had returned to Bordighera to see what was left of their palatial villa. Post-war transport difficulties and food shortages had given the Italian Riviera a strange sense of isolation, a curious feeling of remoteness. As he sat in a grubby, unheated coach, it was clear that the chic luxury of the old *Le Train Bleu* had been forever buried by this war. He was finding himself increasingly dependent on his Swiss patrons emotionally, financially and psychologically. Against his better judgement he drew ever closer to them, especially Helen. She adored him, treasuring him as her 'cherished pianist'. He was fond of her as they had worked together on so many charitable events in Switzerland during the war years, but love in the way one normally understands it hardly entered the picture. Arthur, her husband, seemed perfectly at ease with their mutual friendship, it having evolved into a family unit rather than a romantic *ménage-à-trois.*

After the stresses of war, Eddie welcomed this tender and solicitous care without much analysis. Sabine seemed to have vanished without trace and he preferred not to return to goad that painful memory. He had made some final enquiries of her whereabouts, but with millions of displaced persons wandering Europe, this had been a thankless task. He had made few close friends in the peripatetic lifestyle of a concert artist. The high society that had provided him with such glittering engagements, the platform on which his musical identity had rested, was now largely in ruins and he felt unlikely ever to be restored. He lived in a state of panicked resentment at these threats to his art and independence, more rootless than ever.

Eddie occupied himself through much of 1946 assisting the Siegers to put their villa back in order. The interior had suffered at the hands of troops and the garden was close to being damaged almost beyond restoration. The valuable objects and paintings they had secreted with their Italian friends before their flight were returned. In May 1938 the Windsors had taken a lease on a vast shore-front villa known as La Cröe at Cap d'Antibes which they had fled after the fall of France in 1940. Although rather shabby and lightly looted, it became a refuge in April 1946 when they left Paris with nowhere to live. Eddie often motored across to play for them in these palatial surroundings. 'La Cröe became in effect a kind of distant and enchanted island on which the Duke awaited the call that never came'.*

One morning, an invitation from Paris dropped onto the doormat at Bordighera. Eddie was at once excited and appalled at the prospect of being invited to play before what would certainly be a musically discriminating and critical audience. By far the most important musical success of his life would be this first 'official' recital at the prestigious École Normale de Musique de Paris on 19 March 1947. The concert was at the invitation of his former teacher, the charismatic Swiss-French pianist Alfred Cortot. The event itself was organised and patronised by the glamorous Lady Diana Cooper. Being the wife of Duff Cooper, the British Ambassador, she had gathered together a glittering audience of the French aristocracy.

The École Normale de Musique had been founded in 1919 by Cortot. He was a 'Chopinist' of the greatest distinction. Many of the finest classical musical instrumentalists and composers have performed or lectured there. The audience for this concert read like a gallery of characters from *À la Recherche du temps perdu*. The venue represented the Parnassus of musical excellence in France.

Among the distinguished even exotic audience present at Eddie's recital was the rather unmusical Duff Cooper, British Ambassador to France 1944–48. In September 1944 he had left London for Paris in a plane escorted by forty-eight Spitfires. He was accompanied by the 'beauty of the century' Lady Diana Cooper and their eighteen-

* Bloch, *The Secret File of the Duke of Windsor*, p. 227.

year-old son John Julius Cooper (Norwich). Bulent Rauf also attended, the Turkish-British mystic, spiritual teacher, translator and author. He was accompanied by his wife, the impossibly exotic and glamorous Princess Faiza Rauf, Princess of Egypt and sister of King Farouk.

Luiz Martins de Souza Dantas and his wife accepted the invitation. This heroic former Brazilian Ambassador to France but largely forgotten figure, at great personal risk saved some 400 Jews from the Holocaust during the Occupation and Vichy Government by granting them Brazilian visas. M. Marius Moutet, Eddie's old friend from Switzerland, would not have missed this recital for the world. A surprising guest was M. Gaston Palewski. Born in Paris of Polish-Jewish origin he was Director of General Charles de Gaulle's Private Office. From 1942 he was the long-term unrequited love of the English novelist Nancy Mitford. The 'Colonel' as she called him was a *bon viveur* of charm and wit, highly intelligent and a brilliant conversationalist. He was neither handsome, aesthetic nor aristocratic in appearance and Duff Cooper rather disliked him. At a reception in Paris on New Year's Day 1946 he wrote in his diary 'Gaston Palewski was looking more revolting than usual.' Nancy Mitford described this complete Anglophile to her friend Lady Diana Cooper: 'I say to him, "I love you Colonel," & he replies, "That's awfully kind of you."'*

Mme. Odette Pol-Roger graced the salon, the Grande Dame of the Pol-Roger champagne family and the personification of the *Grande Marque* which bore her name. The highly cultured Mme. Marie-Louise Ritz had admired Eddie at the hotel *soirées* for Lady Michelham. Finally the notorious Louise de Vilmorin, the former Comtesse Louise de Palffy, who was a French novelist, poet and journalist appeared at the recital. Author of the famous novel *Madame de* she was once engaged to the aviator and novelist Antoine de Saint-Exupéry and for many years the mistress of Duff Cooper. He found 'Loulou' ultimately too *au grand sérieux* for his temperament.

Some seventy leading members of French aristocratic families also attended this recital. This gathering of the cream of French *noblesse* who had assembled in a Parisian concert hall to listen to

* Lovell, *The Mitford Girls*, p. 357.

Fryderyk Chopin was surely one of the scintillating final flourishes of a social class facing dissolution. The reviews of the concert were effusive. In the well-known journal *Quatre et Trois* the music critic Lucien Laurent wrote

> Eddie Cahill has conquered Paris. He received the acclamation of the élite who refused to cease applauding his beautiful recital.

In *Musical Week* Paris Mario Facchinetti wrote perceptively

> The personality of Eddie Cahill, Australian pianist, is quite unusual. His exterior appearance expresses the profound morality which is the prerogative of real artists. For his first recital in Paris since the war, Eddie Cahill avoided blustering publicity and, in the elegant arrangements of the estrade of the École Normale, I felt only the influence of the aesthetic sense of the artist and of the charming lady [Lady Diana Cooper] who organised the evening. Eddie Cahill has an excellent technique, a sort of literary conversational play and remarkable strength. But his particular quality is the pleasant clearness which, united to the exact rendering of the musical text, seems to explain and comment on it. So the execution is, at the same time, musical, intellectual and sensitive.
>
> The first part of the programme included Schumann, Schubert and Brahms; the third part a complete series of Chopin's works. The second part, dedicated to Corelli, Scarlatti, Beethoven, Mozart and Bach proved an excellent understanding of classical music and a clever manner of treating the modern piano with the lightness of the harpsichord. [Original in English.]

Marie Segur in the *Freelance Presse* Paris of 22 March 1947 wrote

> The first part of the programme consisted of works by Mozart, Bach, Schubert, Beethoven, Brahms and Liszt. Then came a feast of Chopin. Never since Paderewski have I heard that great master interpreted in such an utterly satisfying manner. So many great instrumentalists seem to want to dominate, to impart the execution of Chopin's works their own personal feelings and reactions. It becomes a duel between composer and exponent.
>
> Eddie Cahill, on the contrary, sinks his own personality and becomes solely Chopin's medium – expressing the beauty and passion, the joy, sorrow, pathos, love of life and premonition of death all of which characterise the great composer's music.
>
> He is off soon to give concerts in Ventimiglia, Bordighera and

> San Remo and then back to Paris and off again in June on tour in Switzerland. He tells me he has just received a food parcel from Australia containing many wonders, amongst which is a ham 'such as even a black marketeer dreams of'.

This recital was in many ways the apotheosis of Eddie's musical career. It was no mean achievement to have traversed with panache such a prodigious social distance from his first piano lessons from the wife of the Beenleigh milkman among the sheep, heat and flies of a tiny rum distilling town of 400 souls in the Australian bush of the 1880s. As I stood on the corner opposite the École Normale de Musique situated in this grand Parisian location, I could not help but ruminate in amazement at the degree of natural talent and infectious charm that had brought Eddie to this point.

* * *

The year 1947 was turning into one of distinction for Eddie. He scaled heights he was never again to achieve. He had acquired an Italian male patron, the adventurous aristocrat Barone Leonino da Zara of Bovolenta, a town near Padua. He was a former Italian pioneering aviator, benefactor of Italian aviation and a Great War air ace. He had unsuccessfully attempted to become airborne in a curious paper and wire monoplane in the famous air race in Brescia in 1909. This extraordinary event attracted the composer Giacomo Puccini, the wild Italian poet Gabriele D'Annunzio and astonishingly Franz Kafka and Max Brod in the role of reporters.* They had a great deal in common, as the Barone had also raced some of the earliest motor cars and was interested in the Brooklands racing circuit which Eddie knew so well.

At the beginning of April Eddie again climbed aboard the *Calais-Méditerranée-Express* to stay at the luxury Albergo Esperia in Bordighera. There was a long period at the end of the nineteenth century during which English visitors stayed at the palatial hotels and villas hidden among the olive trees. Their numbers reached three thousand, significantly outnumbering the local population. The town was appreciated by the English for its excellent winter

* The full account of this extraordinary event is entertainingly told by Peter Demetz in *The Air Show at Brescia, 1909* (New York 2002).

climate and the quietness offered by the numerous walks along the sea front under tall palms. War damage was extensive which prevented Eddie from visiting his adored Hanbury Gardens.* He was to give a *Concerto di beneficenza* at the Museo Bicknell on 12 April 1947.† The concert raised a substantial amount for the poor and those suffering as a result of the wartime destruction. He received many letters of thanks from almost everyone of importance in the region.

In May, on the initiative of the Barone, he was invited to give a recital 'for the poor of Italy' at the Teatro Romano in Ventimiglia on the border of the Italian and French Rivieras as a gesture of Anglo-Italian *rapprochement*. Allied bombing had revealed the ruins of an ancient Roman theatre where there had not been a stage performance for 1500 years. The ancient Roman city of Albintimilium had been established in Liguria near the Via Julia Augusta in the 1st century BC. The theatre flourished between the second and third centuries AD but was abandoned in the fourth century. It held up to 5000 spectators who attended performances of plays, dances and mimes. This modern audience sat on the ancient Roman stones while Eddie played, the piano protected from the Mediterranean sun by a large beach umbrella.‡

Using his influence in Society, the Barone had proposed Eddie for two important Italian civil decorations. While *en route* to recitals in Rome and Naples, he learned that he was to be awarded two prestigious medals for his war work. The Italian decoration and title of *Grande Ufficiale di Merito del Capitolare Militare Ordine dei Cavalieri della Concordia* (Grand Officer of Merit of the Military Order of Knights of Concordia). Elevated to the rank of *Grand'Uff*, he was decorated with the Order of Concordia medal and proudly

---

* The famous gardens were established around 1870 by Sir Thomas Hanbury (1832–1907) on a small, steep peninsula jutting southwards from an altitude of a hundred meters down to the Mediterranean. It contains thousands of important botanical specimens. After suffering severe damage and neglect after the Second World War it is now maintained by the University of Genoa.

† Clarence Bicknell (1842–1918) was possibly the most famous historical English resident of the English colony at Bordighera. He was a Protestant minister, patron and scholar, refined water-colourist, promoter of Esperanto, appreciated botanist, but above all an indefatigable explorer and discoverer of the prehistoric paintings (petroglyphs) in the *Alpes Maritimes*.

‡ A damaged fragment of 16mm movie film exists of this concert which may be accessed on the link printed at the beginning of this book.

reprinted his visiting cards. In addition he would receive the Medal of the Etruscan Institute of Capena at a ceremony in Rome.*

At this time Eva Perón, the first lady of Argentina, was on her 'Rainbow Tour' of Europe, so named after her 14 July 1947 *Time* magazine cover with the caption *Eva Perón: Between two worlds, an Argentine rainbow*. Eddie was asked to give a recital in her honour. She had received a mixed reception in Italy, insisting on wearing a glamorous but ill-advised fox fur cape even in Rome's intense summer heat. She travelled in regal style with a large and expensive entourage and was granted an audience with the Pope. Ordinary Romans appalled her with their crude eighteenth century shouts of '*Puttana Madonna!* Whore!'

On 29 December 1996 the Italian newspaper *La Stampa* carried a retrospective article on her historic visit to Italy

> It was a hot July in 1947. Evita Perón was in Rapallo for a period of rest. The Barone Leonino da Zara convinced her to go to Liguria. Evita arrived in San Remo on Saturday, 13 July, shortly after 1800 hrs in a spectacular black Cadillac. At the Hotel Miramare the Mayor of San Remo expected her for the official reception.

Before the concert Eddie was amused to see Evita change cars on arrival from the ostentatious black Cadillac 'State Limousine' to a more appropriate open Alfa Romeo. The warm and spontaneous reception at San Remo, the joyful shouts of 'Argentina!' were a welcome respite from the medieval insults of Rome. She called emotionally and enthusiastically to the crowds '*Viva Italia!*' Later that evening, although clearly tired, she dressed in a glamorous figure-hugging black sequinned gown for a Grand Gala reception and later appeared at the San Remo Casino. The Barone rushed about hectically as the *chef de réception.* On the Sunday she travelled to Bordighera where various local Italian dignitaries were duly presented to the 'august personage'. She then visited the Roman amphitheatre at Ventimiglia where Eddie had performed in May. Vast swathes of orchids and tuberoses from the *Riviera dei Fiori* had been laid over the ancient stones.

After a lengthy lunch at the Albergo Esperia in Bordighera and as part of the welcoming ceremonies, Eddie gave a recital

* These medals and certificates were found intact in the trunk of his effects and have been preserved.

devoted entirely to Chopin. The programme was similar to that given at the Museo Bicknell in Bordighera in April. Evita was clearly delighted by the performance as she had a particular love of this composer. Through the good offices of the Comtesse Capellini, the 'Argentinean Queen' asked him to join her in a glass of champagne afterwards at her table and 'generously gave me her autograph'. They had a lengthy discussion of opera and singers, she commented knowledgably on Chopin and complimented him on his refined playing, touch and 'beautiful tone quality'. Eddie later confided to his journal that he was 'astounded' to find himself actually playing before this 'amazing creature'. He felt himself flattered almost into speechlessness by her invitation to drink the finest of French champagne with 'a colonial boy from the bush'. The evening came to a close when the mayor presented her with a painting by a local artist and a rose of the deepest red, the emblem of the Riviera of Flowers.

* * *

On his return to Paris for Christmas 1947 Eddie struggled to find remunerative engagements. Blackouts were still common and resentment had built up among Parisians against the 'invasion' of the 'vulgar' Americans. In comparison, the Nazis were considered to have shown 'admirable good manners' during the Occupation. Food shortages were deeply resented. Eddie had come to admire the courage of the Resistance fighters during the episode he experienced at St Gingolph in Switzerland in 1944 and now gave numerous post-war charity recitals in Paris to assist them financially.

Many solo concert pianists with far higher artistic reputations than Eddie were battling to make even a modest living in the capital. He once again reluctantly checked in to Le Grand Hotel but was reduced to giving depressing recitals at second-rate events such as *vernissages* at art galleries. At the beginning of 1948 he gave a single well-attended concert at the most celebrated classical music venue in the capital, the Salle Pleyel. However this was no guaranteed way of earning a living, despite the prestige of the venue. Charity recitals kept him financially afloat to some extent. Norah Collins, later Lady Docker* the notorious English socialite and the Duchess of Windsor asked him if he would give a number of charity recitals to assist and possibly expand the Hertford British Hospital for the British Residents of Paris. Such recitals seldom paid well, but his generous spirit immediately agreed. By 1948, despite the long and honourable tradition of the hospital, there was a funding shortfall of some £15,000.† After the war many British residents in the capital had lost their mansion houses, the contents looted of paintings, silver and valuables by the Nazis, never to be recovered. Much of Eddie's spare time, of which he now had a great deal, was spent writing and delivering papers at the École Normale on academic aspects of music such as 'Voice Production' for singers.

Eddie's friends and patrons in England had not abandoned him during his wartime absence. The celebrations for the Silver Wedding Anniversary of the King and Queen resulted in a personal invitation to attend the ceremony in St Paul's Cathedral on 26 April 1948. This anniversary meant a great deal to Eddie. He had witnessed the wedding of the Duke of York to Elizabeth Bowes-Lyon on his first visit to London on a spring day in 1923 as a gauche young artist.

Not a soul in the cheering crowd massed outside the palace that particular day could have foreseen the destiny that was in store for the Duke and his bride. In the difficult years following the war the security of bourgeois family values were strengthened by this silver anniversary celebration. The event was of utmost importance to the morale of the British people, most of whom continued to suffer severe deprivations caused by the conflict. Eddie felt particularly honoured to be invited. Much had changed for him in these twenty-five years. His former accommodation in Manchester Street was now a heap of rubble waiting to be cleared.

---

* Lady Docker, Norah Royce Turner (1906–83), was a dance hostess at a club in her youth. She married three times, each time to an executive of a luxury goods firm. Her third marriage was to the industrialist Sir Bernard Docker, chairman of BSA motorcycles and its subsidiary the Daimler company. The couple became notorious for extravagant behaviour. She was banned from Monte Carlo by Prince Rainier following an incident when she shredded the Monegasque flag.

† Close to £450,000 in 2015 values. The Hertford British Hospital was founded in 1871 by the English millionaire Sir Richard Wallace for the medical and surgical treatment of 'indigent and sick British nationals in and around Paris'. Sir Richard was a philanthropist and a great connoisseur of art. He acquired a superb and valuable collection that became the famous Wallace Collection in Manchester Square, London.

The general population was only slowly recovering from the hideous loss of life. Unlike Paris, the Americans who flooded London were welcomed, even emulated. In 1948 the country was also still recovering from the appalling weather of the previous year which had brought the worst winter for fifty years, the worst floods for three hundred years, followed by a drought. London was blanketed by the worst fog in living memory that lasted 144 hours. This had profoundly affected the production and distribution of desperately needed food. Australia followed its gift of £25 million in 1947 with, in October, 'the launch of a great food growing scheme to help Britain.'* The country donated a third of its total beef production, valued at some £4 million.† Eddie felt a surge of patriotism and even prouder of being Australian. Emigration from Britain to the 'Lucky Country' increased significantly.

He travelled to see his most devoted friends and the now-widowed Maude Denny at Horwood in Buckinghamshire. He was depressed at what he found. The congenial country house lifestyle he remembered had been swept away forever. Frederick Denny had died in 1941 and Maude Denny was ill and was to die in October 1949. Like so many of his distinguished patrons she was now living in comparatively impoverished circumstances. During the war the house had been requisitioned. A girls' school from the Isle of Wight had been evacuated there. The Dennys were moved out of the 'big house' to The Laundry in Little Horwood, not incommodious but certainly a reduction of estate. Maude Denny was broken-hearted over the loss of her husband and the neglect of her beloved gardens. Like many other wealthy families, they had lost most of their servants which 'made life difficult' for a social class who had become almost completely dependent on them.

The idea of socially exclusive and glamorous musical 'At Homes' organized by 'the distinguished Australian pianist Edward Cahill' were now consigned to the dustbin of history. He sadly decided to dispose of his neglected Alvis motor car as it was now permanently covered with a tarpaulin but parked outside at the mercy of the elements. The sweet pleasures of pre-war motoring in leafy English

---

* £853 million in 2015 values. Official Year Book of the Commonwealth of Australia No. 37, 1946 and 1947, p. 1240–2.

† £136 million in 2015 values.

lanes were severely limited by petrol rationing, private motoring restricted to ninety miles per month. The track at Brooklands had been closed in 1939 and placed under the control of the Ministry of Aircraft Production. The circuit had been severely damaged during the war and repairs found to be uneconomic. Motor racing there as Eddie knew it never resumed.

He took the long train journey back to Switzerland during a heat wave in the last week of July in a deeply disillusioned frame of mind. He had witnessed so many profound changes in England and was now fully cognisant of the shocking loss of life and property among his friends. On the train from Paris weary travellers stood in the corridors without food or water. Then the frontier and the anticipated visual ecstasy of Switzerland and the Val de Travers came into view. Fine food and wine suddenly became available at the Swiss border station. Eddie had a bout of nostalgia at Berne where the sight of the River Aare recalled the historic medieval village of Büren an der Aare where he had given such a moving recital for interned Polish officers in the Siberian winter of 1940. The glittering prosperity and luxury of neutral Switzerland still managed to surprise him after the grim panorama of post-war England, the country of 'the so-called victor'. Switzerland had not been 'laid waste' in the struggle for freedom against the barbarians. Suspicions of Swiss wartime duplicity had not yet fully surfaced.

Eddie was back in the Pays de Vaud, that stronghold of Gallic humanism, back in Helvetia

> a fascinating and unexplored organ of European civilisation … prudent, cautious and unromantic, invincibly bourgeois, but admirably unambitious, unconsciously liberal, wholesomely sceptical of ideologies, and, although too attached to money, independent, wise, tolerant, humane and free.*

At the Sieger's mansion at Pré-Choisi above Clarens on Lake Geneva there were passionate discussions late into the night concerning his future and their own. History had determined that a strong will to continue a classical musical career seemed now to count for nothing.

* Cyril Connolly, *The Selected Essays: Homage to Switzerland,* ed. Peter Quennell (New York 1984), p. 59.

* * *

Arthur Sieger had major business interests in the sisal industry in the former German East Africa. After the Great War the area lay under the control of Britain and was renamed Tanganyika (Tanzania). He was apprehensive of the Cold War that he could see inevitably developing. He felt it would take years for Europe to recover economic competitiveness if it ever did. Even though their life in Switzerland was enviably comfortable within a destitute Europe, they were seriously contemplating moving permanently to the Union of South Africa, where they would be closer to his industrial interests. They could live without care in a mansion they had previously built on an estate at Somerset West, a small town on the coast some thirty miles south-west of Cape Town. Here they could live at ease and maintain a full gallery of servants, something increasingly difficult in Europe. Helen Sieger was still prone to repeat proudly and arrogantly 'You know Eddie, I have never done my own hair in my life and I do not intend to begin now!'

Eddie himself was feeling his sixty-three years and the war had taken a terrible toll on his health. He had developed high blood pressure and suffered heart irregularities in addition to his continuing hearing difficulties from the old mastoiditis operation. Despite loving the cosmopolitan nature of the villages scattered along the shore of Lake Geneva and even the diminished but still hedonistic glamour of Paris, he was practical enough to realise that the previous world he dwelt in as a concert pianist, the exalted lifestyle to which he had become accustomed before the war, had perished forever. He had failed to extend his repertoire sufficiently to rival the greatest pianists of the day now playing on the Continent which might have led to further public engagements. 'Too late now.' The cultured High Society that had sustained him had disappeared forever. Yet Edward Cahill's life was about to take another radical and quite unforeseen turning.

Chapter 19

Ja, Baas – The Colonisation of the Mind

Switzerland was clearly no long-term solution to Eddie's plight. Gaining a permit to reside would be nearly impossible, given his Australian nationality and chronic lack of funds. No official consideration would be given to his charitable war work when applying for residency, only his empty Swiss bank account. He never managed to own any property during his entire life, had no investments, few savings and negligible assets. He spent everything he ever earned either on survival or maintaining appearances among his upper-class patrons. The Siegers in the guise of angels of mercy now offered him the chance to accompany them to Somerset West in the Cape Province 'for a six month extended holiday'. This seemed like an answer to his prayers.

At Southampton he embarked on the luxurious Union-Castle Royal Mail Steamer RMS *Pretoria Castle* berthing at Table Bay in Cape Town on 17 March 1949. With his usual impeccable timing, he had arrived at the time of year that most Capetonians regard as ideal. The irritation of the notorious but health-giving wind known as the Cape Doctor was petering out. Blue lay over the waters where two oceans meet and a blue haze shimmered over curious Table Mountain. The intense azure and bewitching clarity of the light reminded him of Australia. Here a white city of gracious elegance fringed the seashore, the settlement rising part way up the mountain slopes, tentatively embracing the base of it.

Eddie had last visited the Union in 1923 *en route* to London and gave a recital with George Brooke. This time his European celebrity preceded him and numerous newspaper and magazine articles announced the arrival in fulsome terms as 'the man who played for Royalty'. His ego was always pleasantly massaged by this type of introduction. The travellers' insatiable curiosity compelled him to explore the city for a few days before heading for his ultimate destination, Somerset West. The Palladian buildings of Cape Town with their noble Roman porticos spoke of respect for European culture, art and tradition. Overall he thought the manners of the city 'terribly English'. The colonial architecture of wrought iron fringing the verandahs, the eucalyptus trees and exotic birds, the smell of the sea, decaying fish and the business of the docklands forcefully reminded him of Queensland coastal towns.

The people 'of many colours' wandering the streets seemed incongruous against this European background. The White settlers looked far more prosperous than their compatriots eking out a bare existence in a Paris or a London ruined by war. The city seemed dedicated to shopping and recreation, with a plentiful supply of servants to carry the treasures home. English tea rooms were patronised by retired colonels and their wives passing leisurely sunny afternoons. He was struck by the unexpected graciousness and good manners of colonial life in South Africa.

* * *

The Siegers had owned the large estate for some time at Somerset West, located in an area of the Western Cape known as Hottentots Holland. The original light-skinned Khoi Khoi people had been almost exterminated by the Dutch and were known by Whites as Hottentots. In the distant past, before the arrival of the White man, this was an area bounded by sea and encircled by mountains. The land was extensively wooded with sweeping grasslands where game of every variety flourished, the home of nomadic Hottentots herding cattle and fat-tailed sheep.

After the discovery by the Portuguese of the new trade route around the Cape, the Dutch in pursuit of slaves, pepper, cinnamon, musk, ambergris and other spices from the East Indies, decided to establish a small fort or 'refreshment station' for the ships of the internationally powerful Dutch East India Company (VOC). The Commander of the settlement, the resourceful but racially intolerant Jan van Riebeeck, first mentioned this fertile, flat region in his journal in 1652. During his ten rather unhappy years at the Cape the small fort grew to become the sophisticated city of Cape Town.

By the early nineteenth century Hottentots Holland had been ceded to the British, first in 1795 and then once again following the Napoleonic Wars after a brief Dutch interregnum. The English Governor, Lord Charles Somerset, administered the area. In 1817 permission for the erection of a church and village was sought in a place

> consisting of beautiful fruitful land, plentifully supplied with water ... situated in its centre near the sea, and the great public Road [...] His Excellency the Governor and Commander in Chief, has been graciously pleased to allow the new projected village to bear the name of *'Somerset'*.*

Between the World Wars the town slowly grew, its delightful position by the sea becoming increasingly attractive to retired White colonials from Cape Town. Somerset West 'battened down and blacked out, came through World War II with flying colours.'†

The enormous Hudson Super Six motorcar the Siegers sent to Cape Town to collect Eddie ironed out the rutted surface of the old road. The car passed ox wagons slowly groaning towards their destinations, the driver cracking his whip and shouting encouragement as the low hills made the going more difficult. Eddie's forthcoming holiday in the sun and escape from the aftermath of war lifted his spirits, distracting him if only temporarily from the obstacles obstructing his musical career in Paris and London. The pinnacles of the Helderberg Mountains appeared on the horizon wreathed in a blue haze. Soon they were driving through the village of Somerset West which lay at their foot.

Along Main Road an avenue of palm trees had been planted. Eddie recalled Beenleigh whilst touring the shops with their colonial verandahs and sun awnings. The Englishness of the settlement was palpable with its White officer class walking their dogs, matrons in straw hats and wearing sensible shoes holding the hands of well-dressed children. One could almost mistake them for inhabitants of Harrogate except that most of the nannies, delivery boys and

---

* *Cape Town Gazette and African Advertiser* 28 June 1817 quoted in Peggy Heap, *The Story of Hottentots Holland* (Somerset West 1993), p. 107.

† Ibid., p. 124.

drivers were Black or Coloured. Life in Somerset West seemed slow-paced and affluent as the car headed towards the mountains that rose directly behind the village. The Sieger's extensive fifteen-acre estate of Forest Lodge was situated at the base of one of the Helderberg grey-green peaks in an area known as Parel Vallei.

* * *

During the excavation and assembly of the jigsaw that comprised Eddie's life up to his settlement in South Africa, it had not been possible for me to contact a living soul who remembered him at first hand apart from myself. The European society through which he glided together with its many now forgotten but fascinating personalities has vanished forever. However during the period he spent in South Africa and Monaco from the age of sixty-four until his death twenty-six years later, I felt someone may have survived who remembered him. Before leaving for Cape Town I placed an article in the popular Western Cape newspaper *Bolander* under the title *Travel Author on the Trail of his Grand Uncle.* There was one reply from a lady. With some excitement I read that Elizabeth Baumann-Allen had known Eddie when she was fourteen. She agreed to meet me soon after I arrived.

The highway from Cape Town to Somerset West is now a sterile motorway and passes shocking settlements such as Khayelitsha with its thousands of ramshackle shanties thrown together from battered steel sheeting, plastic and cardboard. These shameful dwellings battle together in a chaos of poverty. I searched for the Sieger's home Forest Lodge initially without success, but hopefully discovered a house of a similar name at the base of the Helderberg mountain. I pressed the entry phone button in some excitement.

'Ja!'

Rather like a pistol shot and I jump.

'I am an Australian author researching a book. I wrote to you a week ago. I am looking for some people named Sieger who lived in a house called Forest Lodge in the 1950s. Perhaps you …'

I was roughly interrupted.

'Dis is not Forest Lodge!' he shouted into the speaker with what seemed to me to be an aggressive Afrikaans accent.

'I see. Sorry. But could you help me perhaps?'

'Look it up in de telephone book!' he yelled and hung up.

I press the button again but before I could speak he bellowed: 'Dis area wus farmland in the 1950s. It cannot be here I am tellin' you straight!! Go away or else you'll be regrettin' somethin' very soon!'

A cold click as he hung up. I later discovered the Forest Lodge estate had been divided up for a modern housing development. A Coloured gardener named Louis Cupido worked there for the various owners including the Siegers. I spoke to him in broken English and Afrikaans on the telephone but he was elderly and quite unintelligible. He died not long after I left Cape Town.

* * *

I arranged to meet Elizabeth Baumann-Allen for lunch at a restaurant named *Kaapzicht* overlooking False Bay in a spectacular seaside resort known as Strand, a few miles from Somerset West. Eddie wrote in 1950 that the coast 'resembles the Italian Riviera', but it is now rather over-developed. The population is mainly Coloured with Afrikaans being the predominant language. Elizabeth herself turned out to be a refined and intelligent Cape Coloured woman with the beautiful, flawless complexion and the smooth skin of a high-born Javanese. Her steel-grey hair was scraped back from her brow and temples into a bun.* Lively eyes and excellent teeth. She was in her mid-seventies and immaculately dressed. Seated at a table overlooking the water, conversation was rather stiff at the beginning as we felt our way with each other.

'Do I remind you of Uncle Eddie to look at in any way?' I asked almost immediately wanting to hear her first impression.

'Yes' she replied but failed to elaborate. I must have looked quizzical as she continued, 'Remember I was only fourteen when I met Mr Cahill and only visited Forest Lodge occasionally rather than working there. Not like my Aunt Sybil Barends, who was with

* In Southern Africa the term 'Cape Coloured' is given to an ethnic group of mixed race. They are the predominant population group in the Western Cape. Their ancestry may include European settlers, indigenous Khoisan and Xhosa tribal groups or possibly the descendants of Javanese slaves brought from the Dutch East Indies or a combination of all of these. They were classified as a subset of Coloured South Africans under Apartheid.

them as a maid for years.'

Sybil, another Cape Coloured woman, worked loyally for the Siegers for twenty-two years.

'Eddie recognized me of course and used to wave royally to us children from the big car whenever our paths crossed. Everyone knew each other in Somerset West. It was a small place in those days.'

'So what impressed you most about Eddie when you met him?'

'His hair.'

'His hair? Not his piano playing?' I was more than a little surprised. Another informant, an elderly lady who had heard Eddie play in England when she was a young girl, also only remembered his 'virtuoso's hair'.

'Well, he was a wonderful pianist but I didn't know much about classical music as a girl. Yes, he had a full head of magnificent, silver, shoulder-length musician's hair that he used to take immense pains with – well the servants did anyway! It was very unusual for a man to have such long hair in South Africa in those days. He walked with little determined steps and always dressed immaculately. He took no prisoners. He was unique was Mr Cahill.'

'So he was an interesting character for you?'

'In many ways he brought musical culture to Somerset West for the first time. Mr Cahill was very perceptive. He called Sybil "Cookie". She loved his dog Noni. She had a sister Maggie who he called "the Witch". One day he pointed to a child who lived with us. "That boy is Maggie's son!" he said, which shocked all of us as it turned out to be true.'

The expression in her eyes seemed to drift away and she seemed to become suffused with memories as she began to mentally wander over the geography of her past. A large number of children emerged from a school bus and assembled on the sand for an athletics carnival.

'How wonderful all these children – White, Black and Coloured – so friendly towards each other now!'

'How did Mr Cahill react to apartheid do you think?'

'All I can tell you is that whenever there was a queue of Coloureds at the shops, everyone would stand to attention when he entered! But he would never jump the queue as all White people did. Once the shop assistant gestured for him to come forward from the back and he made his point by saying loudly "Please serve these ladies first!" He would always wait patiently in line. People loved him for this. But I remember he was a bit of a martinet was Mr Cahill! If he wanted a particular type of bread, you had better get exactly what he wanted or else! He was very fair, unlike most Whites, but you did know your place. Even though he was small you knew it when he entered a room! He gave concerts for all those Coloured children. He gave concerts for the underdogs, us Coloureds. There were very few Blacks around in Somerset West those days. Wonderful really, what he did.'

'And he was dependent on the Siegers for financial support?'

'Yes. He was and was generally very pleasant to the staff. I recall two Blacks and three Coloureds including Sybil working there. She was a very tolerant person and cheerful by nature. She went about her duties with enthusiasm and was very willing to please. Of course she had been trained for nothing but cooking and cleaning. She was one of six children and had minimum schooling. Money was tight and work scarce ... she was not White, remember. Eddie loved her because she took such good care of his dog Noni. She died of cancer, poor thing, after returning to South Africa from Monaco after his death.'

A glow spread across her features during what had become a moment of both painful recall and pleasure. Her brow creased as she told me of a pregnant Coloured woman who had wandered onto this beach and was brutally assaulted by a mounted policeman.

* * *

Apartheid in the Cape arose from a simple desire to maintain White supremacy driven by the fear of the gradual erosion of White domination by 'the Native'. It was passionately believed contact as equals between races must be prevented; competition for jobs from 'the Kaffirs' must be thwarted; African urbanisation must be inhibited by separate development (*volksgemeenskappe*). In 1939 the Afrikaner nationalist and champion of apartheid Johannes G. Strijdom, the 'Lion of the North' and future Prime Minister of South Africa from 1954 to 1958, commented

> The European had hitherto been able to maintain himself in South Africa because he was economically and culturally superior to the Native. If the Government went out of its way to civilise and uplift the Native in an unnatural manner, the White man would not be able to maintain his superiority.*

By the time Eddie reached Cape Town in 1949, Afrikaner Nationalism had reached its zenith with the election of the Afrikaner-dominated National Party (*Nasionale Party*). South Africa was already a racist and partially segregated state even before the coming of apartheid. British emigration to the salubrious climate and fertile land threatened to overwhelm, or as they expressed it, to 'plough under' the Afrikaner settlers. Justified resentment simmered over memories of the Boer War. Some believed the war had overpaid and empowered Black Africans to cultivate anti-Boer feelings and assume ideas 'above their station'.

From the Black African point of view, as a remorseful, somewhat sardonic Xhosa aphorism puts it, 'At first we had the land and the White man had the Bible. Now we have the Bible and the White man has the land.' The hated Pass Laws, a variety of 'internal passport' that limited the movement of labour within the country was introduced by the colonial British as far back as 1797. They manacled White employer and African together.

> Under apartheid the scope of the Pass Laws, later known as influx control, was radically extended, enmeshing Africans ever more tightly in bureaucratic coils. No single institution of segregation caused more anger and irritation to Africans.†

Urban Africans were increasingly to be considered merely as 'temporary sojourners' whose permanent home should be in a designated reserve of separate development, the Bantustans or homelands often terrifyingly far from their aboriginal and familiar tribal territories.

The failed social experiment of apartheid, a sterile sometimes desperately imposed ideology, was greatly expanded from the initial British segregationist concept by the brilliant but misguided Dutch intellectual, psychologist and philosopher Dr Hendrik

---

* Quoted in R.F. Alfred Hoernlé, *South African Native Policy and the Liberal Spirit* (Cape Town 1939), p. 1.

† David Welsh, *The Rise and Fall of Apartheid* (Cape Town, 2009), p. 33.

F. Verwoerd.* He published works with titles that revealed an austere mechanistic mentality such as *A Method for the Experimental Production of Emotions* and *Objective Criteria to Determine Personality Types*. The 'separate but equal' system he upheld with an almost Savonarola-like theological blindness was implemented with savagery. Bereft of basic humanity, it resulted in the resettlement of entire populations and devastated countless lives.

The Siegers on their estate mainly employed the racial class known as Cape Coloureds. In analysing their own complex racial mixtures, Coloureds to this day believe they have a momentous but largely ignored social history. Racially they came into being through the sexual congress or intermarriage of Dutch colonial settlers with the original inhabitants of the Cape, the light-skinned Khoi Khoi people or perhaps with Cape Malays and other Eastern artisans. Many officials of the VOC (Dutch East India Company) married beautiful high-class Javanese women and later settled at the Cape and raised children of mixed race with fine-textured amber skin.

As we discussed their tragic history, Elizabeth commented with passion: 'Our skin meant that under apartheid we were not considered white enough and now we are not considered black enough!'

* * *

Eddie's 'holiday' soon turned into something far more permanent. The beauty of the landscape, the relief at having escaped a devastated Europe and the ease of life in the sun with numerous servants acted on him like a narcotic. His cosmopolitan mind slowly began to be colonised by South Africa. The privileged environment in which Eddie was now living seemed to deny or even ignore the fact they were living in part of a vast and magnificent wilderness. Cape Province was always a type of enlightened corrective to the idea of the 'red in tooth and claw' continent of 'pure' Africa. Although there was no physical or romantic contact between Helen Sieger and Eddie, platonically she needed him by her side to define her position in Cape Town society as a discriminating hostess.

---

* Dr Hendrik F. Verwoerd (1901–66) socially engineered and implemented the policy of apartheid. He was Prime Minister of South Africa from 1958–1966.

Arthur Sieger, the husband of this daughter of a Hatton Garden jeweller, shrewdly invested his profits to maintain the domestic clockwork of servants and gardeners that ran Forest Lodge. Personally he was a rather stiff businessman who appreciated Eddie as an artist but was a man who appeared to lack imagination or warmth. As affectionate as he could ever be, Arthur seemed to conceive of Eddie predominantly as a useful and friendly addition to his outpost of post-war civilisation in a colony situated at the extremity of what was considered at the time to be the 'Dark Continent'.

The Siegers were getting on in years and had become unable or disinclined to cope with the minutiae of daily life. Their preoccupations became increasingly religious and medical. They created for Eddie the post of 'personal assistant' to their establishment, providing him with his own self-contained cottage in the extensive grounds and a car. In addition Helen decided she would build a music room furnished with a Blüthner concert grand for his sole use. This annex would be attached to the house. She took professional advice on the acoustics of the room which had a specially designed coved ceiling and was equipped with a magnificent Venetian chandelier.

She decided to hold musical salons and *soirées*, inviting the well-connected and powerful from Cape Town Society for black-tie musical weekends. The road from Cape Town at the time was unlit, narrow and seriously rutted – too poor to permit a convenient return after an evening concert. Audiences would assemble for the weekend of music in the afternoon of a Saturday for the evening recital, followed by a Sunday morning concert and then depart in the afternoon before dark. Invitations were much sought after as Eddie no longer appeared in public recitals.

Somerset West was in essence a re-creation of inter-war England, a place where moral values and manners seemed miraculously preserved. The brutalities of apartheid had not yet begun in earnest and there was hope among some Black Africans and many Whites that something positive might arise from its sophistry. The Mediterranean climate of Cape Town with its mild, wet winters and warm dry summers suited him. The luxuriant vegetation and hundreds of fruit trees in the Sieger estate gardens – guavas, quinces, lemons, plums, apples and almonds – reminded him of Queensland. He managed in the end to calm the inner turmoil of what he considered a prematurely truncated concert career and come to terms with his lingering sense of professional failure. In retirement Eddie settled into a relaxed and affluent colonial way of life.

* * *

Quite soon after his decision to accept the Siegers' offer to reside permanently at Somerset West, Eddie began to give his customary round of society recitals and charity concerts. He needed to feel lionised as he had been in London. He continued to send birthday greetings, Christmas wishes and even fresh narcissi ordered from Switzerland to Queen Mary, possibly as a modest sign of still being 'remembered by royalty'. He sent a letter of sympathy to the Duke of Windsor on the death of his brother King George VI in February 1952 and received a personal telegram of thanks.

Cape Town provided him with unaccustomed social and mental challenges, particularly the increasing cruelties of racial segregation. His strong Australian egalitarianism prevailed despite the existence of the notorious colonial 'White Australia' policy which many of his compatriots supported. Eddie instinctively recoiled from the violent discrimination in South Africa during his thirteen-year residency. In fact he actively and courageously opposed apartheid through his concerts and recitals by insisting that any recital given for Whites should be accompanied by a repeat performance of the identical programme for Black and Coloured folk, often in the same venue. This attitude attracted threats and enmity.

On May Day 1950 he gave a recital at the rather toy-town Palladian Somerset West Town Hall to raise funds for All Saints Church, 'the gallery being reservable for non-Europeans'. Naturally his recent career among the aristocracy of Britain was lauded in the newspapers as 'a story of incredible romance. His personality is utterly original ...' The concert attracted the customary White *haut ton* of Cape Town undeterred by the poor state of the roads. At this concert Eddie made the acquaintance of the amusing 'Ian' Russell, then Marquess of Tavistock, his wife Lydia (née Yarde-Buller) and the well-known travel author H. V. Morton and his wife, all of whom were to become close friends.

His Chopin selections, 'treasures of virtuosity', were much remarked upon in the *Stellenbosch Distrik Mail*

> the poetic nature of his playing in drawing from the piano charming softness in *pianissimo* passages and glorious resonances tinged with the same charming softness in *bravura* and *fortissimo* interpretations.

He also performed the Liszt *Hungarian Fantasy* with the orchestral part rendered on a second instrument played by Madame Buchi, the musically accomplished wife of the Swiss Consul-General. Since performing with George and Sabine, Eddie had shown little interest in performing with other musicians in chamber music or *Lieder*. H.V. ('Harry') Morton, who lived in Somerset West at this time, wrote a monograph on Eddie to accompany the recital, describing him as 'a small, boy-like man' with 'tiny, immaculate hands'.

Eddie repeated the programme in the Town Hall but on this occasion to an audience entirely of Cape Coloured people. He had noticed the seating arrangements in the first concert for 'non-Europeans' was dismally inadequate and many Coloureds had failed to find a place. The audience of Coloured folk packed in to hear Eddie in this recital dedicated to them on 2 May 1950. Dramatically the stage lights failed but he calmly continued playing by candlelight. This concert was his first indirect public statement of where his sympathies lay in the matter of apartheid, racial segregation and musical education.

Arthur and Helen Sieger were staunch, lifelong members of the Seventh Day Adventist Church. Later in May Eddie gave the same recital to an audience of 400 at the Helderberg College in Somerset West. Eddie however remained true to his Irish Roman Catholic roots. Dr McClure, the principal of the college, paid tribute to Eddie, quoting from the H.V. Morton monograph. The spellbound *Stellenbosch Distrik Mail* wrote

> Try to entrance a blind man with your description of a rainbow spanning a gorgeous Alpine landscape, and you may have an idea of the almost impossible task of describing Mr Cahill's performance at the piano to anyone who has not heard him play. To those who have heard him it would be imprudence; to those who have not heard him it would be futile.

In November his commitment to familiarizing children of all races with the finest in classical music became clear when he gave two recitals at the Ashley Street Primary School. On each occasion some 700 non-European, predominantly Coloured pupils attended. Musically minded Black and Coloured youngsters from other schools in the Cape Town area were invited by the progressive headmaster, Mr Golding. As ever, Eddie was introduced as 'the man who played for Royalty' and commented in a racially inclusive address before he played the programme of Schumann, Brahms, Mozart and Chopin

> You must begin with the children if you are to build up a musical community. Those who do not later sing or play can at least learn how to listen and appreciate. Interest them now and they will be concert-goers as adults.

The review in the *Sun*, which appeared on 1 December 1950, was one of well meant hyperbole, referring to his 'dynamic personality' and 'brilliant technique' particularly in the moving Chopin group, singling out for especial praise the B-flat minor Scherzo. The Cape Town recording he made of this work is remarkable and betrays all the elements of the great Theodor Leschetizky's influence on his playing, even if filtered through his former pupil and auxiliary assistant Leonie Gombrich.

> They [the children] sat entranced as they watched the magic fingers of this charming pianist bring out music that carried them on wild flights of fancy… the adult audience sat spellbound as Mr Cahill, playing with obvious inspiration and vigour reached emotions of ethereal heights.

Mr G. J. Golding, headmaster of the school and editor of the *Sun*, was particularly glad of Eddie's courageous recital as a distraction from the all-pervasive contemporary political ferment.

Despite his 'difficult sympathy' with the native people, the grand houses of the wealthy and well-connected in Cape Town continued to provide occasional venues for Eddie to hold charity concerts. He fitted in to Cape Town Society as seamlessly as he had done in aristocratic London. Typical of many was the recital he gave on 9 May 1951 in aid of the Linen Fund for St Monica's Home and Maternity Hospital. This took place at the magnificent Cape Dutch influenced colonial residence known as Luncarty. It was noted that

'Mr Cahill takes a practical interest in the Non-Europeans and has already given several concerts for them.'

* * *

In South Africa Eddie had ample free time to practise and live a more relaxed private life relieved of the pressure of performing and earning a living. His playing improved immeasurably with this increased practice time and he significantly expanded his repertoire. More importantly, at leisure he was able to listen attentively to recordings of outstanding pupils of the Polish pedagogue Theodor Leschetizky such as his beloved Ignacy Jan Paderewski, Artur Schnabel, Ignaz Friedman, Alexander Brailowsky and Benno Moiseiwitsch. This helped him recall the detail of his lessons with Frau Gombrich in Vienna and her invaluable advice.

The conclusions Eddie came to concerning keyboard technique and 'having more to say musically' now than ever before led him to an experiment. Unusual at the time, in 1955 he decided to make a number of expensive private 78 rpm shellac recordings at the Sound and Film Services (SFS) Studios, Radio City, Cape Town on a Grotrian-Steinweg concert instrument, his favourite piano.* These recordings reveal many of the late-Romantic performance practices that embody an aesthetic and sensibility distant from today. Eddie noted a comment by the great Polish pianist Ignaz Friedman 'There are the notes, but there is what is behind the notes and there is what is between the notes.' His performances of Chopin are strikingly 'modern' in their approach, with little cultivation of the extreme individualism that characterised much piano playing during the

* He recorded Chopin's Étude in A-flat major Op. 25 No. 1, the Scherzo in B-flat minor Op. 31, the Waltz in A-flat major Op. 42, the 'Heroic' Polonaise in A-flat major Op. 53 and Liszt's *La Campanella*. Their survival is miraculous, given his peripatetic lifestyle and its reversals. Two 78 rpm shellac discs survived but the Scherzo shellac was broken beyond repair. All were transferred to a master tape some years ago before any further damage to the fragile discs. This tape has now been re-mastered and transferred to CD by *Selene* in Poland with pitch correction by Jonathan Summers, Curator of Classical Music at the British Library. The Scherzo in particular betrays the influence of Cahill's first London teacher Tobias Matthay. His performance is reminiscent of another fine Matthay pupil of much the same age and keyboard refinement, the largely forgotten Irene Scharrer (1888–1971) once famed for her Chopin interpretations. She was one of that great British female trio coached by Matthay that included Myra Hess (her cousin) and Harriet Cohen. These recordings may be downloaded using the internet link in the preliminaries of this book.

latter years of the nineteenth century.

In his playing the suave elegance, colour, charm, richness of tone without attendant roughness, the delicate velocity and luminous clarity of the greatest late nineteenth century pianists is preserved as well as a fine quality of *pianissimo* piano sound. His cultivated *legato* and *cantabile* grew from the years of accompanying the tenor George Brooke. He had full command of the larger works and did not neglect the virile strength, passion and anger that lay within the 'late style' of Chopin. He played 'with meaning and without mauling'.* Eddie seemed to understand instinctively the miraculous expressive balance that the composer achieved between the masculine and feminine aspects of his poetic nature. His rendition of Liszt's *La Campanella* is a spectacular *tour de force* of virtuosity, touch, bell-like timbre and feathery velocity.

The Australian poet Mabel Forrest wrote of Eddie

> The career of Edward Cahill, the Australian pianist, has had over it from the outset the glamour of almost incredible romance.

She wrote a poem in praise of Eddie and the spectrum of sound and impressionist colours he produced from the instrument. He loved to quote the lines of one particular stanza of this poem on any appropriate occasion

> *Diamonds you fling from your fingertips,*
> *And the sudden rose of a ruby's light,*
> *And a garnet warm as a woman's lips,*
> *O'er the hush of lilies tall and white.*

True to his educational mission, Eddie gave a number of lectures at the Seventh Day Adventist Helderberg College. None involved performance but covered voice production, the vital cultivation of personality by the musician and what he termed 'the mechanics of music'. Eddie was particularly well qualified to comment on voice production having spent so many years accompanying George Brooke

> We are not bi-vocal, we have only one voice tone in speech or song. We have sometimes made the remark 'What a charming voice that man has.' If we ask ourselves exactly what we mean

* The opinion of the playing of Irene Scharrer in the *Musical Times*, Vol. LXXVI, April 1935, p. 330, but a phrase singularly appropriate to describe Edward Cahill's approach to Chopin.

> by such a remark, we shall find that the outstanding characteristic that attracts our admiration is the quality of the vocal tone.

The lecture continues in an increasingly technical manner on the nature of nasal resonance, breath control, vowel sounds, consonants, diphthongs and tripthongs. He concludes on the dangers of excessive speed both in singing and piano playing.

He mentioned on many occasions in interview that he considered the development of an individual 'voice' or personality of major importance for an artist. In his lecture *Personality is One of the Keys to Success* he observed:

> Personality makes the difference between failure and success; it is *the* factor deciding whether you go forward, or stand still, or retreat.

Concerning the development of this quality

> The main fault lies with the individual. When father and mother have been suitably blamed, and the environment duly condemned, a glance in the mirror will reveal the party who carries the greater responsibility. Don't confuse personality with character, in the moral sense. Benvenuto Cellini had not much character, but he had a forceful personality. Have you not heard it said of someone you know that 'He's an awful blackguard, but extremely interesting and amusing?'

In a short talk entitled *We are Snobs about Success* he perhaps inadvertently revealed one of the motivating forces behind his own career

> The younger generation of today has done its best to sweep away the old forms of snobbery. We have set up success as the new standard ... Under the old regime one could pass from house party to house party with a birth certificate as one's sole recommendation, but nowadays we have to *earn* our food and drink and our weekend's hospitality.

* * *

In addition to his musical activities in South Africa, Eddie also had time to cultivate new friendships peripherally associated with music. One was with the renowned English travel writer H.V. Morton, the foremost English travel writer between the wars who had come to live in Somerset West around the same time as Eddie. He was one of the most influential writers to perpetuate the national myth of England and English rural life. In the highly influential book that made his fortune, *In Search of England* (1927), he cultivates an idealized image of England as a garden of Eden. He travels around the country in a modest blue 'Bullnose' Morris Cowley motor car which he had christened 'Maud'.

He writes of St Just in Roseland in Cornwall

> I have blundered into a Garden of Eden that cannot be described by pen or paint. There is a degree of beauty that flies so high that no net of words or no snare of colour can hope to capture it.*

With such a love of English landscape and country life why was he living in South Africa, a country increasingly riven by simmering social and cultural divisions? At the end of the war the distinguished Prime Minister Jan Smuts had invited Morton and his wife Mary to the Cape. They loved the experience and a second journey resulted in his book *In Search of South Africa*, published in 1948. Written in a similar style to his previous *In Search of …* books, Morton betrayed a love of motoring when he discovered Somerset West

> One day in November I motored out of Cape Town without a care in the world … South Africa lay before me in vast, hot distances and in bewildering variety, and the road upon which I was travelling was, as recently as a century and a half ago, a lone and perilous track leading to what men called 'the interior'. Travelling eastward, I ran into that little country town whose name would seem to defy the compass, Somerset West, but it orientates itself in relation to another Somerset farther to the east.†

Much the same disillusionment with Europe that Eddie had experienced following the war inspired the Mortons to move to Somerset West. For Eddie, his choice was out of financial necessity. For Morton it was possibly a desperate attempt to retain a threatened English Arcadia still vaguely preserved in this colony. Certainly neither wanted to live and work in the London of 1945 that was

> gruesome in the late-gathering darkness: its bare and wry trees with tufts of leaves at the tips of the branches like the legs and necks of plucked fowl; its masklike fronts of bombed-out houses,

* H.V. Morton, *In Search of England* (London 1927), p. 81.
† H.V. Morton, *In Search of South Africa* (London 1948), p. 97.

with their dark eye-sockets and gaping jaws.*

Nor did they want to live among a people afflicted with

> *la morgue anglaise* [...] suffocating in the general state of mind to which England was now reduced: a combination of competitive spitefulness with exasperated patience.†

Morton built a house called Schapenberg in the hills above Somerset West. After dinner he and Eddie would often meet in the library of his house with its atmosphere of an English gentleman's club and discuss 'the old days'. Both Harry and Eddie loved dogs and Eddie was deeply attached to his Rhodesian Ridgeback 'Noni'. Morton took a number of photographs of Eddie with this handsome animal. The dog would lie quietly on the Turkish rug listening to Eddie practising until it felt it had heard enough. It would then climb up on the piano stool and put its paws on the keys as a signal for him to desist.

The two men shared a motoring interest. Indulging his love of cars, Eddie purchased a new yellow and white Austin Metropolitan coupe: 'The car that thrilled America. The car with 'Zing' both in its looks and in its performance.' Eddie's favourite excursion out of Cape Town was Chapman's Peak Drive, one of the most spectacular and thrilling drives in the world. The precipitous drops and cliffs are Wagnerian in scale and impact. His journal mentions one demanding excursion to the picturesque village of Greyton, which lies about eighty-five miles from Cape Town in the Overberg district lying at the foot of the Riviersonderend mountain range.‡ The village nestles in a nature reserve of crystal streams, abundant birdlife and aromatic *fynbos*. The settlement is made up of carefully restored Cape vernacular houses, art galleries and restaurants, the eaves heavy with cascading bracts of mauve bougainvillea.

Being Christian and educationalist in outlook, Eddie visited the nearby Moravian mission station at Genadendal (Valley of Grace).§

* Wilson, *Europe Without Baedeker*, p. 177.

† *'La morgue anglaise'* is perhaps best understood as the cohabitation of arrogance and death. Ibid., p. 195.

‡ The farm of Weltevreden was purchased by the wealthy Englishman Herbert Vigne in 1846 and in 1854 he established a freehold agricultural village which he named 'Greyton' after Sir George Grey, Governor of the Cape Colony.

§ The mission station was established in 1738 by the young Moravian missionary, Georg Schmidt, to convert the local tribe known as the Khoi Khoi. In 1800 the British built a

Nelson Mandela visited this tiny town in 1995. He was so affected by its 'tangible and intangible history' that he renamed his presidential residence in Cape Town, Genadendal. A large beautifully preserved square of spreading trees and benches is fringed in the manner of a cloister by honey-coloured buildings with an Eastern European feel.* Eddie gave a short lecture and concert there for the native people on a piano whose 'felts were much depleted by moths'. They had never heard the music of Chopin before or any sort of concert pianist and received the music in awed silence.

He also gave a number of recitals at the graceful university town of Stellenbosch in the heart of the Winelands. There was an annual Festival of the Arts here in his day where the great American pianist Rosalyn Tureck performed Bach and in 1958 the Amadeus Quartet played Beethoven quartets. The somnolent atmosphere and whitewashed Cape Dutch gables are redolent of seventeenth-century colonialism. Yet this town turned away from the finest in human achievement to become the cold intellectual heart of Dr H.F. Verwoerd and the evolution of his ideology of Grand Apartheid.†

* * *

Another close acquaintance in South Africa who was fond of music and reminded Eddie of his glamorous London days was the John 'Ian' Russell, then Marquess of Tavistock (later 13th Duke of Bedford) and his second wife, Lydia Yarde-Buller. The couple disliked the cold and damp English climate. The Georgian house they had lived in on the Chenies estate in Buckinghamshire was discovered to be full of dry rot and needed to be demolished. London was expensive, extensively damaged and they wanted somewhere warm to settle and educate their children. In 1948 they

---

church and Genadendal flourished until the end of the nineteenth century, at one time being the largest settlement in the colony after Cape Town.

* The Moravian Church originated in Bohemia (now the Czech Republic) in 1467 as a breakaway from the Roman Catholic Church. Genadendal is the oldest Protestant Church in South Africa.

† 'Petty Apartheid' could be considered the process of racial discrimination on a daily basis, while the evolution of 'Grand Apartheid' during the 1950s (the various phases of the Group Areas Act) was the actual physical relocation of entire racial groups within the country.

too decided to sell up and emigrate to South Africa, buy a farm and run it as a commercial proposition. They purchased a 200-acre fruit and vineyard estate called Waterfall in the Drakenstein Mountains about forty miles from Cape Town. Ian considered his period in the colony as

> the happiest time of my life. [...] There is no doubt that if you can ignore the local politics, it is an almost idyllic part of the world in which to live. [...] Somebody said to me not long ago that it is a wonderful country to live in so long as you don't think, and I am afraid that is true. Even living our relatively isolated farm and country life, the colour-conscious atmosphere and the politics start to weigh you down. The *Afrikaners* have never forgotten the Boer War. [...] The native and Coloured populations live in the most ghastly conditions, with no sanitation, and their dwellings literally strung together out of paper and old squashed petrol tins. It is an appalling state of affairs which got worse all the time we were there ... conditions leave a bitter taste in your mouth.'*

* * *

Although Eddie occupied the prestigious social position of a retired international concert pianist with 'Royal connections', he did miss his days of glamour in Europe. Apartheid was becoming increasingly draconian and the health of his patrons the Siegers more fragile. He became increasingly occupied with arranging their clinical appointments and overseeing the complex labour arrangements at the house. As the decade progressed, the number of his concert appearances began to decline.

By the late 1950s the basic framework of apartheid had been implemented and Eddie and the Siegers, despite the insulation of wealth, could not remain indifferent to the ideological and uncompromising political process taking place in South Africa under Dr Verwoerd. The homelands policy impacted on their own staff quite apart from conflicting with their own fervent Christian religious convictions. Eddie was committed to musical education and was alarmed at the impact apartheid was having on the future generation through the government's emphasis on the limited so-

* John Ian Russell, 13th Duke of Bedford (1917–2002), *A Silver-Plated Spoon* (London 1959), pp. 180–1. This book chronicles the lives of the British aristocracy with, as *The Times* obituary put it, 'bleakly astute realism'.

called 'inherent character' of Black people. In a shameful speech in 1954 Verwoerd stated

> The Bantu must be guided to serve his own community in all respects. There is no place for him in the European community above the level of certain forms of labour. [...] Up till now he has been subjected to a school system which drew him away from his own community and partially misled him by showing him the green pastures of the European but still did not allow him to graze there.*

Did this mean Verwoerd considered Black Africans incapable of appreciating classical music? Eddie had already received various threats as a result of his open educational and tolerant attitudes towards Coloured children at the piano recitals he gave. The Afrikaner Verwoerd was vehemently against education for producing what he termed 'black Englishmen'.

The killing of sixty-nine Africans by police at Sharpeville on 21 March 1960 was the result of a protest against the hated pass laws and a watershed for apartheid. The massacre expressed the dark heart of the ideology as Dr Verwoerd implemented merciless retribution. A storm of international condemnation resulted which developed into a feeling of extreme insecurity among the White population. Three weeks after the Sharpeville Massacre, Verwoerd was shot but miraculously survived, gathering even more support. Undoubtedly the Siegers and Eddie felt the country to be on the brink of revolution and began to make arrangements to leave for Europe as did many other White families.

When the Siegers left to take up residence in Monaco, Eddie stayed behind at Forest Lodge for a time with his beloved African lion dog Noni. Not until she died did he feel he could leave Somerset West and join them. Dr Verwoerd was assassinated on the floor of the House of Assembly in September 1966, but by that time Eddie and the Siegers, together with their South African Coloured maid, Sybil Barends, were safely ensconced in four interconnecting apartments high above the Jardin Exotique and sparkling harbour of Monte Carlo, gay with yachts and conspicuous consumption.

---

* Quoted in Welsh, *The Rise and Fall of Apartheid*, pp. 64–5.

Chapter 20

Life in the Fairy Kingdom

'Have you had your ampoule, Eddie?' asked Mrs Sieger in a tone accustomed to command.

Her jet hair and impassive features under heavy makeup gave her the appearance of a Kabuki theatre mask. She chose a glass phial from the row in front of her plate, worked industriously at the neck with the tiny saw, snapped off the top and poured the yellow contents into a bowl of what appeared to be porridge. She stirred and began to eat with evident satisfaction.

'Just about to, my dear,' replied Eddie his face fringed by a shock of white hair and wearing heavy black spectacles.

The swirling colours of the contents of various ampoules blended together. Seated next to Eddie, Helen's husband Arthur was way ahead of the rest of the diners in ampoule-snapping, no doubt a result of his German efficiency applied to matters of therapy. The Coloured South African maid Sybil stood by awaiting orders. The bleached blonde Monégasque maid glared at her furtively in apparent rivalry. The bizarre, brittle sound of the ampoule saws at work filled the dining room. I gazed over the succulents and cacti of the Jardin Exotique de Monaco and the glittering Mediterranean. The 'dinner' in the bowl that lay before me filled me with horror.

'Are you not hungry, Michel?'

'Well actually, I'd prefer some meat.'

'Meat?' A look of alarm passed over their faces.

'But we have half a ton of Complan health porridge in the garage!' shot out Mr Sieger. His angular frame twitched.*

---

* *Complan*, formerly a Glaxo product, was known as 'the complete planned food' with 23 vital ingredients designed for 'Problem Eaters' and 'Those Too ill to Eat'. It could be mixed with milk as a health drink or eaten as a 'porridge' depending on preference. The company was acquired by *Danone* in 2011.

'Well ... perhaps some fish. We are on the French Riviera!' I replied over-enthusiastically.

Eddie seemed embarrassed by his nephew's *faux pas*.

'We'll arrange to take you down to the village in the morning in the Bentley. We should be able to obtain some veal that has been weaned on milk. You cannot be too careful.'

Sybil brought me some bread and butter and an apple. Clearly hypochondria ruled the household.

'It's time for my preacher!' Helen suddenly cried.

Eddie looked at me and rolled his eyes. She maintained close connections with the Seventh Day Adventist Church and never missed a broadcast. A radio blared the wisdom of choosing the hard rather than the soft road to enlightenment.

* * *

My first visit to Monaco had been in 1962 in my early teens not long after Eddie's own arrival. In 1961 after leaving Somerset West the Siegers had bought four apartments in one of the first high-rise residential blocks known as Le Bermuda, at 49 Avenue Hector Otto, above the Jardin Exotique and the old town. The views over the Port de Fontvieille were spectacular. The absence of income tax attracted them to Monaco, but they mainly came to escape the imminent violence in South Africa for the warm Mediterranean climate and pleasant old world atmosphere of retirees.[*]

In August 1961 they initially stayed at the Hotel Balmoral, a fashionable *belle époque* construction dating from 1896 with superb views over Port Hercule.[†] A Dutchman of their acquaintance commented 'You people taking flats in Monaco are the bravest people and ought to get medals for courage!' The bureaucracy of flat purchases in Monaco was fearsomely complex. Helen wrote to Eddie in South Africa in December 1961 from Monte Carlo 'Arthur

---

* In 1961 the official population of Monaco was 22,812. By 2013 it had grown officially to 30,500, which is significant in a country whose area is a mere 2 sq km. The age of over a quarter of the population has remained constant over the years at 65 years and older. The official language is French but English, Italian and Monégasque are spoken (statistics from NationMaster).

† The hotel has recently been redeveloped into the Résidence Balmoral, one of the most glamorous contemporary addresses in Monaco.

is full of pep and I feel 100! So let us thank our dear Lord for all his manifold blessings.' After the death of his dog Noni, Eddie joined them taking passage on the plush *Pendennis Castle*, arriving in Southampton from the Cape early in 1962. He then boarded the familiar but now significantly less glamorous *Le Train Bleu* to Nice and then on to Monte Carlo.

I remember scarcely anything of this first visit in the summer of 1962 accompanied by my parents. I was fifteen with no conception of the true musical status of my elderly relative. My father was a Medical Officer attached to the Australian Embassy in Rome. I vividly remember our staying at the then slightly down-at-heel Hôtel de Paris, walking with Eddie in the Jardin Exotique and touring the principality by car, an opalescent bronze Mk II Jaguar. My father medically examined the three geriatrics and was horrified at the exotic treatments being meted out to them regardless of expense by the medical 'sharks' of the Principality. We wandered in the gardens and took tea and cake on the balcony. The household was a bizarre spectacle for a young boy. Three elderly folk struggling to keep each other alive high above Monte Carlo harbour.

* * *

The Siegers had never entirely severed their ties with Switzerland. As they aged, they began to take what became an annual summer pilgrimage from Monaco by chauffeur-driven Bentley to health spas, clinics and sanatoria in the Swiss Alps. Each day Arthur used to don his overcoat and hat and pace the diminutive balcony of the Monaco apartment. This clearly had limitations. Helen took no exercise at all, but Eddie often went for long walks and remained very healthy till the end. The Siegers became professional invalids undergoing constant batteries of tests and exotic treatments. The area they chose to recuperate was on the 'Swiss Riviera' close to their former Villa Pré-Choisi at Clarens near Montreux. They oscillated between the luxurious Hotel des Trois Couronnes at pretty Vevey on the shores of Lake Geneva and the Clinique Valmont in the village of Glion sur Montreux, high above the lake. Helen would admire 'the sublime view' from the terrace of the clinic.

Eddie, as their secretary, was entrusted with all the arrangements.

The stress of their increasing demands meant he often needed to accompany them to Switzerland for a 'cure' himself. During these therapeutic absences the Siegers wrote him daily letters.* Arthur and Helen wrote separately to Eddie on the same page of sanatorium notepaper. The contrast in the character of these correspondents was all too apparent. 'My darling Arthur' was predominantly concerned with 'the facts of his own health' and the weather. He writes in spidery handwriting which angles across the page at forty-five degrees. 'My fingers are increasingly freezing up.' Helen is far more open and emotionally transparent. Their deep love of Eddie and concern for his propensity to fret over trifles is clear from their correspondence. 'Please don't worry too much!' proliferates in their numerous letters.

Control of diet and the quality of food were of the greatest importance. 'Helen has been eating her red meat regularly and must today have had 150 gms.' Arthur wrote to Eddie optimistically. Following on below, Helen's usual note: 'My darling Arthur has not been feeling too good in the mornings.' On the passing of a close friend, she writes of the husband in a mood of increasing religious fervour 'perhaps her tragic death will make him fly to his Saviour.'

Their preferred treatment centre over these years was Clinique Valmont. Despite the exorbitant cost, they complained it was often overcrowded and they had to share bathrooms. The weather in summer was often 'infernally hot' or 'clearing after an alpine thunderstorm'. Reports of good weather were always accompanied by the pessimistic rider 'but for how long?' Eddie posted Helen her 'religious tracts' including *How to Pray*, 'which is priceless'. The large supplies of the 'delicious' Complan porridge also arrived safely. Weeks were spent waiting for the results of 'beastly tests' searching for 'the seats of infection'. In July 1966 Helen was placed on a course of antibiotics, had her colon X-rayed and a gynaecological examination under general anaesthetic. 'A nerve-wracking experience!' A bout of bronchitis was erroneously and mysteriously diagnosed as lumbago ('I am very worried!'). Concerning the overworked staff: 'I hope some heavy tipping will

* All quotations that follow are sourced from the large correspondence inherited by the author and addressed to Edward Cahill from the Siegers when resident at various Swiss clinics dating mainly from 1967–69.

see us through'. They were never keen on fraternising with their fellow sufferers. 'The place is packed with Italians, might be Italy. All the women have half-paralysed husbands!'

Arthur was suffering from urinary retention and wrote with disarming enthusiasm and Germanic detail 'Don't worry about "wee"! I filled a pot last night to the very brim! Just a hint of anaemia with 75% red corpuscles and urea 47 but I should be recovered after a long rest.' Constipation was 'bad for the heart if you don't have easy motions' accompanied an urgent request for packets of suppositories. Privately Eddie had told me that he was faintly disgusted by such letters concerning their most basic functions and the constant requests for medication. In fact it drove him 'mad with boredom which is a far cry from the glamour of the Ritz in Paris I fondly remember!' They sent him regular cheques for his needs and expenses, but complained 'You never mention anything of your troubles.' One exotic Swiss treatment in particular fascinated Eddie. Helen assured him in a letter that her brains had been removed, washed, 'ionised' and returned to her. She was now able to think 'far more clearly' after the treatment.

During the annual excursions for treatment, Helen initially preferred to attend the extremely remote Bad und Kurhaus Val Sinestra, high in the Lower Engadine on the other side of the country and then proceed later to Glion. She would spend some weeks there and then be driven to Clinque Valmont to join Arthur for further treatment. She adored this 'Lohengrin's castle' set in a steep-sided valley at an altitude of 1,300 metres. Arthur, who was now 84, could not tolerate the 'thin crystal air' at this altitude, only managing to survive at 300 metres further below.

The chauffeur would drive her the long distance from Monte Carlo, across the Austrian frontier, to the picturesque village of Sent with its charming *sgraffito* decorated houses and baroque gables. Here she would climb aboard an ancient bus to take her along the Val Sinestra to the Kurhaus. Located in the Swiss Canton of Graubünden, it is an unspoiled region of exalted landscapes, alpine meadow and towering granite, where the minority Romansh language is spoken. The final section to the clinic was over an unsurfaced precipitous mountain track running beside chasms protected only by fragile wooden fences, across rickety bridges, the far side of the road a jagged wall of rock. On arrival she was welcomed and shown to her usual well-furnished room by a white-coated attendant, supplied with the whitest of white linen, in a room with white enamelled walls and furnished with a white wash basin. Her balcony opened directly onto a deep pine-forested valley with a rushing stream swirling over boulders.

The intoxicating and pure mountain air from the surrounding snow-covered peaks created an immediate inner peace within the soul of the sufferer. Now a modest hotel, it is in every respect as picturesque and remarkable as Helen Sieger claimed. Her treatments were carefully monitored, attendants running the baths using floating thermometers to achieve the correct temperature, controlling the circulation of the blood. 'I am having my lovely baths. I can't feel my ribs any longer. Heavens! What a mess!' she wrote to Eddie.* Helen had a chronic condition of the veins of the leg only relieved by special bindings wound on by a famous physician from Stuttgart. She wrote happily that she 'no longer waddled' but could now 'at last walk in a straight line'. Helen would telephone Arthur from the Kurhaus every evening at exactly at 6.30 pm.

Clinique Valmont was an exhausting 11-hour drive from Kurhaus Val Sinestra. Helen always arrived in a debilitated state. Arthur writes to Eddie from the clinic in July 1968

> Helen is difficult but with me she is sweet and reasonable. It is going to be a terrible job and she needs a private nurse of superhuman tact and patience! Where is such a one to be found now? She needs a private bath or bidet … This is going to be a terrible struggle in this overcrowded place. All the nurses are overworked as are the doctors. If only she would not exaggerate with her clothes and put on such masses of clothing even when quite warm. She wears a heavy Scotch tweed suit and matching overcoat which she never takes off. I am sure everybody thinks us mad!
>
> You know it is an absurd £100 per day for a private nurse in Monaco now?† I am not surprised that girl Jeanne we know left here for Monte Carlo. So we come here. Most people only come for a check-up that lasts a couple of weeks or so. The fewest stay more than a month as we are doing. I had some anaemia!

---

* Letter to Eddie from Helen at Val Sinestra, 28 July 1968.

† Around £1,600 per day in 2015 values.

> Many thanks for the suppositories! Please send more boxes … Helen uses them too!

And in the same letter Helen takes her turn to write

> My blood count is normal. I was a month in Val Sinestra and that did the trick! I had a wonderful journey from Val Sinestra to here on Sunday. Chatun is certainly a wonderful driver. The way these Swiss go up these mountain passes is simply terrific and many women drivers too!! We certainly were in God's hand every minute of the day! Just think how privileged we are! I have had some ultra sonic ray treatment to my back. The jealously among the doctors is appalling but the food is excellent!'*

They also spent time at the superbly situated Klinik Schloss Mammern on the Rhine in Switzerland not far east of the falls of Schaffhausen. Helen wrote in August 1969 that

> We are both well and kicking among the heavenly trees, good food, good doctors, lovely forests all around, beautiful drives and walks. Full of pep!

Arthur added as his main item of news 'The French have devalued the Franc 12½%'.

During their flight to Switzerland from the Mediterranean heat of summer, Eddie was freed from the role of 'male nurse' to attend concerts, ballet and opera at the Salle Garnier in Monte Carlo. During this period he began his acquaintance with the younger generation of pianists. He listened with tremendous enthusiasm to the early recordings of Martha Argerich and the glorious account by Maurizio Pollini of the Chopin Piano Concerto in E minor made shortly after he won the International Chopin Competition in Warsaw in 1960.

Nice, Cannes, Menton, Antibes and even Saint-Tropez hosted many great pianists during those Riviera summers. He attended a concert given by the legendary Sviatoslav Richter in Nice in November 1964, another in February 1966 at a Gala he attended in Cannes for the benefit of the Musée National Fernand Léger in Biot and in August two 'quite overwhelming' recitals of Chopin, Schubert and Beethoven by this artist in Menton. One particularly memorable recital which brought back bittersweet memories of his musical partner George Brooke took place in Menton in August

* Letter from Arthur and Helen to Eddie, 22 July 1968.

1969 when Richter accompanied Dietrich Fischer-Dieskau in the *Die schöne Magelone*, Op. 33 by Brahms. 'I could scarcely contain myself,' he noted in a letter to his pianist sister Lily in Australia.

* * *

After joining the Siegers, Eddie felt he had reached the pinnacle of retirement ease having been given his own apartment in Monaco, the abode of millionaires and tax exiles. The Principality in the 1960s still retained something of a village feel in comparison to the airless, overcrowded monster it has recently become.

Monte Carlo has developed exponentially since the first casino was established in 1856 to provide revenue for the impoverished Prince Charles III. During one week of March 1857 only one visitor patronised the casino and won two francs. The early croupiers would sit much of the day in the sun on the terrace with one of them given the task of watching the approach roads with a telescope. If a carriage possibly containing a gambler was spotted they would scramble around the gaming tables. Queen Victoria disapproved morally of Monte Carlo and wrote in her diary: 'The harm this attractive gambling establishment does cannot be overestimated.' The English influence on the development of the Côte d'Azur remained dominant, the history described and neatly encapsulated in the title chosen for a book: *When the Riviera was Ours* by Patrick Howarth (London 1977).

Charles Garnier, architect of the Paris Opera, built a new casino and glamorous theatre for opera and ballet which before the Great War attracted such luminaries as Serge Diaghilev, Nijinsky and the Ballets Russes for memorable seasons. However the lack of democracy for the native Monégasques during the 1920s was not pleasant and energy costs were high despite the 'cascades of gold' pouring into the casino.* The development of the motor car made the Riviera more accessible between the wars. Fashionable motoring exploits abounded, such as the race initiated by one of the 'Bentley Boys', Woolf Barnato, who wagered he could beat *Le Train Bleu* from Cannes to his London Club in his Speed Six Bentley. He did.

* *The Times*, 9 April 1929.

British influence was eclipsed after the Second World War. The British continued to suffer under exchange control (happily £75 was now permitted to be taken abroad)* but a few somehow managed to continue living the high life outside the Sterling Area, which naturally attracted the interest of the Inland Revenue and the odium of the less well-off. Maintaining an attractive and comfortable standard of living in Monaco soon became impossible for respecters of the law and hazardous for those who operated outside it, unless they were among the 'happy few' who had business interests abroad. The British were forced to live unaccustomedly drab lives in the Principality. No one much cared for their plight at home in Britain, crippled as they were by their own austerity measures.

The marriage of Prince Rainier III and Grace Kelly in April 1956 completely transformed the Principality. The Hollywood film star brought glamour, charm and class to the rather authoritarian Grimaldi family, softening the rule of its inflexible Prince. In many ways she created the luxurious glittering ambience of modern Monaco.† The 1960s witnessed an upsurge in French infrastructure investment in the Principality in motorways, marinas, supermarkets and hotels, which rapidly exceeded the comparatively modest British investments.

* * *

My second visit to Eddie in Monaco was during the 'Year of European Revolution' 1968. I was to stay with him for six months. My interests had matured over years of family diplomatic travel but we had by now returned to Australia. I had had the good fortune not to have been conscripted to fight in the Vietnam War in the infamous 'birthday ballot'. Along with thousands of other 'Australian intellectuals', I felt trapped between two ghettos – that of a suffocating bourgeois family life, the other being the sterility of regimented studies at university. I fled to Europe.

On arrival in Paris I saw the evidence of the May student revolt, barricades now being dismantled and *pavés* scattered among the remains of burnt-out cars. A few intimidating *flics* wandered

* Around £3,000 in 2015 values.

† Alfred Hitchcock made an amusing, charming and glamorous film set in Monaco around this time starring Grace Kelly and Cary Grant entitled *To Catch a Thief* (1955).

about. Trudging the Latin Quarter among despondent students (who hardly seemed threatening but were merely hungry, poor and disinherited), I noticed scrawled on a wall near the Place de Contrescarpe slogans such as *La société est une fleur carnivore.* In those years I was writing my own experimental *avant garde* texts in the style of the *Nouveau Roman* and was deeply interested in contemporary classical music.* I was planning to attend some of the classes given by the German electronic composer Karlheinz Stockhausen at the *Rheinische Musikschule* in Cologne (Courses for New Music) as an observer together with the Australian composer David Ahern†.

Eddie guided me around 'old Monte Carlo' and we attended gala classical concerts in the rococo Salle Garnier. Everyone from the doorman to the artist seemed to know 'Professeur Caheell'. Eddie had met Diaghilev in London in 1924 and showed me the former rehearsal rooms of the Ballets Russes where it was said Nijinsky leapt so high he almost touched the ceiling. We were both 'transported' by Rudolf Nureyev dancing in Frederick Ashton's *The Dream* (a charming setting of Shakespeare's *A Midsummer Night's Dream*) with music by Mendelssohn at the Third International Ballet Festival in Monte Carlo in July 1968. This was the beginning of his fascination with the Russian dancer.

In the evenings we might cross the marbled atrium of the casino to play roulette under the blazing chandeliers of the Salon Europe (just before its restoration) or *chemin de fer* by private arrangement in the improbably opulent Salle Médecin with a view of the distant wooded peninsula of Cap-Martin. He spoke to me of the Baroness Orczy and encountering members of 'The Scarlet Pimpernel' acting

---

* The *Nouveau Roman* was a variety of *avant garde* French novel which emerged in the 1950s and overturned conventional literary forms. Among the practitioners were Marguerite Duras, Alain Robbe-Grillet, Michel Butor, J.M.G. Le Clézio and Nathalie Sarraute. The movement also influenced *La Nouvelle Vague* cinema of Jean Luc Godard and Alain Resnais in films such as *Last Year in Marienbad* and *Hiroshima, Mon Amour.*

† The composer David Anthony Ahern (1947–88) was born in Sydney. He studied composition first with Nigel Butterley, then with Richard Meale. His first performed work was entitled *After Mallarmé* (Universal Edition 1966) for orchestra, but of the greatest notoriety was the piece entitled *Ned Kelly Music* (1967) for orchestra. The success of this piece elevated Ahern's importance within the Australian *avant garde.* Ahern later studied with Cornelius Cardew in London and later formed the AZ Music Ensemble at the Sydney Conservatorium of Music.

company at Villa Bijou. In a luxurious boutique I bought a burgundy chamois waistcoat with antelope horn buttons for a fabulous sum. But my arrival had clearly thrown the tightly regulated household into turmoil.

We took many excursions to his old haunts in the Bentley, one to the historic village of La Turbie on the Grande Corniche. Dante had dedicated verses to the medieval village in the Divine Comedy on his way into exile in Provence. Tobias Smollett wandered through in 1764 and Lord Tennyson followed later, while the Madonna of Laghet nearby has attracted pilgrims for hundreds of years. The shrine is mentioned in Proust when Charles Swann asks Odette, the Niçoise courtesan, to swear true love on her medal of Our Lady. Napoleon stayed overnight on 2 April 1796 *en route* to Italy. The picturesque town is crowned by the Roman ruins known as the Trophy of Augustus.*

Eddie had what he termed a 'secular passion' for racing cars and Monaco was ideal for him to indulge this sport as a spectator. He had practised for the La Turbie hill climb in 1939 and we chatted about his love of car racing as he showed me the original course of the hill climb. We visited the remarkable private collection of antique cars owned by H.S.H. Prince Rainier III and admired the Type 35B Bugatti that had won the inaugural Monaco Grand Prix.† Together we watched the 1968 Grand Prix, which took place at the end of May despite the threat of power cuts arising from the political unrest. Consummate glamour and excitement reigned. Emergency generators from a film studio had been made ready to light the notorious tunnel if it was suddenly plunged into Stygian gloom by a lightning industrial strike.

Eddie had attended every Grand Prix since he had arrived in Monaco in 1962 and by the time I arrived had organised access to the pits and a superb position for us to watch the race from a balcony at the Hôtel de Paris. These were the most dangerous years of Formula 1 racing. Eddie had witnessed the immolation

* This rare survival commemorates the extension of Roman rule in the Alps from 25 to 14 BC by the Emperor Augustus. Also Ted Jones *The French Riviera: A Literary Guide for Travellers* (London 2004) p. 161–2.

† This museum houses an outstanding collection of 100 important cars including the Type 35 Bugatti that won the inaugural Monaco Grand Prix in 1929 driven by William Grover-Williams.

of the Ferrari 312 of Lorenzo Bandini on the harbour chicane the previous year. The 1968 Grand Prix was held in the shadow of the death of Jim Clark, one of the greatest drivers of all time. Graham Hill in a Lotus 49, known affectionately as 'The Master of Monaco', won that year.

We drove to Saint-Jean-Cap-Ferrat to visit the aesthetic splendours of the Neo-Renaissance Italian Villa Ephrussi created by Baroness Ephrussi de Rothschild. In the past he had often performed there at elegant parties. The villa is surrounded by nine gardens with different themes spread over more than ten acres shaped like the deck of an ocean liner. Ponds, fountains and waterfalls are an integral part of the formality of this French garden with a Temple of Love at the apex. Eddie, the great traveller, also took me on foot along the narrow precipitous streets of the *village perché* of Eze, the narrow cobbled streets ablaze with flowers. Friedrich Nietzsche had walked along a path here where he solved some of the creative problems associated with *Thus Spake Zarathustra.*

Eddie had given recitals at some of the grandest villas on the French and Italian Riviera in the glamorous 1930s. He took me to picturesque Menton, in the French Département des Alpes-Maritimes. In the early 1920s the novelist Katherine Mansfield lived in the Villa Isola Bella. Luminaries ranging from Guy de Maupassant to Nietzsche, R.L. Stevenson to F. Scott Fitzgerald sought cures both physical and psychological at Menton. Aubrey Beardsley spent the last two years of his life here. Vladimir Nabokov visited Menton after finishing *The Gift* in Cannes attracted not by a promise of a cure but by the profusion of butterflies.

The town's colourful past is reflected in its coveted border location. It swung like a pendulum throughout history between rule by the Grimaldi family of Monaco, the Italians and the French. In the 19th century it was popular with English aristocrats as a sanatorium for tuberculosis sufferers. Together with the Russians, they built many luxurious palaces and villas in the elegant area known as Garavan. He showed me the famous Villa Maria-Serena at Menton-Garavan where in 1938 he had stayed and performed as a guest of Hans-Heinrich 'Henri' König, one of his closest friends and patrons.* Eddie reminded me with forgivable vanity that as a fashionable concert pianist he had performed for much of High Society on the Côte d'Azur during that charming, elegant and somewhat decadent period of the Scott Fitzgerald novel *Tender is the Night.*

* * *

In Monaco the Siegers and my great-uncle lived in four interconnecting apartments. During my visit we ate in the 'Eating Apartment' as 'one cannot have cooking smells where one lives'. The fact that no cooking of any consequence took place there was irrelevant. We would leave the table after those geriatric meals of Complan and heave our way to the 'Music Apartment' where Eddie lived. When the summer sun was setting, the interior possessed the romantic burnish of another age.

Eddie had decorated the drawing room with many of the gifts he had been given over the years from admiring music-lovers. Silver candelabra adorned his dining table. A large nineteenth-century *Famille* Chinese fish bowl decorated with figures of dancers and musicians stood on a stand. A marine painting by the seventeenth-century Flemish Baroque painter Bonaventura Peeters in its original carved oak frame, speckled with worm holes, hung on a wall together with classical Italian landscapes. Arabian camel cloths and Caucasian rugs were scattered across the parquet together with a few carefully selected Louis Quinze armchairs. Pride of place was naturally given to the mahogany-cased Blüthner grand piano.

Still meticulously dressed by Savile Row and Jermyn Street, Eddie's sensitive small-boned features were always remarked upon, the silvery hair swept back in the 'waves of inspiration' that had made him the darling of the Mayfair salons in the 1920s. He would begin his evening recitals perhaps with a Chopin mazurka, while Sybil fretted with cups of camomile tea. His passion and approach to the music of Chopin clearly betrayed a rather neurasthenic disposition and *irritabilité nerveuse* that on occasion permeates the music of the Polish composer. He would emphasise the intimate folk character of the mazurka with great sensitivity and sensibility,

* See Chapter 13 for further detail on Hans-Heinrich 'Henri' König.

dwelling on the 'grotesque' rhythmic elements and adventurous harmonies. After playing he often mentioned the influence of the Polish pianist Ignaz Friedman whom he had once heard play Chopin mazurkas 'in an unsurpassed fashion' in Vienna.

The Siegers would fall asleep almost immediately the music began, the long figure of Arthur splayed in the armchair like a praying mantis and Helen collapsed like an abandoned marionette. I noticed with alarm she had 'annexes' constructed on her shoes to incorporate her large bunions. One evening Eddie launched into the opening bars of the Chopin *Revolutionary* Étude, the final study from the Op. 10 set. The Siegers suddenly lurched awake as a fantastically distorted sound like a cry of despair suddenly erupted from the instrument. This was not the result of the anguished music or the onset of sudden illness. The Blüthner was 'a jinxed instrument' Eddie told me later. It had been left off the inventory when they departed South Africa in 1961, which caused endless difficulties and expensive delays with the customs office in Monaco. After surviving the long voyage, the removal men had dropped the piano while unloading it at Avenue Hector Otto and cracked the soundboard. The rich sound was as unctuous as old port until the fatal crack was passed, then a terrifying cacophony rent the air. It had never been successfully repaired.

I felt a mixture of sadness and embarrassment during these recitals. Three elderly people imprisoned in an eyrie desperately dealing with old age and inescapable degenerative disease. The evening *tableau vivant* or rather *tableau de mort* had become a grotesque parody of Eddie's former days of dazzling renown.

Chapter 21

Et in Arcadia Ego

During those months I was with Eddie in Monaco, the hypochondriac Monégasque maid wrapped my knees in rugs and drove me regularly to the village in the Bentley* to purchase perfect fruit and veal (the butcher was carefully quizzed on the weaning of the animal). On Sundays Eddie would take me to the English Church and afterwards to tea at the English Tea Rooms to meet members of the 'English colony'.

At this time I was pursuing the 'calvary' of becoming a concert pianist myself with far fewer natural gifts than my great-uncle. We had long discussions on musical culture, great pianists of the past and modern changes in interpretation, finger technique, particularly the unique fingering of Chopin. We both realised that in a similar manner to the eighteenth-century French *clavecinistes*, the composer gave each finger a distinct character quite different from our notions of industrial equality.

We listened to recordings of the greatest pianists of the day: the young Martha Argerich, Vladimir Horowitz (Eddie confided 'He made my hair stand on end in Vienna!'), Arthur Rubinstein, Emil Gilels, Claudio Arrau and Sviatoslav Richter. He spoke of the wild originality and personality of his friend the pianist and '*Chopinzee*' Vladimir de Pachmann, the glorious Mozart of Annie Fischer, the refinement of touch and tone in the Chopin of Dinu Lipatti, the power of Gina Bachauer. Of the English pianists he had heard, he felt Solomon (Cutner) played Chopin with an almost visionary intensity, as if recreating the work before the audience. Similar to Eddie in artistic sincerity, he did not impose his personality on the music but allowed its inherent emotions to speak.

In person Eddie heard possibly his most favoured modern

* A Bentley S2 in British Racing Green with tan leather upholstery.

pianist, the great Italian artist and teacher Arturo Benedetti Michelangeli, who played Chopin and Debussy in Menton in 1965. Enthusiasm overcame him. 'The nobility of his playing and the majesty of it! His astounding virtuosity, ethereal tone, variety of articulation and dynamic shading. Everything a servant of the music. Aristocratic restraint. The depth of thought in the Chopin G minor Ballade and the joy and sense of fun in his Schumann, say *Faschingsschwank aus Wien* (*Carnival Jest in Vienna*). The tone colour of his Debussy ... Ah Michael! I am just a novice!' Although Eddie had never had any pupils of his own, he taught me much on the broken Blüthner. He was no selfish narcissist.

Eddie told me many stories associated with the glamorous days of the 1920s and 1930s. I had begun to feel a strange affinity with this elegant elderly man, what one might term 'genetic resonance'. However on this second visit I was full of youthful energy and not in a mood to linger over bowls of invalid porridge, faded letters from dowagers, lamentations of lost loves and tales of Hermann Göring's lavish *fêtes champêtres* in pre-war Germany.

I spent my evenings wandering the cafés of Monte Carlo till late and befriended the young members of the brilliant American Harkness Ballet Company led by the dancer Lawrence Rhodes. This small, rather new company of dancers were performing a repertoire in preparation for a season at the Music Box in New York. Eddie was a *balletomane* and had many photographs of Rudolf Nureyev on the walls of his bedroom. Ballet in Monte Carlo is associated with the hovering spectres of Diaghilev, Nijinsky and Stravinsky. These shades fuse with the scene in the movie *The Red Shoes* when the aristocratic dancer Victoria 'Vicky' Page (Moira Shearer) leaps to her death over the balustrade of the theatre terrace. I attended bohemian parties where revellers were using fashionable amyl nitrite 'poppers' for short-lived highs. After a couple of months of enjoying the sybaritic Monte Carlo night life, returning to *Le Bermuda* in the small hours and rising very late, Eddie became nervous of the effect my behaviour was having on the aged household. After all, he was financially dependent on the Siegers and could not afford to upset them with a 'difficult relative'.

Having imbibed the restlessness of the 'revolutionary youth' of the time, I decided to give him a rest from my unpredictability and take a trip to nearby Corsica. For three weeks I drove a hired Citroën *Deux Chevaux* over a mountainous interior landscape truly Wagnerian in majesty and sampled the hedonistic beach life. On my return to Ajaccio, I decided to spend a few nights in the picturesque village of Bains de Guitera some fifty kilometres from the capital. I fell into conversation with a charming young woman named Odile who was sitting in the gathering dusk by a lion fountain in the village square. Green eyes in an adorable face were encircled by an aureole of Venetian blonde hair. One thing led to another. I foolishly ignored the advice given to Boswell by the natives of the place warning that Corsica was old fashioned

> They told me that in their country [Corsica] I should be treated with the greatest hospitality; but if I attempted to debauch any of their women, I might lay my account with instant death.*

I was deported from Corsica for my own safety escorted by the police, absurdly dressed in yellow pyjamas printed with miniature vintage cars. I had telephoned Eddie from the Corsican jail. He was deeply shocked but agreed to meet me at the airport in Nice. A deadly silence reigned during the return to Monte Carlo. Later he explained the difficulties I was now causing for him in particular with the Monégasque maid who was 'tired of serving Michael' and 'tired of his scandals anyway'. He suggested I return to Paris early the following month if not sooner.

* * *

Oddly during those final few weeks before my departure Eddie and I were to have our most productive conversations on music and the piano. Perhaps the Corsican incident had aroused memories of his own colourful youth. He may well have felt subconsciously that in retirement and old age it was time to relate his final conclusions, beliefs and experience concerning the piano to someone who would understand. He increasingly thawed towards me as the days passed.

As we sat together on the terrace of his drawing room overlooking the Mediterranean I asked Eddie about his teachers and their influence. He said he recalled little of Mrs Bale, the wife

---

* James Boswell, *An Account of Corsica, the Journal of a Tour to That Island, and Memoirs of Pascal Paoli* (Glasgow 1768), p. 269.

of the milkman in Beenleigh who guided him through his first childish delights at the piano. He was largely self-taught as a pianist through playing in the silent cinema and vaudeville. 'A great lesson in communication with an audience!' By 1924 he had travelled to London and begun to seriously study the piano 'rather too late' with the distinguished English pianist, teacher and composer Tobias Matthay. But on this final occasion in Monaco he spoke mainly of his studies in Vienna in 1929 with Leonie Gombrich* and later Alfred Cortot in Paris.

Eddie greatly respected the musical discrimination of the Viennese. He had learned a great deal about the great Polish pedagogue Theodor Leschetizky from his pupil Frau Gombrich. This extraordinary musician had studied with Carl Czerny who had been an assistant to Beethoven. A man of the widest culture, he claimed to have read Goethe and Schiller aged seven and performed a Czerny concertino conducted by Wolfgang Amadeus Mozart II (the introverted son of the composer) at the age of nine. Leschetizky remained close to the source of Chopin's inspiration as he was nineteen when the composer died. Although he never met Chopin, he had met his pupils, who passed on their first-hand impressions of 'the Ariel of the piano'.

Famed throughout Europe, he had played for Marie Louise of Austria, the widow of Napoleon. His concert career reached its peak in 1870. Married four times, his second wife and pupil was the renowned pianist Annette Essipova claimed to be the greatest pianist of her day.† Leschetizky was influenced in his own pianistic style by the glamorous and fashionable Bohemian pianist and composer Julius Schulhoff‡ and 'the lion of the keyboard', the great Russian

* For additional pedagogical material on Leonie Gombrich refer to Chapter 8.

† For the material on Theodor Leschetizky I am indebted to James Methuen-Campbell, *Chopin Playing: From the Composer to the Present Day* (London 1981), pp. 58–60. This is a remarkable text for those who appreciate the manifold ways of approaching the interpretation of this composer. Also Ethel Newcomb, *Leschetizky As I Knew Him* (New York 1967) is a fascinating personal account of the man by possibly his favourite assistant. Additionally, Annette Hullah *Theodor Leschetizky* (London 1906).

‡ Julius Schulhoff (1825–98) was a pianist and composer born in Prague. The music of this forgotten friend of Chopin was enormously popular among amateur pianists in the mid-nineteenth century. The glorious tone he produced on the piano while playing his own *Chant de Berger* (the first of a set of pieces entitled *Trois Idylles*, Op. 25) had a profound impact on the twenty-year-old Theodor Leschetizky: 'my heart overflowing with indescribable emotions as I listened … the melody standing out in bold relief ... a legato

pianist Anton Rubinstein.* His influence on modern pianism has been immense. He attracted all manner of pupils and pianists who were themselves to become piano legends.† Leschetizky remarkably never forgot the appearance of the hand of any pupil he had once taught. 'People seemed exhilarated by his presence.'‡ With such a colourful background as Eddie had, Leschetizky, a great *bon viveur*, would never have needed to shout gruffly: 'Don't play in such a bourgeois manner! I hate everything bourgeois!' When Eddie told her he was Australian, Leonie Gombrich commented how unusual for him to be a resident of Vienna. She jokingly mentioned Leschetizky's question to one newly arrived American pupil 'Are you a European or a cannibal?'

Eddie believed (along with Arthur Rubinstein) in the ability of an outstanding pianist to communicate with the audience through a type of intimate 'electrical emanation' that permeates the concert hall. The soul and spirit of the performer create all the unnotated subtle nuances and minute hesitations, the slight variations in *tempo rubato,* the inspired phrasing, touch and tone colour of any significant interpretation. Given an equally commanding technique, only a unique personality will lead to a unique interpretation.

> The score is only a vague indication of a composer's imagined musical intentions. The dots on the page are only the starting point for an interpreter, not a strait-jacket. What is happening *between* the bar lines I ask myself. The quality of the silences between the sounds is what creates the music. What did Chopin say? 'I only suggest, the listener must complete the picture' or

such as I had not dreamed possible on the piano, a human voice rising above the sustaining harmonies! ... Overwhelmed with a sense of inadequacy and unable to control myself, I fled to the farthest room and burst into tears. From that day I tried to find that touch.' Leschetizky ceased playing pieces and concentrated on exercises to achieve a tone and touch which now obsessed him.

* Anton Rubinstein (1829–94). 'Russians call me German, Germans call me Russian, Jews call me a Christian, Christians a Jew. Pianists call me a composer, composers call me a pianist. The classicists think me a futurist, and the futurists call me a reactionary. My conclusion is that I am neither fish nor fowl – a pitiful individual.' Anton Rubinstein, *Gedankenkorb* (Basket of Thoughts) 1897.

† Among them are to be considered such piano luminaries as Annette Essipova, Richard Buhlig, Ignaz Friedman, Ignacy Jan Paderewski, Artur Schnabel, Mark Hambourg, Alexander Brailowsky, Alexander Winkler, Benno Moiseiwitsch, Paul Wittgenstein, Ossip Gabrilowitsch, Elly Ney, Natalia Polnazkovski and Mieczysław Horszowski.

‡ Ethel Newcomb, *Leschetizky As I Knew Him*, p. 279.

> something like that. He scarcely ever played the same piece in the same way twice. After the greatest performances by say a Cortot, Lipatti, Friedman or a Hofmann, there is simply nothing left to say. I hope sometimes I achieved that type of eloquent silence!*

His harsh experience on the vaudeville and music hall stage taught him early in life that audiences attend concerts primarily for social reasons, entertainment and to marvel at keyboard virtuosity. Rarely do they come for musical education. 'I tried to give something to everyone. I tried to carry the audience with me and feel what I feel. Touch them with electricity. I do hope I succeeded!' As a 'society pianist' Eddie possessed sufficient technique, charm and command of the art of programming to enable him to seduce educated audiences. It was often commented on that Eddie possessed a magnetic charisma, expressed a luminous sense of heartfelt feeling of immense subtlety, the refinement of a gracious salon, a type of nostalgic magic in his playing, a quality the music critic Neville Cardus described as 'the pathos of distance'.†

* * *

The renowned Swiss-French pianist and conductor Alfred Cortot had perhaps the most profound influence on the fastidiousness of Eddie's playing and even his personality, in particular on his interpretation of Chopin and Schumann. Eddie found him 'one of the most curious, magnetic and fascinating creatures I have ever met. Music seemed to act like a drug on him!' It was the inner musical meaning of Chopin that was of paramount importance to Cortot. Eddie indicated there are 'good wrong notes' played by great virtuosi and 'bad wrong notes' played by amateurs. Cortot appeared able to hypnotise the audience with music despite his lapses in accuracy.

> With him, control over details always appeared to be improvised on the spot. Nothing seemed musically contrived with Cortot. Everything had an inevitable inner logic. He always tried to create an atmosphere and tell me a story around the work we studied, usually a very poetic one or some sort of personal

* Edward Cahill in conversation with the author Monaco 1968.

† Neville Cardus (1888–1975), the fine music and cricket critic, in 'Friedman's Recital' *Sydney Morning Herald*, 30 July 1941.

> fantasy of bizarre images inspired by the music. He encouraged me to do this myself. When I recorded the Chopin Waltz in A-flat major Op. 42 years later in Cape Town I remembered he had told me to imagine the dancing of a flirtatious countess and her dashing cavalier puffed up with vanity like a peacock. We studied this work closely together. Cortot was just as wonderful in Schumann, particularly in his luminous understanding of the ambiguous titles and innocent visions he brings to his performance of *Kinderszenen*.*

We listened closely to his large number of Cortot recordings. The radiant tone, beauty and subtle sensibility of the Nocturnes brought Eddie close to tears. He considered the performance of the Chopin Preludes Op. 28 Cortot made in Paris in 1942 a supreme account. He felt the complete cycle formed a universe, a planetary system in matched synchronicity, fragments evoking worlds within worlds. However Eddie did not believe that one should perform them as a cycle as it detracted from the full appreciation of the significance of each as an individual masterpiece however brief.

> Cortot creates an extraordinary degree of intimacy and refinement. His integration of the contrapuntal and melodic in Chopin, so difficult to achieve without exaggeration or contrivance, is masterful. The touch and rich tone of Cortot is magical! His phrasing is absolutely exquisite! Don't you think so Michael?

Eddie loved his 1930 recording of the Chopin Waltzes, often played 'in the old style' with the hands slightly separated to emphasise the legato melodic line. Cortot was in control of a subtle and perfectly natural *rubato* which lifts the quality of his performance far above those of most pianists.

Rachmaninoff once commented unkindly to Horowitz on hearing Cortot play the Chopin Études on the radio with many wrong notes 'Cortot is so musical. The more difficult the etude, the more sentimental he gets.'† Cortot felt a particular affinity with the music of the Polish composer. For many Chopinists, Cortot is the foundation stone of 'correct' interpretation

> subtle, melancholic, heroic, deeply communicative and 'full' [...] he aims at a deeper Chopin, a Chopin of sentiment but not senti-

---

* Edward Cahill in conversation with the author, Monaco 1968.

† Quoted in Plaskin, *Horowitz*, p. 188.

mentality, of structural cohesion but not academic formality.*

Cortot convinced many doubters that Chopin was indeed among the greatest of composers for the instrument, a view which was not universal after the Second World War.

* * *

'How do you understand Chopin, Eddie?' I ventured one afternoon over tea and biscuits.†

'Chopin is one of the most difficult of composers to interpret and begs for a cultivated mind of sensibility and poetry with a proper understanding of his cultural milieu and noble, 'classical' historical style. Subtle *legato* sustaining a singing melodic line, colour, texture of the sound, mood contrasts and natural *rubato* dictated by the heart, brought into being at the moment of recreation. Paderewski despite his faults understood this more than almost any pianist save Lipatti, Cortot, Rubinstein, Friedman and Hofmann. Percy Grainger and particularly Solomon were greatly underestimated Chopin interpreters. The intense nobility of Małcużyński ... '

'And young pianists?'

'The world young artists have inherited is loud, cruel and violent, a world dominated by technology that prizes physical power, speed and the body above intelligence, morality and the soul. The style of playing Chopin is affected by this of course. Many pianists are simply too young for the pain and mystery of Chopin. How far we have moved from the composer! They treat the keyboard, as Ferruccio Busoni once remarked, as if it was a gymnasium attached to a musical instrument! They listen to too many modern recordings early in their careers and imitate, do not *meditate* on the music. A pianist must have something individual to say about Chopin but say it with charm and poetry! Remember he adored Bach and Mozart!

The joy inherent in the *style brillant* of Chopin's early years influenced by Hummel, the concertos for example, suits the

* Methuen-Campbell, *Chopin Playing*, pp. 86, 87.

† Edward Cahill's observations that follow were compiled from the author's 1968 journal and notes concerning Cahill's career, his teachers, Chopin and the art of the piano noted down during many discussions. Numerous conversations of a musical nature took place over the six month period I resided with him in Monaco in 1968.

younger player but his later works, say the *Polonaise-Fantaisie*? These are far more complex and profound expressions of mortality. Chopin balances the masculine and feminine in his music in perfect equilibrium. Too many young pianists today emphasise one at the expense of, even exclusion of, the other! The intimate way I performed in aristocratic salons for small audiences in London and Paris in the 1920s and 1930s was much closer to the authentic Chopinesque ambience than our regular huge concert halls, which I nearly always hated.'

He reminded me that Chopin remained faithful to the impressions of his childhood and youth. Amidst the angst and suffering, almost half Chopin's output was dance music and Eddie suggested I actually learn to dance the waltz, mazurka and polonaise in addition to singing, the better to understand the phrasing and capture the significance of the breathing. He pointed out for example that many of the grander Chopin waltzes open with a fanfare, a 'call to the floor', which at the time would have been interpreted as a summons to the dance. Few pianists understand these declamatory opening phrases.

Eddie was also a mine of recondite information concerning the composer. Chopin was a fine organist and gave many impressive improvisatory concerts in Warsaw and smaller towns as a young man. It explains much of his *legato* fingering in his piano pieces, which appear on the face of it to be unnecessary on a sustaining instrument with pedals such as the piano, even the early *Pleyels* which do not sustain as well as a modern instrument.

He told me how the music of Chopin was received differently by the various nationalities. 'The Poles no longer own Chopin! Other pianists can play mazurkas perfectly well!' he once said with heat. He told me the Russians regarded Chopin as a revolutionary Slavic nationalist, his French surname led Parisians to regard him as a poet and dreamer. One clearly deaf English literary critic lamented that George Sand, an apostle of the French Catholic priest, philosopher, and political theorist Lamennais, had become involved with 'the artistic zero' that was Fryderyk Chopin!

He continued: 'Chopin was an ebullient young man fond of a practical joke! He possessed that characteristic Polish individuality curiously combined with French graciousness. Of course when "the

Sand" got hold of him he became emotionally desperate enough to compose those haunted masterpieces.'

'Was this a good thing?'

'Creatively yes. It was a catalyst for many masterpieces but for his personal happiness and peace of mind definitely not!'

'Were they in love do you think, George and Fryderyk?' I asked.

'I expect they complemented each other beautifully,' he said with a wry smile.

Eddie then told me a celebrated story to illustrate the quality of their relationship and the roles played within it by the writer and musician, at least in the later stages. The anecdote was originally related by Wilhelm von Lenz, pianist and friend of Chopin and Liszt. Sand was seated one evening by a drawing room fire. After she had insulted the Russians as barbarians and was generally unpleasant towards the assembled company, while seemingly preoccupied and gazing into the flames, Mme Dudevant took out a large cigar, glanced over her shoulder and called peremptorily across the room 'Frédéric, a light!'

* * *

It was some years later I briefly visited Monaco in 1974 to console Eddie in tragically reversed circumstances. His Swiss patrons had finally died in a Monaco clinic after prolonged struggles. Both had become victims of the medical, legal and religious parasites that feed in the geriatric waters of the Principality. To the last Sybil had remained loyal to her employers and was now caring for Eddie. He had suffered a stroke under the strain of dealing with their illnesses. Drifting in and out of consciousness, suspended in that realm of heightened perception between life and death and in search of a more permanent truth, he still managed to haltingly speak with me. With some difficulty, he managed to extract a pledge from me to travel to Poland at some time in my life and visit the places Chopin had frequented as a young man. 'A country that can produce a man of the stamp of Ignacy Jan Paderewski deserves your undivided attention!'

Knowing he was not far from death, he implored me to scatter a handful of his ashes over the Mazovian plain near Chopin's poetic birthplace at the hamlet of Żelazowa Wola, fifty kilometres from Warsaw. At this request I confess to remaining silent.

He was finally left paralysed and aphasic by another major stroke not long after the death of Helen Sieger late in 1974. His Italian valet assisted Sybil with his care and shaved him each day, moving him from bed to wheelchair. Eddie was condemned by the stroke to repeat endlessly 'I know, I know, I know…' Sybil felt this meant 'I know who you are!' but it had the existential ring of a final and disturbing philosophical conclusion on life. He died in Monaco on 11 February 1975 and, like Mozart, was buried in an unremarkable 'third-class' grave in the Monaco cemetery one bleak and rainy afternoon, the ground merely rented for a period. At the funeral, the maid whispered financial demands into my ear as the coffin was being lowered into the earth.

After his death I sorted as many of his possessions as remained and transported them to London where they remained in limbo until I felt impelled to piece together the history of this artist.

* * *

The year was 2010. Breakfast on the terrace of my pension was an absolute French delight, the sublime view of Eze and Cap Ferrat through the haze, power boats slicing in slow motion across the Mediterranean leaving scars of white, vast Russian yachts at anchor, a scene of affluent calm of which one could never tire. Soft croissants, *pain au chocolat,* home-made jam in rustic containers, smelly cheeses, breads of every description and excellent coffee. I decided to drive to Monaco and try and find Eddie's old address. I took an orange from the basket in the portico, patted the dog Fiona and set off.

The airless rabbit warren of twisting streets drive most visiting motorists to distraction. I at last found Avenue Hector Otto, the street where Eddie had lived, without much drama as it was high above the city, not secreted in the airless labyrinth below. However I spent some time finding the actual block of flats as during the intervening thirty-five years since his death Monaco high-rises had spread like giant mushrooms. In desperation I asked a wrinkled old lady who managed a Tabac about the apartment Le Bermuda above the Jardin

Exotique. 'You will find only the entrance after the parking station. Go up in the lift.' The concealed entrance was to a block of flats clearly built long ago. I took a photograph and was suddenly accosted by a Canadian who emerged. He spoke first in French and then English.

'Why are you taking a picture of our decrepit entrance?' he asked in amazement.

'My great-uncle the concert pianist Edward Cahill retired here from 1962–75 where he died. Might you perhaps remember him?' I asked.

'No-one is young enough to remember!' he observed. 'But wait! Here are two ancient types who might know something! I know they have lived here for eons.'

Two elderly folk with liver-spotted skin came out of the entrance. Both were stooped and walked with sticks. He introduced me but these unfortunates were clearly in their nineties and in some stage of dementia. They remembered nothing of the former residents. Their conversation kept straying off to the gravely serious shopping expedition they intended to do in the town. I gathered that very few expatriate exiles live, die and are buried here.

The next day on an impulse I decided to try and rediscover Eddie's grave. I hoped it would not take me six months of tortuous Monégasque bureaucracy. Searching for his grave in the grand Monaco cemetery during a stifling, humid and scorching summer was less than pleasant. I had almost given up when surprisingly I spied a small, bijou cottage in one corner of the graveyard with stained glass windows, white linen cushions lying on wrought-iron chairs, a tiny conservatory with flowering plants. In short the cottage possessed a general air of habitation and civilised life. A fine-boned rather attractive Monégasque woman approached me from the cemetery steps, barefoot in jeans. A large silver cross hung about her neck and some silver bangles jingled around her wrists. Her crinkly hair was held back with a clip and she had an air of spiritual or possibly alcoholic intoxication.

'Can I 'elp you, Monsieur?' she asked.

'Well, perhaps you can,' I replied without the slightest confidence. I told her briefly of Uncle Eddie's history of thirteen years' residence in Monaco.

'Ah! 'E was your uncle. A relative of you! We must find 'im. *C'est très important!* Can you tell me the year 'e dead ?'

'He died in 1975, but I don't know the exact date.'

'If you can tell me plus or minus five years will be alright! I look in ze books!' she answered brightly.

I was astounded as she went to a small cupboard in the cottage and brought out a couple of battered leather-bound ledgers. She ruffled through the pages of the 1975 volume.

'What 'is name you say? I am forgetting pronunciation English names quickly.'

'Edward Cahill' I repeated and I wrote it on a piece of paper even less optimistically and handed it to her. Within two minutes the entry was found.

'Come out and take ze picture of the book but near some green!' she said.

I asked her name.

'Joy!' she exclaimed.

'How ever did you come to be working here?'

'I was owning a *boutique* in Monaco and the Mayor of Monaco 'e asked me to 'elp 'im to work one day. I am now 'ere ten years!'

'How did your friends feel about it?'

'I 'ave no friends. These are my friends. All my friends are 'ere!' she said warmly gesturing to the tiers of graves in a grand sweeping movement of her arm.

Led by Joy, I walked in the blistering heat to the grave itself, now empty. A porcelain plaque with an enamelled bird in bright plumage lay on the stone. By the most perfect coincidence it read in French *Berce son repos de ton chant le plus beau* (Cradle his rest with your most beautiful song).

Prince Rainier had allocated a special part of the cemetery called 'Piquet' or more sensitively 'Jacaranda' for the poor residents of Monaco who could not afford the expensive funerals of the Principality. After the expiry of the five-year grace period, our family could have rented Eddie's plot for another 30 years but the cost was exorbitant. Immortality and the remembrance of life also has a price. Eddie had lain in grave No. 50 for five years before being cremated and his ashes ultimately placed in a common grave in the area of the cemetery called 'Le Jardin de Souvenir'. This garden plot had a miniature Palladian entrance arch, a tiny stream flowing over rocks and a commemorative marble urn circled in flowers where ashes are placed communally. A cloud of butterflies vividly danced over it in the sun.

* * *

And so this journey of exploration to assemble the life story of a member of my family, my great-uncle the concert pianist Eddie Cahill concluded. A tale greater than I could ever had anticipated that dismal afternoon had unfolded before me like a Persian rug. The discovery of so many family traits genetically carried through the generations was indeed a salutary yet deeply enlivening experience. I no longer felt ashamed of my weaknesses and prouder of my strengths. The journey over these last six years that began one lovelorn, wet afternoon in London has been extraordinarily enriching.

Edward Cahill's musical voice remains alive in the survival of the few precious recordings he made of Liszt and Chopin. Throughout his colourful and successful life 'Uncle Eddie' passionately held the belief he once energetically expressed in Monte Carlo before his final decline

> 'My dear young man, personality, temperament and character are the mainstays. They are everything! Cultivate your individuality above all else. Don't be afraid to be *you!*'

His story is surely a fine example of the truth of this conviction. And then he said something surprising rather *sotto voce,* a curious remark and to me unforgettable

> 'Michael, when you play try and communicate with passion and intensity the *sexual electricity* contained within music without fear. As in relationships select the right tempo and all will be well. Play with your heart and soul, your sensibility. Technique is merely their servant. This is the paramount feature of all the greatest pianists. True musical art creates an inexhaustible desire for itself.'

Then suddenly in a more forthright tone of power and confidence

> 'And less poetically Michael. You must really *want it,* this being a pianist! Rid yourself of all inessentials not directly serving the pupose of music. Work, my boy, work with courage and heart!'

Bibliography

Papers in the author's private collection

Edward Cahill's personal collection of letters, journals, manuscripts, music reviews, scrap books, newspaper articles, official documents, personal period photographs, memorabilia, film and 78 rpm shellac and tape recordings

Interviews with informants who remembered the pianist or the historical period in question

Edward Cahill personal interviews with the author in Monaco in 1968 during 6 months residence and more briefly in 1974

Material from publicly accessible archives

John Oxley Library (State Library of Queensland)

Queensland Museum

National Trust of Queensland

National Film and Sound Archive of Australia

Australian Teachers of Media (ATOM) No: 8 *The Story of the Kelly Gang* (Melbourne 2007)

National Trust of Queensland, Report on the Beenleigh Hotel, 1975

Logan River & District Family History Society Inc.

Picture Australia – National Library of Australia

Newspapers – National Library of Australia

Digital Collections – National Library of Australia

National Film and Sound Archive of Australia

National Portrait Gallery London

Hansard: Punjab Disturbances. Lord Hunter's Committee

HC Deb 08 July 1920 vol. 131 cc.1705–822 cc.1705–819, Army Council and General Dyer

Musical archive resources, British Library, London

Newspaper resources, British Library outstation, Croydon

Theatre Collection, University of Bristol

British Cartoon Archive, University of Kent

Southeast Asia Visions Collection Cornell University

TROVE (Online digitised newspaper resource of the National Library of Australia)

YouTube

Music reviews and articles taken from selected Australian newspapers 1909–1935 include

The Argus (Melbourne)

Australasian (Melbourne)

Barrier Miner (Broken Hill)

Brisbane Courier

Cairns Post

Courier-Mail (Brisbane)

Morning Bulletin (Rockhampton)

Punch (Melbourne)

Queenslander (Brisbane)

Sydney Morning Herald

Telegraph (Brisbane)

SECONDARY SOURCES

Reference Material

Australian Dictionary of Biography

Oxford Dictionary of National Biography

Summers, Jonathan, *A-Z of Pianists*, Reference Book plus 4 CDs (NAXOS, London 2007)

Books

Acton, Harold, *Memoirs of an Aesthete* (London 1948)

Agate, James, *The Selective Ego: The Diaries of James Agate,* Tim Beaumont ed. (London 1976)

Baigent, Michael and Leigh, Richard, *Secret Germany: Claus von Stauffenberg and the Mystical Crusade Against Hitler* (London 1994)

Balfour, Patrick, Lord Kinross *Society Racket* (Tauchnitz Edition, Leipzig 1934)

Barenboim, Daniel and Said, Edward W., *Parallels and Paradoxes* (London 2003)

Barrow, Andrew, *Gossip: A History of High Society from 1920 to 1970* (London 1978)

Barry, John, M., *The Great Influenza* (New York 2004)

Bartholomew, Michael, *In Search of H. V. Morton* (London 2004)

Beethoven, Ludwig van, *Heiligenstadt Testament* 1802 trans. John V. Gilbert

Beevor, Antony and Cooper, Artemis, *Paris After the Liberation 1944–1949* (London 1994)

Berry Bros & Rudd *'Number Three'* Autumn (London 1976)

Bird, John, *Percy Grainger* (London 1976)

Blainey, Anne, *I Am Melba* (Melbourne 2008)

Bloch, Michael, *The Secret File of the Duke of Windsor* (London 1988)

Boswell, James, *An Account of Corsica, the Journal of a Tour to That Island, and Memoirs of Pascal Paoli* (Glasgow 1768)

Brink, André, *Looking on Darkness* (London 1974)

Brockway, Fenner, *Hungry England* (London 1932)

Brown, Gordon, *Courage: Eight Portraits* (London 2007)

Brown, David, *Tchaikovsky: The Crisis Years, 1874–1878* (New York 1983)

Buchanan, Alfred Johnson, *The Real Australia* (London 1907)

Bullock, Alan, *Hitler: A Study in Tyranny* (London 1952)

Bullock, John, *Fast Women: The Drivers Who Changed the Face of Motor Racing* (London 2002)

Cannon, Michael, *The Long Last Summer: Australia's Upper Class Before the Great War* (Melbourne 1985)

Carrington, Dorothy, *Granite Island: A Portrait of Corsica* (London 1971)

Channon, Henry, *The Ludwigs of Bavaria* (London 1952)

Charles-Roux, Edmonde, *Chanel* trans. Nancy Amphoux (London 1976)

Chester, Fay and Young *The Zinoviev Letter* (London 1967)

Christie, Agatha *The Mystery of the Blue Train* (London 1928)

Churchill, Winston S., ed. *Never Give In! The Best of Winston Churchill's Speeches* (London 2003)

Clare, George *Last Waltz in Vienna: The Destruction of a Family 1842–1942* (London 1981)

Clark, Kenneth, *Another Part of the Wood* (London 1974)

Clarke, Hugh, & Burgess, Colin, *Barbed Wire & Bamboo: Australian POW Stories* (Sydney 1992)

Clarke, Jonathan, Construction History Vol. 18. *Like a huge birdcage exhaled from the earth: Watson's Esplanade Hotel, Mumbai (1867–71), and its place in structural history* (Cambridge 2002)

Collett, Nigel, *The Butcher of Amritsar: General Reginald Dyer* (London 2005)

Colley, Linda, *Captives: Britain, Empire and the World 1600–1850* (London 2002)

Collins, E.J.T., ed. *The Agrarian History of England and Wales* Volume VII 1850–1914 Part 1 (Cambridge 2000)

Comte, Martin, *Australian Pianists* (Melbourne 2010)

Connolly, Cyril, *The Rock Pool* (London 1936)

_____, *The Selected Essays* ed. Peter Quennell (New York 1984)

Conradi, Peter, *Hitler's Piano Player: The Rise and Fall of Ernst Hanfstaengl, Confidant of Hitler, Ally of FDR* (London 2005)

Cooper, Diana, *The Rainbow Comes and Goes* (London 1959)

_____, *The Light of Common Day* (London 1959)

_____, *Trumpets from the Steep* (London 1960)

Cooper, Duff, *Old Men Forget: The Autobiography of Duff Cooper* (London 1953)

Cortot, Alfred, *Rational Principles of Piano Technique* (Paris 1928)

d'Almeida, Fabrice, *High Society in the Third Reich* (Cambridge 2008)

Demetz, Peter, *The Air Show at Brescia, 1909* (New York 2002)

Dostoevsky, Fyodor, *The Gambler*, trans. Ronald Meyer (London 2010)

Douglas, James, *Bombay and Western India: A Series of Stray Papers* 2 vols., (London 1893)

Douglas-Home, Jessica, *Violet: The Life and Loves of Violet Gordon-Woodhouse* (London 1996)

Duke of Bedford, John, *A Silver-Plated Spoon* (London 1959)

Duleba, Władisław *Wieniawski* (Warsaw 1984)

Dwivedi, Sharada and Barwani, Manvendra Singh, *The Automobiles of the Maharajas* (Bombay 2003)

Eade, Philip, *Sylvia, Queen of the Headhunters* (London 2007)

Earl, John, *British Theatres and Music Halls* (Risborough 2005)

Eigeldinger, Jean-Jacques, *Chopin Pianist and Teacher As Seen by his Pupils* (Cambridge 1986)

Elton, Charles I., *An Account of Shelley's Visits to France, Switzerland and Savoy in the Years 1814 and 1816* (London 1894)

Evans, Allan, *Ignaz Friedman: Romantic Master Pianist* (Bloomington 2009)

Evans, Raymond, *A History of Queensland* (Cambridge 2007)

Fisher, Marshall Jon, *A Terrible Splendour: Three Extraordinary Men, a World Poised for War, and the Greatest Tennis Match Ever Played* (New York 2009)

Forster, E.M., *Maurice* (London 1999)

Fry, Helen, *Music and Men: The Life and Loves of Harriet Cohen* (Stroud 2008)

Fry, Michael, *Hitler's Wonderland* (London 1934)

Furtwängler, Wilhelm, *Notebooks 1924–1954* trans. Shaun Whiteside ed. Michael Tanner (London 1989)

Gaines, James R., *Evening in the Palace of Reason* (London 2005)

Gardiner, Juliet, *The Thirties: An Intimate History* (London 2010)

Gilmour, David, *The Ruling Caste: Imperial lives in the Victorian Raj* (London 2005)

Goldberg, Ronald Allen, *America in the Twenties* (New York 2003)

Goldring, Douglas, *The Nineteen Twenties* (London 1945)

Griffiths, Richard, *Fellow Travellers of the Right: British Enthusiasts for Nazi Germany, 1933–1939* (London 1980)

Gunther, John, *The Lost City* (London 1964)

Hale, Julian, *The French Riviera: A Cultural History* (Oxford 2009)

Hamilton, David, *The Monkey Gland Affair* (London 1986)

Hamilton, Kenneth, *After the Golden Age: Romantic Pianism and Modern Performance* (Oxford 2008)

Hanfstaengl, Ernst, *Unheard Witness* (Philadelphia 1957)

Hastings, Selina, *The Secret Lives of Somerset Maugham* (London 2009)

Heap, Peggy, *The Story of Hottentots Holland* (Somerset West 1993)

Henderson, Carol and Tovey, Heather, *Searching for Grace* (Wellington, New Zealand 2010)

Her Highness Princess Marie Louise *My Memories of Six Reigns* (London 1956)

Hoernlé, Alfred R.F., *South African Native Policy and the Liberal Spirit* (Cape Town 1939)

Hofmann, Josef, *Piano Playing with Piano Questions Answered* (New York 1909)

Hotchner, A.E., *The Man Who Lived at the Ritz* (London 1981)

Howarth, Patrick, *When the Riviera was Ours* (London 1977)

Hughes, Angela, *Chelsea Footprints: A Thirties Chronicle* (London 2008)

Hughes, Robert, *The Fatal Shore* (London 1987)

Hullah, Annette, *Theodor Leschetizky* (London 1906)

James, Robert Rhodes, ed. *'Chips': The Diaries of Sir Henry Channon* (London 1967)

Johnson, Bob and Stuart-Findlay, Derek, *The Motorist's Paradise: Early Motoring In and Around Cape Town* (Cape Town 2007)

Jones, Nigel, *Rupert Brooke: Life, Death and Myth* (London 1999)

Jones, Ted, *The French Riviera: A Literary Guide for Travellers* (London 2004)

Jordis, Christine, *Bali, Java, in My Dreams* (London 2002)

Kelly, David, *The Ruling Few or the Human Background to Diplomacy: The Memoirs of Sir David Kelly G.C.M.G., M.C.* (London 1952)

Keneally, Thomas, *The Great Shame: A Story of the Irish in the Old World and the New* (London 1998)

Kershaw, Ian, *Making Friends with Hitler* (London 2004)

Kessler, Charles, trans. & ed. *Berlin in Lights: The Diaries of Count Harry Kessler (1918–1937)* (London 1971)

Kipling, Rudyard, *Land and Sea Tales* (London 1923)

_____, *From Sea to Sea: Letters of Travel* (New York 1913)

Kozubek, Lidia, *Arturo Benedetti Michelangeli as I Knew Him* (Frankfurt Am Main 2011)

Kramarz, Joachim, *Stauffenberg: The Life and Death of an Officer* trans.

Richard Barry (London 1967)

Lafayette, Maximillien de, *America in the Twenties. Photos and Reports.* Volume 1 (New York 2011)

Lambert, Angela, *Unquiet Souls: The Indian summer of the British aristocracy* (London 1984)

Lambert, Gilles, *The Conquest of Age: The Extraordinary Story of Dr Paul Niehans* (New York 1959)

Langfield, Valerie, *Roger Quilter His Life and Music* (Rochester 2002)

Lannoy, Richard, *Benares Seen from Within* (Bath 1999)

Larson, Erik, *In the Garden of the Beasts* (New York 2011)

Lenz, Wilhelm von, *The Great Piano Virtuosos of our Time* (New York 1899)

Lewis, Wyndham, *The Apes of God* (London 1930)

Logan River & District Family History Society Inc. *They Chose Beenleigh: A Tribute to the Immigrant Landholders and Pioneers of the Beenleigh and Eagleby, Queensland, Australia prior to 1885* (Beenleigh 2009)

Lovell, Mary S., *The Mitford Girls: The Biography of an Extraordinary Family* (London 2001)

Lowe, Keith, *Savage Continent: Europe in the Aftermath of World War II* (London 2012)

MacCarthy, Fiona, *BYRON: Life and Legend* (London 2002)

MacKrell, Judith, *Flappers: Six Women of a Dangerous Generation* (London 2013)

MacMillan, Margaret, *Peacemakers: The Paris Conference of 1919 and Its Attempt to End War* (London 2001)

MacQueen-Pope, W., *The Melodies Linger On: The Story of Music Hall* (London 1950)

Mallarmé, Stephane, *The Poems in Verse* Translation and Notes by Peter Manson (Miami 2012)

Marks, Martin Miller, *Music and the Silent Film: Contexts and Case Studies 1895–1924* (New York 1997)

Marquess Tokugawa *Travels Around Java in 1920s* (Tsukuba 1996)

Marsh, Edward Howard, *Georgian Poetry, 1911–1922* (London, 5 volumes)

Maude, Aylmer, *The Life of Tolstoy: The First Fifty Years* (London 1917)

Maugham, Somerset, *A Writer's Notebook* (London 1949) Readers Union Edition 1951

______, *The Casuarina Tree* (London 1926)

Mayor, Edward, *Petwood: The Remarkable Story of a Famous Lincolnshire Hotel* (London 2004)

McEwen, Britta, *Sexual Knowledge: Feeling, Fact, and Social Reform in Vienna, 1900–1934* (New York 2012)

McKibbin, Ross, *Classes and Cultures: England 1918–1951* (Oxford 1998)

Methuen-Campbell, James, *Chopin Playing: From the Composer to the Present Day* (London 1981)

Mitchell, John Hanson, *The Rose Café* (Emeryville 2007)

Mitford, Jessica, *Hons and Rebels* (London 1960)

Mitford, Nancy, *The Pursuit of Love* (London 1945)

Morris, James, *Pax Britannica: The Climax of an Empire* (London 1968)

Morton, H.V., *In Search of England* (London 1927)

_____, *H.V. Morton's London* being *The Heart of London, The Spell of London* and *The Nights of London* in one volume (London 1940)

_____, *In Search of South Africa* (London 1948)

Mosley, Leonard, *The Reich Marshal* (London 1974)

Muggeridge, Malcolm, *The Thirties: 1930–1940 in Great Britain* (London 1940)

Mulvagh, Jane, *Madresfield: The Real Brideshead* (London 2008)

Murray, Robert, *The Confident Years: Australia in the Twenties* (London 1978)

Nelson, Michael, *Queen Victoria and the Discovery of the Riviera* (London 2001)

Neuhaus, Heinrich, *The Art of Piano Playing* (London 1973)

Newcomb, Ethel, *Leschetizky As I Knew Him* (New York 1967)

Nicholas, Lynn H., *The Rape of Europe* (New York 1994)

Nicolson, Harold, *Diaries and Letters 1930–39* (London 1966)

Norwich, John Julius, ed. *The Duff Cooper Diaries 1915–1951* (London 2005)

Orczy, Baroness, *Links in the Chain of Life: The Autobiography of Baroness Orczy* (London 1947)

Parris, Matthew, *Great Parliamentary Scandals* (London 1995)

Patterson, Shelia, *Colour and Culture in South Africa* (London 1953)

Penn, Lyle, *The Picture Show Man* (Melbourne 1977)

Peres da Costa, Neal, *Off the Record: Performing Practices in Romantic Piano Playing* (Oxford 2012)

Peter Hill *Stravinsky: The Rite of Spring* (Cambridge 2000)

Petropoulos, Jonathan, *Royals and the Reich: The Princes von Hessen in Nazi Germany* (Oxford 2006)

Petrovic-Njegoš Thompson, Milena *My Father, the Prince* (Xlibris, Bloomington 2000)

Pidoux, Edmond, *The Castle of Chillon* (Neuchatel 1975)

Plaskin, Glenn, *Horowitz: A Biography* (London 1983)

Prendergast, Roy M., *Film Music: A Neglected Art* (New York 1977)

Price, George Ward, *I Know These Dictators* (London 1937)

Prieberg, Fred K., *Trial of Strength: Wihelm Furtwängler and the Third Reich* (London 1991)

Pugh, Martin, *We Danced All Night: A Social History of Britain Between the Wars* (London 2008)

Quattrocchi, Angelo and Nairn, Tom, *The Beginning of the End* (London 1968)

Reade, Eric, *Australian Silent Films: A Pictorial History 1896–1929* (Melbourne 1970)

Révész, G., *The Psychology of a Musical Prodigy* (Amsterdam 1924)

Robinson, John Martin, *Felling the Ancient Oaks: How England Lost its Great Country Estates* (London 2011)

Rosen, Charles, *Piano Notes: The Hidden World of the Pianist* (London 2003)

Ross, Alex, *The Rest is Noise* (London 2008)

Ross, Cathy, *Twenties London: A City in the Jazz Age* (London 2003)

Rousseau, Jean-Jacques, *Julie or the New Héloïse: Letters of Two Lovers who live in a small town at the foot of the Alps* Philip Stewart and Jean Vaché trans. (Hanover, New England 1997)

Rowse, A.L., *Homosexuals in History* (New York 1977)

Rubinstein, Arthur, *My Young Years* (London 1973)

_____, *My Many Years* (London 1980)

Sackville-West V., *English Country Houses* (London 1941)

Saikia, Robin, ed. *The Red Book: The Membership List of the Right Club – 1939* (London 2010)

Saili, Ganesh, *Mussoorie Medley: Tales from Yesteryear* (New Delhi 2010)

Schama, Simon, *Landscape and Memory* (London 1995)

Schnitzler, Arthur, *Selected Short Fiction* trans. J.M.Q. Davies (London 1999)

Scott Fitzgerald F., *Tender is the Night* (New York 1934)

_____, *'Early Success'* from *The Crack Up* (New York 1945)

Sereny, Gitta, *Albert Speer: His Battle with Truth* (London 1995)

Sharp, Ilsa, *There is Only One Raffles: The Story of a Grand Hotel* (London 1981)

Shirakawa, Sam H., *The Devil's Music Master: The Controversial Life and Career of Wilhelm Furtwängler* (Oxford 1992)

Skeaping, John, *Drawn from Life: An Autobiography* (London 1977)

Souhami, Diana, *Edith Cavell* (London 2010)

Speer, Albert, *Inside the Third Reich: Memoirs by Albert Speer* trans. Richard and Clara Winston (London 1970)

Szulc, Ted, *Chopin in Paris: the Life and Times of the Romantic Composer* (New York 1998)

Tampke, Jürgen, *The Germans in Australia* (Cambridge 2006)

Taylor, D.J., *Bright Young People. The Rise and Fall of a Generation: 1918–1940* (London 2007)

Thomas, Lowell, *The Land of the Black Pagoda* (New York 1930)

Tinniswood, Adrian, *The Long Weekend. Life in the English Country House Between the Wars* (London 2016)

Tolstoy, Leo, *The Kreutzer Sonata* (Oxford edition 1924)

Twain, Mark, *Following the Equator: A Journey Round the World* (Hartford, Connecticut 1897)

Venables, David, *Brooklands: The Official Centenary History* (Yeovil 2007)

Vestey, Pamela, *Melba: A Family Memoir* (Melbourne 1996)

Vickers, Hugo, *Behind Closed Doors: The Tragic Untold Story of the Duchess of Windsor* (London 2011)

_____, *Cecil Beaton* (London 1985)

Vincent, Patrick, ed. *Chillon: A Literary Guide* (Geneva 2010)

Voronoff, Serge, Dr, *The Sources of Life* (Toronto 1943)

Waal, Edmund de, *The Hare with Amber Eyes: A Hidden Inheritance* (London 2010)

Waitzman, Mimi S., *The Benton Fletcher Collection at Fenton House: Early*

Keyboard Instruments (London 2003)

Wake, Jehanne, *Princess Louise: Queen Victoria's unconventional daughter* (London 1988)

Wakeman, Rosemary, *The Heroic City: Paris 1945–1958* (Chicago 2009)

Waterhouse, Richard, *From Minstrel Show to Vaudeville: The Australian Popular Stage 1788–1914* (Sydney 1990)

Watson, Stephen, ed. *A City Imagined* (Johannesburg 2006)

Waugh, Evelyn, *Decline and Fall* (London 1928)

_____, *Vile Bodies* (London 1930)

_____, *Brideshead Revisited* (London 1945)

Weir, Alison; Williams, Kate; Gristwood, Sarah and Borman, Tracy, *The Ring and the Crown: A History of Royal Weddings 1066–2011* (London 2011)

Wells, H.G. *Kipps* (London 1905)

Welsh, David, *The Rise and Fall of Apartheid* (Cape Town 2009)

Wilson, Edmund, *Europe Without Baedeker* (London 1948)

Wlaschin, Ken, *The Silent Cinema in Song, 1896–1929* (Jefferson 2009)

Wylie, Neville, *Britain, Switzerland and the Second World War* (Oxford 2003)

Zamoyski, Adam, *Paderewski* (London 1982)

Zweig, Stefan, *The World of Yesterday: An Autobiography by Stefan Zweig* (New York 1943)

ACKNOWLEDGEMENTS

This project has been assisted by the Australian Government through the Australia Council for the Arts, its arts funding and advisory body.

Most of the long period of gestation, writing, travel and research was carried on alone however I must acknowledge rare encouragement from a number of directions. First and foremost, Elizabeth Baumann-Allan, one of only two people living save myself who remembered Edward Cahill, having met him in Somerset West, South Africa, when she was 14. Her affection for him and unwavering enthusiasm for the project were an inspiration. Anne McIntyre of the Logan River and District Family History Society was tireless in assisting me to trace the family and early life of this famous son of Beenleigh. Dianne Byrne, Curator of Original Materials (Queensland Memory) at the State Library of Queensland was helpful far beyond the call of duty, one of the few who recognized the importance of the preservation of both story and recordings. Staff at the John Oxley Library were similarly dedicated.

Michał and Stanisław Dybowski of Selene Records in Poland successfully with skill re-mastered from wretched open reel tapes the precious private recordings Edward Cahill left behind. Jonathan Summers, Curator of Classical Music at the British Library, was impressed with the quality of Cahill's playing and corrected the pitch. His own extensive knowledge and discrimination concerning historical pianists and performance practice was enlightening and an inspiration.

The pianist and teacher Elizabeth Powell gave me invaluable assistance with descriptions of her teacher Leonie Gombrich who also taught Cahill. Valerie Langfield selflessly shared her own discoveries concerning the lives of the Quilter family. Marion Wasdell gave up valuable time to take me on a tour of H.V. Morton's home *Schapenberg* in Somerset West where she lives privately. The late Roger Beardsley made available to me the extraordinary re-mastered direct metal transfer recordings of the soprano Dame Nellie Melba, an artist of seminal influence on Edward Cahill. The Rolls-Royce Enthusiasts' Club (South African Section) was an unlikely source of great practical assistance during my period in Cape Town. Roman Zołtowski remained unfailingly positive of the value of writing this life and tirelessly read the earliest unedited versions. A correspondence with Aaron Voronoff was most helpful on the Riviera details of Dr Serge Voronoff, the exotic acquaintance of Cahill.

The writer, critic, broadcaster and film-maker Robert Carver expressed rare faith in the project from the outset as did the author Dr Mark St. Leon. The brilliant travel writer Rory McClean has unswervingly encouraged my writing career throughout. I could not have continued without the encouragement of the musician and educationalist Richard Berkeley. My sister, the musician, painter and writer Trishaa Perrin unfailingly bolstered my shattered nerves. John Wieneman, an authority on the Duke and Duchess of Windsor and Andrew Ian Henry Russell, 15th Duke of Bedford, assisted me with various family connections.

Heartfelt thanks to Nick Walker, my publisher at Australian Scholarly Publishing, the sole Australian publisher who recognized the importance of preserving this historical record. Amelia Walker provided the imaginative cover designs. Anastasia Buryak showed remarkable patience with my lengthy corrections during the final proofing stages. Two of the longest suffering members on my particular wailing wall are my editor George Miller and my companion Barbara Adam. How they put up with my fluctuating moods over the last six years is anybody's guess but medals they certainly deserve.

Michael Moran
Warsaw
October 2016

MAP OF CONTENTS

EC Edward Cahill GB George Brooke SA Sabine Adler

Early Life and Career (1885–1919) 1–21

Indian & Southeast Asian Tour (1919–1920) 21–51

- EC forms Cahill-Brooke Concert Party with the tenor GB 21
- Frederick Shipman, the well-known impresario, arranges extensive Southeast Asian and Indian Tour before London 22

Tour engagements:

- Darwin 22–3
- First Singapore concert – later Raffles Hotel 23, 41–4
- Kolkata (Calcutta) 23–5
- Chennai (Madras) 25–6
- Bengaluru (Bangalore) 26
- Secunderabad 26–7
- Pune (Poona) 27–8
- Mumbai (Bombay) 28–30
- Jaipur 30–1
- Mussoorie 31–4
- Amritsar atrocity – Brigadier-General Reginald Dyer 34–6
- North-West Frontier – concert in military fort 36
- Varanasi (Benares) – Maharajah of Benares 36–9
- Yangon (Rangoon) – Josie Westaway marries 40–1
- King of Siam – Bangkok 44–5
- Sarawak – Sylvia Brooke – Astana Palace concert 46–9
- North Borneo – Kota Kinabalu (Jesselton) concert 46
- Indonesia – Jakarta (Batavia) 49–50
- Java 50–1

First Australian Tour (1921–1923) 52–6

- Returns to Beenleigh and the harsh realities of Queensland in 1920 52–3
- February 1921 appears with variety vaudeville act known as *The Sparklers* (songs, popular operatic arias, comedians and ballet) in Brisbane's Palace Gardens Theatre – distinguished audience 53
- Death of father Edward Cahill, 21 May 1921 53
- November 1921 – luncheon at Government House, Melbourne – acquires patronage of Countess Helena, Lady Stradbroke. Meets Dame Nellie Melba once again 53–4
- Announces London visit but not before a series of 'Farewell

Recitals' around Australia and New Zealand including Melbourne, Wellington, Sydney, Cairns, Rockhampton 54–5
• EC & GB become more serious about classical music and increasingly disillusioned with vaudeville 54–5

First British Tour (1923–1926) 56–97

• Carries letters of recommendation from Lady Stradbroke and Labor Premier of Queensland, Ted Theodore to London 56
• Royal Wedding – Prince Albert, Duke of York to Lady Elizabeth Bowes-Lyon 62
• Opening concert in Glasgow 9 July 1923 63
• Series of London concerts 63–6
• Buckingham Palace 'Afternoon Parties' 63
• Source of the 'The Pocket Paderewski' moniker 63
• London Concerts 64–5
• James Agate – *Sunday Times* theatre critic observations on their concert 70–1
• Brooklands Motor Racing Circuit 1924 73–4
• Lansdowne House Banquet 76
• Victoria Palace Theatre. London debut 76–8
• Performance for Queen Mary 1 July 1924 at 69 Brook Street, Mayfair. Appearance in Court Circular 79
• Author's Eccentric Club Dinner, 69 Brook Street London 80–1
• Ireland – Dublin concert 81–2
• Horwood House, Buckinghamshire – Maude Denny 83
• Paris and meeting with Alfred Cortot 85–6
• First BBC radio broadcast on 2LO October 1925 91–2
• Sir Francis Lloyd concert 92–3

Second Australian Tour (1926–1927) 97–102

• 'See the Conquering Hero Comes' 97
• Civic Reception Brisbane April 1926 97
• Report on state of European music 98–9
• Complimentary Public Welcome Beenleigh 99–100
• GB marriage to the widow Mrs. Margaret Hardman 101
• 1926–27 Australian concert season EC & GB give series of concerts – Melbourne, seven in Brisbane, Sydney and Adelaide. Tours with the J.C. Williamson vaudeville circuit 101–2

Third Australian Tour (1930–1934) 139–58

- Reports in Fremantle on the state of music in Europe 139–41
- German piano scandal 144
- 38 Queensland concerts with the Grotrian-Steinweg piano including Maryborough, Bundaberg, Rockhampton, Mackay, Townsville, Cairns, Atherton 146–7
- Grave health crisis. Sudden death of GB – brain tumour 147–8
- Memorial concert for GB at Lennons in Brisbane 149
- Appendectomy 150
- Eddie and George relationship subject to press speculation 150–1
- House fire, tragic losses 151–2
- Death of Mary Dauth, EC's mother 24 July 1932 152
- *Anni horribiles* 156–7
- EC 'a divided man'. Conflicts concerning his musical future 153
- Series of musical lectures at Queensland schools with bass-baritone Peter Dawson 154–5
- SA arranges concerts in Austria and Germany. Maude Denny arranges others in England 157
- EC leaves Australia 1934 never to return 158

Third English Period (1934–1938) 158–68

- Social conditions in England in the 1930s 158–62
- Marriage of Prince George, Duke of Kent and Marina, Princess of Greece and Denmark. Recital for King George II of Greece 162–3
- Bust of EC sculpted by Felix Weiss de Weldon 164–5
- Travelling by *Le Train Bleu* – assignation with a Russian Countess en route 165–6
- Audience with Pope Pius XI in Rome 167–8

German Tour and Vienna (March 1935–June 1935) 170–93

- Travels to Germany 170
- Nazi sympathisers and pro-Germans EC knew and performed for in England 170–5
- Meets SA in Berlin 175
- EC repelled by Nazi militarism, anti-Semitism and thirst for war 176

INDEX

About the Author

Michael Moran was born and educated in Australia and Europe. He lectured for many years at a Swiss Educational Foundation in London whilst pursuing piano and harpsichord studies. A Fellow of the *Royal Geographical Society* and an incessant traveller, he lives in Warsaw.

The Author, Michael Moran.
Photographer: Mirosław Malczewski

www.ingramcontent.com/pod-product-compliance
Ingram Content Group UK Ltd.
Pitfield, Milton Keynes, MK11 3LW, UK
UKHW041633190726
13854UKWH00006B/2466